Nuclear Weapons an...

Are nuclear weapons useful for coercive diplomacy? Since 1945, most strategic thinking about nuclear weapons has focused on deterrence – using nuclear threats to prevent attacks against the nation's territory and interests. But an often overlooked question is whether nuclear threats can also coerce adversaries to relinquish possessions or change their behavior. Can nuclear weapons be used to blackmail other countries? The prevailing wisdom is that nuclear weapons are useful for coercion, but this book shows that this view is badly misguided. Nuclear weapons are useful mainly for deterrence and self-defense, not for coercion. The authors evaluate the role of nuclear weapons in several foreign policy contexts and present a trove of new quantitative and historical evidence that nuclear weapons do not help countries achieve better results in coercive diplomacy. The evidence is clear: the benefits of possessing nuclear weapons are almost exclusively defensive, not offensive.

TODD S. SECHSER is Associate Professor of Politics at the University of Virginia.

MATTHEW FUHRMANN is Associate Professor of Political Science at Texas A & M University.

Nuclear Weapons and Coercive Diplomacy

TODD S. SECHSER
University of Virginia

MATTHEW FUHRMANN
Texas A & M University

CAMBRIDGE
UNIVERSITY PRESS

CAMBRIDGE
UNIVERSITY PRESS

University Printing House, Cambridge CB2 8BS, United Kingdom

One Liberty Plaza, 20th Floor, New York, NY 10006, USA

477 Williamstown Road, Port Melbourne, VIC 3207, Australia

4843/24, 2nd Floor, Ansari Road, Daryaganj, Delhi – 110002, India

79 Anson Road, #06–04/06, Singapore 079906

Cambridge University Press is part of the University of Cambridge.

It furthers the University's mission by disseminating knowledge in the pursuit of education, learning, and research at the highest international levels of excellence.

www.cambridge.org
Information on this title: www.cambridge.org/9781107106949

© Todd S. Sechser and Matthew Fuhrmann 2017

First published 2017
Reprinted 2017

Printed in the United States of America by Sheridan Books, Inc.

A catalogue record for this publication is available from the British Library.

ISBN 978-1-107-10694-9 Hardback
ISBN 978-1-107-51451-5 Paperback

For our growing families.

Contents

Tables

Figures

Acknowledgements

This book is the product of more than five years of research into the role of nuclear weapons in world politics. In the course of writing the book, we benefited tremendously from the support of many institutions and individuals.

The Program on Strategic Stability Evaluation ("POSSE"), sponsored by the Carnegie Corporation of New York, deserves much of the credit for sparking the collaboration that led to this project. The Program's meetings in Atlanta, Washington, D.C., Monterey, and Vienna gave us the opportunity to refine our ideas over the course of several years. We are indebted to William Potter and Adam Stulberg, the co-directors of POSSE, for including us as core group members in this important program and for supporting our work since the book's inception. We are also grateful to Carl Robichaud at the Carnegie Corporation for his enthusiastic and enduring support of POSSE.

We are also indebted to the Stanton Foundation for sponsoring our Nuclear Security Fellowships at the Council on Foreign Relations (CFR) in Washington, D.C., where we wrote portions of the book. These fellowships are intended to cultivate a new generation of nuclear security scholars, and we have benefitted tremendously from them. Special thanks are due to Elisabeth Allison and Erica Carere at the Foundation for supporting our work in critical ways. We also thank Victoria Alekhine, Kate Collins, Steven Cook, Janine Hill, Michael Levi, James Lindsay, Paul Stares, Ray Takeyh, and Micah Zenko for the support they provided during our time at CFR.

Our home institutions – the University of Virginia and Texas A&M University – also gave key support to the project. At the University of Virginia, the Quantitative Collaborative and the Vice President for Research provided financial support at critical junctures. The College of Liberal Arts and the Department of Political Science at Texas A&M also provided key funding for the project. We thank all of our colleagues at our respective universities who provided encouragement and helpful feedback as we worked on the book, especially William Clark, Dale Copeland, Hyeran Jo, Michael Koch, David Leblang, Jeffrey Legro, Quan Li, Erica Owen, John Owen, James Rogers, and Ahmer Tarar.

James Fearon, Dan Reiter, and Allan Stam read large portions of the manuscript for a workshop at Texas A&M in May 2013; Alexander Downes, Charles Glaser, Paul Huth, Yonatan Lupu, and Caitlin Talmadge did the same for a second workshop at George Washington University. These individuals graciously took time from their busy schedules to help us improve the book, and their extensive feedback resulted in substantial revisions over the last three years. Their astute suggestions came at a key juncture, helping us to recognize dead-ends and strengthen key elements of the argument. The final product is much sharper due to their generosity.

Many other friends and colleagues read parts of the book at various stages of the project or provided helpful feedback. For their efforts, we would like to thank: James Acton, Graham Allison, Daniel Altman, Robert Art, Victor Asal, Kyle Beardsley, Emma Belcher, Linton Brooks, Robert Brown, Albert Carnesale, Jasen Castillo, Jonathan Caverley, Christopher Clary, Elbridge Colby, Alexandre Debs, Bryan Early, Lynn Eden, Mark Fitzpatrick, Benjamin Fordham, Taylor Fravel, Erik Gartzke, Francis Gavin, Michael Gerson, Michael Glosny, Michael Horowitz, Colin Kahl, Jeffrey Kaplow, Jeffrey Knopf, Gregory Koblentz, Mark Kramer, Sarah Kreps, Matthew Kroenig, David Lake, Michael Levi, Jeffrey Lewis, Keir Lieber, James Lindsay, Jason Lyall, John Mearsheimer, Rupal Mehta, Steven Miller, Alexander Montgomery, Nuno Monteiro, Neil Narang, Vipin Narang, William Norris, Robert Pape, Jonathan Pearl, George Perkovich, Barry Posen, Daryl Press, George Quester, William Reed, Bruce Russett, Scott Sagan, Anne Sartori, Elizabeth Saunders, Karthika Sasikumar, Joshua Shifrinson, Henry Sokolski, Nikolai Sokov, Paul Staniland, Marc Trachtenberg, Jane Vaynman, Stephen Walt, and of course, Club Couture. We apologize to anyone we inadvertently excluded from this list.

We presented parts of the book at research workshops organized by colleagues at MIT, the University of Chicago, the University of California at San Diego, and the Nuclear Studies Research Initiative, as well as the Stanton Foundation's annual conferences for its Nuclear Security Fellows. We thank all of the participants in these workshops for their helpful feedback.

Several of our students provided critical research assistance throughout the process of writing this book. We thank Josiah Barrett, Molly Berkemeier, Marie Bernes Cabanne, Lauren Corbett, Benjamin Harris, Hannah Moody, Abigail Post, Matt Scroggs, and Benjamin Tkach for their expert assistance.

At Cambridge University Press, John Haslam was enthusiastic about this project from an early stage. We are grateful for John's support, as well as the help we received along the way from everyone at the press. Thanks are also due to the two anonymous reviewers who provided us with critical feedback that improved the book.

Last, and most important, we wish to thank our families. Their patience allowed us to devote the late nights and frequent travel that this book required. Their love gave us a welcoming sanctuary to recuperate from writing. And their support helped push us over the finish line. It is to them that we dedicate this book.

Portions of Chapter 3 were previously published as Todd S. Sechser and Matthew Fuhrmann, "Crisis Bargaining and Nuclear Blackmail," *International Organization* 67(1): 173–195 (Copyright © 2013 The IO Foundation). Thanks to Cambridge University Press for providing permission to reprint sections of this article. The authors contributed equally to this book.

PART I

The Logic of Nuclear Skepticism

1 | Nuclear Blackmail in International Politics

In the early hours of July 16, 1945, in New Mexico's Jornada del Muerto desert, the United States detonated the world's first nuclear device: a single test bomb with the explosive power of more than 18,000 tons of TNT. The shock wave from the explosion was felt over 100 miles away, but its effects reverberated around the world. Over the next several decades, the United States spent trillions of dollars building and maintaining a vast nuclear arsenal.[1] At its peak in the mid-1960s, America's stockpile consisted of more than 30,000 atomic warheads. Seventy years into the nuclear age, it is time to ask: what exactly has the United States gained from its investment in the bomb? What has it been able to do with nuclear weapons that it could not have done without them?

The United States is not the only country interested in the answers to these questions. Nine other countries have built nuclear weapons since 1945 (see Table 1.1). All of these states made tremendous sacrifices in order to acquire atomic weaponry. Zulfikar Ali Bhutto, the former prime minister of Pakistan, famously boasted that his countrymen would "eat grass" in order to produce the Pakistani bomb. Pakistan ultimately built a nuclear arsenal – but only at a tremendous financial cost. The production of China's atomic bomb likewise required a significant readjustment of national priorities. Beijing's official guidelines for building the bomb indicated that all "other projects for our country's reconstruction will have to take second place to the development of nuclear weapons."[2] More recently, North Korea endured years of crippling economic sanctions and international isolation in order to join the nuclear club. Are the benefits that stem from

---

[1] One study calculated that the United States spent $5.5 trillion on its nuclear arsenal between 1940 and 1996, amounting to nearly one-third of all U.S. military spending for that period (Schwartz, 1998).

[2] Quoted in Perkovich (1999, 80).

Table 1.1 *States that have acquired nuclear weapons.*

Country	Year Acquired
United States	1945
Soviet Union	1949
Great Britain	1952
France	1960
China	1964
Israel	1967
India	1974
South Africa	1979*
Pakistan	1987
North Korea	2006

* South Africa dismantled its arsenal in the early 1990s.

possessing nuclear weapons sufficient to justify these kinds of sacrifices? What have Pakistan, China, and other nuclear powers gained from privileging nuclear weapons programs at the expense of their economic development and other national priorities?

Scholars and politicians have puzzled over the political effects of nuclear weapons for decades. Yet most thinking about nuclear weapons has been devoted to a single idea: the ability of nuclear weapons to deter aggression. In 1953, the physicist Robert Oppenheimer – the so-called father of the atomic bomb – famously likened the emerging American-Soviet rivalry to "two scorpions in a bottle, each capable of killing the other, but only at the risk of his own life."[3] Most research about nuclear diplomacy over the last seven decades has sought to determine the conditions under which this tenuous balance can hold. A key question in this literature, for example, is whether nuclear weapons contributed to the "long peace" that emerged among the great powers after World War II.[4]

But deterring external aggression is just one-half of the equation. It is also possible that nuclear weapons have *coercive* utility. In other words, nuclear weapons might help countries throw their weight

[3] Monk (2012, 610).
[4] See Gaddis (1987).

around to force changes that serve their political interests.[5] Nuclear-armed countries could, for example, try to compel others to relinquish territory, dismantle military bases, pay reparations, or even alter their domestic policies. Just as in nuclear deterrence, the goal is to threaten punishment so severe that the target will capitulate to avoid the possibility of being attacked with nuclear weapons. Are nuclear weapons useful for these more assertive forms of political leverage?

Military coercion has been called "the dark side of international relations."[6] Using, or threatening to use, military force to advance one's political interests is sometimes perceived as morally reprehensible, particularly if nuclear weapons are involved. Nevertheless, when it is successful, coercive diplomacy can be an efficient way for a state to advance its interests. If states can get what they want in world politics without actually having to fight, they can avoid potentially costly wars and other military adventures. For example, the United States was ultimately able to expel Saddam Hussein from Kuwait in the 1991 Persian Gulf War – but Washington surely would have preferred if its military threats had been sufficient to accomplish that objective. Indeed, the most effective threat, as Thomas Schelling argues, is one that never has to be implemented.[7] It is therefore important to understand when and how states can exercise coercive diplomacy effectively.

An emerging wisdom in international relations scholarship says that countries armed with large nuclear arsenals can bully other states into submission by raising the prospect of nuclear punishment. Even some national leaders seem to share this view. This perspective is consequential because if nuclear weapons are powerful tools of coercion, then the United States might benefit from building a larger nuclear arsenal – and from using military force to destroy other nations' nuclear programs. Indeed, many influential observers advocate for these policies today.

This book, however, challenges this emerging consensus. It asks whether nuclear-armed states have advantages in coercive bargaining. We show that nuclear weapons have far less utility for coercive diplomacy than many people believe. For all the money spent on

---

[5] We use the term "coercion" to refer to the use of threats to revise the status quo. Note, however, that some scholars use the term more broadly to refer to all military threats, including deterrent threats. See Schelling (1960), George and Smoke (1974) and Art (2003).

[6] Pape (1996, 3).

[7] Schelling (1966, 10).

atomic bombs, they have bought precious little coercive leverage for
states.

A Fresh Look at Nuclear Weapons in the 21st Century

The political effects of nuclear weapons have puzzled scholars and
strategists ever since the United States dropped the first atomic bomb
on Hiroshima, Japan, in August 1945. Deterrence theorists produced
reams of scholarship on the role of nuclear weapons in the Cold War
superpower standoff between the Soviet Union and the United States.[8]
They wanted to know whether nuclear weapons had any political utility in a world of mutually assured destruction (MAD), where a nuclear
first strike by either the Americans or the Soviets would likely result in
the annihilation of both countries. These scholars focused heavily on
high-profile superpower crises in Berlin, Cuba, and elsewhere.

Over the last two decades, however, the world has changed in ways
that the nuclear deterrence literature did not anticipate. We no longer
live in a world in which two superpowers face one another with tens
of thousands of nuclear warheads at their disposal. Instead, we find
ourselves in a "unipolar" world with one superpower – the United
States. In this new global landscape, regional nuclear powers, like India
and Pakistan, are increasingly important. However, most theories of
nuclear coercion were designed to explain the behavior of superpowers – not regional nuclear powers. These theories may not apply to
today's strategic environment.

Moreover, nuclear deterrence theory has little to say about how
nuclear states interact with nonnuclear rivals. Yet these interactions
are increasingly important in the post–Cold War world – especially for
the United States. Many of Washington's most important adversaries
over the last several years have been so-called rogue regimes that did
not possess the bomb, such as Iraq, Iran, and Syria. Many of the theories developed during the Cold War have little to say about whether
nuclear weapons can be used to coerce nonnuclear states.

This book provides a theory of nuclear coercion that is updated for
the 21st century. It shows that nuclear weapons have little coercive
utility in today's world. Even during the Cold War, nuclear arsenals

---

[8] See, for example, Brodie (1959), Schelling (1966), Betts (1987), Jervis (1989),
   and Trachtenberg (1991).

were far less useful for coercion than many people believe. The opposing view – that nuclear weapons aid coercive diplomacy – is badly
misguided.

The Nuclear Coercionist School

According to one view, nuclear weapons help countries intimidate and
blackmail their adversaries – not just deter them. The nuclear "coercionist" school, as we call it, traces its roots back to the early days
of the atomic age, when many American officials saw the U.S. nuclear
monopoly as a tool for molding Soviet behavior to their liking. During
the Cold War, the coercionist perspective receded as deterrence, not
compellence, emerged as the cornerstone of U.S. nuclear policy. Since
the end of the Cold War, however, the coercionist view has enjoyed
something of a renaissance, drawing adherents both from those who
fear aggression from new nuclear states as well as those who see
nuclear weapons as a useful tool for U.S. coercive diplomacy. The
coercionist viewpoint comes in several different flavors, with important differences – and a few disagreements – between them. But they
all share a basic belief that nuclear weapons are useful for more than
just self-defense.

There is a widespread assumption among international relations
scholars that nuclear weapons provide coercive leverage. Though this
belief is not universal, scholars often assume that nuclear weapons
allow countries to coerce their adversaries. Consider the following
conclusions from prominent studies of coercive diplomacy:

- "Nuclear weapons provide more than prestige, they provide leverage. They are useful in coercive diplomacy, and this must be central
  to any explanation of why states acquire them."[9]
- "Even if the coercer's nuclear resources are limited, the prospect of
  damage far worse than the most intense conventional assault will
  likely coerce all but the most resolute defenders."[10]
- "Coercion is more likely to work ... if the coercer enjoys a unilateral
  nuclear advantage."[11]

---

[9] Beardsley and Asal (2009b, 297).
[10] Pape (1996, 38).
[11] Horowitz and Reiter (2001, 163).

- "When the compeller enjoys a monopoly over nuclear weapons, he can virtually dictate conditions to the compellee."[12]
- "States that enjoy nuclear superiority over their opponents are more likely to win nuclear crises."[13]
- "Nuclear weapons aid the coercive capabilities of the United States."[14]
- "Nuclear weapons are inherently valuable for political (especially coercive) purposes."[15]

The coercionist perspective begins from a simple and irrefutable observation: nuclear weapons are terrifyingly destructive. When deciding to back down or stand firm in a crisis, countries must consider whether they could prevail in an eventual war at an acceptable cost. Armed conflict with a nuclear-armed coercer could result in the destruction of a state's major cities and the killing of hundreds of thousands – and perhaps millions – of its civilians. Countries have obvious incentives to avoid this kind of punishment. By threatening to inflict massive amounts of pain, nuclear nations therefore can compel targets to reverse unfavorable policies or hand over disputed items.

Absolutists and Relativists

The nuclear coercionist school encompasses a wide array of views about the conditions under which nuclear weapons can be useful tools of coercion. Most, however, fall into one of two camps, which we label *absolutists* and *relativists*. Nuclear absolutists suggest that the mere possession of a nuclear arsenal – of any size – allows states to blackmail and intimidate other states, regardless of others' military capabilities. Proponents of this view suggest, for example, that if Iran builds a nuclear arsenal, it would be able to coerce the United States and Israel – even though both of those states would have overwhelming nuclear superiority over Iran. Indeed, whenever a nondemocratic regime appears on the cusp of acquiring the bomb, it is seemingly pro forma for senior officials in the United States to raise alarm about the danger of nuclear blackmail. In the 1950s, for instance, Secretary

---

[12] Merrill and Peleg (1984, 34).
[13] Kroenig (2013, 141).
[14] Thayer and Skypek (2013, 43).
[15] Dittmeier (2013, 494).

of State John Foster Dulles argued that nuclear weapons "might in the future get into the hands of irresponsible dictators and be used as a form of international blackmail."[16] Half a century later, President George W. Bush echoed the same view when he asserted that countries such as Iran, Iraq, and North Korea would be able to "blackmail" the United States and its allies if those regimes acquired the bomb.

Nuclear relativists, on the other hand, focus on the nuclear balance. For relativists, a state's ability to use its arsenal for coercive leverage is conditional on having a nuclear advantage over its opponent. Relativists are divided, however, on just how much of an advantage is necessary for nuclear weapons to be useful tools of coercive bargaining. Some argue that nuclear states cannot use their arsenals for coercive purposes if their opponents also possess the bomb. According to this perspective, a state with a large arsenal could coerce non-nuclear opponents, but not countries that might retaliate with nuclear weapons, since the latter could impose unacceptable damage in a retaliatory attack.

Other relativists, however, assert that nuclear coercion can be effective, even against other nuclear powers. What matters, these scholars argue, is whether the coercing state enjoys "nuclear superiority" over its opponent. Nuclear-superior states – those with larger and more sophisticated nuclear arsenals – have an important advantage, in this view. As Robert Jastrow once claimed (with no trace of irony), "he who can blow the world up three times has more power than he who can blow it up only twice."[17]

Brinkmanship and the Manipulation of Risk

In a crisis with two nuclear states, carrying out a nuclear threat would likely mean mutual suicide. How, then, can nuclear coercion be effective against other nuclear states? For some scholars, nuclear brinkmanship provides an answer.[18] According to brinkmanship theory, a nuclear state can coerce its opponent by taking dangerous escalatory actions that increase the risk of an unintended disaster.

[16] Dulles (1957).
[17] Jastrow (1983).
[18] Classic studies of nuclear brinkmanship include Schelling (1960), Schelling (1966), and Powell (1990).

Although both sides understand that the other would not rationally start a nuclear war, the possibility of accidental nuclear escalation can turn seemingly incredible threats into credible ones.

To illustrate, consider a colorful illustration offered by Schelling in his classic book *Arms and Influence*. Imagine two mountain climbers that are tied together, standing near the edge of a cliff. If one climber wants to intimidate the other, perhaps he could threaten to jump over the edge. The problem is that this threat would not be credible, since it would be suicidal. But by moving ever closer to the edge of the cliff, the climber can raise the chance that some unforeseen accident – loose gravel, a gust of wind, momentary vertigo – might cause one climber to slip and carry both to certain death. The longer he stands near the edge, and the closer he gets to the chasm, the more likely it becomes that the other climber will lose his nerve and give in.

Nuclear coercion theory argues that this dynamic is what drives confrontations between nuclear-armed countries. Nuclear states prevail in crises with other nuclear states, according to this view, by raising the risk that a crisis will spiral out of control and result in a war that neither side would rationally choose. Some theorists contend that states with a nuclear advantage are particularly likely to utilize brinkmanship tactics.[19] They can take greater risks in crises – and enhance their odds of victory – because their opponents will suffer more than they will if war breaks out. This argument seemingly offers an elegant solution to the problem of incredible threats, showing how states can derive coercive value from their nuclear arsenals even if they would never rationally use them.

Another strand of nuclear coercion theory goes even further, suggesting that nuclear brinkmanship – or an explicit nuclear threat – is not necessary for nuclear states to derive coercive leverage from their arsenals. According to this view, nuclear weapons loom in the background of international crises even when states do not make explicit nuclear threats. In 1956, before he became the Pentagon's second-in-command

---

[19] See, for example, Trachtenberg (1985, 139) and Kroenig (2013). However, other brinkmanship theorists – most notably Jervis (1984) and Powell (1990) – reject the notion that nuclear superiority makes states push harder in crises. These scholars argue instead that the balance of resolve determines a state's willingness to generate risk in a crisis. Despite this key difference, both of these perspectives embrace the notion that states can extract coercive utility from their nuclear arsenal when nuclear threats might appear incredible.

official, Paul Nitze argued that "whether or not atomic weapons are ever again used in warfare, the very fact of their existence, the possibility that they could be used, will affect all future wars ... In this sense even the cold war is an atomic cold war."[20] Nuclear states therefore should be able to coerce their adversaries without ratcheting up the risk of nuclear war. Nuclear alerts, nuclear deployments, and explicit verbal threats are not needed for states to gain political leverage over their adversaries: simply possessing the bomb is often enough. One study put it bluntly: "even if a state never makes an explicit nuclear threat, the mere presence of nuclear weapons may exert a powerful coercive role in low-level militarized disputes."[21]

Problems with the Nuclear Coercionist School

The nuclear coercionist perspective offers some useful insights into the dynamics of nuclear blackmail, but it also has significant limitations. One problem is that it does not seem to explain the historical record very well. Nuclear-superior states have often failed to get their way in coercive disputes with other nuclear powers. Soviet pronouncements of its nuclear superiority, for example, did not help achieve a more favorable resolution to its territorial disputes with China in the late 1960s. The United States likewise has not had much luck altering North Korea's aggressive policies since Pyongyang's first nuclear test in 2006. Moreover, nuclear states frequently have failed to coerce even nonnuclear adversaries. The shadow of America's nuclear arsenal did not convince Afghan leaders to hand over al Qaeda operatives after the group conducted terrorist attacks against American targets in 1998 or 2001. Great Britain could not coerce Argentine forces to withdraw from the Falkland Islands without a fight in 1982, despite deploying nuclear forces to the South Atlantic. The Soviet Union could not force Iran or Turkey to hand over disputed territory in the early 1950s, after Moscow acquired the bomb. China has similarly been unable to make relatively weak states – including, Brunei, Malaysia, Philippines, Taiwan, and Vietnam – abandon their claims to the disputed Spratly Islands in the South China Sea.

---

[20] Nitze (1956).
[21] Horowitz (2009, 251).

Why does nuclear coercion theory produce so many historical anomalies? We argue that it suffers from two key limitations that constrain its explanatory power. First, it overlooks key factors that limit the credibility of coercive nuclear threats. The coercionist school acknowledges that implementing nuclear threats can be costly for the attacker. But it conceives of these costs narrowly, focusing mostly on the possibility of military retaliation. In reality, states that carry out coercive nuclear threats would likely suffer a host of political and economic consequences, in addition to possible military punishment. Downplaying the nonmilitary consequences of nuclear coercion produces overly optimistic conclusions about the credibility of nuclear threats, particularly if the target is nonnuclear and cannot launch retaliatory nuclear strikes. Making coercive nuclear threats believable becomes decidedly more difficult once one accounts for the full range of costs that attacking states could suffer.

Second, the coercionist view exaggerates the utility of nuclear brinkmanship as a solution to the credibility problem. Brinkmanship theory assumes that leaders are willing to escalate crises, potentially causing them to lose control of events, and that targets will correctly detect and interpret signals of resolve. Both of these assumptions are often wrong, a point that we will return to below. Brinkmanship may be an effective strategy under specific conditions, but its record of success is less than advertised.

The Logic of Nuclear Skepticism

This book argues that nuclear coercion theory is overly optimistic about the coercive utility of nuclear weapons.[22] There is no doubt that the bomb can inflict catastrophic damage on target countries. Yet the standard arguments fail to fully appreciate several key challenges that nuclear states face in coercive bargaining. Taken together, these problems render atomic weapons ineffective tools of blackmail – despite their tremendously destructive power.

In the broadest sense, coercion involves the use of threats to change the behavior of another actor. Three main considerations influence whether coercion works: (1) the challenger's ability to impose its

---

[22] We have made similar arguments in other writing as well; see Sechser and Fuhrmann (2013a, 2014).

will militarily, (2) the stakes in a dispute, and (3) the costs of military conflict. Drawing on this framework, we argue that three factors combine to render coercive nuclear threats ineffective in the modern international system.

First, the military utility of nuclear weapons is limited – and often redundant to the capabilities of conventional weapons. In coercive diplomacy, the coercer often seeks to destroy a disputed item, or wrest it away from the target. A target is likely to capitulate in these episodes if it believes that the challenger will ultimately end up with the object anyway. However, a coercer's nuclear capabilities typically do not affect the target's perception about whether it can maintain control over a disputed item. The reason is that a nuclear-armed challenger's conventional power is usually (though not always) sufficient to seize or eliminate a contested object. To illustrate, in 1981 Israel demanded that Syria remove surface-to-air missiles from Lebanese territory or face an Israeli military attack. Syria and Lebanon had little reason to fear a nuclear attack since Israel could easily destroy the missiles in a conventional strike – which it ultimately did. Nuclear weapons added little to Israel's ability to achieve its objectives by force.

Nuclear weapons have at least two military advantages over conventional firepower. A key feature of atomic weapons is that they can destroy cities and kill civilians more efficiently than conventional forces. This makes the bomb a potentially useful tool of punishment in coercion. Pakistan, for example, could attempt to wrest Kashmir from India by threatening to attack key Indian cities if it did not get its way. On the surface, one might expect such a threat to work because India would surely want to avoid losing its cities. Another advantage of nuclear weapons is that they can destroy some "hardened" targets, like underground military facilities, more efficiently. The nuclear option, therefore, may be useful for some coercive military missions.

Yet even when nuclear weapons offer advantages over conventional weapons, a second credibility problem can inhibit the effectiveness of nuclear threats: carrying out a coercive nuclear threat would be tremendously costly for the challenger, even if the target does not possess the ability to retaliate with nuclear weapons. A state that launched a nuclear attack to achieve a coercive objective – that is, to obtain something it did not have already – would provoke an enormous backlash from the target, from other states, and from the broader public. Their collective responses could threaten the coercer's security, prosperity, and the political fortunes of its leaders. In addition, carrying out a coercive nuclear threat would harm a state's long-term interests by setting a dangerous precedent and encouraging others to align against it.

The current crisis between China and Japan over the Senkaku Islands (called the Diaoyu Islands in China) is instructive in this regard. Tokyo currently administers the islands, but Beijing believes that they belong to China. China has threatened to use military force to resolve the dispute, and some officials have suggested that Beijing could bring a quick end to the crisis by launching a nuclear attack against Japan.[23] Yet Japanese leaders show no sign of backing down in the dispute, presumably because they understand that such an attack would not only trigger retaliation from Japan's allies (including the United States) but also encourage countries to actively align against China, frustrating Beijing's efforts to assert its influence in Asia.

Of course, the costs of enacting a threat are only one part of the equation, and these costs might be worth paying if one's survival were at risk. This brings us to a third credibility problem: states making coercive threats rarely face such dire circumstances. Indeed, a key feature of coercion is that the coercer typically seeks something that it has already been living without – such as a piece of disputed territory, monetary reparations, or reversal of an unfavorable policy. While these stakes are hardly trivial, in most cases they are not so vital to the coercer's security as to outweigh the inevitable backlash that would follow an offensive nuclear strike. Pakistan would desperately like to acquire Kashmir from India, but having lived without it for decades, Pakistan's survival hardly depends on possessing it. The very nature of coercion thus works against the effectiveness of nuclear coercive threats.

The three problems discussed above – the limited military utility of nuclear weapons relative to conventional power, the high costs of implementing coercive nuclear threats, and the relatively low stakes for coercers – render most coercive nuclear threats incredible. Potential targets know this and therefore have little reason to worry about nuclear strikes in coercive crises. India may worry about war with Pakistan – the two states have fought four wars since their independence

---

[23] See Garnaut (2013).

from Britain in 1947 – but it is unlikely that Islamabad would implement a coercive *nuclear* threat over Kashmir.

None of this is meant to imply that nuclear coercion never works. Indeed, nuclear blackmail can be effective when states are able to overcome the credibility problems discussed above. This is most likely to happen under three conditions. The first is if a challenger's conventional power is insufficient to achieve a desired objective; nuclear weapons in this circumstance would add a coercive capability that was not previously there. Second, coercive nuclear threats may become more credible if a challenger faces an extreme provocation by the target. In this case, the costs of implementing a nuclear threat would decline to some degree, partially alleviating the second credibility problem. A third condition under which threats could be credible is if a challenger found itself in a desperate situation with its back against the wall. This would mitigate the third credibility problem by raising the coercer's stakes in a crisis considerably. States in such positions might also be more willing to use dangerous nuclear signals to bolster the seriousness of their demands. However, the reality is that these conditions are rarely satisfied. While nuclear coercion can in principle be effective, in practice it almost always fails.

Nor do we mean to imply that nuclear weapons are irrelevant in international politics. It is quite plausible, and indeed likely, that nuclear weapons are useful for deterrence. As we noted previously, the stakes are higher when its objective is to deter. Moreover, many of the costs of making threats would be reduced in a deterrence context. Nuclear deterrent threats, therefore, are likely to be more credible – particularly when a state's survival is at risk. Thus, states may reap some benefits from their investments in atomic weapons. However, enhanced coercive leverage is not one of those perks.

The Limitations of Nuclear Brinkmanship

Can nuclear states make their coercive threats more credible by engaging in brinkmanship, as Schelling and others have suggested? This logic too has important shortcomings.

First, leaders tend to be hesitant to manipulate the risk of accidental war when their goals are coercive in nature. Being seen as reckless can have significant and costly consequences, even for "rogue" regimes. In major crises, therefore, leaders usually strive to maximize their control over events, not cede it.

Second, even if states make dangerous escalatory moves – for example, by ordering a nuclear alert – nuclear signals may not be detected or properly interpreted. For example, President Richard Nixon alerted U.S. nuclear forces in October 1969 to signal America's willingness to use whatever means necessary to end the war in Vietnam. But neither North Vietnam nor the Soviet Union received the appropriate message, and Nixon's gambit failed. This case is hardly anomalous: as we show in the following chapters, signaling failures routinely occur in serious nuclear crises.

What's at Stake in the Nuclear Coercion Debate?

The nuclear coercionist school and nuclear skepticism theory offer fundamentally different perspectives about the role of nuclear weapons in world politics. Knowing which view is correct carries important implications for how we think about international politics.

The questions addressed in this book speak to longstanding debates about the political effects of military power. Scholars dating as far back as ancient Greece have argued that military capabilities bring political influence. According to this line of thinking, power in international politics is analogous to money in a market economy. With enough money, an individual can purchase anything she desires. Similarly, power enables states to buy influence in international politics. The greater a state's military capabilities, the more it will be able to sway others. As Robert Art writes, "Militarily powerful states have greater clout in world politics than militarily weak ones."[24]

Yet others have challenged this view of military power. An alternative perspective argues that converting military power into political leverage is not as simple as trading money for goods. Power provides states with an imperfect ability to achieve political objectives. In fact, militarily powerful states may actually be at a *disadvantage* vis-à-vis weaker countries. Academic research has highlighted the potentially perverse effects of power in crisis bargaining, warfighting, institutional

---

[24] Art (1996). See also Organski (1958); Snyder and Diesing (1977); Cable (1994); Baldwin (2002); and Mearsheimer (2001).

politics, and other contexts.[25] These studies – all of which demonstrate the challenges that powerful states face in achieving political objectives in world politics – call into question standard views about the effects of military power.

This book provides useful insights into the power debate. Nuclear weapons are the most destructive weapons known to mankind, so they ought to be especially valuable as tools of international influence. Yet our research ultimately supports the less sanguine view of military power. It demonstrates that nuclear weapons do not carry the coercive leverage that their extraordinary power might suggest. The ability to destroy does not necessarily convey the ability to coerce.

The study of nuclear coercion speaks to another key question in international relations: what are the likely consequences of nuclear proliferation?[26] Do nuclear weapons bring peace to the international system, or do they incite instability? Scholars who argue that nuclear proliferation is dangerous sometimes suggest that having a nuclear arsenal helps countries change the status quo with greater ease. This is a legitimate concern if nuclear weapons are, in fact, useful for military blackmail. This book shows, however, that they are not. Nuclear weapons support primarily defensive – not offensive – objectives. The spread of nuclear weapons may therefore be less harmful for international security than many believe. While this may be good news from the standpoint of peace and stability, it is bad news for countries that invest heavily in nuclear weapons. Indeed, states that develop nuclear arsenals to enhance their political leverage will likely be disappointed.

Of course, this does not mean that we should welcome the spread of nuclear weapons. Nuclear proliferation may influence world politics in a variety of ways, some of which could undermine global security. The global spread of nuclear weapons, for example, may raise the danger of catastrophic destruction as a result of miscalculation, terrorism, or sabotage. While evaluating these scenarios is beyond the scope of this book, our research suggests that nuclear blackmail is not among the negative consequences of nuclear proliferation.

---

[25] Sechser (2010, 2016b), Sullivan (2007), Lyall and Wilson (2009), and Voeten (2004).

[26] Scholars have fiercely debated how nuclear weapons affect the stability of the international system. See, for example, Feaver (1995), Karl (1996), Seng (1997), Karl (2001), Sagan (2001), Sagan and Waltz (2002), Karl (2014), Kapur (2007), Fuhrmann and Kreps (2010).

These conclusions carry important lessons for policymakers. Nuclear proliferation is a persistent problem, perhaps more intractable than any other security-related issue in the post–World War II era. Since the beginning of the nuclear era, intellectuals and leaders have worried about how nuclear proliferation might transform world politics. In the 1950s, nuclear anxiety centered around France, Sweden, West Germany, and other European countries that were exploring their nuclear options. In the 1960s, concerns about the Chinese and Israeli nuclear programs dominated the nonproliferation landscape. In the 1970s, the superpowers considered how best to prevent South Africa, South Korea, and Taiwan from crossing the nuclear threshold. Iraq and Libya were the main proliferators of concern during the 1980s, while the Indian and Pakistani nuclear tests caused a stir during the 1990s. In the 2000s, the main proliferation-related problems stemmed from North Korea and Syria. Today, Iran is the principal country of concern in the world of nonproliferation.[27] Tomorrow, it will be someone else.

When future proliferation problems emerge, policymakers will have to make decisions about how to respond – just as they have done in the past. One option will be to launch preventive military strikes against a proliferator's nuclear facilities to delay its ability to build the bomb. This is an option that officials in a diverse set of countries – including India, Russia, Taiwan, and the United States – have seriously contemplated. Israel actually carried out two "bolt from the blue" raids to destroy nuclear facilities, in Iraq in 1981 and Syria in 2007. Countries seeking to limit nuclear proliferation have also opted for less aggressive options such as imposing economic sanctions and offering positive inducements. Still another possibility is to do nothing, tacitly accepting another state into the nuclear club.

Which of these options will make the most sense in the next proliferation crisis? The answer will depend, in part, on whether nuclear weapons are useful for coercion. Advocates of using military force to prevent proliferation often assert that new nuclear states will be able to bully and intimidate their adversaries with ease. If this view is correct, aggressive nonproliferation policies might be justified. However,

---

[27] In July 2015, the United States and several other countries reached an agreement with Iran that appears to have resolved the crisis over Iran's nuclear program for the time being. However, it remains unclear whether this deal will succeed in preventing Iran from acquiring nuclear weapons.

if the bomb is useful primarily for deterrence, the benefits of military strikes may not justify their high cost.

A second policy implication pertains to the future of nuclear weapons in existing nuclear states. In several countries – including Britain, Russia, and the United States – several prominent former officials have called for deep reductions to global nuclear stockpiles, arguing that nuclear weapons are expensive and accident-prone relics of a bygone era. But arms control critics contend that such measures would undermine their governments' influence around the world. These critics argue that maintaining nuclear superiority is critical for shaping international affairs to their country's advantage. The utility of nuclear coercion plays an important role in this debate: if nuclear weapons are reliable instruments of coercion and can compel adversaries to act in line with their foreign policy goals, then policymakers should be cautious about making major cuts to their nuclear arsenals. However, if nuclear weapons are not useful as tools of coercion, the case against significantly reducing nuclear stockpiles would be significantly weakened.

This book points toward the latter view. The debate about nuclear arms reductions is complex, and this book admittedly does not explore that debate in detail. However, our research suggests that the coercive potential of nuclear weapons is not a compelling reason to eschew nuclear arms reductions: if history is to be believed, cutting a nuclear arsenal is unlikely to have any meaningful impact on the strength of a country's coercive diplomacy.

Approach of the Book

How do we know which view of nuclear coercion is correct – the nuclear coercionist school or nuclear skepticism theory? This book takes a two-pronged approach to collecting and analyzing evidence. First, we use statistical analysis to identify broad trends in nuclear coercion. We explore, in particular, whether nuclear states generally fare better at coercive diplomacy than their nonnuclear counterparts. We evaluate the role of nuclear weapons in two main coercive contexts: crisis diplomacy and territorial disputes. Our analysis of hundreds of cases of attempted coercion shows that, on average, nuclear states fare no better during high-stakes confrontations, nor in longstanding territorial disputes.

Second, we delve deeply into history's most serious coercive nuclear crises. Coercive nuclear threats are rare: nuclear weapons have been invoked to achieve coercive goals less than two dozen times since 1945. We study each of these episodes, drawing on declassified documents when possible. Our analysis includes well-known Cold War superpower standoffs, like the Cuban missile crisis, as well as post–Cold War nuclear crises involving newer nuclear powers. In all of these cases, countries brandished nuclear weapons by issuing verbal threats, alerting nuclear forces, or conspicuously deploying their arsenals. The evidence we present underscores the limits – not the virtues – of nuclear weapons for coercive diplomacy.

This book offers the most comprehensive assessment of nuclear coercion to date. Other books have evaluated the effectiveness of nuclear coercion by conducting in-depth case studies of crises in which nuclear weapons appeared to play a significant role. However, these books focus heavily on a small number of crises, most of which involve the United States during the Cold War. By contrast, this book covers the full spectrum of nuclear coercion attempts, analyzing dozens of historical and contemporary cases using quantitative and qualitative methods. Unlike other studies, we also examine the effectiveness of nonnuclear coercion, allowing us to determine whether nuclear weapons help, hurt, or have no impact on the effectiveness of military coercion in international politics. Moreover, our historical analysis covers cases of nuclear brinkmanship that have received less attention from scholars – for example, the Bangladesh War, the 2001–2002 Indo-Pakistani border standoff, and the 2013 Korean crisis.

Roadmap of the Book

In the chapters that follow, we develop nuclear skepticism theory and test it against the historical record. The book continues in four parts.

In Part I, we explore the dynamics of coercion in world politics and explain why nuclear powers get little coercive leverage from their arsenals. We also discuss in greater detail why many scholars and policymakers hold the opposite view.

Parts II and III present the evidence. Part II, which includes Chapters 3 and 4, introduces quantitative evidence that nuclear weapons are generally not useful for coercive bargaining. Chapter 3 analyzes the relationship between nuclear weapons and explicit coercive threats. We show that nuclear states do not make more effective threats than nonnuclear states. In addition, contrary to the expectations of the nuclear coercionist school, nuclear states are not more likely than their nonnuclear counterparts to escalate coercive crises. In Chapter 4, we shift our attention away from explicit threats and focus on international bargaining over disputed territory. Our analysis reveals that nuclear and nonnuclear states in territorial disputes extract concessions at a similar rate, suggesting that nuclear arsenals do not help countries redraw the map through coercive diplomacy. Moreover, there is scant evidence that nuclear powers are more willing than nonnuclear states to use military force during territorial disputes. Nuclear weapons therefore do not seem to allow states to more effectively seize disputed land with their conventional military forces.

In Part III, we examine the most important historical and contemporary nuclear crises. Chapter 5 looks at nine failures of nuclear coercion, including Nikita Khrushchev's attempt to expel Western forces from Berlin in the late 1950s and early 1960s, and Richard Nixon's ill-fated nuclear alert during the Vietnam War. Chapter 6 addresses the cases that seem to pose the greatest challenge to nuclear skepticism theory: the Korean War, crises in the Taiwan Strait during the 1950s, the Cuban missile crisis, the 1969 border war between China and the Soviet Union, the Yom Kippur War, and several others.

Part IV concludes by assessing the myths and realities of nuclear coercion. Chapter 7 identifies ten widely held beliefs about nuclear coercion, and explains why those views – like the nuclear coercionist school – are off the mark.

2 | *Nuclear Coercion and Nuclear Skepticism*

Do nuclear weapons provide countries with advantages in international bargaining? If so, under what conditions? Scholars and policymakers have debated these questions for decades. Remarkably, nearly seventy years into the nuclear age, we still lack consensus about the coercive value of nuclear weapons. Our goal in this chapter is to add greater clarity to the nuclear blackmail debate.

We start by describing the basic complexion of coercion in international politics. Next, we develop a generalized framework of coercion that yields several conclusions about the conditions that favor coercive success, and then ask whether nuclear weapons help bring about – or bolster – these conditions. In the end, we conclude that they do not. Nuclear weapons may be useful for deterrence and self-defense, but they are not useful for coercion.

Coercion: An Introduction

In its broadest sense, coercion involves using threats – either explicit or implied – to motivate someone to act.[1] At its core, then, coercion is about behavior modification. A coercer aims to persuade a victim to alter its behavior by taking actions that serve the coercer's interests. The coercer's objective is to change the target's behavior without actually having to execute the threat. Executing threats can be costly not only for the target, but also for the challenger. Coercers therefore would prefer that their words be sufficient. As Clausewitz wrote: "The

---

[1] Our use of the term "coercion" closely matches Schelling's "compellence," a term he invented to describe a "more active kind of threat" whose purpose is to provoke action rather than prevent it (1966, 71). Some scholars (including Schelling) use the term "coercion" to refer to deterrent objectives as well. However, we instead follow other contemporary scholars of coercive diplomacy in using "coercion" synonymously with "compellence." See George and Simons (1994), Pape (1996), and Art and Cronin (2003).

aggressor is always peace-loving...he would prefer to take over our country unopposed."[2] Coercion, then, is at its most effective when no punishment is ever imposed.

In our lives, as in international politics, coercion is inextricably woven into the daily rhythms of human interaction. A parent threatening to withhold a toy from a misbehaving child, a boss warning an insubordinate employee, or a homeowner threatening to sue a builder for breach of contract are all engaging in coercion. In each case, the coercer holds out the possibility of some unpleasant consequence unless the target behaves to the coercer's liking. Consider the following (hypothetical) scenarios:

The dog next door has been terrorizing the neighborhood for months. One day, the dog attacks a child who was playing in her own front yard. The child's mother promptly marches to the door of the dog's owner, looks him in the eye, and issues a stern warning: "We've had enough. If you don't get rid of that dog today, then I will."

★   ★   ★

Walking home just after midnight, a man decides to take a shortcut through a darkened alley. As he turns the corner, a figure steps out from the shadows and points a gun: "Your money or your life."

★   ★   ★

After a long committee hearing, a congressman returns to his office to find an unopened envelope on his chair. The envelope contains incriminating photographs of the Congressman involved in an extramarital affair, along with an unsigned note: "Kill the banking bill, or my next letter goes to the *Times*."

★   ★   ★

These stories all describe various forms of coercion. They illustrate two distinct ways that a coercer can attempt to achieve its aims. First, a blackmailer can threaten to impose its will by force if the target does not comply with a demand, a strategy known as "coercion by denial." In the first vignette above, the coercer's objective is to rid the

---

[2] Clausewitz (1976, 370).

neighborhood of a dangerous animal. The coercer (the child's mother) attempts to compel the neighbor to do the dirty work himself by threatening to act alone if the neighbor is uncooperative. Getting her way does not necessarily require the ability to hurt the neighbor. Indeed, she is not threatening to inflict pain on the neighbor at all. Pain, however, plays a much more central role in the other two scenarios. The alleyway mugger hopes to obtain the man's wallet by threatening to shoot him if he does not hand it over willingly. In the congressional blackmail scenario, the coercer threatens to hurt the target in another way: by ruining his career and his marriage. Strategies such as this are sometimes referred to as "coercion by punishment."[3]

Coercion in World Politics

In world politics, just as in everyday life, the object of coercion is to induce a target to alter its behavior. The target of coercion may be asked to relinquish territory, pay reparations, return hostages, end a blockade, abandon an ally, or even depose a leader. Coercers can attempt to get what they want by threatening to impose their will on other countries (coercion by denial) or by threatening to inflict pain on those states if they fail to heed demands (coercion by punishment). Countries frequently employ both forms of coercion to advance their interests in international relations.

When engaging in coercion by denial, coercers typically threaten to attack "counterforce" targets – armed forces or military facilities. A key feature of this type of coercion is that the coercer can – at least in principle – achieve its objective unilaterally, by using military force to remove, destroy, or seize the object in dispute. Weapons of mass destruction facilities, for example, can be destroyed in air raids. Missile sites can be bombed. Leaders can be assassinated. Armies can be forcibly expelled. Disputed territory can be seized and held. While the coercer in these cases would undoubtedly prefer that the target comply with its wishes, it could also achieve its objectives by acting unilaterally. The target's compliance, in other words, is preferable but not necessary for the coercer to accomplish its goals. Consider a few prominent examples:

---

[3] On the distinction between denial and punishment in coercion, see Pape (1996, 13).

- In 1991, President George H.W. Bush warned Saddam Hussein to remove Iraqi military forces from Kuwait, or the U.S. military would forcibly expel them.
- In the lead-up to the July 2015 nonproliferation deal with Iran, Israeli leader Benjamin Netanyahu repeatedly threatened to destroy Iran's nuclear facilities unless Tehran curtailed its nuclear program.
- In 2011, Azerbaijan threatened to seize Nagorno-Karabakh – territory it lost to Armenia after a war in the 1990s – if Armenia did not hand over the disputed territory peacefully.

In all of these cases, coercers hoped to get their way by convincing targets that the coercer would ultimately achieve its objectives by force if necessary. President Bush sought to coerce Saddam Hussein by suggesting that Iraqi troops would be forced out of Kuwait even if he resisted American demands. Netanyahu wanted Iran to think that its nuclear capabilities would be damaged if it did not comply with Israeli threats. And Azerbaijan tried to persuade Armenian leaders that they would inevitably lose control over the disputed territory, so resistance was futile.

Some coercive demands, however, revolve around things that cannot be physically seized: policy changes, apologies, elections or plebiscites, and reparations payments. These issues lie indelibly under the control of the target. Target states must therefore cooperate in order for the coercer to achieve its goals. In these cases, coercers can only get what they want by threatening to inflict pain on targets. Since the coercer cannot simply wrest its objective from the target's hands, it must persuade the target to cooperate by threatening punishment if it resists. In the hypothetical blackmail scenario described earlier, the blackmailer could not kill the congressional bill himself, so he had to threaten punishment in order to persuade the congressman to do it for him.

Punishment strategies usually rely on "countervalue" threats against targets that do not have direct military value, such as cities. Terrorist organizations, for example, typically employ coercion by punishment, hoping to compel governments into making concessions by threatening to inflict damage on civilian targets if they do not comply.[4] In coercive diplomacy, countries likewise utilize punishment strategies when their coercive objectives cannot be achieved by force alone. By threatening

---

[4] Pape (2003).

instead to cause unacceptable pain, they hope to motivate the target to comply. If the coercer can credibly threaten to harm items of value to the target, then the target will be more prone to capitulate. For instance:

- During the Peloponnesian War in the fifth century BCE, Athenian generals threatened to execute civilians on the island of Melos unless the Melian government agreed to join the war on Athens' side.
- In 1923, the Italian government threatened to bombard civilian targets on the Greek island of Corfu until Greece agreed to pay reparations for the death of an Italian military officer.
- After the 9/11 attacks, Pakistani leader Pervez Musharraf claimed that the United States threatened to bomb Pakistan "back to the stone age" if he did not assist Washington with counter-terrorism operations in Afghanistan.[5]

Coercers in these cases hoped to get their way by threatening to punish recalcitrant targets – not by seizing disputed objects directly. In each instance, the coercer hoped that the threatened costs of contin- ued resistance would compel the target to capitulate. The Athenians, for example, tried to alter the Melian government's behavior by threatening to inflict pain on civilians residing on the island.

While distinguishing between denial and punishment is analytically useful, coercive behavior in practice often straddles the lines between these two types. The line between "countervalue" and "counterforce" targets is often blurry: targets of military strikes may have value as both military and civilian assets. For example, the city of Hiroshima, Japan, which suffered the first atomic bomb attack in August 1945, was both a significant military target as well as a home to 250,000 civilians. Further, coercive military threats often do not specify exactly what the target of military action will be, leaving it to the recipient of the threat to infer whether the coercer plans a counterforce or coun- tervalue operation. And of course, coercive threats often contain both counterforce and countervalue components, raising the possibility of attacks against both military and civilian targets. In practice, then, denial and punishment can be difficult to disentangle.

---

[5] Goldenberg (2006).

Coercion Versus Deterrence

Coercion is often contrasted with its counterpart, deterrence. Coercion aims to spur an adversary to action, whereas deterrence aims to keep the adversary at bay. Successful coercion is marked by a change in the status quo: the adversary relinquishes a possession, changes a policy, removes or destroys something objectionable, or otherwise takes action in accordance with the coercer's wishes. Deterrence, by contrast, succeeds when the adversary does nothing at all. A deterrent threat draws a red line and warns the target not to cross it, whereas coercion draws a line and commands the adversary to step across it, or else.

Perhaps the most widespread piece of conventional wisdom about coercion is that it is more "difficult" than deterrence. Robert Art, for instance, writes that "compellence may be easier to demonstrate than deterrence, but it is harder to achieve."[6] Robert Pape likewise asserts that deterrence and compellence "pose distinct theoretical problems because coercion is harder. Threats that deter may not coerce."[7]

Why might this be the case? One key difference between coercion and deterrence is that the state issuing a deterrent demand already possesses the item at the center of the threat. The United States, for instance, made deterrent threats repeatedly throughout the Cold War to protect territories and possessions that it had held for years or even decades. By contrast, the issuer of a coercive demand generally has lived *without* the item in question for a period of time. This difference is critical because, as psychologists have long noted, individuals tend to place greater value on possessions they already own, compared to possessions they do not yet have in their custody.[8] In other words, "the party who already possesses something will value it higher than another who covets it."[9]

Coercion: A Basic Framework

Before evaluating the impact of nuclear weapons on the effectiveness of coercion in international relations, we must first paint a general picture of the factors that play into coercive success and failure. The

[6] Art (1980, 8).
[7] Pape (1996, 6).
[8] Kahneman and Tversky (1979) and Kahneman et al. (1990).
[9] Snyder and Diesing (1977, 24–25).

goal in this section is to describe the basic mechanics of coercion, and identify the broad characteristics of coercive encounters so that we can answer the question: When is coercive success more likely? Our framework incorporates familiar concepts in the study of coercion, including resolve, stakes, and military power. Once our baseline predictions are established, then we introduce nuclear weapons into the analysis and specify how they change (or do not change) the dynamics of the general framework.

Threat Credibility and the Structure of Coercive Episodes

Coercion is an interactive process. It depends on strategic choices made by at least two actors. Each actor's decision depends both on its own circumstances as well as its expectations about the likely behavior of the other actors. Figure 2.1 illustrates a simple two-step version of this interaction. After receiving a coercive demand, the target of the coercive attempt must decide whether to resist or comply. If it resists, the coercer has two basic choices: carry out its threat or walk away.

Successful coercion occurs when the target decides to comply. However, the target's decision depends in part on its belief about the credibility of the coercer's threat. If the coercer is believed to be willing to carry out its threatened punishment, then coercion is more likely to work, other things being equal. If it is not, then the target will be less likely to comply. Explaining today's behavior therefore requires us to understand what the actors expect to happen in the future. In other words, the proper way to understand Figure 2.1 is to read it backward: first, develop an expectation about whether the coercer will enforce its demands in the last stage, and then make predictions about how the target will behave in light of those expectations.

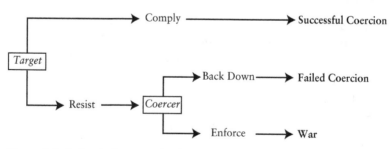

Figure 2.1 A simple framework of coercion.

An analysis of this process should address two questions. First, what factors influence a coercer's decision to enforce its threat? Second, what impacts the target's decision to comply or not?

Consider first the coercer's decision to enforce its threat. Coercers seek to maximize their net gain from engaging in coercion: to obtain the greatest benefits at the lowest cost. Enforcing a threat, however, is costly. Coercers therefore must think carefully about the likely effects of their actions before resorting to military means. Military action entails a variety of costs, including risks to soldiers' lives, damage to costly equipment, the financial expense of high-tempo military operations, and the possible reputational costs of military aggression. Further, the benefits are uncertain: war outcomes are notoriously difficult to predict, and minor unanticipated events can exert an inordinate influence on who wins and loses. Even a clear military advantage is no guarantee of success in wartime. Coercers must weigh all of these factors when deciding whether or not to carry out a military threat in the name of a coercive objective.

Targets of coercive demands face equally precarious choices. It may be painful to part with a swath of valued territory or a preferred policy, but enduring military punishment could be equally or more costly. Even if a target prevails in an eventual military conflict, the price of doing so could be prohibitively high. Targets therefore must balance the costs of surrender against the price of resistance when deciding whether to acquiesce to a coercive demand. A critical part of their calculation, as noted above, is whether they perceive the challenger's threat as credible. Coercion has a low probability of success if the target does not believe that the challenger will carry out its threat.

Key Factors: Power, Costs, and Stakes

We now have the basic skeleton of a model of coercion. Now we add some muscle to that skeleton and specify more precisely the factors that play into the decisions of each actor in coercive encounters. According to our framework, three main factors influence the outcomes of coercive episodes:[10]

---

[10] A fourth factor – the benefits of military conflict – is also potentially significant. Coercers that enforce their threats may gain in reputation or prestige, yielding dividends in future coercive episodes. Resistance may also

1. *The coercer's ability to impose its will.* A coercer that meets resistance has two choices: back down or escalate to military force. As we discussed earlier, states may have an opportunity to achieve their objectives forcibly. If another state will not voluntarily relinquish a piece of disputed territory, for example, then perhaps it can simply be seized by force. If the coercer has the military capability to do so, then the target will have strong incentives to back down rather than fight a costly and hopeless war.

2. *Crisis stakes.* Coercive episodes are fundamentally about disputed political issues. In every coercive encounter, the coercer has a material objective that it would like to wrest from the target, whether it be territory, a disputed policy, or another issue. The stakes may not be of equal value to both sides in a crisis. In a hypothetical crisis between China and the United States over Taiwanese independence, for instance, it is likely that the stakes would be higher for Beijing than for Washington. The central question is: how much is obtaining the objective worth to the coercer, and how much is it worth to the target to keep it? The answer has an important bearing on military coercion dynamics.

3. *The costs of military conflict.* Military conflict is costly: indeed, a central purpose of engaging in it is to impose costs on one's adversary. If a coercer wishes to enforce its military threat against a target, both sides will likely endure costs. Although leaders can never be sure how a military conflict will play out, it is reasonable to assume that they enter into coercive disputes with at least some expectation of the costs they will pay if the dispute escalates to violence.

When Does Coercion Work?

What does our framework imply about the conditions under which coercion is more likely to succeed? Table 2.1 summarizes how the variables described above affect military coercion dynamics. We discuss each of these factors in turn.

---

entail reputational benefits for coercive targets, even if the ultimate outcome is unfavorable. For simplicity's sake, we set aside these factors and focus our attention on the actors' immediate costs and benefits.

Table 2.1 *Factors shaping the success of coercion.*

Variable	Effect on Probability of Successful Coercion
Coercer's ability to impose its will	+
Crisis stakes: coercer	+
Crisis stakes: target	−
Costs of conflict: coercer	−
Costs of conflict: target	+

Coercer's Ability to Impose Its Will

The first factor of interest is the coercer's (perceived) ability to impose its will on the target by prevailing in a military conflict. This ability stems directly from the coercer's relative military strength. It is important to note, however, that we treat the coercer's ability to impose its will separately from the costs that a military conflict might entail. Although one might suppose that the expected costs of a conflict are related to the balance of military strength, we treat them distinctly here in order to gain a more precise sense of the factors that impact coercive outcomes.

The coercer's ability to impose its will is positively related to successful coercion. This is, of course, quite intuitive and consistent with most literature on coercive diplomacy: other things being equal, more powerful coercers are better able to convince their targets to back down.[11] If the challenger can act alone, then the target will be more likely to comply with its coercive demands, knowing that the coercer is likely to impose its will anyway. Given that resisting could be costly and yield little chance of prevailing, the target may view compliance as the least unattractive option. Conversely, a coercer's inability to destroy the target object in cases of coercive denial will often lead to failure. Had the United States lacked sufficient airpower to destroy Soviet ballistic missile sites in Cuba in 1962, for example, it is unlikely that the Soviets would have acquiesced to U.S. demands to remove them. The credible threat of a U.S. strike was central to the Soviet Union's decision to back down.

---

[11] However, Sechser (2010, 2016a,b) argues that more powerful coercers succeed less often both because they make larger demands and because their opponents have greater incentives to defend their reputations.

To illustrate further, let us return to the hypothetical stories described earlier in this chapter. The mother's threat to remove the aggressive dog from the neighborhood is much more likely to carry weight if the child's mother owns a rifle and is known as an expert sharpshooter. On the other hand, if it was not an adult making the threat, but rather a small child, the threat would be considerably less meaningful. A similar logic applies to the thief in the alleyway: his ability to take the man's wallet by force is a critical element of his threat. If he clearly cannot do so – if, for example, he is unarmed and the victim is a world-class sprinter – then the threat will have little effect.

Military capability, then, is a key condition for the credibility of coercive threats. Indeed, if a coercer clearly lacks the ability to enact the threat, then there is little point to making it. Nevertheless, there are some historical cases of implausible coercive threats that provide a nice illustration of the linkage between capability and credibility. One such example is provided by the former Libyan leader Muammar Qaddafi, who demanded in 1975 that Oman expel foreign forces from its territory – primarily Iranian fighters – or Libya would "unleash a war." Being hundreds of miles away and lacking the ability to project air, land, or naval power, Libya's threat was absurd. The Omani government clearly thought so as well, ignoring Libya's demands and continuing to use Iranian assistance to prosecute its fight against domestic rebels.

However, material factors are only part of the equation. A coercer's ability to impose its will also depends critically on the issue at stake. The distinction between denial and punishment presented earlier in the chapter illustrates this point. Other things being equal, the challenger's ability to impose its will is likely to be highest when denial is the objective, since the coercer need only destroy certain targets (for instance, missile bases or civilian settlements) or seize disputed items in order to achieve its objectives. The more difficult cases are those in which the coercive objective is a policy change or other intangible item that the coercer cannot simply seize or destroy. In these cases, coercion must be achieved by punishment, rather than denial.

Crisis Stakes

The substantive issues behind coercive disputes impact coercive outcomes in an intuitive way as well. The more a coercer values the issue, the more likely it will be to fight for it. Once the value of the issue exceeds a critical threshold, then the coercer will choose to enforce its demand if pressed, and only highly resolved targets will escalate. A similar logic applies to the target. A target will choose resistance over acquiescence – even knowing that the coercer will fight – if it values a disputed item highly. Overall, coercion is more likely to succeed when the coercer values the stakes highly and the target does not. It is possible for both sides to place a high, low, or sharply differing value on the stakes in question.

The man in the mugging scenario may turn over his wallet if the contents are not that valuable. However, he is more likely to resist if his wallet contains his entire life savings in cash. The congressman may balk at the blackmailer's threat if he had spent his entire career working for the passage of the banking bill. However, if the bill was a trivial piece of legislation about which he cared little, he would be more likely to comply. In the realm of international politics, leaders often resist demands that put their survival or other critical interests at stake – even if they know that intransigence will lead to a fight. For instance, in 2003 Saddam Hussein resisted the American demand that he step down from power since he was highly resolved to stay in office; he might have been more likely to capitulate in the face of an imminent attack if the United States had merely demanded that he reverse an important but not critical policy.

Costs of Conflict

The fact that war is costly is the central reason coercion can be effective. If there were no costs for resisting a coercive threat, after all, then war would always be preferable to acquiescing. The possibility of averting these costs gives targets an incentive to capitulate.

The magnitude of these costs, however, exerts opposing effects on coercive outcomes. For the target, greater costs mean greater incentives to avoid fighting and simply acquiesce. If the target's expected costs of fighting are greater than its expected costs of resisting, then the target will prefer to give in rather than fight a war in defense of the stakes. The more costs a coercer can impose on the target, then, the more effective coercion is likely to be.

Consider, for instance, the congressional blackmail scenario discussed earlier. The coercer in this case attempts to get what she wants by threatening punishment: if the congressman does not comply, the blackmailer will release the incriminating photographs to a newspaper.

A critical element of this sort of coercion is the magnitude of the threatened punishment, and the harm it would inflict on the victim. If the punishment is too small, the threat will fail. The blackmailer's threat would be meaningless in this instance if the incriminating photos instead pictured the congressman gardening or reading a book. There would be no cost to the target for resisting such a threat. The challenger's ability to inflict pain likewise affects coercion in world politics.

Equally important is the pain that the coercer would suffer from carrying out the threat. The greater costs the coercer stands to pay from executing a threat, the less effective the threat will be. In the congressional blackmail story, for example, imagine that the lover pictured in the incriminating photos is also the blackmailer, and that she is a high-ranking government official with a family of her own. Her threat to release the photos now would ring hollow, because she would pay a tremendous price for releasing them. Coercive threats lose their potency when the coercer would pay prohibitive costs for implementing a threat.

Note that it is not the *balance* of costs – or the actors' relative ability to impose them – that matters for coercive outcomes. Whether one side can impose more costs than the other is irrelevant. Rather, the effectiveness of coercion depends on each side's ability to impose costs that outweigh the other side's benefits from resisting a threat. A coercer does not necessarily need to be able to inflict more harm than its opponent; it need only threaten sufficient harm to exceed the target's expected benefits from resisting. In this way, even the weak can coerce the strong.

★   ★   ★

In the following sections, we evaluate the coercive utility of nuclear weapons in light of this general theoretical framework. First, we review why many scholars believe that nuclear coercion works. Then, we draw on the framework presented above to explain why nuclear weapons are poor instruments of military blackmail – despite their enormous destructive power.

Nuclear Weapons and Coercion: The Coercionist View

Nuclear weapons revolutionized military strategy, according to many scholars, because of their destructive power. Strategist Bernard Brodie reportedly said to his wife after reading about the dropping of the atomic bomb on Hiroshima, "Everything that I have written is obsolete."[12] The headline on the front page of the *New York Times*, where Brodie learned of the attack, left little doubt about why he reached that conclusion: "FIRST ATOMIC BOMB DROPPED ON JAPAN; MISSILE IS EQUAL TO 20,000 TONS OF TNT; TRUMAN WARNS FOE OF A 'RAIN OF RUIN.'" Just one atomic bomb could kill hundreds of thousands of civilians, destroy thousands of buildings, and render large portions of land uninhabitable. Nuclear weapons are not necessary for large-scale destruction or civilian victimization, but no other weapon can cause so much damage so swiftly. The sheer speed with which they can cause massive amounts of destruction, and their potential to cause radioactive fallout, make atomic weapons truly exceptional.[13] Given that nuclear weapons provide states with the ability to inflict catastrophic damage on their adversaries, many scholars have argued that nuclear weapons fundamentally changed international politics.[14]

Yet a key question persists: does the power to hurt translate into the power to coerce? According to the nuclear coercionist school, the answer is affirmative. As Victor Asal and Kyle Beardsley write, "nuclear actors should be better able to make other states *back down short of war*, whether they are defending the status quo or not."[15]

This view relies heavily on one particular dimension of our framework: the challenger's ability to punish its adversary. Because nuclear weapons are so destructive, states have little choice but to heed the wishes of nuclear-armed challengers. Resistance is simply too costly when countries face opponents that can impose nuclear punishment. As Pape argues, "Nuclear weapons can almost always inflict more pain than any victim can withstand ... even the most determined opponents can be overwhelmed."[16] For this reason, Pape goes on to argue, "nuclear coercion works better than conventional coercion." Many other scholars share the view that the costs of resistance are too high when targets face nuclear-armed challengers.[17] According to this

---

[12] Caldwell and Williams (2012, 49).

[13] See Schelling (1966) for a further discussion of this point.

[14] For example, Kahn (1960), Schelling (1966), Jervis (1989), Powell (1990), and Waltz (2003a).

[15] Asal and Beardsley (2007, 144). Emphasis added.

[16] Pape (1996, 9).

[17] For example, Bueno de Mesquita and Riker (1982), Feldman (1983), Mearsheimer (1993), Kraig (1999), Simon (2004), Beardsley and Asal (2009b).

line of thinking, in a crisis, rational cost-benefit calculations dictate state behavior.[18] Nuclear-inferior opponents realize that they are outgunned, and they capitulate to avoid the consequences of resistance.

Nuclear coercion theory often assumes that nuclear threats are not necessary to invoke the coercive power of nuclear weapons. In other words, in this view, atomic weapons play a role in any dispute involving a nuclear power, even when their use is not explicitly threatened.[19] According to this view, simply possessing the bomb is sufficient to get one's way in international politics. Nuclear powers need not make explicit nuclear threats, put their nuclear forces on alert, or engage in other signaling activities in order to extract coercive leverage from their arsenals. As one recent study put it, "nuclear weapons loom in the background of any contest with a nuclear state."[20]

The nuclear coercionist perspective has emerged as the standard view about the political effects of nuclear weapons in scholarship, particularly over the last decade. A key theme emerging in this literature is "that nuclear weapons increase the coercive bargaining power of the states that possess them."[21] Many policymakers share the belief that nuclear weapons are useful for blackmail because of their sheer power. For instance, President Kennedy believed that a Chinese nuclear test would be the "most significant and worst event of the 1960s," in part because a nuclear arsenal would enhance Beijing's influence.[22] Condoleezza Rice expressed a similar fear about Iraq in September 2002: "It wants to blackmail its neighbors, and it will eventually want to blackmail the entire international community. If we wait until that blackmail includes the ability to blackmail with a nuclear weapon, we will have made a grave mistake."[23]

Prominent journalists routinely espouse the coercionist view. Indeed, the mainstream media seems to take for granted that a nuclear-armed Iran would be able to bully other states into submission. David Sanger, for example, wrote matter-of-factly in the *New York Times*:

---

[18] Nitze (1956) and Betts (1987).
[19] See, for example, Nitze (1956).
[20] Gartzke et al. (2014, 488).
[21] Horowitz (2009, 234). See also Pape (1996), Asal and Beardsley (2007), Gartzke and Jo (2009), Beardsley and Asal (2009b), and Beardsley and Asal (2009a).
[22] Quoted in Burr and Richelson (2000/2001, 61).
[23] Rice (2002).

The Iranians know exactly what the bomb would make them: the dominant regional power in the Middle East. Iran would become, in a stroke, more powerful than the Saudis, an even greater influence than it is today over a Shiite-controlled Iraq, and, arguably, as powerful as Israel. And the better Iran's missile technology becomes, the greater its influence and ability to blackmail.[24]

Nuclear coercion theory comes in different varieties. Each strand of the theory accepts that nuclear weapons are useful for purposes other than deterrence, but makes slightly different claims about the conditions under which nuclear blackmail works. We distinguish between two types of nuclear coercion theory: *absolutists* and *relativists*. Absolutists imply that nuclear powers have coercive advantages regardless of their opponents' capabilities. Once a state acquires nuclear weapons, this view suggests, it can impose its will on nuclear and nonnuclear adversaries alike. Analysts frequently make this argument about Iran.[25] If Tehran builds nuclear weapons, they contend, it will be able to coerce Israel and the United States – two states with vastly superior nuclear arsenals – as well as nonnuclear countries such as Saudi Arabia and the UAE. In sum, what matters for nuclear absolutists is simply whether a state has nuclear weapons, not how its arsenal compares to others.

Relativists instead focus on the nuclear balance. Some posit that the coercive leverage of a state's nuclear arsenal is neutralized against a nuclear-armed target, especially if the target has a second-strike capability.[26] As Pape writes, "nuclear coercion can work ... only when the coercer enjoys superiority so great that it need not fear retaliation in kind."[27] According to this line of thinking, a state will refrain from executing a coercive nuclear threat if doing so will bring about nuclear retaliation. Nuclear targets therefore are free to resist demands made by nuclear-armed challengers. This logic suggests that Iran would not be able to blackmail the United States or Israel – even if Iran someday builds a larger arsenal than either country. Conversely, neither Israel nor the United States would be able to coerce a nuclear-armed Iran. Nuclear weapons, in this view, are a prescription for stalemate.

---

[24] Sanger (2006).
[25] For example, Bolton (2015).
[26] Beardsley and Asal (2009b).
[27] Pape (1996, 173).

Other relativists, however, believe that nuclear states can coerce other nuclear powers, as long as they have larger arsenals.[28] Nuclear superiority, then, is the key to coercive victories. In a crisis with two nuclear-armed states, the side that wins will be the one that has more nuclear forces at its disposal. The logic here is that although nuclear war would be catastrophic for both states, it would be relatively worse for the nuclear-inferior state. To illustrate, consider a hypothetical crisis between North Korea and the United States in which Washington makes a coercive demand. If North Korea had the capacity to deliver nuclear warheads on long-range missiles, it could perhaps destroy a handful of U.S. cities on the West coast with its small atomic arsenal. The United States, on the other hand, has an arsenal large enough to destroy every city in North Korea. In a nuclear war between these two countries, therefore, North Korea would suffer more than the United States. Because the costs of war for North Korea are high relative to those same costs for the United States, Pyongyang should capitulate, according to this particular relativist argument. Scholars have used similar logic to explain Soviet-American crises during the Cold War. They argue that overwhelming U.S. nuclear superiority during the early Cold War period provided America with significant coercive advantages in its dealings with the Soviets. However, the loss of nuclear superiority during the 1970s "diminished U.S. political leverage."[29]

Brinkmanship and the Manipulation of Risk

Nuclear states hoping to coerce other nuclear powers face a tall order: they must make seemingly suicidal threats believable. They can do this, some theorists argue, by manipulating the shared risk of accidental nuclear war. For a coercer, the purpose of manipulating risk is to generate coercive leverage in a situation where a threat otherwise would not be credible. When states introduce the possibility of inadvertent catastrophe, they can alter the behavior of their enemies even in a world of mutually assured destruction.

---

[28] For example, Bueno de Mesquita and Riker (1982) and Kroenig (2013).

[29] Betts (1987, 15). Pape (1996, 37) accepts this line of thinking, arguing that "Although Britain in the Suez crisis and the Soviet Union in the Cuban missile crisis had some nuclear retaliatory capabilities, both were tremendously overmatched and both conceded."

Schelling conceptualized risk manipulation as a tactic to be used by the superpowers during the Cold War, noting that a threat to launch a global nuclear war inherently lacks credibility because of the enormous costs it would impose on both sides.[30] For Schelling, the strategic problem in such a scenario is how to coerce one's opponent when one cannot credibly threaten to intentionally launch a war. Brinkmanship offers an answer. According to Schelling, brinkmanship involves "the deliberate creation of a recognizable risk of war, a risk that one does not completely control. It is the tactic of deliberately letting the situation get somewhat out of hand ... It means harassing and intimidating an adversary by exposing him to a shared risk [of war]."[31] In order to coerce intransigent targets, challengers therefore must increase the probability that an inadvertent war will occur.

To illustrate how this might be done, Schelling describes an imaginary scenario:

I should have a little black box that contains a roulette wheel and a device that will detonate in a way that unquestionably provokes total war. I then set this little box down, tell the Russians that I have set it going so that once a day the roulette wheel will spin with a given probability ... that, on any day, the little box will provoke total war. I tell them ... that the little box will keep running until my demands have been complied with and that *there is nothing I can do to stop it*.[32]

Hypothetical stories like this one usefully illustrate the theory behind risk manipulation. However, no country actually possesses a "little black box." How, then, can countries blackmail their adversaries by raising the danger of nuclear punishment? In other words, how might leaders deliberately risk accidental war in order to intimidate their foes?

Most nuclear powers maintain assertive civilian control over their arsenals. For example, in the United States – except in rare contingencies – a nuclear attack can occur only with authorization from the president and confirmation by the Secretary of Defense. Measures such as this are instituted to prevent the risk of an accidental nuclear launch. States may be able to effectively manipulate risk for coercive purposes by removing safety-related measures and decentralizing the command

[30] Schelling (1960).
[31] Schelling (1960, 200).
[32] Schelling (1960, 197). Emphasis in original.

structures of their nuclear arsenals.[33] One approach involves leaders "pre-delegating" the authority to order the use of nuclear weapons to local military commanders. When states take decisions about nuclear use away from civilian leaders, they run the risk that "rogue military officers could take matters into their own hands and release nuclear weapons."[34] Delegating launch authority to local commanders is therefore dangerous – and that is precisely why it could be an effective way to manipulate risk. Predelegation therefore may be one way that states can *deliberately* manipulate the risk of nuclear war, thereby instilling fear in their opponents.

To illustrate how accidents can inadvertently occur during nuclear crises, consider an example from the 1962 Cuban missile crisis. During the crisis, the United States alerted its nuclear forces to signal its resolve.[35] As a consequence of the alert, military commanders were granted effective launch authority over some nuclear forces. This raised the possibility, however unlikely, that nuclear weapons could be launched without the approval of top political authorities. One such scenario came frighteningly close to playing out. Shortly after the U.S. nuclear alert, the pilot of a U-2 based in Alaska became disoriented and accidentally ventured into Soviet airspace. The Soviets scrambled MiG fighter jets to intercept the spy plane, and the United States sent aircraft to usher the U-2 back to Alaska. Because of the nuclear alert, the U.S. fighters were carrying nuclear warheads – and the pilots had control over the firing of those weapons.[36] The U-2 returned to American airspace without a military confrontation, but it is not hard to imagine that this incident could have triggered a catastrophic clash – even though this is an outcome that the Americans and the Soviets desperately hoped to avoid. Actions like these, according to this perspective, help resolve crises by revealing which side in a nuclear crisis has a greater ability to tolerate risk.

Other deterrence theorists, such as Robert Powell, conceive of risk manipulation somewhat differently than Schelling.[37] They argue that risk is an inherent feature of nuclear crises – it is not something that leaders deliberately manipulate to coerce their enemies. The risk of

[33] Sagan (1985, 132).
[34] Narang (2013, 14).
[35] See Sagan (1985).
[36] Allison and Zelikow (1999, 240).
[37] Powell (1990).

disaster, according to this view, simply increases the longer that states remain in a crisis. As Powell explains, "Because the risk that a crisis will go out of control rises as the crisis continues, deciding how long to hang on is equivalent to deciding how high a state is willing to let the risk go before quitting."[38] The way states raise the risk of inadvertent war, then, is by simply standing firm during crises. The longer that states remain in a crisis, the greater the risk that an accident will lead to mutual disaster. According to this view, leaders do not enthusiastically bid up the risk of a catastrophic war; they do so reluctantly, and leaders' willingness to remain in a crisis does not necessarily imply that they are being reckless.[39]

While they disagree about the nature of risk during crises, brinkmanship theorists generally agree that a coercer can make its threats more effective by raising the possibility that a crisis will spiral out of control if the target does not back down. Some scholars contend that nuclear states "win" crises precisely by manipulating this level of risk. States with a nuclear advantage in a crisis, they argue, are more likely to take actions that raise the likelihood that the crisis will get out of hand.[40] Nuclear war would be costly for both countries, but it would be comparatively worse for the state with nuclear inferiority. Relatively weak states, then, cannot outlast adversaries with nuclear superiority during competitions in risk taking. Nuclear-superior states, in short, can coerce their adversaries by raising the risk of an event that neither side would intentionally choose.

Other brinkmanship theorists argue that the balance of resolve – not nuclear superiority – determines which crisis actor will manipulate risk more effectively.[41] Countries that have more at stake in a crisis, this view holds, will march closer to the nuclear brink, increasing the likelihood of a crisis victory. This line of thinking is partially consistent with the nuclear coercionist logic, but somewhat at odds with it: while it downplays the significance of strategic superiority, this view nonetheless accepts that countries may derive coercive value from their arsenals even when nuclear threats are seemingly incredible.

---

[38] Powell (2014, 94).
[39] Powell (2014, 90).
[40] See, for example, McDonough (2006); Kroenig (2013).
[41] See, for example, Jervis (1984, 9); Powell (1990).

Implications for Nuclear Statecraft

Nuclear coercion theory encompasses several different views about the role of nuclear weapons in world politics, as the preceding discussion illustrates. Scholars in this theoretical tradition may accept some tenets of nuclear coercion theory while disagreeing with others. In general, however, the nuclear coercionist school yields three specific implications that we investigate in the following chapters.

Implication #1: Nuclear powers are more successful at coercive diplomacy. The first and most obvious claim of the coercionist perspective is that nuclear weapons are useful tools of coercive diplomacy. If this is true, a review of the historical record should reveal that states with nuclear capabilities achieve their objectives more often in coercive diplomacy. For nuclear absolutists, this means that coercive diplomacy will be more effective regardless of how many nuclear weapons a coercer possesses; for relativists, only states with a nuclear advantage over their opponents will enjoy this benefit. But the central implication is the same: nuclear weapons and successful coercion go hand in hand.

Implication #2: Nuclear coercers push harder in crises. A second claim of the coercionist viewpoint is that nuclear weapons embolden states to take escalatory actions in crises. States with a nuclear advantage push harder and take more aggressive military actions, according to this view. For the coercionists, a nuclear advantage translates into an advantage in the war of nerves.

Implication #3: Brinkmanship works. Finally, many coercionists expect that when nuclear coercion works, it works primarily through the mechanism of risk: targets back down because the risk of an accidental or inadvertent conflict is intolerably high. This logic is especially applicable to crises between nuclear states, where launching a nuclear strike would likely invite devastating retaliation. In these cases, we should observe that the targets of nuclear coercion back down not because they believe that the coercer will intentionally launch a nuclear attack, but because they fear an accidental war if the crisis persists.

Flawed Logic: Problems with the Nuclear Coercionist View

The nuclear coercionist view at first glance seems sensible: it is intuitive to suggest that more powerful states have greater influence in world politics. However, there are a variety of problems with the coercionist view of nuclear statecraft.

First, the nuclear coercionist school focuses largely on just one of the elements of successful coercion that we identified earlier in this chapter – the target's costs of resistance – while downplaying the others. It is understandable that this view focuses on the target's punishment costs given that the destructive power of nuclear weapons is what separates them from other military technologies. However, factors other than punishment affect whether nuclear coercion succeeds. A complete theory must account for the advantages *and* the limitations of nuclear weapons for military blackmail. Once we account for all of the relevant factors, the coercive utility of nuclear weapons declines considerably.

To their credit, most scholars in the coercionist camp acknowledge that carrying out nuclear threats could be costly for the attacker. But they conceive of these costs narrowly, focusing on potential for military retaliation. Implementing a nuclear threat could also result in significant political and economic consequencs for the coercer, but most coercionist theories do not fully incorporate these costs. As a result, these scholars overstate the circumstances under which nuclear threats may be credible.

Second, the assumption that nuclear weapons loom in the background of every crisis involving a nuclear power is problematic. In fact, in most crises, the possibility of an atomic attack is so remote that leaders are unlikely to spend time worrying about nuclear punishment. For example, Israel and Syria have experienced numerous crises over Damascus' support for terrorist organizations. Israel has frequently demanded that Syria end support for these groups, and it has occasionally used military force to signal its resolve. According to the nuclear coercionist school, nuclear weapons should have loomed in the background of these crises even though their use was not explicitly threatened. However, in reality there is virtually no evidence of a looming nuclear shadow: Syria does not appear to have seriously considered the prospect of nuclear punishment if it failed to curtail its support for terrorist groups.

Of course, some disputes, like the Cuban missile crisis, carry a real risk of nuclear escalation. But to insert nuclear weapons into a crisis, coercers have to deliberately invoke their arsenals. Indeed, the possibility of nuclear use emerges only after states make verbal threats, issue nuclear alerts, conspicuously deploy nuclear forces, or send other nuclear signals. For some nuclear coercionists, these measures aid coercive diplomacy. By manipulating risk with their nuclear arsenals, these scholars argue, coercers can make even seemingly incredible threats believable.

This brings us to a third limitation of the nuclear coercionist school: it overstates the degree to which brinkmanship can solve the credibility problem in nuclear coercion. To be sure, the manipulation of risk may sometimes aid nuclear statecraft. But there are two critical problems with brinkmanship theory. First, most leaders want to maintain control during crises rather than cede it. The same thing that makes brinkmanship effective – namely, that it is dangerous – often makes leaders unwilling to use it. Second, even if leaders are willing to invoke their arsenals in crises, nuclear signals are often interpreted incorrectly or missed altogether. We revisit the limitations of brinkmanship later in this chapter.

We are hardly the first to argue that nuclear weapons have limitations as instruments of coercion. Robert Jervis, for example, argued that nuclear weapons are tools for preserving the status quo, not for changing it.[42] Kenneth Waltz likewise contended that "nuclear weapons are poor instruments for blackmail."[43] These scholars typically make two arguments. First, coercion is difficult, and rarely works under any circumstances. Second, nuclear weapons are such effective deterrents that a coercive nuclear threat would never work against another nuclear power. For the most part, however, these skeptics have not provided systematic evidence to support their claims.[44]

More importantly, existing scholarship about the limitations of nuclear weapons leaves several gaps in our understanding of nuclear coercion. First, although coercion is indeed intrinsically difficult, as these studies argue, it is possible that nuclear coercers may nevertheless

---

[42] Jervis (1989, 29–35).

[43] Sagan and Waltz (2002, 17). Others have made similar claims: see, for example, Paul (1998, 2009), Walt (2000), Byman and Waxman (2002), and Russett (2011).

[44] Two important exceptions are Bundy (1984) and Halperin (1987), who evaluate the effectiveness of coercive threats in several nuclear crises.

succeed more often than other states. Simply knowing that coercion is hard does not necessarily refute the logic of nuclear coercion. Second, most previous scholarship on nuclear coercion has little to say about the use of nuclear threats against nonnuclear adversaries.[45] Are nuclear weapons useful for coercion when a defender cannot retaliate in kind? Third, skeptics of nuclear coercion have not adequately explained why countries cannot overcome the credibility problems inherent in nuclear coercion through brinkmanship, as Schelling and others have argued.

Below, we aim to correct these theoretical gaps, explaining why nuclear coercion is uniquely difficult compared to other types of coercion – even against nonnuclear adversaries. In addition, we challenge the classic logic of brinkmanship, explaining why the coercionist view is overly optimistic about the possibility of manipulating nuclear risk in order to prevail in crises.

Nuclear Skepticism Theory

We offer a theory of nuclear statecraft that more accurately reflects the role of nuclear weapons in international relations. To begin, we return to the above conditions for successful coercion. We ask a simple question: do nuclear weapons help challengers achieve these conditions? They often do not, according to nuclear skepticism theory. One key reason has to do with threat credibility.

The Credibility Problem in Nuclear Coercion

According to our general framework described earlier, successful coercion depends partially on the target's beliefs about the credibility of the coercer's threat. If the target believes that the coercer might carry out its threat, the target will be more likely to comply, all else being equal. However, coercion has a very low likelihood of success when the target views the coercer's threat as incredible.

Nuclear powers hoping to gain political leverage from the bomb face a major problem: threats to use nuclear weapons for coercion usually lack credibility. Three problems combine to render coercive nuclear threats incredible (see Figure 2.2). First, in many cases the

---

[45] For an exception, see Paul (1998).

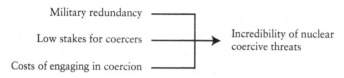

Figure 2.2 The coercive limitations of nuclear weapons.

coercer can accomplish its objectives by relying exclusively on its conventional power. Second, nuclear powers would likely pay tremendous military and political costs for launching offensive nuclear attacks. Third, coercers may care about the issues at the heart of their disputes, but the stakes are rarely high enough to offset the costs of a nuclear first strike. These problems combine to make nuclear weapons poor instruments of coercion.

Nuclear credibility problems are not unique to coercive threats. Deterrence theorists have long recognized that it can be difficult to make deterrent nuclear threats credible – especially deterrent threats meant to protect allies.[46] But the conditions for success identified above are more likely to be present in deterrence, making nuclear weapons relatively more useful for preserving the status quo than for changing it. It seems likely, for example, that the American commitment to use nuclear weapons if the Soviets invaded West Germany – a promise that was backed by the NATO alliance – helped preserve peace in Europe during the Cold War.[47] Nuclear deterrence worked in part because the American nuclear threat was sufficiently credible. The stakes were high for Washington (although, to be sure, protecting Europe was less important than defending the homeland). Even though using nuclear weapons to defend West Germany would have been costly for the United States, those costs would have been reduced to some degree if the Soviets had initiated the confrontation by launching an invasion. On top of this, the United States was conventionally outgunned in Europe throughout much of the Cold War. As a result, conventional threats alone may have been insufficient to thwart a Soviet invasion, raising the credibility of the U.S. threat to escalate.

---

[46] For example Schelling (1960), Snyder and Diesing (1977), Powell (1990), and Morgan (2003).
[47] See Mearsheimer (1984), Gaddis (1987), and Fuhrmann and Sechser (2014b).

Problem #1: Redundancy

According to our general theory of coercion, military technologies can benefit coercive challengers by enhancing their ability to do one of two things: (1) impose their will militarily or (2) punish recalcitrant targets. Nuclear weapons may be sufficient to accomplish both of these objectives. But, when it comes to coercion, they are often unnecessary.

States often use coercive diplomacy to eliminate sensitive military facilities, remove obstinate leaders from power, or seize disputed objects, like territory. When it comes to destroying disputed objects, nuclear weapons are generally far more powerful than needed.[48] Moreover, nuclear weapons have little utility for warfighting in disputed territory: carrying out nuclear attacks on contested territory would destroy the very land that the coercer hopes to possess. Overall, then, nuclear weapons are not useful for coercion by denial.[49] Simply put, nuclear weapons usually do not help challengers achieve their foreign policy objectives forcibly.

Nuclear coercion theory sometimes acknowledges that nuclear weapons do not increase a country's ability to impose its will militarily in coercive crises.[50] Instead, they argue, nuclear weapons have coercive value because of their ability to impose punishment on targets. But here too, nuclear weapons often are redundant to a coercer's conventional capabilities. For instance, in 1997 the United States threatened to punish Iraq if it did not readmit UN weapons inspectors tasked with verifying the dismantlement of the country's weapons of mass destruction programs. To be sure, the United States could have inflicted vastly more pain on Iraq by unleashing its nuclear arsenal. Yet Washington also had the capacity to hurt Baghdad with conventional strikes, and in the end the threat of conventional punishment was sufficient to achieve a coercive victory.[51]

There are two main conditions under which nuclear weapons are likely to make a unique contribution to a state's ability to achieve

---

[48] See Huth and Russett (1984).

[49] Nuclear weapons are much more relevant militarily for *deterrence* by denial. Atomic weapons may deter invasions, in part, because they can blunt advancements by an enemy's military forces.

[50] See Pape (1996, 36).

[51] Saddam Hussein temporarily heeded the U.S. demand before permanently expelling the weapons inspectors in 1998. For more details, see Byman (2000/2001) and Alterman (2003).

coercive victory. First, if the coercer seeks to destroy hardened targets buried deep underground, conventional firepower may be insufficient. In the mid-1990s, for example, the United States detected a suspected chemical weapons plant in Libya known as Tarhunah. Washington threatened to destroy this facility if Libya did not curtail its chemical weapons program, and at least one U.S. official publicly raised the specter of a nuclear attack. A senior U.S. Defense Department official remarked during the crisis, "If we wanted to destroy [Tarhunah], B-61 will be the nuclear weapon of choice."[52] In cases such as these, nuclear weapons may offer military capabilities that conventional weapons cannot. Second, conventionally weak coercers may depend more heavily on nuclear arsenals to prevail in coercive diplomacy. Nuclear weapons are often unnecessary for the United States because it has robust conventional forces. Yet, for countries such as North Korea and Pakistan, nuclear weapons may be the only way to effectively punish an adversary, or credibly threaten it with military defeat. Under some conditions, then, the redundancy problem may be less significant. Yet for most nuclear states, nuclear weapons are redundant for achieving coercive objectives.

Problem #2: The Costs of Nuclear Coercion

Whether a coercive threat succeeds depends, in part, on the challenger's costs of implementing the threat. A challenger that carried out a coercive nuclear threat almost certainly would face tremendous costs.[53] We group these costs into three general categories: direct backlash, long-term containment, and precedent setting.

Direct Backlash. The use of nuclear weapons for reasons other than self-defense would likely result in direct backlash for the coercer. A country that implemented a nuclear threat may face stiff military responses from other countries, as nuclear coercion theory acknowledges. Yet the immediate costs for the nuclear user are by no means limited to military retaliation. Nuclear blackmailers may suffer political and economic consequences, too. The international community may shun nuclear users, potentially leading to political isolation or loss in foreign investment. John Foster Dulles, Secretary of State in

---

[52] See Burns (1996).
[53] For a further discussion of these costs, see Fuhrmann (2016).

the Eisenhower administration, made this point when considering the general use of the bomb in East Asia: "If we resort to such a use of nuclear weapons," he said, "we will in the eyes of the world, be cast as a ruthless military power, as was Germany."[54]

In addition, implementing a coercive nuclear threat could result in domestic backlash that jeopardizes a leader's job security. Indeed, the public may oppose the first use of nuclear weapons, and seek to punish leaders who use atomic forces offensively. Expectations about domestic political fallout may constrain leaders' options when it comes to nuclear weapons. For example, in the 1950s, most officials in the U.S. State Department opposed nuclear use "because of the disastrous effect of such a policy on public opinion."[55]

Long-Term Containment. A state that used nuclear weapons could encourage others to align against it. They might, for instance, balance against the nuclear user by forging military alliances. American policymakers were certainly aware of this risk during the Cold War. Washington was cautious when dealing with China, in particular, because it recognized that countering nonnuclear threats with nuclear weapons would push friendly nations into the arms of Beijing.[56] Even a state's allies could turn against it following an unprovoked nuclear attack. At the very least, nuclear blackmail may complicate alliance relationships. According to President Eisenhower, this is one reason the United States did not use nuclear weapons during the Korean War: "an American decision to use them ... would have created strong disrupting feelings between ourselves and our allies."[57]

Nuclear coercion could also encourage nuclear proliferation.[58] The targets of nuclear blackmail may be motivated by their experience to seek nuclear weapons for deterrence. For example, China built nuclear weapons in part to reduce its vulnerability to American nuclear threats in the wake of the Taiwan Straits crises of the 1950s.[59] Other states may seek nuclear weapons as well, even if they were not the target of

---

[54] Quoted in Paul (2009, 56).
[55] Quoted in Paul (2009, 56).
[56] Burr and Richelson (2000/2001, 78).
[57] Eisenhower (1963, 180).
[58] Sagan (2004).
[59] Lewis and Xue (1988).

a threat. After learning of the American nuclear bombing of Japan, for instance, Soviet leader Josef Stalin told his advisers, "Hiroshima has shaken the whole world ... build the bomb – it will remove a great danger to us."[60]

Precedent Setting. The first-use of nuclear weapons might set a dangerous precedent – namely, that it is acceptable to use the bomb to settle international disputes. Once a state develops a reputation as a "nuclear user," it may be easier for others to justify using nuclear weapons against it. This concern weighs on the minds of the American public: survey research suggests that Americans who oppose the use of nuclear weapons tend to hold that view because they worry that a nuclear strike would encourage similar attacks against the United States in the future.[61] Launching a nuclear attack might also legitimize a rival's use of atomic weapons against a third party. If, for example, the United States had used nuclear strikes to coerce China or North Korea during the Cold War, the Soviet Union might have perceived that it had the right to use nuclear weapons to resolve its own disputes in East Asia or Europe.[62]

Problem #3: Low Stakes

Military technologies – including nuclear weapons – generally do not affect the stakes in coercive bargaining. Yet the stakes in a coercive dispute bear on the effectiveness of coercive challenges. In coercion, a challenger often hopes to gain sovereignty over disputed territory, reverse an adversary's policy, or extract reparations. These things are obviously important to the coercer; it would not have attempted to blackmail its enemy in the first place if that was not the case. These issues, however, rarely threaten the coercer's vital interests. Instead, such disputes often involve bargaining over issues that the coercer has already learned to live without – suggesting that it could continue to do so. Consequently, the costs of coercion will loom especially large for nuclear coercers.

The stakes in a dispute are likely to be somewhat lower for the coercer, other things being equal, than they are for the target. Psychological experiments have demonstrated that individuals tend to

---

[60] Quoted in Sagan (1996, 58).
[61] Press et al. (2013).
[62] Paul (2009, 50–51).

fear losses more than they value equivalent gains.[63] Leaders therefore may care more about avoiding setbacks to their country's standing than they do about improving their country's position. Indeed, policymakers usually expend more effort to defend the status quo than they do to overturn it.[64] Challengers are therefore likely to find themselves up against more resolved targets. Although a coercer may be highly motivated to acquire a given possession, it has already demonstrated that it can live without that possession. By contrast, targets can usually claim that giving up a disputed possession would threaten their existing level of national security. This will not always be the case, of course, depending on the particularities of the dispute. But, on the whole, the targets of coercive demands are likely to value the stakes in a crisis more than the coercer. Consider the Soviet Union's attempts to grab territory from Iran and Turkey after World War II. Moscow was much more powerful than either of those states, but it had an inherent bargaining disadvantage – losing territory would have hurt Iran and Turkey more than gaining it would have benefited the Soviet Union.

Reputational factors also influence the balance of stakes: targets have strong incentives to resist challengers in coercion for the sake of reputation building.[65] Since the target of a coercive threat must act – rather than not act – to comply with a coercive demand, it is difficult for a compliant target to avoid the perception that it was bullied into making concessions. Targets therefore could develop a reputation for being irresolute if they capitulate, which might invite additional coercive challenges in the future. By contrast, resisting a coercer, especially one armed with nuclear weapons, can strengthen a state's reputation for toughness. Standing up to U.S. threats during the 1968 U.S.S. *Pueblo* episode, for instance, arguably enhanced the domestic and international stature of Kim Il Sung, North Korea's leader.

The Limits of Nuclear Brinkmanship

A key reason nuclear coercion does not work, according to our theory, is that coercive nuclear threats are incredible. However, some deterrence theorists have been arguing for decades that states can use their

---

[63] Kahneman and Tversky (1979).
[64] Berejikian and Early (2013).
[65] Sechser (2010, 2016b).

arsenals for influence even when nuclear threats lack credibility.[66] They can do so, these scholars hold, by manipulating the shared risk of war. But just how useful is nuclear brinkmanship?

We acknowledge that in some cases states may be able to make nuclear threats credible by manipulating risk. However, brinkmanship theory is overly sanguine about risk manipulation as a solution to the credibility problem in nuclear crises. We reach this conclusion for three main reasons.

Coercion and the Inherent Risk of Nuclear War

According to brinkmanship theory, refusing to back down in a crisis increases the risk of inadvertent nuclear war. According to some proponents of this view, the risk of inadvertence is an inherent feature of nuclear crises – and increases as a crisis drags on. Yet the historical record does not support this view. Many lengthy crises carry little risk of accidental nuclear war, while some relatively short crises are rife with danger. The Cuban missile crisis – perhaps the most dangerous nuclear crisis of the Cold War – lasted only thirteen days. In contrast, the crisis between the Soviet Union and the United States that ensued following the Soviet invasion of Afghanistan in 1979 persisted for more than two months with little danger of an inadvertent nuclear war. How can we account for this disparity?

History suggests that the risk of inadvertence is not an ever-present feature of nuclear crises. Instead, it emerges primarily from the purposive actions of leaders. If crisis actors do nothing to introduce risk, there will be little danger of an unintended disaster – regardless of how long a crisis lasts. However, the risk of inadvertent escalation can be quite serious if states adopt measures that increase the possibility of an accident. Consider the U-2 incident discussed above. The risk of an accidental nuclear exchange did not emerge simply because the United States stood firm during the Cuban missile crisis. Rather, it resulted from a specific policy decision – President Kennedy's authorization of the nuclear alert. If Kennedy had not put U.S. air units on alert, effectively transferring nuclear launch authority to pilots, the danger of an inadvertent nuclear strike would have declined considerably. Circumstances were different during the Soviet-American crisis over Afghanistan. Neither side seriously worried about an inadvertent

---

[66] For example, Schelling (1966) and Powell (1990).

atomic exchange because the participants in the crisis refrained from taking actions that could have manipulated the risk of nuclear war, such as alerting nuclear forces.

Instead, Schelling's conception of risk manipulation is a more plausible depiction of real-world crises. States must do something intentional – such as spinning the metaphorical roulette wheel – that raises the likelihood of accidental nuclear conflict in order to generate risk. However, this brings us to a second point: leaders often lack the desire to manipulate risk with their nuclear arsenals.

The Will to Manipulate Risk

Manipulating risk is not free. As Schelling noted, the central drawback of risk manipulation – but also the very reason to do it – is that it could backfire and accidentally trigger a costly war. Moreover, there are potential political drawbacks to employing a "threat that leaves something to chance." Leaders that are seen to be reckless could pay a domestic price, if the leader's constituents judge risky behavior as a sign of incompetence. Even if a leader prevails in a crisis and successfully coerces an adversary by spinning the roulette wheel, the leader's political constituency may be sufficiently unnerved to replace her with one who can maintain better control of the nation's military forces. These factors will reduce a coercer's inclination to use stochastic risks to compensate for incredible threats.

In addition, psychological predispositions inhibit the use of risk manipulation as a coercive strategy. As a broad tendency, individuals generally are inclined to maximize control and minimize random chance in decision making, especially when the stakes are high. Individuals prefer to keep control of their options in high-stakes decisions, not release control over them.[67] When a crisis erupts, the experience of high stress leads individuals to maximize control, not relinquish it.[68] In leaders, this effect may be exacerbated by the process through which national leaders generally acquire their positions: whether in a democracy or authoritarian regime, political leaders who favor tight control and leave little to chance are more likely to rise to power. Even if risk manipulation might be an effective coercive strategy under some circumstances, these perspectives lead us to expect that it will

[67] Brehm (1956) and Shin and Ariely (2004).
[68] Rosen (2005).

be employed only very rarely. President Kennedy and his advisers, for example, famously worried about the risk of unintended provocations during the Cuban missile crisis.[69] But Kennedy did not respond to this risk by capitulating: instead, he sought to exert greater control over events, taking pains to ensure that the ships establishing the naval quarantine received "as detailed instructions as possible."[70]

Countries may use nuclear signals if the stakes in a crisis are high, as they often are in deterrence. Consider the case of nuclear deterrence in Europe during the Cold War. Although the conditions for coercive success were generally met in that case, some still questioned the credibility of the U.S. nuclear threat. It is well known, for instance, that French leader Charles de Gaulle and others doubted that the United States would be willing to sacrifice New York or Washington in order to defend Paris or London. Washington therefore needed to do more work to convince the Soviets (and the Europeans) that it would in fact use nuclear weapons in the event of a Soviet invasion – and it was willing to put in the requisite effort because of the importance attached to defending Europe. To signal its commitment, the United States stationed tactical nuclear weapons in West Germany and other European countries.[71] It then went a step further and provided launch authority to local commanders in the event of war, raising the possibility that nuclear weapons would be used without authority from the leadership in Washington. By manipulating risk in this fashion, the United States bolstered the credibility of its nuclear deterrent threat. However, the United States did not show the same willingness to manipulate risk to coerce the Soviet Union in peacetime. The United States did not, for example, purposefully alert its nuclear forces to compel Moscow withdraw troops from Afghanistan in 1979.[72] States sometimes take measures to preserve the status quo – including relaxing control over their nuclear arsenals – that they are unwilling to take for the purposes of coercion.

---

[69] Blight et al. (1987).

[70] Allison and Zelikow (1999, 232).

[71] On the use of forward nuclear deployments in extended deterrence, see Fuhrmann and Sechser (2014a,b) and Sechser (2016c).

[72] The United States did, however, alert its forces in November 1979 and again in 1980 in response to a false warning of a Soviet missile attack. See Burr (2012).

Risk and Signaling

Even if states undertake actions that they believe increase the risk of accidental conflict, brinkmanship nonetheless may fail to pay coercive dividends. At least two factors can undermine the effectiveness of brinkmanship as a coercive tool.

First, there is no guarantee that coercers' attempts to manipulate risk will be noticed by the other side. To be sure, states monitor their adversaries' military maneuvers closely, particularly during crises. But it is nonetheless possible for crisis participants to miss nuclear signals sent by their opponents. Nikita Khrushchev's movement of nuclear missiles into East Germany during the 1958–1959 Berlin crisis, for example, seems to have gone undetected by the United States.[73]

Second, even if signals are detected, they may not be correctly perceived by adversaries. Leaders often assume that their motives are as clear to others as they are to themselves.[74] Thus, when a coercer sends a nuclear signal, it may assume that the target understands the appropriate message. However, a signal's meaning is not always obvious, particularly when it could be interpreted in multiple ways, as is often the case in nuclear brinkmanship. Imagine, for the sake of illustration, that a coercer moves nuclear-capable missiles out of a storage facility during a crisis, as Pakistan is alleged to have done during the Kargil War in 1999. This move could be interpreted in at least three ways: (1) as a signal that the coercer might use nuclear weapons if the target fails to comply with a demand; (2) as a sign that the coercer might launch a nuclear response if the target attacks first; or (3) as a measure to reduce the coercer's vulnerability to a pre-emptive strike. The deployment therefore could be coercive (interpretation #1), deterrent (interpretation #2), or defensive (interpretation #3) in nature. These three motives have very different implications. Which of these inferences is correct may be clear only to the coercer itself. Yet coercers often wrongly assume that their signals are clear to others as well.

Consider President Richard Nixon's nuclear alert during the Vietnam War, in October 1969. Nixon ordered a secret airborne alert of nuclear-armed bombers to signal to the Soviets and the North Vietnamese that he might be willing to use nuclear weapons to end the war – in other words, to support a coercive demand to strike a peace

[73] We discuss this episode in detail in Chapter 5.
[74] Jervis (1976, 1982).

deal. Moscow detected the alert, but did not interpret it as a signal
of resolve in the context of Vietnam, contrary to what Schelling and
other brinkmanship theorists might expect.[75] Nixon's motives may
have seemed obvious to him, but they were opaque to his counterparts
in Moscow and Hanoi.

Even if the target understands the intended purpose of a nuclear
signal, it may nonetheless doubt the sincerity of a coercive nuclear
threat. Indeed, targets may experience cognitive dissonance:[76] if they
do not think a nuclear threat is believable – because of the high costs
for the coercer and the low stakes in coercion – they may dismiss new
information suggesting that the coercer is, in fact, willing to use nuclear
weapons. As a result, nuclear signals may be ignored or downplayed by
targets, further reducing the likelihood that brinkmanship will work.
The U.S. nuclear alert during the 1973 Yom Kippur War provides one
illustration. In contrast to the 1969 episode, the Soviets appear to have
detected the alert, but did not update their beliefs about U.S. resolve
as brinkmanship theory would expect.[77]

Implications for Nuclear Statecraft

If nuclear skepticism theory is correct, at least three things should be
true.

**Implication #1: Nuclear powers are not more successful at coercive
diplomacy.** Our theory leads to a pessimistic conclusion for states
hoping to extract coercive leverage from their nuclear arsenals. Targets should recognize the coercive limitations of nuclear weapons, and
dismiss most nuclear threats as incredible. All else being equal, then,
nuclear challengers should not get their way more frequently than their
nonnuclear counterparts.

To be sure, these arguments do not imply that nuclear coercion
never works. Nuclear weapons could provide states with coercive
leverage if the challenger's conventional power is insufficient to meet
its objectives, the stakes in a crisis are exceedingly high, or the costs
of nuclear first use are substantially curtailed. To illustrate, imagine

[75] Sagan and Suri (2003, 179).
[76] See Festinger (1957) for a general theory of cognitive dissonance.
[77] This case is discussed further in Chapter 6.

a hypothetical scenario in which a coercive nuclear threat might be credible. Imagine that Libya had not terminated its nuclear weapons program in 2003, and that it possessed a small nuclear arsenal on the eve of the 2011 revolution that ultimately brought down the Qaddafi regime. Imagine also that the United States nonetheless intervened in Libya's civil war, and publicly declared that its objective was to remove Qaddafi from power. Then, when Libya's army teetered on the cusp of a crushing defeat, Qaddafi threatened to use nuclear weapons against advancing U.S. troops. It is plausible that such a threat might have been perceived as credible by U.S. leaders. The stakes in this hypothetical scenario would be extremely high for Qaddafi: using nuclear weapons might be his only hope for preserving his regime. Even though carrying out the threat would be costly, and potentially suicidal, the circumstances might justify a dramatic gamble. As a former State Department official put it, "there is no question [Qaddafi] would have used whatever he felt necessary to stay in power."[78]

In the real world, though, the conditions for successful nuclear coercion are exceedingly rare. Even if challengers are conventionally weak, the combination of low stakes and high costs will render nuclear weapons impotent in most coercive contexts, despite their unparalleled destructive power.

Implication #2: Nuclear coercers do not push harder in crises. Our theory also has implications for the behavior of coercers during coercive episodes. According to nuclear skepticism theory, nuclear-armed coercers are no more likely to escalate disputes than other states. Since nuclear weapons are unlikely to come into play, even if crises escalate, having the ability to inflict massive amounts of punishment on an adversary will not embolden coercers to escalate. To be sure, nuclear powers like the United States often use military signals to demonstrate resolve during crises.[79] However, nuclear arsenals should not be associated with greater escalatory behavior.

This prediction is not unique to nuclear skepticism theory. Brinkmanship theorists who emphasize the balance of resolve would also agree that a nuclear advantage does not cause a country to run

[78] Quoted in Sanger (2011).
[79] See Sechser and Post (2015).

greater risks in a crisis.[80] However, in contrast to nuclear skepticism theory, these scholars accept the view that brinkmanship works, at least under certain conditions. This brings us to the third implication of our theory.

Implication #3: Nuclear brinkmanship rarely succeeds. The manipulation of nuclear risk by coercers should be an uncommon tactic, employed only under rare conditions. Schelling's rich metaphors notwithstanding, the reality of nuclear politics is that leaders are not inclined to leave war in the hands of fate; it is a decision they prefer to make themselves, even if doing so undermines the credibility of coercive threats. Of course, leaders have occasionally used nuclear brinkmanship – including verbal threats to use nuclear weapons, conspicuous nuclear deployments, and nuclear alerts – to coerce their adversaries. Our theory holds, however, that the manipulation of risk is of questionable utility in bringing about coercive success. Nuclear signals may be misinterpreted by targets, or missed altogether. Even if targets receive the correct message, they may nonetheless dismiss nuclear threats as incredible.

Are Nuclear Weapons Irrelevant?

It is important to clarify that the above arguments do not imply that nuclear weapons are irrelevant in world politics.[81] While coercive threats are unlikely to meet the conditions for success that we enumerated above, deterrent threats are more likely to do so.

First, vital national interests – including national survival – are more likely to be on the line in cases of deterrence. States are willing to accept considerable costs to preserve these interests. As Schelling observed long ago, few people doubt that the United States would expend considerable effort to defend California.[82] On the other hand, it is less obvious that Washington would be sufficiently resolved to obtain a new piece of territory, even one that was identical to California. Because countries generally care more about preserving the status

---

[80] Jervis (1984, 9) and Powell (1990).

[81] Some scholars, however, do argue that nuclear weapons are irrelevant. See, for example, Mueller (2009) and Wilson (2013).

[82] Schelling (1966, 35).

quo than changing it, deterrers are likely to be more resolute than coercers.

Second, the costs of nuclear coercion are less applicable to nuclear deterrence. It is easier for a country to justify the use of nuclear weapons in response to aggression – particularly if an attack has placed its survival in jeopardy. The backlash resulting from defensive nuclear use, then, would probably be less severe, although the fallout could still be quite substantial. In addition, because nuclear users may be perceived as victims if they suffer an attack first, the likelihood of provoking long-term containment is likely to be lower, even it does not disappear altogether. Using nuclear weapons following a failed deterrent threat may set a dangerous precedent. But the established precedent would be less threatening than the prospect of lowering the barriers to nuclear blackmail by other states. In the former case, a state would be vulnerable to nuclear retaliation only if it attacked another country; however, in the latter instance, any state could be subjected to a nuclear strike even if it did not initiate hostilities.

Overall, our theory implies that nuclear weapons are useful in world politics for deterrence, but not coercion. Nuclear weapons are not useless, as some scholars assert. But they are not a diplomatic magic wand. As weapons of self-defense, they are irreplaceable; as tools of coercion, they are of little value.

Conclusion

In this chapter, we performed three tasks. First, we discussed the nature and meaning of coercion in international relations, taking care to distinguish between coercion and deterrence. Second, we developed a general framework of coercion and detailed the comparative effects of power, interests, and resolve on coercive outcomes. Third, we applied this framework to nuclear coercion and asked a simple question: do nuclear weapons bolster any of the factors that make successful coercion more likely in international crises? We found that they do not: while nuclear weapons are credible tools of self-defense, when the stakes are lower – as they generally are in cases of coercion – nuclear threats lose their potency. Further, although a great deal of scholarship suggests that states can "manipulate risk" – intentionally increasing the chance of an accidental conflict – in order to coerce adversaries,

Table 2.2 *Competing theories of nuclear coercion.*

Nuclear Coercionist School
1. Nuclear weapons enable coercers to threaten extraordinary punishment.
2. Nuclear weapons loom in the background of every confrontation involving a nuclear power.
3. Nuclear weapons embolden states to escalate crises and use conventional force to achieve coercive aims.
4. Nuclear powers succeed more often in coercive diplomacy.
   a. *Nuclear absolutists*: the possession of any nuclear weapons enables more successful coercion.
   b. *Nuclear relativists*: only nuclear-superior states enjoy coercive benefits from nuclear weapons.
5. Nuclear states can coerce by raising the risk of accidents and inadvertent escalation.

Nuclear Skepticism Theory
1. Nuclear weapons usually add little to a coercer's ability to achieve its objectives by force.
2. Coercive nuclear threats are not credible, even against nonnuclear or inferior opponents.
3. Nuclear states are no more likely to escalate crises or resolve them by force.
4. Coercive threats from nuclear states are not more likely to succeed.
5. Leaders seek to maximize control and minimize the risk of accidents during crises. But even when brinkmanship is attempted, it will usually fail.

we argued that such behavior is neither common nor effective in international crises.

Nuclear skepticism theory and the nuclear coercionist school make fundamentally different predictions about the role of nuclear weapons in world politics (see Table 2.2).[83] Ultimately, only the empirical record can tell us which theoretical perspective is closer to reality. We turn to the evidence in the next four chapters.

---

[83] The table includes the three main predictions of each theory discussed in the preceding pages, as well as two other key implications that emerge from each argument's logic.

Trends

Roadmap for Part II

Do nuclear weapons provide states with coercive advantages in world politics? The nuclear coercionist school suggests that atomic bombs do, in fact, give their owners political leverage. Nuclear skepticism theory, by contrast, contends that they do not. Which of these views is correct?

There are two main ways that we could find out.[1] First, we could look at serious nuclear crises – like, for example, the Cuban missile crisis – and assess whether nuclear weapons helped states achieve more favorable settlements. Many seminal books on nuclear diplomacy take this approach.[2] But there is a second possibility: we could examine a large number of cases, including nonnuclear crises, to determine whether states with nuclear weapons fare better in diplomacy than their nonnuclear counterparts.

In this latter approach, nuclear weapons are analogous to a "treatment" in a randomized experiment. Imagine, for the sake of illustration, that a medical researcher wanted to know whether a particular drug could cure cancer. The scientist might randomly assign the drug to some cancer patients and give others a placebo. She could then compare the degree to which cancer progressed in both groups of patients as time passed. If people who received the drug showed greater improvement, on average, than those who got the placebo, she might reasonably conclude that the treatment is effective.

In the study of nuclear weapons, the possession of nuclear weapons might be considered equivalent to the drug in a pharmaceutical study: by comparing states that possess them to states that do not, we can begin to discover whether nuclear weapons offer coercive benefits to

---

[1] The discussion in this roadmap draws heavily on Fuhrmann et al. (2014) and Sechser and Fuhrmann (2014).

[2] See, for example, Betts (1987), Bundy (1988), Jervis (1989), and Trachtenberg (1991).

their owners. Of course, we cannot perfectly replicate this kind of study when evaluating the political effects of nuclear weapons – it is neither realistic nor desirable to randomly give atomic bombs to some states and not others. We can, however, follow the same basic intuition to assess the role of nuclear weapons in world politics.

We adopt both methodological approaches in this book. Part II uses statistical analysis to identify general trends in coercive diplomacy. We assess, in particular, whether nuclear states make more effective coercive threats (Chapter 3) or achieve better territorial dispute settlements (Chapter 4) than nonnuclear states. In Part III, we examine the role of atomic weapons in the most serious nuclear crises since 1945, drawing on archival sources whenever possible. We view these approaches as complementary: the strengths of one help compensate for the weaknesses of the other. A multimethod assessment therefore provides a more complete test of the theories described in the previous chapter.

The Strengths and Limitations of Statistical Analysis

Many scholars are skeptical about the use of statistical analysis to study nuclear politics.[3] As Francis Gavin recently wrote, "Statistical analysis does not strike me as the best method for understanding complex, interactive political decision making about issues of life and death," like nuclear statecraft.[4] Critics of the quantitative approach raise several objections, five of which we highlight here.

First, they argue that statistical studies may not explain the most important historical cases, even if they account for general trends. It might be problematic, for instance, to have a theory of war that explains most armed conflicts but cannot account for World War I and World War II, the two most significant wars of the last century.[5] In the context of nuclear security, these scholars argue, general trends are less important than knowing how well a theory applies to the most important nuclear crises.

Second, critics find it odd that one would look at crises without an overt nuclear component, including disputes between nonnuclear

---

[3] See, for example, Montgomery and Sagan (2009) and Gavin (2014).
[4] Gavin (2014, 32).
[5] On this point, see Fuhrmann (2012, 47).

states, to understand the efficacy of nuclear threats. Based on this line of thinking, we cannot learn much about nuclear statecraft by looking at cases where the nuclear option was clearly off the table. For example, the 1994 Haiti crisis – during which the United States restored democratically elected president Jean-Bertrand Aristide to power – tells us little about the coercive value of nuclear weapons because Washington made no attempt to invoke its arsenal. It would be better, according to this view, to focus on cases where there was clearly a danger of a nuclear attack.

Third, when it comes to nuclear politics, the universe of relevant cases is very small. Just ten countries have built nuclear arsenals, and atomic weapons have not been used in war since 1945. Moreover, serious nuclear crises are relatively rare: by our count, nuclear weapons have been openly brandished in support of coercive objectives around twenty times over the last seventy years. The rarity of these events, critics contend, makes statistical analysis an inappropriate tool. One particular concern is that, in light of the small number of relevant cases, statistical findings may be driven by a small number of events. A few small changes to a data set, skeptics of quantitative analysis suggest, can often overturn results generated from statistical models.

Fourth, statistical analysis requires researchers to quantify their concepts of interest, and critics argue that this raises problems. Seemingly straightforward issues, like who prevailed in a crisis, are often deceptively complex. Consider, for example, the Cuban missile crisis. Most analysts treat this episode as a victory for the United States, since the Soviet Union agreed to withdraw its missiles from Cuba after a tense thirteen-day standoff. However, Moscow extracted some concessions as well: the United States pledged not to invade the island, and agreed to withdraw nuclear missiles from Turkey. It is overly simplistic, then, to say that the United States "won" in Cuba and the Soviet Union "lost." Yet the nuance of this case is lost, critics assert, when a researcher must assign a single quantitative value to its outcome.

A fifth limitation of statistical analysis lies in the challenge of assessing causation. Quantitative studies can usefully identify correlations between two variables – but factors that are highly correlated may not be causally connected. Consider, for instance, that the amount of U.S. crude oil imports from Venezuela correlates highly with the per capita consumption of high fructose corn syrup in the United States.[6] This does not imply, of course, that consuming more corn syrup *causes* the United States to import more oil. This correlation is almost certainly spurious: some third variable, perhaps economic growth or per capita income, probably creates a greater demand for oil and also makes people more likely to purchase food items that contain high fructose corn syrup, like soda. Scholars who use statistical analysis to study nuclear proliferation must be mindful of this issue. Countries do not build nuclear weapons on a whim. They instead seek nuclear bombs when they believe that it is in their interest to possess them. The factors that cause states to proliferate, rather than nuclear weapons themselves, might account for patterns that we observe in the world. Some studies show that nuclear weapons are positively associated with the initiation of military disputes.[7] This relationship might emerge because getting nuclear weapons causes countries to be more aggressive. Yet it is also possible that states get nuclear weapons when they want to be more assertive in world affairs, and this desire could account for the observed relationship between nuclear possession and military disputes.[8]

A related problem is that multiple explanations may account for the same relationship. To illustrate, consider the so-called "democratic peace." Most political scientists accept the finding that democracies are unlikely to fight other democracies. However, multiple factors could account for this finding, and debate persists about why the democratic peace exists. It could be because of shared values that exist among democratic states, institutional constraints that democratic leaders face, or some other factor. The problem is that quantitative analysis does not tell us which of these theories is correct, because it is difficult to statistically disentangle them.

This issue applies to the study of nuclear coercion as well. In Chapter 2, we identified multiple reasons why nuclear weapons are not especially useful for military coercion. Our statistical tests, however, will not directly test the logic of our argument. Even if our quantitative analysis shows that nuclear states fare no better at coercive

[6] For this and other entertaining examples of spurious correlations, see the list compiled by Tyler Vigen at www.tylervigen.com.
[7] See, for example, Gartzke and Jo (2009).
[8] See Bell and Miller (2015).

diplomacy than nonnuclear states, we will not necessarily know why this is the case. This finding could emerge because of the logic of nuclear skepticism theory – but we could also observe this pattern for other reasons that are not captured by our argument. Using statistical analysis alone, it is difficult to assess whether our theory – or some competing explanation – best explains the patterns that we observe.

These criticisms are not entirely without merit. Like any method, quantitative analysis has drawbacks. However, critics focus too much on the limitations of this approach, while neglecting its strengths. In our view, the approach we take in Part II – using statistics to compare the success rates of nuclear and nonnuclear states in coercive diplomacy – offers five main advantages over qualitative historical analysis.

First, quantitative analysis allows us to compare a large number of cases. In any social scientific study, a researcher attempts to understand how the world works by analyzing a subset of relevant cases. However, looking at too few cases can produce misleading conclusions. Consider, for example, the relationship between gender and international conflict. Margaret Thatcher, to the surprise of some, launched a war to expel Argentine troops from the Falkland Islands in 1982. Does this mean that female leaders are more likely to become involved in wars? Not necessarily, because the Falklands case may not be representative of a broader trend. To fully appreciate this relationship, we would want to look at a large number of leaders and compare the conflict propensities of men and women. A recent study that takes this approach shows that a leader's gender is a poor predictor of whether he or she will be involved in military disputes.[9] Yet if we focused on high profile conflicts that involved female heads of state – like the Falklands War, the 1971 Bangladesh War (India's Indira Gandhi), or the 1973 Yom Kippur War (Israel's Golda Meir) – we might reach the opposite conclusion. It is only after accounting for the behavior of hundreds of leaders over a long time span that we understand the true relationship between gender and conflict.

This issue bears on the study of nuclear coercion as well. Scholars often focus on the most dangerous nuclear crises, but these cases may be anomalous. The Cuban missile crisis has received much attention in scholarship precisely because it was *not* like other cases – it brought the

---

[9] Horowitz et al. (2015).

world closer to nuclear war than any crisis before or since. Conclusions that emerge from this case, therefore, may not be generalizable. By collecting information about hundreds of international disputes – rather than just one or two – we can gain insights into whether the patterns we observe in any individual case are representative of broader trends.

Second, focusing on nonnuclear cases serves an essential analytical purpose: it provides a basis for comparison. Without studying both nuclear and nonnuclear states, it is impossible to to know whether the former achieves better coercive outcomes than the latter. In the hypothetical cancer study above, for example, analyzing only people who received the drug – and ignoring those who received the placebo – would be a grave mistake. It is only after looking at the treatment and control group that we can know whether the drug worked. The same logic holds in the case of nuclear statecraft. Consider a hypothetical finding: imagine that we discover that nuclear states issue successful coercive threats one-third of the time. What might this mean? It would be tempting to conclude, on the basis of this information, that nuclear weapons are not very useful for coercion, since nuclear states fail more than they succeed. However, that conclusion could be erroneous. It might be the case that nonnuclear states are successful even less often. If that were true, nuclear weapons would appear to increase the likelihood of success. Without a basis for comparison, there is simply no way to know whether nuclear weapons help or hurt (or do not matter one way or the other) in coercive diplomacy.[10]

A third advantage of the approach we take in Part II is that it accounts for disputes with nuclear states that did not include overt nuclear brinkmanship. Studying lower-profile cases helps avoid stacking the deck in favor of nuclear skepticism theory. The most dangerous crises tend to be the ones where coercive (or deterrent) threats were initially unsuccessful. If the threats had worked, the target would have backed down before things escalated to dangerous levels. Consider the 1970 Cienfuegos crisis: the United States demanded that the Soviet Union close a submarine base under construction in Cuba, and Moscow complied without much resistance. U.S. coercive diplomacy was successful – even more so than in the much higher-profile 1962

---

[10] In fact, we find in Chapter 3 that nuclear coercers succeed roughly twenty percent of the time, whereas nonnuclear coercers have a thirty-two percent success rate.

Cuban missile crisis – precisely because the dispute did not escalate. If we were to focus only on the most high-profile cases, we might miss successful cases, like the Cienfuegos case, thereby biasing the evidence in our favor.

Moreover, even if states do not invoke their arsenals in crises, they may still benefit from possessing nuclear forces. Some scholars have suggested that nuclear weapons cast a looming shadow over any crisis involving a nuclear state, even in the absence of nuclear threats. For example, Marc Trachtenberg argues that the U.S. nuclear arsenal helped the West coerce China and the Soviet Union at the end of the Indochina War in 1954 despite the fact that Washington mostly refrained from publicly brandishing nuclear weapons. "It was not that they [the Chinese and the Soviets] thought an American nuclear attack was imminent," Trachtenberg argues, "They just would not want to come anywhere near the point where an American nuclear attack could become a real possibility."[11] Thus, we cannot fairly assess claims made by nuclear coercionists without looking at a wide variety of cases, including those that did not include overt nuclear brinkmanship.

Fourth, statistical analysis forces us to be transparent about our methods, judgments, and conclusions. To carry out a statistical study, one must clearly identify and code each case in a data set. To be sure, this can be a difficult task. We agree with critics who suggest that it is sometimes difficult to code key concepts of interest. However, once a quantitative data set exists, the measurements in the data set are open for all to see. If someone disagrees with a particular coding decision, they can easily modify the data set and repeat the analysis. Through this process, others can determine how sensitive statistical findings are to particular coding decisions. Transparency thus facilitates external quality control, and ultimately the advancement of scientific knowledge.[12]

Finally, statistical analysis can help us uncover patterns that may be hidden from plain view. Looking at what leaders say or write – as opposed to how they behave – can sometimes lead researchers

---

[11] Trachtenberg (2013, 20).

[12] Qualitative analysis is becoming more transparent through the use of "active citations," a trend that we welcome. See, for example, Saunders (2014).

astray. Indeed, there are some pitfalls associated with relying exclusively on archival sources or other primary materials, like memoirs written by crisis participants. Two key issues are worth highlighting here.

One is that we cannot always accept information contained in the historical record at face value. Crisis participants – both challengers and targets – have incentives to misrepresent the efficacy of nuclear threats. Issuing effective threats makes leaders look tough and competent in foreign policy. They therefore may wish to claim that their nuclear threats worked – even when they did not. Indeed, in their memoirs and public interviews, leaders sometimes boast about their skillful nuclear diplomacy. Nikita Khrushchev, for example, believed that his nuclear threat during the 1956 Suez crisis coerced Britain and France, but other evidence makes it difficult to substantiate this view. Targets, by contrast, may wish to minimize the the effects of nuclear weapons, particularly if they back down in a crisis. Admitting that they capitulated because of a nuclear threat could harm a leader's reputation and encourage future atomic blackmail. Thus, analysts should be suspicious when leaders claim that they were not worried about nuclear escalation during a crisis. Such a claim may, in fact, be true, but it could also be a smokescreen to avoid the appearance of weakness.

Another limitation of archival research is that existing documents may not provide direct insights into the question at the heart of this book: how do coercive nuclear threats influence a target's decision making? Leaders are sometimes conspicuously silent on this issue during meetings with their advisors. Consider Indian general Ved Prakash Malik's statement about the role of nuclear weapons during the 1999 Kargil War with Pakistan: "The nuclear factor too must have been weighing on the minds of the prime minister and his [Cabinet Committee on Security] colleagues," he said, "though this aspect was never mentioned or discussed in the meetings."[13] Thus, nuclear weapons may influence the way that leaders behave, even if they do not say so. When officials do not express their views during crises – only commenting on the issue afterwards, if at all – it is difficult to determine their true feelings. Needless to say, smoking gun evidence for nuclear skepticism theory (or the nuclear coercionist school) is often difficult to find, even when we have access to troves of declassified documents.

[13] Malik (2006, 126).

In sum, nuclear weapons may play a role in crisis dynamics regardless of whether officials say so. By focusing on the way that leaders behave, rather than what they say, statistical analysis can reveal connections that are difficult to identify in the documentary record alone.

The preceding discussion is not meant to suggest that qualitative historical analysis should not be used to study nuclear statecraft. In fact, we see it as an indispensable tool. In Part III of the book, we employ qualitative historical analysis, taking care to explain how it helps address some of the weaknesses of the statistical tests that follow in the next two chapters.

3 | *Standoffs: Nuclear Weapons in Crisis Bargaining*

In the previous chapter, we developed a theory about coercion in international politics. At its core, coercion is about persuading an adversary to get out of the way so that a state can achieve its foreign policy objectives without war. This endeavor is more likely to work if the coercer can convincingly say, "If you don't get out of the way, I'll either push you out of the way myself or cause you so much pain that you'll acquiesce just to make it stop." A coercive target is more likely to concede without a fight if it is faced with inevitable defeat, or if the price of victory is too much to bear.

We argued that nuclear weapons fall short as instruments of coercion. For military conquest, nuclear weapons have limited utility. Nuclear weapons can accomplish some missions better than conventional weapons (such as destroying hardened targets), but those missions are few in number and extremely rare. More importantly, they tend not to be the kinds of missions required for successful coercion. Coercion often involves seizing objects: taking territory, rescuing hostages, or liberating victims of conquest. Nuclear weapons are not useful for any of these tasks. Instead, nuclear weapons are best for inflicting pain: they destroy, irradiate, and kill indiscriminately. But their extraordinary lethality is what limits their usability in coercive contexts. For self-defense, nuclear weapons can be credible and persuasive tools of punishment. For coercion, however – when the challenger's survival is rarely at stake – they are simply too costly to be credible.

We now turn to the empirical record to evaluate these claims. Does the evidence support our argument about the irrelevance of nuclear weapons in coercion? In this chapter, we examine coercion in its most explicit form. We analyze more than 200 instances in which one state made an explicit *compellent threat* against another state, and we assess the effect of nuclear weapons on the outcomes of these threats. The evidence is clear: states that possess nuclear weapons enjoy no more success when making compellent threats, even when they enjoy nuclear superiority over their opponent. Moreover, we find that nuclear states are not "manipulating risk" in the way that 1960s-era nuclear strategists and some contemporary game theorists expect them to. To the contrary, leaders frequently pass up opportunities to leverage their nuclear arsenals, even when doing so might mean political defeat. In short, nuclear weapons are of little use as instruments of coercion.

Theoretical Predictions: The Nuclear Coercionist School Versus Nuclear Skepticism Theory

In international politics, leaders would prefer to get their way without having to use military force. As a result, leaders often issue explicit warnings and threats to allow adversaries the opportunity to back down before escalating to military combat. Often these threats take the form of deterrent warnings, intended to prevent an adversary from taking certain prohibited actions. However, states also use verbal threats for coercive purposes – that is, to persuade an adversary to change its behavior or relinquish a possession. In his canonical work about military coercion, *The Strategy of Conflict*, Thomas Schelling termed these "compellent threats" – threats designed to compel an opponent into taking action that it would not otherwise take.[1]

Compellent threats represent coercive diplomacy in its most overt and explicit form. For this reason, they are a useful place to begin our inquiry about the coercive effects of nuclear weapons. Before looking at the empirical record, however, we first clarify what our theory – and its chief competitor – expects to find. Each theory makes competing predictions about how nuclear weapons influence (1) the efficacy of coercive threats and (2) the level of escalation during crises.

Do Nuclear Weapons Make Coercive Threats More Effective?

The most obvious way that nuclear weapons could aid coercive diplomacy is by making a challenger's threats more effective. Are countries armed with nuclear weapons more likely to issue successful threats than nonnuclear states?

---

[1] Schelling (1960). Schelling discussed compellence in even greater detail in another classic book, *Arms and Influence* (1966).

The Nuclear Coercionist View: Nuclear Arsenals Produce Coercive Victories

Nuclear weapons are the most destructive weapons known to man. The prospect of facing an attack with nuclear weapons therefore ought to be sobering for any leader engaged in a diplomatic confrontation. This basic logic underlies the nuclear coercionist prediction about nuclear weapons and compellence: that a leader faced with a coercive threat is more likely to capitulate peacefully if the adversary has nuclear weapons at its disposal. In this view, few issues short of a nation's own survival would be worth enduring a nuclear attack. When a nuclear state issues a compellent demand, the argument holds, the odds of success multiply.[2]

An important element of this claim, as we discussed previously, is that nuclear states possess a coercive advantage even when they do not make explicit nuclear threats. Indeed, the use of nuclear weapons has rarely been threatened explicitly in conjunction with a compellent threat. Art, for instance, notes that nuclear compellent threats historically have been "guarded, ambiguous, or leave sufficient room for backtracking."[3] Yet many scholars argue that nuclear weapons exert implicit crisis bargaining leverage even when they are not invoked. Henry Kissinger, for instance, warned that "overt threats have become unnecessary; every calculation of risks will have to include the Soviet stockpile of atomic weapons and ballistic missiles."[4] Beardsley and Asal argued along similar lines, asserting that "the possession of nuclear weapons helps states to succeed in their confrontations with other states even when they do not 'use' these weapons."[5] In short, according to this perspective, the mere possession of nuclear weapons enables states to make more successful threats:

Nuclear Absolutist Prediction: *Compellent threats from nuclear states are more likely to succeed, on average, than compellent threats from nonnuclear states.*

A more qualified version of this argument asserts that the compellent effects of nuclear weapons depend on the target's retaliatory

---

[2] Pape (1996, 38).

[3] Art (1980, 21).

[4] Kissinger (1956, 351).

[5] Beardsley and Asal (2009b, 296).

capabilities. If a target has nuclear weapons, this view holds, the compellent leverage of a nuclear arsenal will be neutralized. In this view, the compellent effects of nuclear weapons are particularly powerful when nuclear capabilities are one-sided – that is, when a challenger possesses nuclear weapons but the target does not. Since the target cannot threaten nuclear retaliation in response to the threat, it cannot match the challenger's bargaining leverage. When a nuclear-superior state issues a compellent threat, the logic goes, the target will be more likely to back down rather than risk provoking the challenger into exercising its nuclear advantage:

Nuclear Relativist Prediction: *Compellent threats from nuclear states are more likely to succeed, on average, than compellent threats from nonnuclear states only if the coercer has a nuclear advantage over the target.*

Nuclear Skepticism Theory: Nuclear Weapons Contribute Little to Coercive Diplomacy

The theory developed in the previous chapter disagrees sharply with the nuclear coercionist viewpoint. We maintain that even if nuclear weapons might be effective for defending against threats to national survival, they generally are not useful for compelling adversaries to relinquish possessions or change their behavior. There are three main reasons why this is the case.

First, there are very few military missions that nuclear weapons can accomplish but conventional weapons cannot. Indeed, for many critical missions, nuclear weapons are actually less useful. Compellent threats often center on disputed cities and territories that a challenger seeks to obtain from the target state. Coercive demands for these objects would be more effective if the challenger could threaten to seize the item by force, since the target might decide to forgo costly fighting if it expects to lose the object anyway. Nuclear weapons, however, contribute little to a challenger's ability to seize possessions. Although nuclear weapons can destroy enemy forces that stand in the way of an invading military, an offensive nuclear attack could destroy the very object that prompted the dispute. Except in rare conditions, it will be difficult for a nuclear state to use its arsenal to physically wrest away an item that the target refuses to relinquish.

Instead, a nuclear state might hope to coerce a target by threatening to attack the target's valued possessions. A challenger could threaten to incinerate a target state's capital city, for example, unless it relinquished a disputed territory. But this possibility highlights the second major limitation of nuclear weapons: the costs of executing nuclear punishment would likely be tremendous. A state that launched a nuclear attack to achieve compellent objectives would provoke international backlash, potentially triggering economic sanctions and international isolation, encouraging nuclear proliferation, and provoking other states to align against it. Faced with such costs, crisis challengers will find it difficult to threaten nuclear punishment credibly except under extreme circumstances.

A third and related problem is that the stakes in coercive crises are rarely dire for the coercer. The exorbitant diplomatic, economic, and political costs of executing a nuclear threat might be worth paying if the benefits of doing so were equally high – but for coercers, this is rarely the case. Whereas states issuing deterrent threats are more likely to believe that their existence (or that of their governing regime) is at risk, coercive threats generally address less dire issues such as disputed territory or an objectionable policy. This is not to say that the stakes for coercers are low – from the coercer's perspective, they certainly are not. But they are rarely so high as to outweigh the tremendous price that the coercer would pay for using nuclear weapons against a target, especially a nonnuclear target.

Consider a few illustrative examples. Possessing nuclear weapons did not help China compel Vietnam to terminate its invasion of Cambodia in 1979. Nuclear forces also did not aid Britain's attempt to compel Egypt to peacefully reopen the Suez Canal in 1956, nor did they help the United States and its allies expel Iraqi forces from Kuwait without a fight in 1991. These cases are all notable because the issue at stake was important enough to the coercer that the use of nuclear weapons might have been considered plausible, but the challenger's threats failed. Compellent threats from nuclear-armed challengers have even failed in instances when the target's acquiescence would have been relatively inconsequential for its national security. For instance, nuclear weapons did not help South Africa coerce several of its neighbors into cracking down on African National Congress (ANC) insurgents during the 1980s. And the U.S. nuclear arsenal did not help in securing the release of hostages held at the American embassy in Tehran from 1979 to 1981.[6]

---

[6] The hostages were released in 1981, but not as a result of American compellent threats.

In principle, nuclear states could overcome credibility problems by making coercive threats that "leave something to chance," as Schelling and others have suggested. They could, for example, order a nuclear alert or forward-deploy nuclear missiles after making a demand. However, nuclear brinkmanship is costly, and leaders prefer to maintain control rather than cede it. Most of the time, then, leaders lack the will to do what it takes to make coercive nuclear threats potentially believable. Assuming that they recognize this in advance, leaders are unlikely to view nuclear brinkmanship as a solution to the credibility problem.

Thus, our theory suggests that nuclear weapons provide challengers with little, if any, additional compellent leverage in crises:

Nuclear Skepticism Prediction: *Compellent threats from nuclear states are no more effective, on average, than threats from nonnuclear states.*

Do Nuclear Weapons Influence Crisis Escalation?

Nuclear weapons may affect the dynamics of crisis bargaining in another respect: they could influence the way that coercers behave during disputes, even if they do not ultimately force targets to capitulate. In particular, having nuclear weapons might embolden challengers to escalate military crises. Do nuclear weapons embolden states to take dangerous risks during crisis encounters?

The Nuclear Coercionist View: Nuclear Coercers Push Harder in Crises

According to the coercionist perspective, nuclear weapons motivate states to escalate crises and launch risky gambles. In turn, these risky gambles, according to the logic of brinkmanship, are the reason nuclear states prevail more often. The reason nuclear states are more willing to escalate is simple: from the standpoint of nuclear-armed coercers, war would be relatively more costly for their opponents. Knowing this, nuclear coercers can raise the ante during crises with greater confidence. This logic is fundamental to the nuclear coercionist perspective, particularly the version of the theory that emphasizes brinkmanship as a tool of coercion. Indeed, some scholars in this camp suggest that nuclear states prevail in crises precisely because they push harder during these "competitions in risk taking."[7] This view implies

[7] See, for example, Nitze (1976/1977) and McDonough (2006).

that having nuclear weapons emboldens countries to take greater risks during crises:

Nuclear Absolutist Prediction: *Nuclear states are more likely to escalate coercive crises, on average, than nonnuclear states.*

As before, the degree to which nuclear weapons embolden challengers to engage in brinkmanship may depend on the nuclear capabilities of targets. If the target also possesses nuclear weapons, a nuclear-armed challenger may not be able to impose higher costs than its opponent. In that case, nuclear weapons would not necessarily encourage escalatory behavior. This leads to a more qualified prediction:

Nuclear Relativist Prediction: *Nuclear states are more likely to escalate coercive crises, on average, only if the coercer has a nuclear advantage over the target.*

Nuclear Skepticism Theory: Nuclear Coercers Do Not Take Greater Risks

We argue, by contrast, that nuclear weapons do not cause states to take greater risks during crises. Like targets, challengers recognize that coercive nuclear threats are usually incredible. In most coercive episodes, the likelihood of nuclear use is exceedingly low – so low that challengers often rule out the nuclear option entirely. The possibility of a nuclear attack is rarely even mentioned by leaders. Indeed, scholars have observed a strong inhibition among government officials against even the suggestion of nuclear escalation, especially in the United States.[8] Having nuclear arsenals (or nuclear superiority), therefore, does not necessarily provide a challenger with peace of mind. Even if a crisis escalates to war, the nuclear option will remain off the table most of the time.

To illustrate, consider the U.S. threat against Serbia over ethnic cleansing in Kosovo in 1999. It would be hard to argue that the U.S. nuclear arsenal encouraged President Bill Clinton to push harder during this crisis. No senior U.S. official (to our knowledge) suggested that the use of nuclear weapons might be considered if Serbia did not comply. The United States did, in fact, ratchet up the pressure on Serbia,

[8] Tannenwald (2007) and Paul (2009).

but it strains credulity to suggest that it did so because it had nuclear weapons.

Nuclear Skepticism Prediction: *Nuclear states are not more likely to escalate coercive crises, on average, than nonnuclear states.*

Collecting Data on Compellent Threats

How can we go about evaluating these competing claims? Choosing where to look for evidence is a critical issue in any academic study. The reliability of one's results depends, in part, on whether the evidence is appropriate for the question being investigated. If unreliable or inappropriate data are used, the study will be unable to provide a satisfying answer to the question that inspired it in the first place. A scientist who believes he has stumbled upon a drug for curing cancer should test it on a set of cancer patients – not on patients whose only affliction is a common cold.

One way we could evaluate the effectiveness of nuclear coercion would be to pull a prepackaged collection of historical data off the shelf – like shopping in a grocery store. International relations scholars have many such options. For example, some studies have used the International Crisis Behavior (ICB) data set, a database maintained by scholars at Duke University and the University of Southern California, to evaluate whether nuclear states win crises more often than nonnuclear states.[9] Other studies of coercion in international relations use data from the Correlates of War Project, another large-scale data collection effort that aims to catalog international incidents involving military threats or action.

For our purposes, however, these data sets have significant limitations. For the most part, they were designed to assess the causes and frequency of conflict – not the effectiveness of coercive diplomacy or compellence. As a result, they suffer from several problems that force us to look elsewhere for appropriate data.

First, the data sets used in these studies do not actually contain very many coercive threats. A recent analysis of quantitative data sets in international relations found that roughly eighty-five percent of the crisis observations in the ICB data set do not contain a coercive threat.[10]

---

[9] For example, Beardsley and Asal (2009b).
[10] Downes and Sechser (2012).

The Militarized Interstate Dispute (MID) data set, also commonly used to evaluate crisis outcomes, fared even worse: the same analysis found that barely ten percent of the disputes in the MID data set contain threats. Instead, most crises in these data sets revolve around trespassing fishing boats, minor border clashes, and other trivial events in which no coercive diplomacy was attempted. Yet many studies assume otherwise, leading to historically inaccurate conclusions. For example, the ICB data set lists the 1964 Congolese hostage crisis as a victory for the United States since Belgian paratroopers used U.S. military transports to rescue hundreds of civilians taken captive by Congolese rebels.[11] The data set also lists the crisis as a defeat for the Soviet Union because the Soviets publicly denounced the rescue operation. Quantitative models using the ICB data set therefore consider this a case of one nuclear state achieving "victory" over another.[12] Yet this interpretation is misleading. The United States did not attempt to coerce the Soviets in any way during this crisis: the United States did not make any threats, and the Soviets did not make any concessions. The case therefore does not belong in a data set of coercive threats. Unfortunately, since the ICB and MID data sets do not distinguish cases containing threats from those that do not, researchers studying nuclear coercion cannot readily exclude (or recode) such cases in their empirical analyses.

A second problem is that these data sets often conflate military and coercive outcomes. To determine whether nuclear-armed states make more effective threats, one naturally needs to know the outcomes of threats that are made. Data sets such as ICB and MID provide some of this information – but, crucially, they do not distinguish between crisis victories achieved by brute force from those achieved through successful coercive diplomacy. For instance, many studies of coercive diplomacy treat the 1991 Gulf War as a "crisis victory" for the United States and its coalition partners, on the grounds that the U.S.-led coalition ultimately won the war. Yet the compellent threat associated with this crisis was a clear failure: the U.S. ultimatum demanding Iraq's evacuation from Kuwait was rejected, thus necessitating the war in the first place. This case – like dozens of other military victories in the data set – should not be classified as a success for coercive diplomacy since

[11] Brecher and Wilkenfeld (1997).
[12] For example, Kroenig (2013).

the central purpose of making a threat is to achieve one's objectives without large-scale military action. With so many military victories coded as successes in these data sets, it is unclear whether studies that employ them can tell us anything about the effectiveness of coercive threats.

The Militarized Compellent Threats Data Set

We use a better data set to evaluate the effectiveness of threats made by nuclear-armed states. Sechser's Militarized Compellent Threats (MCT) data set contains information about 210 interstate compellent threats – that is, episodes in which one or more challengers issued a compellent demand against a target and threatened to use force if it did not comply – comprising 242 challenger-target dyads overall.[13] The data set, which spans the years 1918–2001, contains both well-known superpower crises (for example, the 1956 Suez crisis), as well as lesser-known disputes between small states (for example, the 1995 Hanish Islands crisis between Eritrea and Yemen). Likewise, it includes crises in which nuclear weapons seemed to play a central role (for example, the Cuban missile crisis) as well as episodes in which the possibility of nuclear attack was never mentioned (for example, the 1993–1994 Bosnian crises). It is important to note that the data set does not include compellent demands made by states already at war.[14]

The structure of the MCT data set is ideal for assessing the coercive utility of nuclear weapons. First, it contains only compellent threats, defined as *"interstate demands to change the status quo* which are *backed by the threat of military force."*[15] Episodes in the MCT data set have two components: a coercive *demand* and a *threat* to use military

---

[13] Sechser (2011). The number of challenger-target dyads (242) is greater than the number of threat episodes (210) because some demands are jointly issued by more than one challenger. However, the findings below are largely unaltered if we include only one challenger (the principal challenger) for each multilateral threat in the MCT data set.

[14] In Chapters 5 and 6, we examine several cases of wartime nuclear coercion.

[15] Sechser (2011, 379). Emphasis in original. Deterrence and compellence are often difficult to distinguish, of course, because disputants often disagree about what constitutes the legitimate status quo. The MCT data set requires that compellent threats contain a demand for a material change in the status quo in order to be included in the data set. This helps address the problem of subjectivity by establishing an objective reference point for differentiating deterrence and compellence. See Sechser (2011, 380–382).

force. While threats to use force are often transmitted verbally, they may also be communicated implicitly through militarized actions such as troop maneuvers or exercises. Both varieties are included in the MCT data set. However, the data set consciously excludes military clashes, raids, and wars in which coercive demands were not made. It therefore allows us to distinguish coercive diplomatic successes from military victories, thus providing a more valid assessment of the extent to which nuclear weapons make compellent threats more effective.

Second, the MCT data set is not restricted to nuclear crises; it contains threats made by nuclear and nonnuclear challengers alike.[16] This variation is essential because it allows us to answer a central question in the study of nuclear coercion: do nuclear challengers succeed more often than nonnuclear challengers? Studies that examine nuclear crises alone fail to answer this question since they have no baseline against which nuclear states can be compared. The research design employed here addresses this problem by comparing threats made by nuclear and nonnuclear states, thus yielding more reliable inferences about the relative benefits of nuclear possession.[17]

Evaluating the Coercive Effects of Nuclear Weapons

The central objective of our analysis is to determine whether nuclear-armed states enjoy consistently higher odds of success when making compellent threats. To achieve this, we use a common statistical model designed for precisely this purpose. Using our database of compellent threats, this model estimates the effect that a variety of factors – both nuclear and otherwise – exert on the probability that a given compellent threat will succeed.

Our approach first requires us to determine which threats in the database were successful, and which were not. We use the information contained in the MCT database to measure the target's level of compliance with the challenger's demands. We define a successful compellent threat as a threat that meets two criteria: first, the target

---

[16] In the MCT data set, forty-nine of 242 challengers (twenty percent) possessed nuclear weapons at the time they made compellent threats.

[17] For this reason, it is appropriate to include cases occurring before 1945, since the prenuclear era provides valuable information about the outcomes of compellent threats made by nonnuclear states. As we note below, however, the results are unchanged if the study sample is limited to the nuclear age.

voluntarily complied with all of the challenger's demands, and second, the challenger did not have to use military force to achieve its goals. By this definition, more than thirty percent of the compellent threats in the data set were successful, suggesting that successful compellent threats are quite common, even if compellence is indeed "harder" than deterrence.[18]

Next, we need to measure the possession of nuclear weapons by the states in the database. Which states had nuclear weapons? Which enjoyed some level of nuclear advantage over their opponents? Which states had the greatest advantage? We measure nuclear capabilities in five different ways. First, we simply distinguish between states that possess nuclear weapons and those that do not. Second, we count the actual number of nuclear weapons that states possess, to obtain a more accurate measurement of their nuclear arsenals. Third, we devise a crude measure of nuclear "superiority" by determining which state in a "dyad" pair had more operational nuclear warheads in its arsenal. Fourth, we calculate the ratio of a crisis challenger's warheads to those of its target. Fifth, we measure how many more (or fewer) nuclear weapons the challenger possessed than the target, since a ratio would not necessarily account for large numerical disparities in nuclear arsenal sizes.[19]

Our analysis also accounts for several other factors that are often believed to influence coercive diplomacy outcomes, including the balance of conventional power and the history of conflict within each dyad. Two additional factors are worth mentioning here. First, relative stakes are important for explaining crisis outcomes. States with critical interests at stake should be more tolerant of costs and less likely to back down without a fight. Specifically, issues related to territory and leadership are generally thought to be more important to states than matters of policy and ideology. We therefore distinguish between threats made over territory or leadership issues – roughly sixty-eight percent of the compellent threats in the data set – and threats made over smaller stakes.

Second, signals of resolve during a crisis could impact a threat's credibility: specifically, challengers who signal their willingness to use force

---

[18] Schelling (1966).

[19] For example, a warhead ratio of 2:1 would yield the same value as a ratio of 20,000:10,000, even though the numerical gap is significantly larger in the latter case.

may be more likely to prevail.[20] We address this by identifying demonstrations of military force and conspicuous military mobilizations undertaken by challengers.[21]

The Evidence: Nuclear Weapons and Compellent Threats

Coercive Threat Success

Is nuclear possession correlated with successful coercion? Figure 3.1 offers a first glimpse at the answer, reporting overall threat success rates for both nuclear and nonnuclear challengers. It demonstrates that challengers possessing the bomb are not more likely to make successful compellent threats overall. Indeed, they actually may be somewhat less likely to make successful threats: we observe success in just twenty percent of the cases involving nuclear challengers, compared to thirty-two

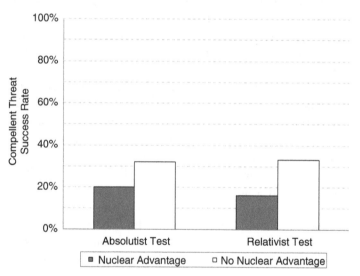

Figure 3.1 Nuclear weapons and compellent threat success.

---

[20] Fearon (1994).

[21] One could argue that nuclear-armed challengers may be more likely to signal their resolve during crises, because they are more powerful than their nonnuclear counterparts. If true, the effects of nuclear possession could be picked up by the resolve variable. We address this issue in the appendix by replicating all of our regression models without the measure of resolve, and the results are similar.

percent of nonnuclear challengers.[22] Of the more than 200 compellent threats in the data set, just ten involve successful coercion by nuclear weapons states. Having a clear nuclear advantage does not seem to make things any better for challengers, as implied by nuclear relativists. When they have a dyadic nuclear "monopoly," nuclear-armed challengers make effective threats sixteen percent of the time, compared to thirty-three percent otherwise.[23]

We now turn to a more complex statistical analysis, the details of which are described in the appendix, to find out whether this result holds up under scrutiny. This analysis accounts for the nuclear status of the challenger and the target, as well as the other variables described above. The coercionist school expects that we should find measures of nuclear possession to be positively associated with successful compellent threats, indicating that challengers possessing nuclear weapons (or nuclear superiority) are more likely to issue successful coercive challenges. Our theory of nuclear skepticism, however, expects that possessing nuclear weapons should have little effect on compellent threat outcomes.

The findings from this analysis are unambiguous: nuclear skepticism receives strong and consistent support, whereas the nuclear coercionist school finds barely any support at all. Based on our statistical model, the predicted probability of successful coercion declines by twelve points (from forty-one percent to twenty-nine percent) when the challenger's status changes from nonnuclear to nuclear and all other factors are held constant.[24] However, from a statistical standpoint, the challenger's nuclear status is insignificant: the success rates for nuclear and nonnuclear challengers are statistically indistinguishable. Even against nonnuclear targets, nuclear-armed challengers do not enjoy a coercive advantage. Indeed, our findings contradict the nuclear relativist prediction: when facing nonnuclear opponents, the predicted probability of success for nuclear challengers is twenty-four percent, compared to forty percent when nonnuclear coercers square off against other nonnuclear states.[25]

It could be the case, however, that the size of one's nuclear arsenal, rather than the mere fact of nuclear possession, influences compellent threat outcomes. We therefore repeated our statistical models using

---

[22] This difference is statistically significant at the ninety percent level.
[23] This difference is statistically significant at the ninety-five percent level.
[24] These calculations are based on Model 1 in the appendix.
[25] These calculations are based on Model 2 in the appendix.

several alternative ways of measuring nuclear capabilities, as described earlier. However, *none* of the other measures of nuclear capabilities yielded results supportive of the nuclear coercionist hypotheses. In every case, a challenger's nuclear weapons – or nuclear advantage – was unrelated to the likelihood that its threats would succeed.

We then repeated our analyses using two more lenient measures of successful compellent threats. First, whereas our original coding scheme defined a successful threat as one that achieved compliance with no military force, we created a new dependent variable that reclassified compellent threats as successful even if the challenger used limited military force, as long as the target suffered fewer than 100 fatalities. A second reclassification adopted this 100-fatality threshold in addition to a more lenient standard for compliance, coding threats as successful if the target complied with any (as opposed to all) of the challenger's demands. The results remain the same: nuclear weapons do not make for more effective compellent threats.[26]

The Manipulation of Risk

Do nuclear weapons embolden challengers to escalate crises? If it were true that atomic arsenals give states advantages during metaphorical games of Russian roulette, we should have found that coercive threats issued by nuclear challengers were more effective, on average, than demands made by nonnuclear states. Instead, we found that nuclear states do not prevail more frequently than nonnuclear states in coercive crisis bargaining. We explore this issue further here, examining more directly whether nuclear states are greater risk takers during international crises.

Figure 3.2 suggests that they are not. This figure compares the escalatory behavior of nuclear and nonnuclear states during the crises in our data set of compellent threats. Specifically, it reports how often each type of state engaged in some sort of military demonstration or show-of-force during the crisis – precisely the sort of behavior that nuclear coercionists see as central to brinkmanship and the escalation of risk. The figure shows that there is actually very little difference between nuclear and nonnuclear challengers in terms of

---

[26] As a further check, we replicated these analyses using a limited sample that includes only post-1945 observations. The findings remain similar.

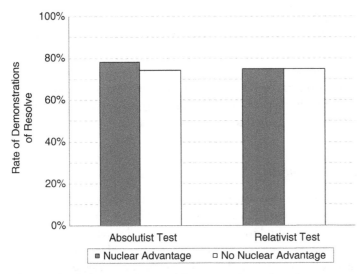

Figure 3.2 Nuclear weapons and demonstrations of resolve.

their propensity to take military risks during coercive crises. Nuclear-armed challengers engage in escalatory behavior roughly seventy-eight percent of the time, compared to seventy-four percent for nonnuclear challengers.[27] Moreover, the rate at which states escalate when they have a nuclear monopoly is identical to the rate of escalation when they do not (seventy-five percent in both cases). If nuclear weapons systematically made states more willing to accept the risk of war in coercive crises, as the nuclear coercionist school suggests, the difference in the behavior of nuclear and nonnuclear challengers should be far more striking that what we actually observe.

This initial analysis could be misleading. It does not account for other factors that might influence escalatory behavior, so the simple comparison depicted in Figure 3.2 may not reflect the true relationship between nuclear weapons and crisis risk taking. We carry out a more rigorous statistical analysis that accounts for several other relevant considerations: the stakes in a crisis, the relative balance of conventional military power, whether the challenger and the target are both democracies, geographic contiguity, and the distance between the challenger and the target.[28] Our findings reaffirm our earlier conclusion.

---

[27] This difference is not statistically significant.

[28] These same variables are included in a recent study that supports the nuclear coercionist position that nuclear weapons embolden challengers to take greater

Regardless of how we measure the challenger's nuclear status, it is not statistically associated with a greater likelihood of military escalation. Even when challengers have nuclear superiority, they are not more likely than nonnuclear states to display resolve. Overall, the evidence supports our theory that coercive nuclear threats lack credibility at a fundamental level: the behavior of coercive targets and challengers is not systematically related to the nuclear balance.

Possible "Selection Effects"

These results suggest that neither nuclear possession nor nuclear superiority is associated with more effective compellent threats. However, it is possible that this finding is due to what social scientists call "selection effects" in the data.[29] Broadly speaking, a selection effect is a hidden process that subtly influences the kinds of cases we observe, while causing other cases to not appear at all. If not addressed, selection effects can cause scholars to draw the wrong conclusions from observational data by systematically hiding cases that would alter those conclusions.

When studying the relationship between nuclear weapons and compellent threat outcomes, selection effects are a potentially serious problem. Specifically, it could be the case that nuclear states tend to issue threats over more valuable issues, thus selecting themselves into crises in which threats are inherently less likely to work.[30] If true, then the coercive benefits of nuclear weapons might be obscured in the compellent threats we observe, since nuclear and nonnuclear states would not be playing on a level field. We might then conclude that nuclear states succeed at lower rates than nonnuclear states, when in reality the lower success rate was the result of other factors. To definitively test this possibility, one would need to conduct a controlled experiment, randomly assigning nuclear weapons to some compellence challengers while holding other crisis conditions – in particular, the issues at stake – constant. Since this is obviously an unrealistic solution, we use three

---

risks during crises. Adopting that study's design, therefore, should make it harder to find evidence in favor of nuclear skepticism theory. See Kroenig et al. (2015).

[29] Morrow (1989) and Fearon (2002).

[30] Fearon (2002).

alternative techniques to evaluate the severity of selection effects in the data.

First, we examine the cases in the data set to determine whether failed compellent threats from nuclear states indeed tend to be over high-stakes issues. Table 3.1 lists all episodes in the MCT data set in which nuclear challengers failed to compel their adversaries according to our rules. This list provides little support for the selection effects hypothesis: most cases on the list are not, in fact, high-stakes crises, but rather crises in which the target could have acquiesced without significantly harming its national security. For example, in the *Pueblo*, *Mayaguez*, and Iran embassy crises, U.S. threats failed to compel non-nuclear adversaries to release American hostages, even though their release would have had little material consequence for the target state. In these cases, the issue at stake was considerably more important to the challenger than the target, yet nuclear superiority did not make the challenger's compellent threats effective. This suggests that the failure of compellent threats by nuclear states has been due to the limited coercive potential of nuclear weapons rather than disproportionately difficult crisis conditions.

More concretely, we can measure the frequency of high-stakes demands – that is, demands over leadership or territory – in the MCT data set to evaluate whether nuclear powers are more likely to be involved in high-stakes crises. If crises involving nuclear challengers are disproportionately likely to involve high stakes, then the STAKES variable would detect this trend. However, nuclear powers are actually less likely than nonnuclear states to make compellent demands over high-stakes issues: fifty-one percent of demands made by nuclear challengers in the MCT data set are related to territory or leadership, compared to seventy-two percent for nonnuclear challengers.

A second method for evaluating selection effects is to assess whether the coercive effects of nuclear weapons depend on the stakes of a crisis. If self-selection into high-stakes crises puts nuclear challengers at an inherent disadvantage, then the analysis should distinguish between high- and low-stakes crises in order to properly estimate the effects of nuclear possession. It turns out, as shown in the appendix, that nuclear states neither enjoy a consistent advantage in high-stakes crises (when nuclear threats might be most credible) nor in low-stakes crises (when the risk of nuclear punishment is most likely to outweigh the issue at stake).

Table 3.1 *Unsuccessful compellent threats from nuclear-armed challengers, 1945–2001.*

Challenger	Target	Year	Demand
China	India	1965	Withdraw from outposts in Kashmir
China	India	1965	Destroy military structures along Chinese border
China	Vietnam	1979	End occupation of Cambodia
France	Serb Republic	1993	Accept Bosnian peace plan
France	Serbia	1998	Stop ethnic cleansing in Kosovo
Great Britain	Saudi Arabia	1952	Withdraw from Buraimi Oasis
Great Britain	Egypt	1956	Open Suez Canal
Great Britain	Argentina	1982	Withdraw from Falkland Islands
Great Britain	Iraq	1990	Withdraw troops from Kuwait
Great Britain	Serb Republic	1993	Accept Bosnian peace plan
Great Britain	Serbia	1998	Stop ethnic cleansing in Kosovo
Great Britain	Iraq	1998	Readmit weapons inspectors
Great Britain	Afghanistan	2001	Extradite al Qaeda leaders
India	Pakistan	2001	Suppress terrorist organizations
Israel	Egypt	1967	Reopen Gulf of Aqaba to Israeli shipping
Israel	Lebanon	1970	Suppress Palestinian commandos
Israel	Lebanon	1972	Expel Palestinian guerrillas
Israel	Syria	1978	Stop shelling Beirut
Israel	Syria	1981	Remove surface-to-air missile batteries

Country	Target	Year	Demand
South Africa	Mozambique	1981	Stop supporting African National Congress (ANC) rebels
South Africa	Lesotho	1985	Stop supporting ANC rebels
South Africa	Botswana	1985 (×2)	Stop supporting ANC rebels
South Africa	Zimbabwe	1985	Stop supporting ANC rebels
South Africa	Zambia	1985	Stop supporting ANC rebels
Soviet Union	Yugoslavia	1949	Stop repression of Soviet nationals
Soviet Union	Czechoslovakia	1968	Reverse political reforms*
Soviet Union	China	1969	Withdraw from Zhenbao Island
Soviet Union	China	1969	Participate in territorial dispute negotiations*
Soviet Union	China	1979	Withdraw from Vietnam
United States	Vietnam	1964	Stop supporting Viet Cong
United States	North Korea	1968	Release USS Pueblo
United States	Cambodia	1975	Release USS Mayaguez
United States	Iran	1979	Release American embassy hostages
United States	Panama	1989	Remove Manuel Noriega from power
United States	Iraq	1990	Withdraw troops from Kuwait
United States	Serb Republic	1993	Accept Bosnian peace plan
United States	Serbia	1998	Stop ethnic cleansing in Kosovo
United States	Afghanistan	1998	Extradite Osama bin Laden
United States	Iraq	1998	Readmit weapons inspectors
United States	Afghanistan	2001	Extradite al Qaeda leaders

NOTE: Targets denoted with asterisks complied after minor military combat. These cases are recoded as successful threats under a looser definition of compellence success.

Third, we employ a statistical model that is designed to account explicitly for the possibility of selection effects (see the appendix). This model simultaneously estimates both the likelihood that a compellent threat will be made and the probability that it will succeed. By modeling these two outcomes jointly, we address the possibility that nuclear states may coerce their adversaries without having to make threats at all. However, the findings do not change significantly: states possessing nuclear weapons are not more likely to issue successful compellent threats, even when we adjust for factors that explain the onset of crises. This analysis also casts doubt on the notion that nuclear weapons embolden states to behave more aggressively. We find that nuclear states are not more likely than their nonnuclear counterparts to issue compellent threats in the first place.

A Look at the Cases

Let us now take a a brief look at the cases in our quantitative data set to be sure that the statistical models are not missing important dynamics.[31] The overall picture confirms our theory of nuclear skepticism, illustrating the minimal role played by nuclear weapons during coercive crises in the last seven decades.

A useful place to begin is Table 3.1, which lists all forty-one cases in the MCT data set in which nuclear-armed challengers failed to compel their adversaries. This list includes a wide variety of cases, including failed efforts by China to coerce territorial concessions from India without force during the 1960s, unsuccessful Soviet attempts to coerce China in the 1960s and 1970s, and failed efforts by the United States to compel North Korea, Iraq, Iran, and other adversaries.

One lesson that jumps out immediately from this list is that compellent threats from nuclear-armed challengers have often failed even under conditions that ought to have facilitated their success. In many such cases, it was at least conceivable that the use of nuclear weapons might be considered, yet the challenger's threats failed. Britain and France, for example, tried to coerce Egypt into reopening the Suez Canal in 1956 – an issue viewed by both countries as having vital national economic and security importance. Despite Britain's possession of nuclear weapons, however, the threat was unsuccessful, and the two allies had to resort to war. Similarly, the United States attempted

---

[31] We thoroughly examine the most serious nuclear crises in Part III.

to coerce the government of Afghanistan into surrendering Osama bin Laden following the 2001 terrorist attacks against New York and Washington, D.C. Afghanistan, however, refused, despite America's keen interest in finding bin Laden and its overwhelming level of nuclear superiority.

These cases illustrate the three central components of our theory of nuclear skepticism. First, in almost all of the cases in Table 3.1, nuclear weapons were either militarily useless or redundant to conventional capabilities for achieving the coercer's objectives. Using nuclear weapons against a poor and rural Afghanistan in 2001, for example, would not have helped the United States find Osama bin Laden – indeed, it required more than a decade of careful military and intelligence work to achieve that objective. In the Suez crisis, Britain might have been able to use nuclear weapons to destroy Egyptian military formations near the canal, but it already possessed conventional capabilities adequate for the job. The remaining cases in Table 3.1 have a similar flavor: either nuclear weapons had little military utility, or they were redundant to the coercer's existing capabilities. In each case, nuclear weapons added little to the challenger's coercive leverage.

Second, although we can never know for certain what costs might have been imposed on the coercers in Table 3.1 for using nuclear weapons, one can surmise that they would have been severe. Britain and France faced an international uproar simply for using conventional force in the Suez crisis; using nuclear weapons likely would have triggered a much higher level of backlash. Likewise, had the United States used nuclear weapons against any of the opponents listed in the table – all of whom were nonnuclear at the time – the diplomatic and political reaction would have been unprecedented.

Although such costs might be worth paying in some circumstances, Table 3.1 affirms that for coercive challengers, the stakes are rarely high enough to justify such costs. In none of the cases on this list was the survival of the coercer – or even the coercer's government – at stake. This is not to say that the stakes in these cases were trivial – surely they were not, as evidenced by the fact that the challengers in these cases often opted for war. However, they were not worth the price of violating an important international opprobrium and risking the wrath of friends and enemies alike.

It is also telling that challengers rarely "manipulated risk" with nuclear weapons in the cases listed in Table 3.1. In two of these cases – the Sino-Soviet crisis of 1969 and the Indo-Pakistani crisis of

Table 3.2 *Successful compellent threats from nuclear-armed challengers,
1945–2001.*

Challenger	Target	Year	Demand
France	Serb Republic	1994	Withdraw heavy artillery from Sarajevo
Great Britain	Serb Republic	1994	Withdraw heavy artillery from Sarajevo
Soviet Union	France	1956	Withdraw forces from Suez canal region
Soviet Union	Great Britain	1956	Withdraw forces from Suez canal region
United States	Dominican Republic	1961	Permit elections following Trujillo assassination
United States	Soviet Union	1962	Withdraw missiles from Cuba
United States	Soviet Union	1970	Cease construction of submarine base in Cuba
United States	Serb Republic	1994	Withdraw heavy artillery from Sarajevo
United States	Haiti	1994	Restore Jean-Bertrand Aristide to power
United States	Iraq	1997	Readmit weapons inspectors

2001–2002 – countries did engage in significant nuclear brinkmanship.[32] Yet, as we will show later in the book, these crises fail to clearly
support the conventional wisdom about nuclear superiority and risk
manipulation.

This does not necessarily imply, however, that nuclear weapons
have *never* been useful for coercive diplomacy. In fact, there are ten
instances in the MCT data set in which a nuclear-armed challenger
issued a successful coercive threat. Table 3.2 lists these cases. After
accounting for compellent threats made jointly by multiple challengers,
these observations represent a total of seven crisis episodes. If there is
any evidence that nuclear weapons aid compellent threats, we would
find it in these episodes. In two crises (Suez and Cuba), threats of

---

[32] Some have suggested that Soviet nuclear coercion worked against the Chinese
in 1969. We classify this case as "apparently successful" in Part III, and discuss
it at length in Chapter 6.

nuclear attack were implied, but even then the coercive effects of nuclear weapons were ambiguous (see Chapter 6). The other cases are noteworthy for the total absence of nuclear threats, implicit or otherwise. None of the seven cases provide clear support for the view that nuclear weapons convey the ability to blackmail other states.

Conclusion

Do nuclear weapons improve the effectiveness of compellent threats? Using a database of more than 200 militarized compellent threats from 1918 to 2001, this chapter presents evidence that they do not. Compellent threats from nuclear states have not been more successful than threats from nonnuclear states, even after accounting for other factors that influence coercive diplomacy outcomes. Moreover, this finding is robust to a wide variety of measurements of nuclear superiority, compellence success, and possible selection effects. In contrast to what Schelling and others have argued, this chapter showed that countries rarely manipulate risk with their nuclear arsenals to coerce their adversaries. Collectively, these results support our argument that nuclear weapons are not credible instruments of compellence in international politics.

To be sure, the findings presented here should not be taken to imply that nuclear weapons have no compellent value whatsoever. The analysis in this chapter showed that nuclear weapons do not provide additional compellent leverage to their possessors beyond what is already afforded by their conventional capabilities. But this does not mean that nuclear weapons have never played a role in crises triggered by compellent threats. As the Suez and Cuban missile crises illustrate, nuclear weapons have indeed weighed heavily on the minds of decision makers throughout the nuclear age. The contribution of this chapter is simply to suggest that, on the whole, the outcomes of compellent threats are not systematically different when nuclear weapons are present.

4 | Stalemates: Territorial Disputes and Nuclear Politics

Kashmir. The Panama Canal. West Berlin. The Senkaku Islands. These are all territories that once were – or are still – claimed by more than one state. Territorial disputes such as these exist because two or more states want what only one country can have. States must therefore bargain over how to divide up the proverbial territorial pie. This chapter addresses how nuclear weapons affect this bargaining process. Are nuclear states able to settle territorial disputes more favorably than other countries?

There are two main ways that states can resolve territorial disputes in their favor. First, they can try to extract concessions from their opponents during negotiations. Second, they can impose their will by using military force to seize disputed land. According to the nuclear coercionist school, nuclear weapons should help countries do both of these things more effectively. Nuclear-armed states have an easier time extracting concessions during negotiations, in this view, because the prospect of a nuclear attack looms in the background if their opponents stand firm. In addition, nuclear coercion theory posits that nuclear weapons serve as "shields" that enable states to forcibly take disputed land and then deter retaliation with their nuclear arsenals.

Nuclear skepticism theory, by contrast, holds that nuclear weapons generally do not provide states with any special advantages in territorial disputes. Coercive nuclear threats usually lack credibility, even in potentially high-stakes conflicts over territory. It is therefore difficult for countries to use their arsenals to redraw the map, either directly (by threatening to launch nuclear attacks if the target does not hand over disputed territory) or indirectly (by seizing land militarily and then threatening nuclear escalation if the target attempts to reclaim it).

Which of these views is correct? In this chapter, we attempt to answer this question by analyzing 348 territorial disputes between 1919 and 1995. The findings provide strong support for nuclear skepticism theory. Nuclear states do not extract concessions during negotiations at a higher rate than nonnuclear states. Moreover, nuclear powers are not more likely than their nonnuclear counterparts to gain disputed territory after using force. In addition, contrary to the assertions of many nuclear coercionists, nuclear arsenals do not embolden states to use military force during territorial disputes or escalate existing military confrontations. In the end, the advantages of nuclear weapons in territorial disputes are few.

The Advantages of Studying Territorial Disputes

Territorial disputes arise when states make competing claims to the same piece of land.[1] China and its neighbors, for instance, disagree about which country has sovereignty over several island chains in the South China Sea. Territorial disputes are particularly conflict prone: research shows, for example, that territorial claims are more likely to result in wars and rivalries than disagreements over other issues.[2] Even a casual glance at a list of wars fought over the last fifty years underscores that territorial issues can provoke military confrontations. China and India fought a war in 1962 over a disputed Himalayan border; Chad and Libya clashed over the Aouzou Strip in the 1980s; the dispute over the enclave of Nagorno-Karabakh led to a war between Armenia and Azerbaijan in the early 1990s; and the Badme War of 1998–2000 erupted over an Ethiopian-Eritrean territorial dispute along their shared border.

Military force is widely believed to be "an effective instrument for achieving territorial goals."[3] Nuclear weapons, in particular, are likely to be in play – even if their use is not explicitly threatened – because territorial disputes are highly salient and prone to escalation. As Pape argues, states "will attempt [nuclear] coercion only when they have important interests at stake," and "the principal issue in serious international disputes is usually control over territory."[4] If nuclear weapons are useful for coercion, then, we should find supporting evidence when examining these disputes.

---

[1] See Huth (1996) for a more detailed definition.
[2] See, for example, Vasquez (1993), Huth (1996), and Fuhrmann and Tir (2009).
[3] Huth and Allee (2002, 31).
[4] Pape (1996, 16, 37).

In addition, studying territorial disputes helps address some of the limitations of our analysis in the previous chapter. First, the cases evaluated in the previous chapter all contained explicit coercive demands. Yet demands are not always explicit in international politics; countries may get their way without ever issuing a clear threat. Territorial confrontations in particular are often distinguished by the absence of clear and explicit demands. By focusing on territorial dispute outcomes, we can determine if nuclear weapons provide states with bargaining advantages regardless of whether states engage in explicit military blackmail.

Second, as we discussed in Chapter 3, compellent threats may have selection problems: disputants know one another's nuclear status at the outset of the crisis, so it could be that only highly resolved states become targets of threats.[5] Less resolute targets may back down before a formal threat is issued, potentially obscuring cases of successful coercion by nuclear powers. Nuclear weapons, in other words, may aid coercion in unobservable ways. Although we presented evidence in the previous chapter suggesting otherwise, this issue nonetheless warrants additional attention.

Territorial disputes provide a useful venue for addressing the selection issue because they often persist for a long time. It is therefore possible for disputants to acquire nuclear weapons during an ongoing territorial dispute, an event that we call a "nuclear shock." When a state obtains the bomb after a dispute has begun, its opponent cannot strategically avoid a fight – the fight has already started. Instead, the principal way to skirt a possible nuclear confrontation following a nuclear shock is to make concessions, since avoiding the dispute in the first place is not an option. Nuclear shocks therefore should make it easier to observe the coercive effects of nuclear weapons if they do, in fact, exist.[6] We will analyze the coercive effects of nuclear weapons following nuclear shocks, thus reducing a potentially thorny selection problem. In addition, we will compare the effects of nuclear

---

[5] See Fearon (1994).

[6] For example, when Jordan first challenged Israeli sovereignty over land along demilitarized zones, Israel did not possess nuclear weapons. A fear of nuclear escalation could not have deterred Jordan from challenging Israel. Yet this dispute was still ongoing after Israel acquired the bomb. At that point, the nuclear coercionist school would expect Jordan to capitulate. Jordanian concessions therefore would be observable since the two countries were already entangled in a dispute.

weapons acquired during disputes to those obtained prior to the onset of a crisis.

Third, nuclear weapons may provide states with indirect benefits that were not captured by our analysis of compellent threats. Many scholars have argued that nuclear weapons allow countries to use conventional force with greater ease in world politics.[7] Nuclear weapons, according to this view, serve as a shield: nuclear powers can commit conventional aggression against their adversaries and then deter retaliation with their atomic arsenals. Territorial disputes offer an opportunity to assess this argument given that "bolt from the blue" land grabs are widely believed to be more feasible when states possess nuclear weapons. Some have argued, for instance, that Pakistan could be more aggressive in its dispute with India over Kashmir once it obtained the bomb.[8]

Theoretical Predictions: The Nuclear Coercionist School Versus Nuclear Skepticism Theory

Throughout the book we have discussed two competing arguments about the coercive effects of nuclear weapons: the nuclear coercionist school and nuclear skepticism theory. In this section, we review these two theories and discuss how they apply to territorial disputes. As in Chapter 3, each theoretical perspective makes distinct predictions about both coercive outcomes and intra-dispute behavior.

Do Nuclear Arsenals Help States Redraw the Map?

The clearest way in which nuclear weapons might influence territorial disputes is by helping states obtain territory that they did not previously possess. Do nuclear-armed countries have an advantage in obtaining land through territorial concessions?

The Nuclear Coercionist School: Nuclear Arsenals Help States Grab Territory Through Diplomacy and Force

According to the nuclear coercionist school, nuclear states achieve more favorable territorial dispute settlements. Realizing that they are

---

[7] Ganguly and Wagner (2004), Kapur (2007), Beardsley and Asal (2009a), and Bell and Miller (2015).

[8] For example, Kapur (2007).

outgunned, opponents of nuclear powers should make concessions to avoid the possibility of escalation to the nuclear level. Even if the chance of nuclear attack seems remote, the consequences of being targeted with atomic weaponry are so unthinkable that countries would rather back down in a dispute than run the risk of mass destruction. By contrast, when there is no risk of nuclear escalation, states have fewer incentives to concede. All else being equal, then, disputes without nuclear powers should result in fewer concessions than conflicts with a nuclear-armed actor. This logic implies that nuclear weapons directly benefit states in bargaining over disputed territory.

Few academic studies have evaluated the role of nuclear weapons in territorial dispute settlements. Yet some scholarly research supports the notion that nuclear states have bargaining advantages in these conflicts. In perhaps the only quantitative study dedicated to this issue, Gartzke and Jo find that nuclear powers tend to resolve disputes over territorial and maritime issues quicker and more favorably than nonnuclear states.[9] Similarly, although they do not focus on territorial disputes specifically, Beardsley and Asal show that nuclear powers generally experience shorter crises – some of which arise from competing claims to land.[10] These studies demonstrate, according to some scholars, that "the primary effect of nuclear proliferation on international politics is ... greater international influence for their possessors."[11]

It is also possible that states obtain indirect benefits from their arsenals in territorial disputes. In particular, nuclear-armed challengers may be able to seize disputed territory without warning and then deter counterattacks by threatening nuclear retaliation. It is often assumed that Iran, like Pakistan, would use a nuclear arsenal in this fashion. Iran's regional goals could include wresting territory – including, potentially, Iraqi oil fields – away from other states. As Stuart Gottlieb, a former foreign policy adviser to Senator Charles Schumer, wrote in the *New York Times*: "with territorial (and other) disputes against

---

[9] Gartzke and Jo (2009). Note, however, that their analysis includes the Western Hemisphere and Western Europe only. Gartzke and Jo's analysis therefore excludes seventy percent of the states that have possessed nuclear weapons, including China, India, Israel, North Korea, Pakistan, Russia, and South Africa.

[10] Beardsley and Asal (2009b).

[11] Gartzke and Kroenig (2009, 158).

nearly all of its neighbors, Iran could ...use a nuclear deterrent to try to alter the map of the Middle East."[12]

Whether nuclear weapons help states extract concessions or seize disputed territory with conventional military force, the preceding discussion implies that they provide coercive advantages in territorial disputes. Some nuclear coercionists argue that nuclear weapons have an absolute effect on international politics. Possessing the bomb, these scholars argue, allows states to get their way in international politics irrespective of their opponents' capabilities. Others suggest that the bargaining advantages of nuclear powers may be contingent on the nuclear status of their opponents. Nuclear states are likely to have a harder time pushing around other nuclear powers, according to this perspective, when targets can retaliate with nuclear forces. The coercive value of nuclear weapons therefore may be neutralized when both actors in a territorial dispute possess the bomb, or when the target has a superior arsenal.[13]

Two general predictions follow from this logic. The first conjecture suggests that nuclear weapons provide all states with coercive leverage, while the second offers a more qualified assessment based on the nuclear capabilities of the opponent:

Nuclear Absolutist Prediction: *Nuclear-armed states experience more favorable territorial dispute settlements than nonnuclear countries, on average.*

Nuclear Relativist Prediction: *Nuclear-superior countries, on average, experience more favorable territorial dispute settlements than nuclear-inferior or nonnuclear states.*

Nuclear Skepticism Theory: Nuclear Arsenals Are Mostly Unhelpful for Changing the Territorial Status Quo

We argue, in contrast, that nuclear weapons present states with three problems in coercive bargaining: nuclear weapons are often unnecessary to achieve coercive victories; implementing nuclear threats is costly; and the stakes are generally low in coercion relative to deterrence. These problems collectively render the bomb a poor instrument

---

[12] *New York Times* (2012). See also Kahl et al. (2012, 12).
[13] See, for example, Beardsley and Asal (2009b).

of blackmail, and they are at least as acute – and potentially more severe – in territorial disputes.

To begin, it is important to note that nuclear weapons are not particularly useful for seizing disputed territory. It is hard to imagine, for example, that China would attempt to resolve its territorial dispute with the Philippines by using nuclear weapons in the contested Spratly Islands. If nuclear weapons provide bargaining advantages during territorial disputes, it likely comes from their ability to punish.

It is theoretically possible for nuclear states to try to resolve conflicts by threatening their opponents' capital cities or other highly populated areas outside the contested lands. Such a use of military force would certainly be costly for the target country. However, using nuclear weapons to resolve a territorial dispute would also be costly for the attacker. Doing so might invite international condemnation, motivate other states to retaliate or align against it, and encourage proliferation. Despite the salience of territorial disputes, they are rarely important enough to coercers to justify such severe consequences. Threats to use nuclear weapons – whether they are explicit or implicit – are therefore not credible in most territorial disputes. Accordingly, there is little reason to expect that nuclear weapons would compel states to make concessions during negotiations.

What about the possibility that nuclear weapons could indirectly benefit states by serving as shields for aggression? We do not claim that nuclear arsenals are never useful for this purpose. However, nuclear coercionists are overly optimistic about the indirect benefits of possessing the bomb. To effectively use nuclear arsenals as shields for aggression, states must make nuclear threats credible following conventional military maneuvers. Yet this is a difficult task to accomplish. Nuclear powers hoping to use their arsenals to support conventional attacks face many of the same problems encountered by states in coercion – even if demands are technically deterrent in nature. The costs of implementing nuclear threats following conventional uses of force would likely be high relative to the stakes, in part, because countries that attack first would be viewed as aggressors in the eyes of international audiences. Target countries therefore may dismiss nuclear threats issued following conventional aggression as incredible, just as they downplay the possibility of nuclear punishment in coercive diplomacy. The conditions that sometimes make deterrent nuclear threats credible – in particular, higher stakes for the state issuing the threat, combined with lower costs of nuclear use – are less likely to hold when states attempt to use their arsenals as shields for aggression.

In sum, our argument implies that nuclear weapons provide few coercive advantages during bargaining over territorial disputes. This leads to the following prediction:

Nuclear Skepticism Prediction: *Nuclear states are not more likely than nonnuclear states, on average, to achieve favorable territorial dispute settlements.*

Do Nuclear Arsenals Influence Military Escalation?

Nuclear weapons may also influence a state's propensity to escalate territorial disputes by using military force. Do nuclear weapons embolden states to push harder in disputes over territory?

The Nuclear Coercionist View: Nuclear Arsenals Embolden Countries to Take Greater Risks

The nuclear coercionist logic expects that nuclear-armed states should behave differently from their nonnuclear counterparts during territorial disputes. According to some coercionists – particularly those who emphasize brinkmanship – having nuclear weapons (or nuclear superiority) increases the odds that states will take dangerous actions that could result in costly military confrontations.[14] Nuclear powers push harder in crises, in this line of thinking, because they have greater confidence that they will prevail in the event of escalation.

Indeed, many analysts have argued that nuclear-armed states are more likely to initiate military disputes, believing that their arsenals will limit the target's response to aggression.[15] The argument that nuclear weapons are a "shield" in territorial disputes also carries this implication: in order to orchestrate a *fait accompli*, a country must first seize land militarily. In addition, once a military confrontation has started, nuclear states may act with less restraint than other countries. Nuclear powers, in particular, may be quicker to mobilize in response to aggression and more likely to act belligerently following an initial provocation.[16]

[14] For example, Nitze (1976/1977) and McDonough (2006).
[15] See, for example, Bell (2015, 93).
[16] Bell (2015, 99).

This perspective yields two predictions about military escalation:

Nuclear Absolutist Prediction: *Nuclear-armed states are more likely than nonnuclear to use military force during territorial disputes, on average.*

Nuclear Relativist Prediction: *Nuclear-superior countries, on average, are more likely to use military force during territorial disputes than nuclear-inferior or nonnuclear states.*

Nuclear Skepticism Theory: Nuclear Arsenals Are Unrelated to the Use of Military Force

Our theory, however, leads to a different conclusion about the link between nuclear weapons and resolve in territorial disputes. Nuclear weapons are off the table in most territorial disputes, even in the event of escalation. Whether or not states choose to escalate a dispute by using military force often has little to do with their nuclear capabilities, according to the logic of nuclear skepticism theory.

The "nuclear shield" argument is seemingly intuitive, but we question just how often nuclear states will attempt sudden territorial seizures. First, this argument assumes that states can swiftly take territory without their adversaries noticing. However, taking and holding territory requires the mobilization of military forces, and enemies may be able to observe these maneuvers. Targets thus may have time to react and potentially deter land grabs before they occur.[17] Second, when nuclear states commit aggression, they become threatening to others – particularly to states invested in limiting the risk of nuclear war. Conventional attacks, therefore, may prompt third-party interventions, which can be bad news for states that initiate military conflicts. For example, Pakistan attempted to use its nuclear weapons as a shield in 1999, when it seized a slice of territory in Kashmir. The attempt prompted military retaliation by India and significant diplomatic pressure from the United States. President Bill Clinton summoned Pakistan's prime minister to Washington in an attempt to prevent the war from escalating. Shortly after his visit, Pakistan ordered its forces to stand down.[18] Nuclear powers – particularly non-superpowers – may anticipate these kinds

[17] Waltz (2003b, 114).
[18] Joeck (2009).

of international responses, and this may deter them from initiating conventional disputes.

Nuclear skepticism theory predicts, therefore, that nuclear arsenals are not associated with a greater risk of conflict initiation or dispute escalation:

Nuclear Skepticism Prediction: *Nuclear states are not more likely than nonnuclear states, on average, to use military force during territorial disputes.*

Collecting Data on Territorial Disputes

We test the above hypotheses using Huth and Allee's data set of 348 territorial disputes from 1919 to 1995.[19] Their data set contains most of the information necessary to test the above hypotheses. First, it identifies challenges to the territorial status quo. At any point in time, challengers in territorial disputes have three options: (1) doing nothing, (2) calling for negotiations, or (3) initiating militarized challenges to demonstrate resolve.[20] Huth and Allee's data set records which option challengers pursued throughout the duration of each dispute. In sixty-seven percent of the cases, challengers opted to maintain the status quo, while they initiated talks twenty-seven percent of the time and resorted to military action in six percent of the cases. Second, the data set provides information about what happened after states initiated negotiations or used military force.[21]

There are 1,528 rounds of negotiations documented in Huth and Allee's data set. Once states come to the negotiating table, each party must decide whether to make concessions. The challenger can make concessions during talks, leading to a more favorable settlement for the target.[22] For example, China called for negotiations in 1962 to

---

[19] Huth and Allee (2002). This data set is frequently used by other scholars to study the causes and effects of territorial conflict. See, for example, Tir (2005) and Gibler (2007).

[20] Huth and Allee (2002, 142).

[21] Huth and Allee provide three versions of their "outcome" data set; we use version 1 for the relevant tests in this chapter.

[22] This is a key difference between the territorial dispute data set and the compellent threat data set used in Chapter 3. The territorial dispute data set contains information about concessions made by both the challenger and target, whereas the compellent threat data set examined only the target's behavior.

resolve its border dispute with Mongolia and then renounced its claims to the disputed land.[23] Alternatively, the challenger can "win" the dispute by extracting concessions from the target. Panama, for instance, brought the United States to the negotiating table to resolve a dispute over the Canal Zone and ultimately gained full sovereignty over the disputed territory as a result of American concessions.[24] Our analysis below accounts for the behavior of both challengers and targets during territorial dispute negotiations.

The data set also contains 374 military confrontations.[25] Once a challenger initiates a military dispute, it must decide how much force it is willing to employ in pursuit of territorial gains. Challengers used large-scale military force after initiating confrontations in eighty-nine cases (twenty-four percent), while they refrained from escalation in the other 285 disputes (seventy-six percent). If the challenger escalates, the target must decide how to respond. It could stand firm at the risk of war or capitulate to avoid a potential costly armed conflict. Targets refrained from high levels of escalation in 307 of the confrontations (eighty-two percent) in the data set. They stood firm and escalated in the other sixty-seven disputes (eighteen percent).[26]

Three features of this data set make it particularly well suited for the analysis carried out in this chapter. First, it contains both well-known territorial disputes as well as some more obscure conflicts, such as the dispute in the 1920s between Finland and Sweden over the Aaland Islands. This type of variation is important for our analysis, just as it was when studying coercive threats in the previous chapter. The most salient territorial disputes – for example, the British-Argentine conflict over the Falkland Islands – tend to be disputes that seemingly drag on forever. Focusing too heavily on these cases may unfairly disadvantage the coercionist school in our empirical tests, since longer disputes may be more likely to give the impression that nuclear weapons do not provide bargaining leverage.

---

[23] Huth and Allee (2002, 408).

[24] Huth and Allee (2002, 453)

[25] Huth and Allee (2002, 53–54).

[26] The data set does not technically indicate who "wins" territorial disputes. However, we are able to identify winners and losers based in part on case descriptions provided by Huth and Allee. See Huth and Allee (2002, 305–460).

Second, the data set contains both nuclear and nonnuclear territorial disputes. We therefore have sufficient variation to evaluate whether nuclear powers fare better than nonnuclear states when it comes to territorial dispute settlements. Moreover, nuclear shocks occurred in a sizable number of disputes. Using the Huth and Allee data set, we can exploit variation in the timing of nuclear proliferation to evaluate the relative effects of nuclear shocks vis-à-vis predispute bomb possession.

A third important feature of this data set is that it spans most of the twentieth century. This allows us to analyze how states' fortunes changed once they built the bomb, something that we could not do as easily if we limited our analysis to the post-1945 period. The temporal coverage of the data set is particularly ideal for testing the nuclear shock argument, which predicts that territorial disputes that have festered for years will end abruptly if one party acquires nuclear weapons. We would lose valuable information – particularly for the first three nuclear powers: the United States, the Soviet Union, and Britain – if we did not account for disputes that preceded the nuclear age.

We now turn to our analysis. As in Chapter 3, while we do not discuss the technical aspects of our findings here, we encourage interested readers to consult the methodological appendix for further details.

The Evidence: Nuclear Weapons and Dispute Outcomes

There are two ways in which countries can attempt to prevail in territorial disputes: extracting concessions through negotiations or using military force. We consider whether nuclear weapons help states end disputes through either of these means.

Territorial Concessions

We begin our analysis by asking a simple question: do states make concessions in territorial dispute negotiations more often when their adversary possesses nuclear weapons? Figure 4.1 shows that they do not. The rate at which targets make concessions is virtually identical when the challenger is nuclear (thirty-five percent) and when the challenger does not possess the bomb (thirty-six percent). Challengers actually concede at a greater rate (forty percent) when facing nonnuclear targets than when they square off against nuclear targets (twenty-nine percent). These patterns could emerge because nuclear

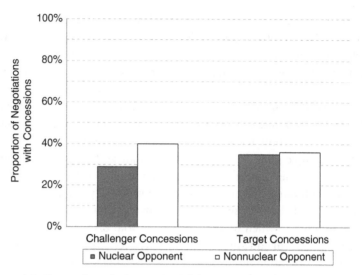

Figure 4.1 Concessions during territorial disputes.

shocks affect negotiations differently from nuclear weapons acquired prior to the start of a dispute, as implied by the earlier discussion. Yet a similar pattern emerges when comparing talks that follow nuclear shocks to other negotiations. When facing challengers that acquire nuclear weapons in the middle of a dispute, targets make concessions thirty-four percent of the time, compared to thirty-six percent when such shocks do not occur. Challengers similarly concede at a lower rate (thirty-four percent) following nuclear shocks, relative to nonshock cases (thirty-eight percent).

Nuclear relativists assert that states need a nuclear advantage in order to extract coercive leverage from their nuclear weapons. However, the evidence does not support this contention. Having nuclear superiority – that is, possessing more nuclear weapons than an adversary – does not provide countries with coercive advantages in bargaining over territory. When we account for nuclear superiority, rather than just nuclear possession, the trends are similar to those depicted in Figure 4.1.

Taken together, this evidence contradicts the nuclear coercionist perspective, but supports nuclear skepticism theory. From a statistical standpoint, nuclear states do not extract more concessions from their opponents in territorial disputes.[27]

---

[27] Note that the higher concession rates for nuclear and nuclear-superior states should not be taken to imply that nuclear weapons are disadvantageous for

We need to carry out more sophisticated tests, however, before declaring victory for our argument. Challengers and targets may consider factors unrelated to nuclear weapons when deciding whether to make concessions. In addition, the decisions made by challengers and targets during territorial dispute negotiations are obviously linked: a challenger's willingness to make concessions may depend on whether the target gives some ground, and vice-versa. Failing to account for both of these things could produce misleading results. We conduct further statistical tests to determine how nuclear weapons affect the probability of concessions while accounting for strategic interactions between challengers and targets and controlling for other factors that could influence whether either party concedes. Our analysis accounts for the challenger's conventional capabilities relative to the target's, the presence of shared strategic interests between the challenger and the target, the ethnic and strategic value of the disputed territory, whether either state has other territorial disputes, and whether the challenger and the target are democracies.

The findings from our more sophisticated statistical analysis continue to support nuclear skepticism theory. Neither challengers nor targets are more likely to concede when facing nuclear-armed adversaries. These results hold when we distinguish between nuclear shocks and nuclear weapons acquired before disputes began, and when we use more fine-grained measures of nuclear status. Nuclear weapons do not appear to provide states with bargaining advantages even when their opponents are nonnuclear, a result that undermines the nuclear relativist hypothesis.

Accounting for Statistical Patterns: An Overview of the Cases

To illustrate the above findings, it is useful to consider some specific cases contained in our data set. One observation is that nuclear states are sometimes successful in obtaining territorial concessions. In three territorial disputes, nuclear challengers extracted major concessions without giving much ground themselves: China's dispute with Portugal over Macau (1974–1975); China's border dispute with the Soviet Union (1987); and India's border dispute with China (1981). However, only in the case of Macau can the challenger be said to have

coercers in territorial dispute negotiations: the differences between nuclear and nonnuclear coercers generally are statistically insignificant, meaning that we cannot reliably conclude that their success rates are meaningfully different.

"won" the territorial dispute, and it would be hard to argue that China's nuclear arsenal contributed to this outcome. In the other two disputes, the conflicts did not end on terms that were favorable to the challengers.

But there are far more cases in which nuclear-armed challengers failed to extract major concessions from targets. Indeed, Table 4.1 shows that nuclear challengers were unable to obtain meaningful concessions in seventy-four negotiation rounds across eighteen different territorial disputes. In several of the disputes listed here, nuclear weapons clearly played little role. For instance, it is hard to imagine that Russia would have seriously contemplated using nuclear weapons against Azerbaijan to settle a dispute over basing rights in the early 1990s. Likewise, we have seen no evidence that Bangladesh ever worried about a nuclear strike from India as a means to settle their territorial dispute. Cases such as these are noteworthy because, as we have underscored throughout the book, some nuclear coercionists believe that nuclear weapons provide their possessors with bargaining advantages even when the possibility of nuclear attack is not invoked. A casual glance at Table 4.1 casts significant doubt on that claim.

What is more interesting, in our view, is that nuclear powers failed to coerce their adversaries in higher-stakes territorial disputes where the perceived risk of nuclear punishment might have been higher. The Soviet Union, for example, attempted to grab territory from Turkey in the immediate aftermath of World War II, and many analysts at the time believed that Moscow might use military force to get what it wanted. Yet the Soviets actually became less aggressive after becoming a nuclear power in 1949, and they eventually abandoned their territorial claims. This outcome is especially surprising, from the nuclear coercionist standpoint, because Moscow pursued claims against Turkey under Josef Stalin, who is widely regarded as one of the most ruthless leaders of the post-1945 era. George Patton, the famous U.S. Army general, summed up the way that many Americans viewed the repressive Soviet dictator: "We'll need Almighty God's constant help if we're to live in the same world with Stalin and his murdering cutthroats."[28] A common refrain from nuclear coercionists is that dictators like Stalin are not constrained by the costs of nuclear first use to the same degree as other leaders. It is telling, therefore, that even

[28] Brighton (2009, 376).

Table 4.1 *Failed attempts by nuclear challengers to extract concessions during negotiations, 1945–1995.*

Challenger	Target	Year(s)	Brief Description
Britain	Saudi Arabia	1952	Claims to islands near Bahrain
Britain	Saudi Arabia	1955	Claims to ill-defined border areas
Britain	Saudi Arabia	1956, 1963–1964	Claims to Buraimi Oasis
China	Bhutan	1985–1989, 1993	Claims to border areas
China	Japan	1972, 1974, 1978, 1992	Claim to Senkaku Islands
China	Kyrgyzstan	1993, 1995	Claims along border
China	Soviet Union	1964–1965, 1970, 1972–1975, 1977–1979, 1982–1985, 1995	Border from Central Asia to Manchuria
China	Tajikistan	1993, 1995	Claims along border
China	Vietnam	1975, 1977, 1990, 1992	Claims to Paracel and Spratly Islands
East Germany (with Soviet Union)	United States	1951, 1954–1955, 1957, 1960, 1964, 1967–1969	Claims to West Berlin
India	China	1982–1990	Restoration of pre-1962 border
India	Bangladesh	1980, 1994	Claims to border areas
Israel	Syria	1967	Disputes over demilitarized zones
Pakistan	India	1988–1990, 1993–1995	Claims to Kashmir and Jammu
Russia	Azerbaijan	1994–1995	Military base rights
Russia	Ukraine	1995	Base rights for Black Sea fleet
Soviet Union	Turkey	1953	Claims to Kars and Ardahan; base rights
United States	Canada	1974, 1977, 1979, 1984	Claims to Seal Island and other territories

NOTE: Sources: Huth and Allee (2002). Huth and Allee list only East Germany (not the Soviet Union) as the challenger in the Berlin dispute.

Stalin suffered territorial defeats despite possessing a weapon that is unmatched in terms of its punishment potential. China's territorial disputes provide fitting illustrations, too, and they are worth considering in a bit more detail.

A Tool with Little Utility: Nuclear Weapons in China's Territorial Disputes. Beijing's acquisition of nuclear weapons in 1964 appears to have had little effect on its propensity to make (or extract) territorial concessions: China gave substantial ground in seventy percent (seven of ten) of its territorial disputes from 1949 to 1963 and seventy-seven percent of its conflicts from 1964 to 2005.[29] These figures actually suggest that China's bargaining power lessened slightly after it built a nuclear arsenal.

Consider, for example, that China's nuclear arsenal has not been of much use in resolving its dispute with India over Arunachal Pradesh, which is located along the eastern Sino-Indian border. In 1986–1987, a crisis arose after India's Parliament moved to make Arunachal Pradesh a state in the Indian Union. China responded by demanding territorial concessions from India. Beijing then built up its military presence along the border and reportedly stockpiled nuclear weapons in Tibet and aimed them at India.[30] The crisis ended shortly thereafter without either side making significant concessions. According to the nuclear coercionist school, India should have heeded China's demands – particularly after Beijing issued an implicit nuclear threat. Why didn't this happen? Consistent with our theory, the costs of nuclear first use were exceedingly high for China, and the stakes in the dispute were too low to justify the risk. As George Perkovich explains, implicit nuclear threats over Arunachal Pradesh lacked credibility: "a Chinese nuclear threat would destroy Beijing's international credibility and subject it to severe counterpressures from the United States and Russia, among others. India and the Sino-Indian border dispute were not important or threatening enough to risk this."[31]

China's ongoing dispute with Japan over the Senkaku Islands (called the Diaoyu Islands in China) is also instructive. These islands are a group of uninhabited rocks in the East China Sea. Japan has

[29] Fravel (2005, 56–57).
[30] Perkovich (1999, 289).
[31] Perkovich (1999, 440).

maintained control over them since 1972, when they were handed over by the United States along with Okinawa. However, China has attempted to change the status quo by asserting that the Senkakus rightfully belong to Beijing. China first began to assert sovereignty over the islands in the early 1970s, after the international community learned that they contained oil deposits. Since that time, a number of Chinese attempts to coerce Japan have brought the two East Asian rivals to the brink of armed conflict.

In September 2012, for instance, the Japanese government purchased three of the islands from a private citizen.[32] This move prompted implicit nuclear threats from China. The state-run *Beijing Evening News* suggested how China could settle the Senkaku Islands dispute: "Just skip to the main course and drop an atomic bomb. [It would be] simpler."[33] Around the same time, Xu Caihou, vice chairman of China's Central Military Commission, said that the Chinese army should "be prepared for any possible military combat," a statement that could be interpreted as a veiled reference to nuclear weapons.[34] Colonel Liu Mingfu also invoked nuclear weapons when speaking about the dispute over the Senkakus. If Japan commits aggression, he said, "how do you know it wouldn't receive another nuclear bomb?" making a reference to the atomic bombings of Hiroshima and Nagasaki.[35] He went on to say, "The world would hail if Japan receives such a blow."[36] These provocative statements were followed up with displays of military force intended to coerce Tokyo. Koichiro Genba, the foreign minister of Japan, aptly summarized the situation when he recently wrote, "China appears to be attempting to make the practice of dispatching government vessels to [the Senkaku Islands] an everyday affair, and change the status quo through coercion."[37]

Yet China's coercive diplomacy has so far failed to settle the Senkaku Islands dispute. There were four rounds of negotiations from 1972 to 1995, and Japan did not make any concessions during these talks;

---

[32] See Wiegand (2012, 103–104) for a discussion of earlier crises over the Senkaku Islands.
[33] Tatlow (2012).
[34] Xinhua (2012).
[35] Garnaut (2013).
[36] Garnaut (2013).
[37] Genba (2012).

China, on the other hand, made concessions on two occasions.[38] Japan has continued to stand firm in more recent years. Tokyo refuses to even acknowledge that there is a territorial dispute, claiming that it is the only country with a rightful claim to sovereignty over the islands. Lacking crystal balls, we do not know how the current crisis will play out. However, there are no signs that Japan is willing to give any ground to China – even with nuclear weapons potentially looming in the background. Foreign Minister Genba indicated, "We cannot make any concessions where sovereignty is concerned."[39] Prime Minister Shinzo Abe likewise stated, "Japan must not yield to the Chinese government's daily exercises in coercion around the Senkaku Islands."[40]

China's repeated failures to diplomatically or militarily wrest territory from its opponents is illuminating. When it acquired a nuclear capability in the 1960s, China was the consummate rogue regime in the eyes of American policymakers. Many elites in Washington believed that a nuclear-armed China would be able to throw its weight around in Asia and force the United States to withdraw from the region. As Francis Gavin notes, "the threat posed by a nuclear-armed China under Mao Zedong was far more terrifying than anything Iraq's Saddam Hussein or current 'rogue' rulers could muster ... Mao's internal policies had led to the deaths of millions of Chinese citizens, and he had already declared that nuclear war with the United States was not to be feared."[41] Yet dire predictions about how the world would look if China acquired the bomb turned out to be incorrect – particularly with respect to the settlement of Beijing's territorial disputes.

Do Nuclear States Get What They Want by Using Military Force?

Our analysis up until this point has not accounted for the role of military force in territorial bargaining. This is an important limitation because the "nuclear shield" argument – and the nuclear coercionist school more generally – asserts that nuclear powers can take what

---

[38] Huth and Allee (2002).
[39] Genba (2012).
[40] Abe (2012).
[41] Gavin (2012b, 75–76).

they want with force more effectively than other states, even if they do not, on average, obtain peaceful concessions more frequently than nonnuclear countries. To find out whether this is true, we examined all cases in our territorial dispute data set where nuclear challengers took up arms during territorial disputes. We then identified whether the challenger's use of military force contributed to a successful settlement.

In our database, nuclear challengers initiate military conflicts about six percent of the time. Table 4.2 lists the cases in the data set where conflict occurred among nuclear-armed challengers. The first thing to notice is that military conflict involving nuclear challengers is relatively rare: twenty-three military confrontations occurred within seven different territorial disputes from 1945 to 1995.[42] Were these confrontations effective from the standpoint of the challenger?

To find out, we examined the outcomes of these conflicts. In our judgment, seventy percent of the time, the use of military force did not result in major territorial gains. The list of failures includes some salient cases. For instance, China's frequent use (and threatened use) of military force against Vietnam – including a war in 1979 – did little to alter the territorial status quo. Nuclear weapons should be especially useful in asymmetric nuclear relationships such as this one, according to the nuclear coercionist school, since the target cannot retaliate with atomic forces. The failure of China to take territory from Vietnam, even after initiating conventional military confrontations, is therefore particularly noteworthy. In addition, it is telling that Kashmir appears on this list given that scholars frequently use this case to support the view that nuclear weapons offer a shield for aggression. Although nuclear weapons may have encouraged Pakistan to act aggressively, Islamabad has still failed to wrest Kashmir away from India.

Nuclear-armed challengers successfully used military force less than thirty percent of the time (two of seven cases). Britain and Russia were able to get their way in disputes with Saudi Arabia and Georgia, respectively. However, we found no clear evidence that their nuclear arsenals contributed to these victories.

---

[42] This includes the Berlin dispute, which Huth and Allee treat as a conflict between East Germany (challenger) and the United States (target). We add the Soviet Union as a challenger, since Moscow's role was central in the conflict over Berlin (see Chapter 5).

Table 4.2 *Military confrontations initiated by nuclear challengers, 1945–1995.*

Challenger	Target	Brief Description	Year(s) of Military Conflict	Outcome: Military Confrontation Successful?
Britain	Saudi Arabia	Claims to Buraimi Oasis	1953, 1955	Yes
China	Portugal	Sovereignty over Macau	1967	No
China	Soviet Union	Claims to border regions	1964, 1967, 1969	No
China	Vietnam	Claims to land border and Paracel and Spratly Islands	1974, 1979, 1980–1981, 1983-85, 1987, 1988	No
East Germany (with the Soviet Union)	West Germany (with Britain, France, and the United States)	Status of Berlin	1949, 1959, 1961	No
Russia	Georgia	Russian military bases	1993	Yes
Pakistan	India	Claims to Kashmir and Jammu	1987, 1990–1992	No

NOTE: Territorial disputes drawn from Huth and Allee (2002). Only East Germany (not the Soviet Union) is listed as the initiator of military conflict in the Berlin dispute in the original Huth and Allee data set.

The Evidence: Nuclear Weapons and Dispute Behavior

The preceding analysis showed that having nuclear weapons does not help states achieve more favorable *outcomes* in territorial disputes. But what about the behavior of nuclear states *during* these disputes? Do nuclear states act differently from their nonnuclear counterparts in territorial disputes? This is important because nuclear skepticism theory and the nuclear coercion school offer very different answers to this question. We assess whether nuclear states are more likely to either initiate military challenges or escalate military disputes once they occur.

Do Nuclear States Initiate Military Challenges More Frequently?

Are nuclear states systematically more likely to initiate militarized challenges during ongoing territorial disputes?[43] Figure 4.2 provides the answer, comparing how frequently nuclear challengers signal their resolve by using limited displays of military force compared to

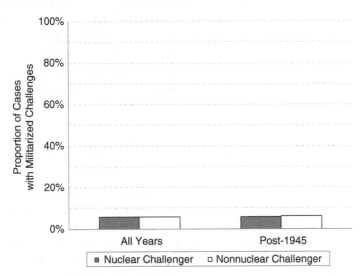

Figure 4.2 Nuclear weapons and military challenges.

[43] For our purposes here, a military confrontation is the use or threatened use of military force to reverse the territorial status quo.

nonnuclear challengers.[44] The columns on the left hand side of the figure include all observations from 1919 to 1995; the columns on the right limit the sample to the nuclear age. As the figure shows, the rate at which nuclear and nonnuclear states signal their resolve is virtually identical. This pattern remains similar if we restrict our analysis to nuclear shocks: states are slightly more likely to start military disputes following nuclear shocks (seven percent) than they are otherwise (six percent), a statistically-insignificant difference.

Contrary to claims made by nuclear relativists, states are not more aggressive when they have a nuclear advantage. Among non-nuclear targets only, the rate of conflict initiation is similar for nuclear challengers (five percent) and their nonnuclear counterparts (seven percent). Further, there is no difference in the rate of military challenges between nuclear-superior and nuclear-inferior states: both groups initiate conflicts at a rate of six percent. This evidence strongly suggests that nuclear weapons do not embolden states to initiate military challenges, even when they have nuclear advantages over their opponents.

However, our preliminary analysis does not account for other factors that could affect military conflict initiation. As a next step, we conduct more rigorous statistical tests to analyze how the challenger's possession of nuclear weapons influences its willingness to use military force, while controlling for other variables – such as the balance of conventional capabilities. The results confirm that the challenger's nuclear status is unrelated to the probability of conflict initiation – regardless of whether the target possesses the bomb or not. Moreover, the findings continue to support our argument when we use more fine-grained measures of nuclear status, including the challenger's arsenal size, an indicator of nuclear superiority, the ratio of nuclear capabilities possessed by the challenger, and the difference in arsenal size between the challenger and the target.

It could be the case, however, that nuclear weapons benefit states once they become embroiled in military disputes over territory. Indeed, a key claim made by nuclear coercionists is that nuclear weapons enable states to escalate crises with greater ease. Before concluding that the evidence supports our theory, therefore, we must address the relationship between nuclear forces and dispute escalation.

---

[44] Our analysis here focuses exclusively on challengers, since only one country can start a military conflict.

Are Nuclear Powers More Likely to Escalate?

We assess whether nuclear powers show a greater propensity to escalate crises over territory once they have begun. We first compare the rate of escalation among nuclear and nonnuclear states. Figure 4.3 shows that nonnuclear challengers escalate twenty-four percent of the time, while nuclear states escalate at a rate of nineteen percent. Thus, nuclear challengers are actually *less* likely to escalate disputes than their nonnuclear counterparts. However, the difference in escalation rates between nuclear and nonnuclear challengers is statistically insignificant. We cannot conclude, therefore, that nuclear challengers behave any differently from nonnuclear countries when it comes to escalatory behavior during territorial conflicts. It appears at first glance that nuclear targets escalate at a slightly higher rate than their nonnuclear counterparts (twenty percent compared to eighteen percent). Yet, once again, this distinction is far from being statistically significant. In some cases – most notably Israel's disputes with Egypt, Jordan, and Syria – nuclear states escalated after being targeted with military force. This does not appear to be part of a broader trend, however.

The patterns depicted in Figure 4.3 are similar when we focus on nuclear shocks only, excluding cases where states acquired the bomb before a territorial dispute began. Additionally, the results continue to

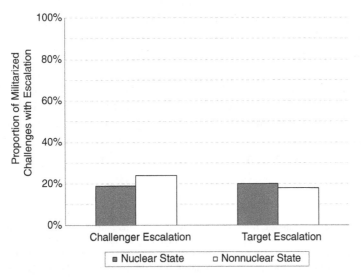

Figure 4.3 Nuclear weapons and escalation of ongoing military conflicts.

support nuclear skepticism theory when we account for the atomic capabilities of one's opponent. Neither challengers nor targets are statistically more likely to escalate when they have a nuclear advantage over their adversary, further undermining the nuclear relativist hypothesis.

As before, we conduct further statistical tests to determine whether these initial relationships survive additional scrutiny. We analyze how nuclear weapons affect the probability of escalation while controlling for other factors that could affect escalatory behavior: the strategic and ethnic value of disputed territory, the conventional military balance, whether the disputants are democracies, and other variables. Our analysis also accounts for the possibility that a target's willingness to escalate depends on whether the challenger does so, and vice-versa.

The evidence from our more sophisticated statistical tests calls into question the notion that nuclear states are more likely to turn up the heat during crises. According to some nuclear coercionists, nuclear powers win disputes because they have greater resolve, making them more willing to take escalatory actions that manipulate the risk of war. The results from our analysis show, however, that, at least when it comes to territorial disputes, nuclear powers are not more likely than nonnuclear states to escalate with military force. If anything, nuclear states are *less* likely to escalate military confrontations. In any case, countries do not seem to take much comfort in having atomic firepower at their disposal during conflicts over territory.

It is telling that escalation by nuclear states is exceedingly rare. Nuclear-armed challengers escalated in just four of the twenty-one opportunities they had to do so. All of the instances of challenger escalation in the data set come from one territorial conflict: China's border dispute with Vietnam. Nuclear targets escalated at a slightly higher rate, but they still ramped up military pressure in just eight of the forty total opportunities. These trends emerge, in our view, because nuclear weapons do not provide any special advantages in coercive disputes of this nature.[45]

---

[45] A critic might assert, however, that we observe this pattern because nuclear powers do not have to escalate to get their way in military conflicts over territory. According to this perspective, opponents of nuclear states realize they are outgunned and decide to give ground before escalation becomes necessary. If true, this suggests that nuclear powers have an easier time getting their way

Finally, it is worth pointing out that nuclear brinkmanship is quite rare in territorial disputes. To be sure, nuclear weapons loomed in the background in some cases analyzed in this chapter. For example, as discussed above, China pointed nuclear weapons at India during their ongoing border dispute and recently made nuclear threats to compel Japan to hand over the Senkaku Islands. However, even in these cases, nuclear states generally behaved cautiously and sought to minimize the possibility that something could go awry. Pakistan, one of the few countries whose nuclear posture is based on a delegative command structure, is the possible exception to this statement.[46] Particularly in crisis situations over Kashmir, Pakistan has opted to give local commanders a substantial degree of control over the the country's nuclear assets. Yet states engaged in overt nuclear brinkmanship in fewer than five percent of the territorial disputes included in our analysis.[47]

Conclusion

There are two ways that states can get their way in territorial disputes: by extracting concessions during negotiations or by using military force. This chapter shows that nuclear weapons do not bolster a state's ability to do either of these things. Nuclear-armed challengers do not gain territorial concessions at a higher rate than nonnuclear states, on average. This is true regardless of whether states possessed nuclear arsenals before disputes began or acquired bombs during ongoing conflicts. In addition, states that possess the bomb are not more likely to use conventional military power to gain control over disputed land.

Overall, this chapter throws cold water on the argument that nuclear weapons are useful for redrawing the map. If nuclear weapons do anything in these disputes, they preserve the status quo. Based on history, then, fears that Iran or other future proliferators will suddenly be able to grab territory with ease appear to be unfounded.

---

once they use military force, regardless of whether they escalate or not. Our earlier analysis showed, however, that this is not the case.

[46] Narang (2009). Note however, that Pakistan has pursued this posture only since 1998 when it conducted a round of nuclear tests.

[47] This includes the cases mentioned above and several others analyzed in Part III of the book: the Berlin crises from 1958 to 1961, Arab attempts to recover territory lost during the 1967 war with Israel, the Suez crisis, and the Falklands War.

Cases

Roadmap for Part III

The evidence offered in Part II of the book is an important pillar of support for nuclear skepticism theory. We demonstrated that nuclear states do not issue more successful compellent threats (Chapter 3) or obtain more favorable territorial dispute settlements (Chapter 4) than their nonnuclear counterparts, on average. Most of the time, then, nuclear weapons do not appear to provide countries with special benefits when it comes to coercion in world politics. However, the preceding analysis leaves an important question unanswered: does nuclear coercion work when states deliberately invoke their arsenals in crises?

In many of the cases that we analyzed in the previous two chapters, countries did not consciously use their nuclear arsenals for coercive purposes. Indeed, nuclear threats were notably absent from the majority of coercive threats and territorial disputes that we studied. We are not surprised that countries rarely brandish their nuclear arsenals, since our theory expects explicit brinkmanship behavior to occur infrequently. Yet a critic might argue that cases in which the danger of nuclear war was exceedingly low, like the 1999 Kosovo War, tell us little about the utility of nuclear weapons. Nuclear weapons would not play a role in these crises, according to this view, since states made no attempt to engage in atomic blackmail.

In the next two chapters, we address this concern by studying cases in which countries clearly attempted nuclear coercion. Instead of comparing the success rates of nuclear and nonnuclear states in coercive diplomacy, as we did in Chapters 3 and 4, the following chapters analyze whether nuclear brinkmanship works when it is tried.

A crisis must meet three conditions to be included in our analysis. First, at least one crisis participant must issue an explicit or implicit nuclear threat. This can be done by threatening to use nuclear weapons, alerting nuclear forces, deploying atomic weapons,

125

or conducting tests of either nuclear weapons or ballistic missiles.[1] However, these actions alone do not necessarily make a dispute a serious nuclear crisis. Some nuclear threats certainly bring states to the brink of nuclear war, but others do not.

This brings us to our second criterion: the crisis must carry a nontrivial risk of nuclear escalation. We excluded cases in which nuclear use seemed implausible, based on our review of available documents and secondary literature. To illustrate, in a 1977 crisis with Guatemala, Great Britain deployed the aircraft carrier HMS *Achilles* to Latin America. Because the *Achilles* carried nuclear-capable delivery systems, some analysts classify this episode as a nuclear threat.[2] Yet we find it hard to believe that the nuclear option could have played any meaningful role in the crisis, so we exclude this case from our analysis. Another example is a potentially veiled nuclear threat President George W. Bush made against Iraq during a March 13, 2003 press conference: "Again, all options are on the table," he said, "But one thing I will not allow is a nation such as Iraq to threaten our very future by developing weapons of mass destruction." This case, too, does not have the flavor of a serious nuclear crisis. Indeed, there is no evidence that the United States seriously considered using nuclear weapons against Iraq during the 2003 invasion.

Setting a high bar for what constitutes a nuclear threat serves an important analytic purpose. Imagine that a nuclear power makes an oblique reference to nuclear weapons in a public speech, and then issues a threat that ultimately fails (as in the Iraq case above). One might claim that such a case supports our theory. Yet a critic of our argument might respond that the challenger simply was not serious, and that the threat might have succeeded if it had been. Focusing on nuclear crises in which the participants engaged in clear brinkmanship behavior addresses this problem by excluding cases that may not provide a fair test of nuclear coercion theory.

Third, the nuclear threat must be linked to a coercive demand. We excluded cases in which states intended to preserve the status quo

---

[1] Threats to proliferate are beyond the scope of our study. We therefore do not examine the 1994 North Korean crisis, during which Pyongyang used the threat of proliferation to extract concessions from the United States and its allies. Likewise, because our interest is in the effectiveness of coercive nuclear threats – rather than actual nuclear strikes – we exclude the 1945 atomic bombings of Japan from our analysis.

[2] Black (2010).

rather than overturn it, even if they made a conscious effort to invoke their nuclear arsenals. For instance, we exclude a U.S. nuclear threat that may have been conveyed to Iraq prior to the 1991 Persian Gulf War. In a letter to Saddam Hussein dated January 5, 1991, President George H. W. Bush stated that he and his country would "pay a terrible price" if it used chemical or biological weapons. Even if this statement was, in fact, a reference to nuclear weapons, its purpose was clearly to deter rather than coerce.[3] U.S. nuclear threats against the Soviet Union during the 1948 Berlin airlift and the 1958 Lebanon crisis were likewise deterrent in nature, as was President Nixon's threat against Iraq and Syria during the 1970 Jordan crisis. We therefore do not analyze these cases in detail, focusing instead on clear attempts at nuclear blackmail.

It is important to note that we are primarily interested in *direct* nuclear coercion. These are cases in which one state attempts to coerce another by threatening to launch a nuclear attack against it. However, we also address some cases involving nuclear coercion against third parties.[4] In these cases, a nuclear state attempts to coerce a target by threatening to attack a third party rather than the target itself. During the 1973 Yom Kippur War, for example, Israel allegedly threatened to attack its Arab rivals with nuclear weapons to compel the United States to provide it with additional military support.

We identified thirteen cases that clearly met these three criteria. These cases are listed in Table III.1. Another six borderline cases nearly met our criteria; we included these six cases in our analysis as well, in part because other scholars have identified them as significant nuclear crises. In the next two chapters, we examine the role of nuclear brinkmanship in all nineteen of these crises, devoting the most attention to the most serious cases.

Table III.1 shows that there is notable variation in the outcomes of coercive nuclear crises since 1945. Nine cases represent clear failures of nuclear coercion. In these crises, consistent with nuclear skepticism theory, states failed to achieve their coercive objectives despite making nuclear threats. The other ten cases, however, were apparently successful: coercers got their way in these disputes after engaging in nuclear brinkmanship. This does not necessarily mean that nuclear threats

---

[3] The effectiveness of this threat is still debated. See, for example, Sagan (2000).

[4] For a more extensive treatment of third-party nuclear compellence, see Narang (2014).

Table III.1 *Cases of attempted nuclear coercion, 1946–2016.*

Nuclear Crisis	Challenger	Target(s)	Year(s) of Nuclear Brinkmanship
Nuclear Coercion Failures			
Berlin ultimatum I	Soviet Union	United States	1958–1959
Berlin ultimatum II	Soviet Union	United States	1961
Seizure of the USS *Pueblo**	United States	North Korea	1968
Vietnam War	United States	Soviet Union/North Vietnam	1969
Falklands War*	United Kingdom	Argentina	1982
Third Taiwan Strait crisis*	China/United States	Taiwan/China/United States	1995
Kargil War	Pakistan	India	1999
Indo-Pakistani border crisis	India	Pakistan	2001–2002
Korean crisis	North Korea	South Korea/United States	2013
Apparently Successful Cases			
Korean War	United States	China/North Korea	1950–1953
Indochina War	United States	China/Soviet Union/Viet Minh	1954
First Taiwan Strait crisis	United States	China	1954–1955
Suez crisis*	Soviet Union	France/United Kingdom	1956
Second Taiwan Strait crisis	United States	China	1958
Cuban missile crisis	United States	Soviet Union	1962
Sino-Soviet border crisis	Soviet Union	China	1969
Bangladesh War*	United States	India	1971
Yom Kippur War	Israel/United States	United States/Egypt/Soviet Union	1973
Kashmir crisis*	Pakistan	India/United States	1990

NOTE: Asterisks designate borderline nuclear crises.

caused states to achieve coercive victories, but the sequence of events seemingly supports the nuclear coercionist school and contradicts nuclear skepticism theory.

The following two chapters split these cases based on their apparent outcome. In Chapter 5, we analyze clear failures of nuclear coercion. This chapter illustrates the logic of nuclear skepticism theory, showing that nuclear signals are sometimes missed by the target, and that coercive nuclear threats may still be dismissed as incredible when challengers engage in potentially dangerous brinkmanship. Chapter 6 evaluates apparently successful cases of nuclear coercion.[5] These cases seem to be outliers for our theory. A careful analysis of these crises, however, shows that the evidence supporting the nuclear coercionist view is quite tenuous. None of these crises offer unequivocal evidence that nuclear coercion works. Together, the evidence we offer in Chapters 5 and 6 leads to a surprising conclusion: nuclear weapons have rarely, if ever, helped countries successfully blackmail their adversaries.

Sources, Methods, and the Value of Qualitative Historical Analysis

In Part II of the book, we analyzed a large number of cases to identify general trends in nuclear coercion. We take a different approach in Part III: we study a small number of serious nuclear crises in greater detail. Each case addresses three main questions. First, what were the issues at stake in the crisis? Second, how did the coercer use nuclear brinkmanship to achieve its objectives? And third, what role did nuclear weapons play in the outcome of the crisis? In addressing these issues, we strive to illustrate nuclear skepticism theory, and cast further doubt on the nuclear coercionist logic.

Our assessment of each crisis comes from a comprehensive review of the historical record. Whenever possible, we consulted declassified documents to determine how the crisis participants themselves thought about the role of nuclear weapons as events unfolded. We also reviewed other primary sources, including memoirs and media

---

[5] The 1969 Sino-Soviet border crisis included two compellent threats, both of which we classified as unsuccessful in Chapter 3. However, the second demand was partially successful according to the MCT data set, and some scholars have argued that Soviet nuclear coercion worked in 1969. We therefore treat this crisis as an apparently successful case of nuclear coercion in Chapter 6.

reports. Finally, we relied on secondary case literature. Given that the crises we study are widely viewed as dangerous, many of them have attracted considerable attention in scholarship. We privileged secondary sources that are viewed as authoritative and credible by other scholars; these are often the studies that rely the most heavily on government documents.

The case studies address two key limitations of the quantitative analysis carried out in Part II. First, Chapters 3 and 4 do not directly test the logic of nuclear skepticism. Instead, they test a key prediction of our theory – namely, that nuclear powers are no more effective at coercive diplomacy, on average, than nonnuclear states. We find this to be true, but this does not necessarily mean that our theory is correct. Other factors unrelated to nuclear skepticism theory could potentially account for this pattern. Looking at the cases allows us to determine whether nuclear skepticism theory actually explains the relatively poor record of coercive diplomacy held by nuclear powers. The evidence will show that it does: the cases demonstrate that credibility problems undermine the efficacy of atomic blackmail, and that manipulating risk does not necessarily make coercive nuclear threats effective.

Second, the purpose of quantitative analysis was to identify general trends – not to explain any single case. Even if the quantitative evidence suggests that our argument is generally correct, nuclear skepticism theory may fail to explain some cases. Why does this matter? The unexplained cases – often referred to as "outliers" – may be particularly salient. All crises are not equally important in the eyes of analysts and policymakers: most people are especially interested in the cases that brought countries close to nuclear war, like the Cuban missile crisis. The historical analysis conducted in Part III allows us to assess how well nuclear skepticism theory fares in these cases. If our theory struggles to explain the most dangerous nuclear crisis, it would be reasonable to question its utility, even if we can account for general trends. However, as we will show, nuclear skepticism theory can explain many of the most high-profile cases, in addition to general trends, which further adds to its appeal.

While historical analysis usefully complements our quantitative tests, it also suffers from some limitations. As we discussed earlier, we cannot always accept information that is contained in the historical record at face value, because leaders have incentives to misrepresent the truth. In addition, key pieces of evidence may be absent from the written record. It is also important to mention that we do not have access to key documents pertaining to many of the crises analyzed in Part III. We can now access large quantities of formerly classified material on U.S. nuclear crises, including the Korean War, the Taiwan Strait crises of the 1950s, and other Cold War disputes. These sources are tremendously helpful in assessing the role of nuclear weapons in American crisis decision making. However, the archives remain closed in many other countries. Some useful Russian documents – particularly pertaining to the Cuban missile crisis – have started to trickle out in recent years. But there is much that we still do not know about the Russian side of that crisis, and others like it. The documentary record is even thinner for China, India, Israel, and Pakistan. And there are virtually no sources that provide insights into North Korean decision making during the crises that we examine. Many of the conclusions from our qualitative analysis, then, are necessarily preliminary. We assess how nuclear weapons influenced crisis outcomes based on the information that we have at our disposal, recognizing that our findings could change as new evidence comes to light.

With these caveats in mind, we can now begin to examine the cases. We start with the nuclear coercion failures, and then turn our attention to the apparent anomalies for nuclear skepticism theory.

5 | Brinkmanship Busts: When Nuclear Coercion Fails

The next two chapters take a close look at the most dangerous coercive nuclear crises since 1945. In this chapter, we discuss nine nuclear coercion failures. These are cases in which countries openly brandished nuclear weapons but still failed to achieve their coercive objectives. The leaders who issued these ill-fated threats – particularly Nikita Khrushchev, Richard Nixon, and Kim Jong Un – followed the nuclear coercionist playbook to the letter. They alerted nuclear forces, forward-deployed atomic weapons, and appeared willing to engage in nuclear conflict. This kind of brinkmanship behavior should make coercive nuclear threats effective, according to nuclear coercionist logic. However, in these cases, it did not.

This chapter illustrates two key features of nuclear skepticism theory. First, it shows that credibility problems in nuclear blackmail are pervasive. In all of the nuclear coercion failures analyzed in this chapter, targets questioned the credibility of atomic threats, albeit to varying degrees. Although it is often difficult to determine precisely why states dismissed threats as not credible, two problems associated with nuclear coercion – the high costs of carrying out nuclear threats and the relatively low stakes in coercive crises – seem to play an important role in most crises.

Second, this chapter underscores that brinkmanship is an imperfect solution to the credibility problem in nuclear coercion. In each instance of failed blackmail, countries tried to make nuclear threats believable. Yet targets nevertheless largely dismissed the possibility of nuclear escalation. Brinkmanship failed to pay coercive dividends, in part, because of signaling failures. Nuclear coercion theory assumes that nuclear signals are easily detected and interpreted. If one state manipulates the risk of nuclear war by alerting its nuclear forces, for example, the other side should notice and understand what the alert is meant to communicate. However, the evidence suggests that this view is overly optimistic. Consistent with our theory, the cases show that nuclear signals are sometimes misinterpreted or totally missed. That atomic threats fail in serious brinkmanship crises – not just in cases with a minimal nuclear dimension, like the Iranian hostage crisis in 1979 – demonstrates that it is exceedingly difficult to engage in credible nuclear blackmail.

The evidence offered in this chapter unequivocally undermines the most extreme nuclear coercion argument: namely, the nuclear absolutist claim that nuclear weapons allow states to blackmail their adversaries regardless of their opponent's capabilities. However, nuclear relativism is harder to dismiss out of hand. Some relativists argue that nuclear threats are not credible against nuclear targets.[1] Much of the evidence we offer here is consistent with this claim. However, two of the cases we analyze toward the end of the chapter – the 1968 *Pueblo* crisis and the 1982 Falklands War – suggest that nuclear weapons do not seem to have much coercive leverage against nonnuclear targets either, which leads one to question this version of nuclear relativism.

Other nuclear relativists place a premium on nuclear superiority.[2] According to this view, states can engage in nuclear blackmail against other nuclear powers, but only if they possess a larger arsenal. Two of the cases we study – the 1969 U.S. nuclear alert during the Vietnam War and the 2001–2002 Indo-Pakistani border confrontation – clearly contradict this argument. In these crises, nuclear coercion failed despite the fact that the challenger had nuclear superiority over the target. The other four serious nuclear crises discussed in this chapter – the Berlin crises in 1958–1959 and 1961, the 1999 Kargil War, and the 2013 Korea crisis – as well as one less-serious case (the 1995–1996 Taiwan Strait crisis) had nuclear-inferior challengers. These cases seem to support the logic of nuclear superiority. However, in the case studies below, we cast doubt on the notion that nuclear blackmail failed because the challenger had fewer nuclear weapons than the target.

The Berlin Crises, 1958–1961

There were two serious superpower crises over the status of Berlin in the first half of the Cold War.[3] In both of these crises, the Soviet

---

[1] See, for example, Beardsley and Asal (2009b).
[2] See, for example, Jastrow (1983).
[3] In addition, a superpower crisis emerged in 1948 after the Soviet Union cut off rail, road, and canal access to West Berlin. As noted previously, the U.S. nuclear

Union used nuclear threats in an attempt to expel Western forces from Berlin, a city located in the heart of East Germany. However, on both occasions, Moscow failed to change the status quo.

Round 1: 1958–1959

Nikita Khrushchev gave the United States and its allies an ultimatum on November 27, 1958. The Soviet leader threatened to sign a peace treaty with East Germany that would effectively end NATO's right to station troops in Berlin unless NATO agreed to declare West Berlin a "free" city within six months. Khrushchev's goal, according to Polish leader Wladyslaw Gomulka, was to "liquidate the western part of Berlin," where NATO forces were stationed.[4] Moscow believed that the presence of Western forces in Berlin threatened the viability of East Germany as a state. Khrushchev therefore wanted the troops gone and he created "a period of extreme tension" in an attempt to force the West's hand.[5]

Soviet Nuclear Brinkmanship

The Soviet Union issued numerous nuclear threats during the crisis. On December 1, 1958, for example, during a discussion with U.S. Senator Hubert Humphrey about Berlin, Khrushchev threatened to unleash nuclear forces against the United States: "We have rockets . . . We mean business," Khrushchev declared.[6] He went on to assert that the Soviets had just detonated a five-megaton hydrogen bomb, a clear attempt to further intimidate the Americans.[7] Six months later, the Soviet leader told Averell Harriman, former ambassador to the Soviet Union, "The West seemed to forget that a few Russian missiles could destroy all of Europe. One bomb was sufficient for Bonn and three to five would knock out France, England, Spain, and Italy." "We will put an end to your rights in Berlin," Khrushchev went on to say, and Soviet "rockets

---

threat conveyed during this crisis was primarily deterrent in nature. See Shlaim (1983, 239).

[4] Fursenko and Naftali (2006, 199).

[5] Fursenko and Naftali (2006, 211).

[6] U.S. Department of State (1958d). A few weeks prior, Khrushchev had made a similar proclamation to Gomulka: "Today America has moved closer to us; our missiles can hit them directly." Quoted in Fursenko and Naftali (2006, 199).

[7] Taubman (2003, 407).

will fly automatically" if the United States started a war.[8] He similarly told Vice President Richard Nixon that the Soviets could "wipe West Germany from the face of the earth, along with the other countries where [U.S.] military bases are located" if the Americans forcefully resisted his Berlin demand.[9]

These are some of the clearest nuclear threats issued in the atomic age. And they were seemingly credible. In March 1955, Moscow hatched a plan, known as "Operation Atom," to deploy R-5M medium-range ballistic missiles to East Germany. The nuclear missiles arrived at bases north of Berlin in November or December 1958, just after Khrushchev issued his ultimatum.[10] They were fully operational by early May 1959.[11] These deployments provided Moscow with the ability, for the first time, to hit London and Paris with nuclear weapons. Khrushchev believed that now, unlike in the 1956 Suez crisis when his nuclear threat rang hollow, he could use the Soviet nuclear arsenal for offensive diplomatic purposes.[12]

The U.S. Response

The United States doubted Khrushchev's willingness to use nuclear weapons over Berlin. Indeed, most U.S. officials believed that Khrushchev was bluffing. According to a previously top secret memorandum, Secretary of State John Foster Dulles calculated that the Soviets would "hold to their position right up until the last minute before giving way," a view shared by French leader Charles de Gaulle.[13] CIA chief Allen Dulles likewise thought that Khrushchev would not risk war over Berlin.[14] President Eisenhower, who reacted "calmly" to the ultimatum, appears to have shared these views.[15] The high costs of nuclear first use and the relatively modest stakes, it seems, caused Washington to dismiss Khrushchev's brinkmanship. The United States simply stood firm, and refused to overturn the status quo in Berlin. Khrushchev ultimately revoked the ultimatum, temporarily

[8] U.S. Central Intelligence Agency (1960, n–o).
[9] U.S. Central Intelligence Agency (1960, p).
[10] Fursenko and Naftali (2006, 194).
[11] Uhl and Ivkin (2001, 302).
[12] Fursenko and Naftali (2006, 194, 213). We discuss the Suez crisis in Chapter 6.
[13] Merchant (1959) and Taubman (2003, 404).
[14] Fursenko and Naftali (2006, 203).
[15] Fursenko and Naftali (2006, 210).

reducing tensions over Berlin. He knew "deep in his heart," according to his son, that his gambit had failed.[16]

A key signaling failure may have contributed to the failure of Khrushchev's ultimatum. The Soviet missile deployment – which was seemingly so critical to Khrushchev's strategy – may have been missed by the United States. Western intelligence sources noticed suspicious Soviet activity north of Berlin, but it is unclear whether President Eisenhower knew for certain that the Soviets had operational nuclear missiles in East Germany during the height of the crisis. To be sure, there are indications that Washington worried about the forward-deployment of Soviet nuclear forces. For example, a cable sent to Washington from Llewelyn Thompson, the U.S. ambassador to the Soviet Union, in November 1958 speculated that Moscow could station "atomic missiles in Poland or East Germany, if this has in fact not already been done."[17] However, according to one study of the crisis, "information on the nuclear missile deployments may not have reached top-level policymakers in the United States until late 1960," well after Khrushchev had already lifted his ultimatum.[18] It seems unlikely, therefore, that the Soviet Union's recently acquired ability to hit European cities with nuclear weapons influenced U.S. decision making during the crisis.[19] This evidence supports a key part of our argument – namely, that nuclear signals can be misinterpreted, if they are received at all. The lack of concrete information about Operation Atom could explain why U.S. officials barely flinched in the face of Khrushchev's nuclear threats.

Round 2, 1961

The 1958–1959 Berlin crisis had a sequel. Khrushchev renewed his ultimatum while meeting with newly elected president John F. Kennedy at the Vienna summit in June 1961. The Soviet leader asserted, once again, that he would sign a separate peace treaty with East Germany if the United States did not turn West Berlin into a free city. Kennedy

---

[16] Taubman (2003, 412).

[17] Thompson (1958).

[18] Uhl and Ivkin (2001, 303).

[19] Washington missed another potentially significant nuclear signal: Khrushchev withdrew the nuclear missiles from East Germany in August 1959 in an apparent attempt to signal cooperative intentions to the West.

responded by making it clear that the United States would not abandon its right to station forces in West Berlin. During a televised address on July 25, he said, "We cannot and will not permit the Communists to drive us out of Berlin ... [W]e do not want to fight, but we have fought before."[20] Then, a few weeks later, the Soviet Union erected the Berlin Wall, dividing the eastern and western parts of the city. The wall was intended largely to stop refugee flows into West Berlin, which were bleeding the East German economy. Khrushchev had an additional motive: he hoped that the wall would compel the United States to negotiate peace treaties with both Germanys that would inhibit Western access to Berlin.[21] His aspiration did not materialize. After a period of tension in the fall of 1961 – including an eighteen-hour standoff that put American and Soviet tanks face to face – Khrushchev dropped his ultimatum. The sequel ended like the original.[22]

Soviet Nuclear Brinkmanship

The superpower standoff over Berlin in 1961 is widely viewed as exceedingly dangerous – even more so than the 1958–1959 crisis.[23] According to Fursenko and Naftali, after Khrushchev renewed his ultimatum in June 1961, "the world moved closer to nuclear war than at any time since the Soviets tested their first atomic bomb in August 1949."[24] Things were especially precarious for the United States because, unlike in 1958–1959, the Soviet Union now had the capacity to hit the U.S. mainland with long-range missiles.[25] Moscow was seemingly resolved to use its nuclear arsenal to force the United States out of Berlin.

The Soviet Union issued nuclear threats, as it had done in 1958–1959. A prominent article in the Soviet newspaper *Izvestia* warned Washington: "[D]o not overestimate your atomic weapons. The

[20] Harrison (2003, 191).
[21] Harrison (2003, 194).
[22] One could argue that the Soviet Union "won" the crisis because it constructed the Berlin Wall in the face of potential American objections. However, Western forces remained in Berlin – which is what the United States cared about most. Indeed, Kennedy believed that the wall was a victory for the United States because it solidified the status quo. Harrison (2003, 207).
[23] Trachtenberg (1991) and Gavin (2012b).
[24] Fursenko and Naftali (2006, 355).
[25] Smyser (2009, 161).

United States ceased long ago to have a monopoly on such arms."[26] Khrushchev threatened British ambassador Sir Frank Roberts, recycling a warning he made two years earlier while speaking with Averell Harriman: "if nuclear war came, six hydrogen bombs would be 'quite enough' for Britain and nine would do for France," Khrushchev reportedly boasted.[27] The Soviet leader also declared to John McCloy, Kennedy's main disarmament advisor, that Kennedy would be the "last president of the United States" if he started a war.[28] Khrushchev then roughed up Kennedy during their meeting in Vienna, leading Kennedy to question whether his counterpart would act rationally in a crisis. Kennedy later recalled with trepidation, "I talked about how a nuclear exchange would kill seventy million people in ten minutes and he just looked at me as if to say, 'So what?'"[29]

Several nuclear signals accompanied these verbal threats. The Soviet Air Force displayed its supersonic bomber, called "Bounder" by NATO, to remind the West of its strategic capabilities. Moscow also invited foreigners to observe Soviet military exercises, providing the army with a chance to show off nuclear-tipped rockets.[30] Most significantly, after threatening Kennedy in Vienna, Khrushchev ordered the creation of the world's largest nuclear weapon, known as *Tsar Bomba*. He hoped to use this bomb "to increase the pressure on the United States to wilt before his Berlin ultimatum."[31] Khrushchev's superbomb was not completed in time to serve this purpose, but the Soviets nevertheless ended their self-imposed moratorium on nuclear testing during the crisis.[32] Moscow conducted more than two-dozen nuclear tests in September 1961 – more tests than it had conducted in any single month up until that point. These nuclear tests were intended to "scare the daylights out of" the United States.[33]

The U.S. Response
Soviet nuclear brinkmanship in 1961 should have been successful, according to the nuclear coercionist school. Khrushchev brandished his

---

[26] Fursenko and Naftali (2006, 368).
[27] Taubman (2003, 501).
[28] Taubman (2003, 502).
[29] Taubman (2003, 500).
[30] Fursenko and Naftali (2006, 385).
[31] Fursenko and Naftali (2006, 410).
[32] The Soviet Union had not tested a nuclear bomb since early November 1958, before Khrushchev's first Berlin ultimatum.
[33] Taubman (2003, 502).

nuclear arsenal, and used signals to convey his seriousness. In addition, the Soviet leader cultivated the perception that he was unpredictible, foreshadowing the "madman strategy" later adopted by Richard Nixon. However, Kennedy stood firm. To be sure, Khrushchev's attempted nuclear blackmail left an impression on Kennedy. The American president was "dreadfully afraid" that a confrontation over Berlin would lead to nuclear war.[34] Yet Kennedy ultimately dismissed Khrushchev's threats as incredible. He told his advisor Kenny O'Donnell that Khrushchev wouldn't follow through on his threats, despite "all his shouting."[35] Several of Kennedy's advisors shared these sentiments. For example, Edwin Lightner, deputy chief of the U.S. Mission in West Berlin, cabled to Washington during the crisis, "I believe Soviet toughness re their Berlin intentions reflects serious desire change Berlin status, but also includes a large element of bluff. I doubt Sov resolve is sufficient to risk thermonuclear war."[36] Lucius Clay, the U.S. commander in Berlin, likewise conveyed to Washington that he "felt he could count on Khrushchev and the Soviets to act carefully and to pull back in a real crunch."[37]

It is unclear, based on the available historical documents, why Kennedy and his advisors thought Khrushchev was bluffing. But one can surmise that it had to do with the relatively low stakes in Berlin and the tremendously high costs of implementing the nuclear threat, the same factors that undermined Khrushchev's nuclear brinkmanship in 1958–1959. These considerations certainly weakened Kennedy's own resolve to use nuclear weapons. He said during the crisis, "If I'm going to threaten Russia with a nuclear war, it will have to be for much bigger and more important reasons than that. Before I back Khrushchev against the wall and put him to a final test, the freedom of all Western Europe will have to be at stake."[38]

Did Nuclear Superiority Matter?

Despite engaging in nuclear brinkmanship, the Soviet Union was unable to coerce the United States over Berlin in 1958–1959 or in

---

[34] Smyser (2009, 161).

[35] Quoted in Kempe (2011, 260).

[36] Harrison (2003, 174).

[37] Quoted in Gavin (2012b, 69).

[38] Kempe (2011, 258). Kempe quotes Kennedy as saying "treat" instead of "threaten," but the latter is correct.

1961. This undermines the nuclear absolutist assertion that nuclear weapons allow states to blackmail their adversaries regardless of their opponent's capabilities. Nuclear relativists might argue, however, that nuclear superiority played a decisive role in the outcome of the crisis. The Soviets would have been successful, according to this line of thinking, if they had more nuclear firepower than the United States. Would the outcome of the crisis have been different if the Soviet Union had been the nuclear-superior state? We cannot rerun history in an alternative world where the Soviet Union had a larger nuclear arsenal than the United States, so it is impossible to know for certain. However, there are good reasons to doubt whether swapping nuclear arsenals would have produced a drastically different outcome.

First, the problems inherent in nuclear coercion would not have disappeared if the Soviets had nuclear superiority over the United States. Consider, for example, a key issue related to stakes in nuclear blackmail. The United States – as the country seeking to preserve the status quo – still would have maintained a critical bargaining advantage. Once the Americans resisted Khrushchev's initial ultimatum, the Soviet Union found itself in an unenviable position. If it wanted to expel NATO from Berlin, in all likelihood, Moscow would have to be the first to use military force.[39] The United States, in contrast, could sit tight and make it clear that any Soviet provocations would be resisted. Thus, the Soviets – not the Americans – had to initiate actions that could lead to a nuclear exchange. This put Moscow in a "much weaker position" than if it had been defending the status quo.[40] If the Soviet Union had enjoyed nuclear superiority, the burden still would have been on Khrushchev to launch an attack that could lead to mutual disaster. This required a disproportionate level of resolve, which Khrushchev may have lacked in both Berlin crises even in an alternative world where he had the superior nuclear arsenal.[41]

---

[39] However, Khrushchev disputed this, arguing that the United States would be the initiator of any military confrontation. See Gavin (2012b, 69).

[40] Fursenko and Naftali (2006, 209).

[41] Still, the United States may have needed at least a second-strike capability to defend West Berlin since it was outgunned conventionally. According to some scholars, the Berlin crisis would not have occurred if the United States lacked nuclear weapons since, in that case, the Soviets could have simply imposed their will militarily. See, for example, Gavin (2012b).

Second, it is instructive that many American officials discounted the role of nuclear superiority in explaining Soviet behavior during the crisis. McGeorge Bundy, Kennedy's national security advisor, argued that "Certainly there is no compelling evidence that American superiority was decisive for Khrushchev ... I do not think Khrushchev believed that American nuclear superiority inclined either of these two presidents [Eisenhower and Kennedy] toward nuclear risk taking."[42] Kennedy's Secretary of State, Dean Rusk, echoed this sentiment during a television interview on October 22, 1961: "in this confrontation of two great power blocs each side has a capacity to inflict very great damage upon the other. Therefore in terms of handling the relationships between the two power blocs, all responsible governments need to take that into account and not act irresponsibly or frivolously or not supppose that they can press in upon the vital interests of the other side without incurring very great risks."[43] To be sure, this evidence does not mean that nuclear superiority was irrelevant in the eyes of crisis participants: indeed, U.S. officials sometimes alluded quite explicitly to their nuclear advantage during the Berlin crises. John Foster Dulles, for example, told Konrad Adenauer, the West German leader, that we "must have the will ... to use those elements of force in which we are superior," referring to nuclear weapons.[44] Overall, however, statements from officials involved in these disputes cast doubt on nuclear relativism's assertions about strategic superiority.

Indeed, Khrushchev himself did not believe that nuclear superiority mattered. "Missiles are not cucumbers," he reportedly said, "one cannot eat them and one does not require more than a certain number in order to ward off an attack."[45] Khrushchev was the consummate nuclear absolutist: he did not believe that the Soviet Union needed a massive nuclear arsenal to get its way in crises with the United States. It is not clear, then, that his strategy would have changed in 1958–1959 or in 1961 had he represented the nuclear-superior state.

Third, subsequent events cast doubt on the notion that nuclear superiority mattered in the Berlin crises. The Soviets made the most significant concessions over Berlin when they were in a favorable

---

[42] Bundy (1988, 378).

[43] Quoted in Bundy (1988, 383). Rusk made these remarks in response to a question about the Vienna summit.

[44] U.S. Department of State (1958b, 347).

[45] Gavin (2012b, 68).

strategic position vis-à-vis the United States. By 1969 the United States no longer had the ability "to wield nuclear primacy in a conflict over Berlin," but this did not significantly enhance Soviet bargaining power.[46] In fact, Moscow made greater concessions once it achieved strategic parity than it was prepared to make in 1958–1959 and 1961: in the 1971 Quadripartite Berlin Agreement, Moscow accepted Western rights to Berlin.[47] If nuclear superiority was a critical determinant of who "won" the crisis, the Soviets should have struck a much better deal in the early 1970s, when they had rough strategic parity with the United States.

Finally, at least in 1958–1959, Soviet nuclear coercion appears to have failed partially because its nuclear signals were perceived incorrectly. It is hard to see how having nuclear superiority would have helped Khrushchev more effectively convey his willingness to use atomic weapons. Signals can be botched or misread whether a nuclear arsenal is relatively large or small, as the U.S. experience in Vietnam a decade later would make clear.

Vietnam War, 1969

The United States toyed with the nuclear option at various points during the Vietnam War.[48] Most internal discussions about nuclear use did not reflect a serious interest among U.S. leaders in using nuclear weapons against North Vietnam. However, on at least one occasion Washington made an unambiguous attempt at nuclear blackmail. On October 10, 1969, based on orders from President Richard Nixon, the United States initiated a worldwide nuclear alert. The objective of this gambit was simple: to end the war on terms that the United States found acceptable. Nixon hoped, in particular, that the nuclear alert would force the Soviets to apply pressure on the North Vietnamese.[49] Yet, much to Nixon's chagrin, U.S. nuclear threats failed to extract any meaningful concessions from Moscow or Hanoi.

---

[46] Gavin (2012b, 72).
[47] Huth and Allee (2002, 316).
[48] For a relevant discussion, see Tannenwald (2007).
[49] Burr and Kimball (2003, 129–130).

By 1968, particularly following the Tet Offensive, the American public had grown weary of the ongoing U.S. military effort in Vietnam. President Lyndon Johnson announced in March that he would not seek reelection and that negotiations would begin in Paris to terminate the conflict. The talks moved slowly, however, and there was little progress by the time President Nixon entered office in January 1969. Shortly after Nixon entered office, the president and his advisors began discussing "potential military actions which might jar the North Vietnamese into being more forthcoming at the Paris talks."[50] Nixon made it clear to Hanoi and Moscow that he would be forced to take bold, aggressive actions if the relevant parties could not make progress at the negotiating table by November 1, 1969.[51] The president delivered a written ultimatum to Ho Chi Minh, the North Vietnamese leader: "unless some serious breakthrough had been achieved by the November 1 deadline," Nixon reportedly stated, "I would regretfully find myself obliged to have recourse to measures of great consequence and force."[52] Similar messages were conveyed to Anatoly Dobrynin, the Soviet ambassador to the United States.[53] When Hanoi and Moscow dismissed these threats, Nixon decided to up the ante by playing a dangerous game of nuclear brinkmanship.

U.S. Nuclear Brinkmanship

The president explicitly embraced a "madman theory" of coercive diplomacy.[54] Being perceived as irrational and unpredictable, Nixon believed, enhanced the coercive value of nuclear weapons.[55] As he wrote in 1980, "If an adversary feels that you are unpredictable, even rash, he will be deterred from pressing you too far. The odds that he will fold will increase and the unpredictable president will win another

---

[50] Laird (1969).
[51] This date is one year after President Johnson suspended bombing operations in North Vietnam.
[52] Nixon (1978, 393–394).
[53] Burr and Kimball (2003, 122,125).
[54] Sagan and Suri (2003, 150).
[55] Burr and Kimball (2003, 117).

hand."[56] This logic influenced Nixon's strategy on Vietnam. As Nixon told his future chief of staff, H. R. Haldeman, in the summer of 1968, "I want the North Vietnamese to believe I've reached the point that I might do *anything* to stop the war. We'll just slip the word to them that 'for God's sake, you know Nixon is obsessed about Communism. We can't restrain him when he's angry – and he has his hand on the nuclear button' – Ho Chi Minh himself will be in Paris in two days begging for peace."[57] The United States put this theory to the test in October 1969.

On October 6, Nixon called Secretary of Defense Melvin Laird and expressed a desire to "initiate a series of increased alert measures designed to convey to the Soviets an increasing readiness by U.S. strategic forces."[58] Four days later, the United States sent a top secret message to military commanders to "institute a series of actions ... to test our military readiness in selected areas world-wide to respond to possible confrontation by the Soviet Union. These actions should be discernible to the Soviets, but not threatening in themselves."[59] The order called specifically for an increased ground alert rate of nuclear-capable bombers and tankers, among other measures. Shortly thereafter, the U.S. military directed a task force that included the nuclear-armed aircraft carrier USS *Constellation* to monitor Soviet ships en route to the Bering Sea and North Vietnam.[60] Washington also sought to keep as many nuclear-armed submarines at sea as possible.[61] Then, on October 27, the United States sent another, particularly dangerous signal: B-52 bombers armed with thermonuclear weapons participated in a "show of force" operation code-named "Giant Lance." The bombers crossed Alaska and flew in oval patterns toward the Soviet Union and back.[62] This marked the first time that nuclear weapons were placed aboard a B-52 in flight following a disastrous January 1968 crash in Thule, Greenland.[63]

---

[56] Nixon (1980, 254–256).
[57] Haldeman (1978, 83). Emphasis in original.
[58] Sagan and Suri (2003, 163).
[59] Wheeler (1969).
[60] Burr and Kimball (2003, 140).
[61] Burr and Kimball (2003, 139).
[62] Sagan and Suri (2003, 150).
[63] See Sagan and Suri (2003, 168).

All of these moves were dangerous, which should have made them effective in blackmailing Moscow and Hanoi, according to nuclear coercion theory. Nixon certainly believed that his ploy would be successful. As Laird later recalled in an interview, "Nixon thought it [the nuclear alert] would help in Vietnam ... Nixon said things like, I just want to keep them off balance. Keep them questioning what I will do."[64] Nixon apparently succeeded in cultivating a reputation for irrationality with the Soviet Union: Dobrynin told the Kremlin that "Nixon is unable to control himself even in a conversation with a foreign ambassador," and commented on the president's "growing emotionalism" and "lack of balance."[65] However, American nuclear blackmail ultimately failed.

The Soviet and North Vietnamese Responses

The United States ended its nuclear alert activities on October 30 without much to show for its three-week demonstration of resolve.[66] Neither Moscow nor Hanoi reacted to U.S. nuclear brinkmanship in any meaningful way.[67] In the end, U.S. actions did not result in any significant concessions. And the November 1 deadline passed without the United States carrying out its coercive threat.

We cannot comprehensively assess how Moscow perceived U.S. nuclear signals because the relevant Russian archives remain closed. The available evidence suggests that officials in Moscow knew about the nuclear alert, but were not sure how to interpret U.S. actions. As Burr and Kimball conclude, the Soviets "very likely saw the readiness test [nuclear alert] as a bluff; veiled threats of nuclear coercion against Moscow's Vietnam policy lacked credibility."[68] Although the Soviets knew that Nixon perceived the Vietnam War as foreign policy

---

[64] Sagan and Suri (2003, 158).
[65] Suri (2008).
[66] Sagan and Suri (2003, 174).
[67] Dobrynin requested a meeting with Nixon on October 17, and Kissinger interpreted this as evidence that the nuclear alert was working. See Burr and Kimball (2003, 141–142). However, the meeting three days later hardly suggested that the Soviets were worried about American nuclear escalation over Vietnam.
[68] Burr and Kimball (2003, 147).

"problem No. 1," they might have naturally questioned whether the stakes warranted carrying out a costly nuclear attack.[69]

Nixon also unintentionally gave the Soviet Union reasons to question the sincerity of his nuclear threat. In an effort to conceal the nuclear alert from the war-weary American public, for instance, the administration avoided actions that would easily be observable, such as dispersing bombers to civilian airports. Because Washington had sent such visible nuclear signals in previous nuclear crises, the absence of those measures in October 1969 may have undermined U.S. credibility.[70] In this case, as in many others, concerns about domestic and international blowback at least partially restrained U.S. brinkmanship behavior.

Moscow seemed to be confused about what exactly the United States was trying to accomplish with its nuclear brinkmanship. For example, a few days after the alert ended, Dobrynin told Llewellyn Thompson that "he did not understand why there had been such a big build-up beforehand."[71] Even if Soviet officials took the nuclear threat seriously (which they apparently did not), it is unclear whether they realized that it was related to Vietnam. At the time of Nixon's nuclear alert, the Soviets were in the midst of a dangerous border conflict with China that carried a serious risk of nuclear escalation.[72] It would have been reasonable to assume that the increased U.S. state of readiness was intended to force Moscow and Beijing away from the nuclear brink. This is certainly the view that many scholars and journalists adopted prior to the declassification of key U.S. documents in the early 2000s.[73] Nixon and his advisers did nothing, to our knowledge, to clearly signal to Moscow that its nuclear alert was about Vietnam rather than the Sino-Soviet border confrontation. They assumed, as Sagan and Suri put it, "that the Soviet leadership would rationally analyze and clearly understand the strategic signal sent by a president who wanted to be seen as so irrational that he would do anything to end the war in Vietnam."[74] This assumption turned out to be wrong. Signaling failures, then, played an important role in undermining the efficacy of U.S. nuclear blackmail in 1969.

---

[69] Dobrynin (1969).

[70] Sagan and Suri (2003, 176).

[71] Burr and Kimball (2003, 148).

[72] We discuss the Sino-Soviet border crisis in detail in Chapter 6.

[73] Blair (1993, 180).

[74] Sagan and Suri (2003, 179).

Kargil War, 1999

India and Pakistan conducted reciprocal nuclear tests in May 1998, prompting global fears of nuclear conflict in South Asia. Less than a year later, Pakistan instigated a dangerous crisis that took the South Asian rivals to the brink of nuclear war. In February 1999, Pakistan surreptitiously moved forces into Kargil, a mountainous region on the Indian side of the line of control (LoC) in the state of Jammu and Kashmir. Pakistan hoped to wrest a slice of strategically important territory away from India, and force New Delhi to negotiate over Kashmir under unfavorable circumstances.[75] Further, Pakistani military planners believed that Pakistan's nuclear arsenal would force India to accept the new territorial status quo.[76] The possibility of nuclear escalation, according to their line of thinking, made it too risky for India to take back the territory by force. In the event that India threatened to go to war, Pakistan calculated that other countries – especially the United States – would force India to the bargaining table early in the crisis to diffuse a potentially dangerous conflict.

Events did not unfold according to Pakistan's plan. After detecting the Pakistani incursions in the second week of May, India committed its air, land, and sea power to reclaiming the seized territory: it launched air strikes against Pakistani forces on the Indian side of the LoC, mobilized the Western and Eastern fleets in the Arabian sea, and deployed ground forces along the entire western border with Pakistan.[77] By late May, there was serious fighting along a 150-kilometer front in the mountains of Kargil.[78] Caught by surprise, officials in Islamabad soon began issuing nuclear threats.

Pakistan's Nuclear Brinkmanship

On May 27, Prime Minister Nawaz Sharif boasted that Pakistan could now meet an armed attack from India on "equal terms," a statement widely viewed as a reference to Pakistan's nuclear forces.[79] Sharif later added, "If there is war, or if the present confrontation continues on

---

[75] Chari et al. (2007, 126).

[76] Hoyt (2009, 153).

[77] Malik (2006, 272). The use of airpower was particularly significant since neither country had used air strikes in Kashmir-based operations since the 1971 Bangladesh War. Ganguly and Hagerty (2005, 155).

[78] Riedel (2009).

[79] Malik (2006, 273).

the borders, it will bring so much devastation, the damage of which will never be repaired."[80] Other key Pakistani officials similarly rattled the nuclear sabre. Information Minister Mushahid Hussain declared: "Kashmir has been the natural flash point, and now it has the potential to become a nuclear flash point as well."[81] Foreign Secretary Shamshad Ahmad added on May 31, "We will not hesitate to use *any weapon* in our arsenal to defend our territorial integrity."[82] Raja Zafar ul Haq, the Minister of Religious Affairs, similarly asserted that Pakistan would use nuclear weapons if doing so would bolster its security, adding that "the purpose of developing weapons becomes meaningless, if they are not used when they are needed."[83]

Nuclear signaling may have accompanied these verbal threats. According to Bruce Riedel, a South Asia specialist at the U.S. National Security Council, the Pakistanis readied some nuclear-capable missiles for possible deployment during the Kargil War.[84] Indian foreign minister Jaswant Singh corroborated this account, indicating that there was evidence of Pakistan "operationalizing its nuclear missiles."[85] A subsequent Indian Army chief of staff, General Sundararajan Padmanabhan, is also on record saying that Pakistan "activated one of its nuclear missile bases and had threatened India with a nuclear attack."[86] However, Pakistani officials steadfastly deny that there were any preparations for a nuclear strike. The degree to which Pakistan engaged in nuclear signaling during the Kargil War is still debated today. The balance of the evidence suggests that Pakistan probably moved some nuclear-capable missiles out of their storage sites during the conflict. This does not imply, of course, that Pakistan intended to launch a nuclear attack. The missile movements may have been intended for defensive purposes.[87] The fact that we still do not fully understand Pakistan's intentions underscores the challenges that countries face when trying to send clear signals – a point that we will revisit below.

---

[80] CNN (1999).
[81] Constable (1999).
[82] Dugger (1999). Emphasis added.
[83] Malik (2006, 273).
[84] Riedel (2009, 137).
[85] Riedel (2009, 131).
[86] Hoyt (2009, 159).
[87] Hoyt (2009, 159).

Islamabad's nuclear posture should have bolstered the credibility of its atomic threats, by the logic of nuclear coercion theory. After the 1998 nuclear tests, Pakistan sought to credibly threaten the first use of nuclear weapons in response to a conventional attack. It therefore began to adopt a largely delegative command-and-control structure that gave launch authority to local commanders and placed few physical restraints on the release of nuclear missiles.[88] These procedures – combined with limited civilian oversight – made it easier for Pakistan to deploy and use nuclear weapons quickly in a crisis.[89] At the same time, by ceding some control over its arsenal, Pakistan increased the risk of an inadvertent nuclear launch. This danger made Pakistan's arsenal optimized for a game of nuclear brinkmanship. Moreover, Indian officials understood this. General V. P. Malik, India's chief of army staff in 1999, indicated that a key lesson from the Kargil War is that "the military leadership [in Pakistan] tends to take chances and risks" when it comes to the possible use of nuclear weapons.[90]

The Indian Response

Pakistani nuclear threats, however, did not bring India to the negotiating table. Indian forces continued to fight vigorously, and by mid-June they had retaken key positions in the Kargil heights.[91] The United States began pressuring Pakistan to fully withdraw from the Indian side of the LoC. General Anthony Zinni, the commander of U.S. Central Command, visited Pakistan in late June and urged Sharif to end the conflict. General Zinni further refused to link the Kargil War to the broader Kashmir dispute, frustrating Pakistan's ploy to extract territorial concessions from India.[92] With few remaining options, Sharif traveled to Washington on July 4 to meet with President Bill Clinton. The president lambasted Sharif for "messing with nuclear war," and reiterated the American demand for Pakistan to withdraw its forces.[93] Sharif reluctantly pledged to withdraw from Kargil. The war officially ended in mid-July with the status quo ante restored.

[88] Narang (2014, 85).
[89] Narang (2014, 88).
[90] Malik (2006, 280).
[91] Ganguly and Hagerty (2005, 155).
[92] Ganguly and Hagerty (2005, 155–156).
[93] Riedel (2009, 140).

The Kargil case underscores just how difficult it is to make coercive nuclear threats credible. Pakistan embarked on a serious effort to use nuclear blackmail for offensive diplomatic purposes. However, there is scant evidence that India took Pakistan's coercive threats seriously. As India's former prime minister, Atal Bihari Vajpayee, later said, "We never thought atomic weapons would be used."[94] General Malik similarly downplayed the risk of Pakistani nuclear use: "Jingoistic rhetoric apart, there was no credible evidence or threat that nuclear weapons would be used during the conflict."[95] Brajesh Mishra, India's national security advisor during the war, and George Fernandes, then Defense Minister, apparently shared this belief.[96] Why did these officials discount the likelihood of a nuclear strike?

Mishra provided little doubt about the answer when he stated, "anyone with a small degree of sanity would know that [nuclear war] would have disastrous consequences for Pakistan."[97] Not only could India retaliate with nuclear strikes, but the political costs of nuclear first use would also have been extraordinary. India ultimately calculated that Pakistan would not be willing to pay those costs unless its regime or national survival was on the line. As General Malik explained, the Pakistani Army would not use nuclear weapons "unless Pakistan's vital interests are threatened and its very existence is at stake."[98] New Delhi therefore believed that it could reverse the Pakistani *fait accompli* and avoid nuclear punishment, as long as the Indian army's sole objective was to take back previously seized territory.

Missed Signals and Political Blowback

What about Pakistan's attempts to manipulate the risk of nuclear war? The United States detected movement of Pakistani nuclear-capable missiles and, in Riedel's telling, interpreted this as preparation for a possible nuclear attack. However, it is not clear that India received the same message. General Malik hinted at this when reflecting on

---

[94] Kapur (2008, 79).

[95] Malik (2006, 276).

[96] Kapur (2008, 78).

[97] Kapur (2008, 78).

[98] Malik (2006, 279). This assessment is probably based on statements about Pakistani nuclear use by General Khalid Kidwai, the director of the Army's Strategic Plans Division. Varadarajan (2004). See also Ganguly and Wagner (2004, 483).

Pakistan's use of nuclear signals for coercive diplomacy during the Kargil War: "nuclear signaling on the subcontinent . . . is an imperfectly understood practice . . . Leaders in both countries have to realize that these signals could be misread or misinterpreted. Nuclear signaling during a major crisis gets clouded because the messages are interpreted differently by domestic, crossborder and international audiences at the same time."[99] During the Kargil War, as in many nuclear crises, there was considerable confusion about Pakistan's military deployments, and what they implied about the risk of nuclear war.[100]

Pakistan's coercive nuclear threats did not just fail – they also back-fired. Islamabad was arguably worse off after instigating a dangerous nuclear crisis than it was prior to the Kargil War. Significant political blowback accompanied Islamabad's attempted nuclear coercion. Most of the world blamed Pakistan for starting a dangerous crisis, and increasingly viewed it as an irresponsible nuclear power. One key lesson of the 1999 crisis, as stated in the final report of the Indian Kargil Review Committee, is that "the international community is averse to allowing nuclear blackmail to alter the long-established status quo."[101]

The Deterrent Effect of Pakistan's Nuclear Threats

Pakistan's nuclear threats did not appear to coerce India in 1999, but this does not imply that nuclear weapons had no impact whatsoever on India's behavior. Indeed, nuclear threats may have deterred India from escalating the Kargil War. Unlike in previous wars – particularly the Second Kashmir War in 1965 – India did not cross the LoC or attack elsewhere along the border. Many scholars argue that Pakistan's nuclear brinkmanship contributed to India's restraint.[102] As discussed above, General Malik and other Indian officials perceived that the nuclear option might be on the table if New Delhi threatened Islamabad's vital interests. It is therefore plausible that New Delhi worried about a nuclear response if it pushed the Pakistanis too far.[103]

---

[99] Malik (2006, 280).
[100] Hoyt (2009, 159).
[101] Kargil Review Committee (2000, 209).
[102] See, for example, Ganguly and Hagerty (2005), Chari et al. (2007), and Narang (2014).
[103] Narang (2014, 271–272).

However, scholars disagree about the extent to which Pakistani nuclear threats deterred India from crossing the LoC. Paul Kapur, for instance, argues that tactical and diplomatic considerations – not nuclear threats – better explain why India did not cross the line. According to this view, India remained restrained because it could achieve its objectives without crossing the LoC, particularly in light of the international pressure that was being applied against Pakistan.[104] Escalating the war therefore was unnecessary, irrespective of Pakistan's nuclear brinkmanship.[105]

Both of these perspectives probably contain an element of truth. Either way, the Kargil War, like so many other cases, underscores a key theme of this book: nuclear weapons are far more useful for deterrence than for coercion.

India's Nuclear Restraint

What about the role of India's nuclear arsenal in the 1999 conflict? Did Indian nuclear forces contribute to the outcome of the conflict?

India sent few, if any, nuclear signals during the Kargil War. According to the Kargil Review Committee Report, India did not make any nuclear threats.[106] This assessment is largely correct, but it is important to note that references to nuclear weapons occasionally appeared in the Indian press. Perhaps most notably, in a story published in *The Hindu* on July 1, Indian naval chief Admiral Sushil Kumar stated that the navy could survive a nuclear attack and retaliate with atomic strikes against Pakistan.[107] Overall, though, Indian rhetoric was remarkably restrained, especially when compared to the nuclear threats coming from Islamabad. When Indian officials invoked nuclear weapons, it appeared to be aimed at deterring Pakistani nuclear use rather than coercing Islamabad to back down.[108]

---

[104] Kapur (2008, 79).

[105] Yet even Kapur acknowledges that the Pakistani nuclear arsenal probably deterred India from launching a full-scale war, even if it did not play a critical role in the decision not to cross the LoC. See Kapur (2008, 79).

[106] Kargil Review Committee (2000).

[107] Hoyt (2009, 157).

[108] This is consistent with India's nuclear posture at the time, which was based on a strategy of "assured retaliation." See Narang (2014).

One Indian journalist, Raj Chengappa, claims that India made nuclear-related preparations after detecting Pakistani nuclear activity.[109] He asserts, in particular, that India placed its nuclear forces at "Readiness State 3," so that atomic weapons could be mated with delivery systems at short notice. As far as we are aware, no credible reports have substantiated this allegation. According to Indian officials involved in the conflict, "India had no concerns about going nuclear, there was no excitement and no looking at nuclear issues, [and] there was no alert 3 status."[110] Indeed, U.S. officials have never confirmed that India readied its nuclear arsenal during the conflict.[111] India may have dispersed some of its assets to thwart a disarming Pakistani first strike, but it seems unlikely that India actually assembled any nuclear weapons during the crisis.

In any case, there is little evidence that India's atomic forces played any coercive role in 1999, or that India even tried to engage in nuclear blackmail. The best evidence indicates that Pakistan withdrew its forces behind the LoC primarily because of setbacks on the battlefield and U.S. pressure – not because of implicit Indian nuclear threats.[112]

The Irrelevance of Nuclear Superiority

It is not entirely clear who enjoyed nuclear superiority during the Kargil War. At the time of the conflict, India may have had a larger nuclear arsenal than Pakistan. Pakistani officials at the time, however, boasted that their weaponry and command and control systems were superior to India's.[113] Even if India did have a superior nuclear arsenal, its advantage was not overwhelming – particularly when compared to the degree of U.S. strategic dominance over the Soviet Union in the 1950s. Still, some proponents of nuclear coercion theory assert (or imply) that nuclear superiority played a critical role in the outcome of the Kargil War.[114] Pakistan's nuclear inferiority induced caution, they argue, and ultimately necessitated its retreat. This argument, while seemingly intuitive, is difficult to sustain for at least four reasons.

[109] Chengappa (2000, 437). See also Narang (2014, 271).
[110] Quoted in Chari et al. (2007, 139).
[111] Hoyt (2009, 158).
[112] Chari et al. (2007) and Lavoy (2009a).
[113] BBC News (1998).
[114] For example, Kroenig (2013).

First, the coercionist logic linking nuclear superiority and resolve does not hold up. This particular argument predicts that the nuclear-inferior party should behave cautiously in a crisis, while the state with superiority should push harder, knowing that it has an advantage in the event of nuclear escalation. Yet Pakistani officials were by no means restrained in this instance: they instigated the initial military operation, openly made nuclear threats once fighting began, employed an aggressive nuclear posture, and made nuclear-related preparations. India, by contrast, exercised greater caution, despite possessing nuclear superiority. Having an advantage in terms of the nuclear balance, then, did not appear to embolden New Delhi to take greater risks, contrary to the expectations of the superiority argument.

Second, the onset of the crisis implies that Pakistani officials did not see nuclear superiority as particularly important. Islamabad believed that it could alter the territorial status quo in Kashmir, despite possessing nuclear inferiority. As discussed previously, the perception that its small nuclear arsenal would deter an Indian response motivated Pakistan's daring land grab in the first place. Islamabad's views turned out to be misguided, but it is telling that key decision makers in Pakistan did not appear to view nuclear inferiority as a weakness going into the crisis.

Third, there is little direct evidence to support the view that nuclear superiority enabled India to "win" the Kargil War. The clearest support for the nuclear superiority argument appears to come from a statement made by Defense Minister Fernandes in August 2004, five years after the crisis. Had a Pakistani nuclear strike taken place, he said, "We may have lost a part of our population," but once India retaliated, "Pakistan may have been completely wiped out."[115] Fernandes, however, does not appear to be implying that India's nuclear advantage intimidated Pakistan into backing down – only that it deterred Islamabad from launching a nuclear first strike. Even if Fernandes' comment is taken to mean that nuclear superiority had coercive effects in 1999, there is scant evidence elsewhere to support this view. On balance, the evidence suggests that the nuclear balance had little bearing on Islamabad's decision to withdraw its forces behind the LoC.[116]

Finally, if nuclear superiority helps states win coercive crises, India should have prevailed in subsequent South Asian confrontations, when its nuclear advantage was even clearer. However, it did not. Two years after the Kargil War, another serious nuclear crisis occurred between

---

[115] Kapur (2007, 133).
[116] See Lavoy (2009b, 34).

India and Pakistan. In this instance, India failed to coerce Pakistan despite invoking its nuclear arsenal.

Indo-Pakistani Border Crisis, 2001–2002

On December 13, 2001, Pakistani-backed militants attacked the Indian parliament, leading to a tense ten-month standoff between the two South Asian nuclear powers. The day after the attack, Indian prime minister Atal Bihari Vajpayee called for "a war to the finish."[117] India then initiated Operation Parakram, which led to the mobilization of nearly 800,000 troops, including the deployment of three strike corps along the border with Pakistan.[118] Following this large-scale display of force, officials in New Delhi made two main demands of the Pakistani government: that Pakistan end all cross-border terrorism in Jammu and Kashmir and elsewhere in India, and that Pakistan hand over twenty suspected militants. The possibility of a military attack loomed in the background if Islamabad failed to comply.

India's threats seemed to work – at least initially. On January 12, 2002, in a widely anticipated speech, Pakistani leader Pervez Musharraf vowed to crack down on terrorism. He condemned the December 13 raid on India's parliament and banned two Islamic militant groups that India blamed for the attack. Musharraf's apparent concessions, which were made in response to U.S. pressure, temporarily defused the crisis. Yet, as time passed, Pakistan's actions did not necessarily match Musharraf's words. Cross-border terrorism continued, and Pakistan showed no signs of handing over the two militants wanted by India.

On May 14, 2002, terrorists raided an Indian army base in Kaluchak, Jammu, killing thirty family members of soldiers. India responded by ratcheting up its war rhetoric. Prime Minister Vajpayee asserted, "The time has come for a decisive battle and we will have a sure victory in this battle."[119] New Delhi recalled soldiers on leave, signaling that it was ready for war, and once again demanded that Pakistan end cross-border infiltrations. India further insisted that Pakistan permanently dismantle terrorist camps and the associated support

---

[117] Sood and Sawhney (2003, 94).
[118] Narang (2014, 274).
[119] Stolar (2008, 19).

infrastructure.[120] Sensing that events could spiral out of control, U.S. officials traveled to Islamabad and New Delhi in an attempt to rein in leaders in both capitals. Musharraf privately assured Washington that he would crack down on terrorism in Indian-controlled Kashmir, and these promises were then conveyed to India. Officials in New Delhi reacted positively to Musharraf's pledges, and they prepared to demobilize their forces.[121] Operation Parakram officially came to an end in October 2002.

However, in the end, India's coercive diplomacy did not lead to a significant decline in cross-border violence. Musharraf seemed to backtrack on earlier promises, which were widely viewed as "expedient" rather than "substantive" in the first place.[122] Most observers therefore consider India's gambit to be a failure. One Indian analyst characterizes Operation Parakram as an ill-fated plan that "ended as an ignominious retreat after having failed to secure even its minimum objectives."[123] In their comprehensive treatment of the 2001–2002 crisis, Indian Lieutenant General V.K. Sood and Pravin Sawhney likewise conclude that "little had been achieved by flexing military muscle for ten long months."[124]

India's Nuclear Brinkmanship

The border confrontation heightened fears of nuclear war.[125] Officials in the United Kingdom and the United States, in particular, frequently expressed concerns about the danger of nuclear escalation. British prime minister Tony Blair called the situation "desperately serious," and military chiefs in the country believed that nuclear war was a "real possibility."[126] U.S. Deputy Secretary of State Richard L. Armitage agreed: "the international community was frightened to death that we were on the verge of nuclear war," he said.[127]

---

[120] Sood and Sawhney (2003, 97).
[121] Nayak and Krepon (2006, 37).
[122] Sood and Sawhney (2003, 99) and Nayak and Krepon (2006, 37).
[123] Swami (2002).
[124] Sood and Sawhney (2003, 101).
[125] See, for example, Evans and Webster (2002).
[126] Evans and Webster (2002).
[127] Dugger (2002c).

India helped stoke fears of nuclear war by engaging in nuclear brinkmanship. In December 2001, Defense Minister George Fernandes announced that India's missiles were "in position," and media reports alleged that Prithvi missiles had been moved near the border with Pakistan.[128] Prime Minister Vajpayee proclaimed shortly thereafter that "no weapon would be spared in self-defence. Whatever weapon was available, it would be used no matter how it wounded the enemy."[129] The next day, Fernandes added, "I can't believe they [Pakistan] would ever use it [a nuclear bomb] for the simple reason that they would be inviting a second strike. That could be devastating given Pakistan's size."[130] On January 11, 2002, General Padmanabhan boldly asserted that if any country was "mad enough" to initiate a strike against India, "the perpetrator of that particular outrage shall be punished so severely that their continuation thereafter in any form of fray will be doubtful."[131] India then tested nuclear-capable Agni missiles on January 25.[132] Analysts characterized this particular version of the Agni as a "Pakistan-specific missile."[133] Some officials in New Delhi downplayed the significance of the test, arguing that it did not serve a political purpose.[134] It seems likely, however, that the missile test was part of India's nuclear diplomacy. As General Malik indicated in an interview, "the message frankly is part of the strategy, call it coercive diplomacy or whatever."[135]

India toned down its nuclear-related rhetoric and actions for the first few months of 2002, but its brinkmanship behavior resumed after the May 14 attack in Kaluchak. On May 24, India issued a public reminder that its nuclear-capable missiles had been deployed near Pakistan for "some time."[136] Verbal nuclear threats followed this statement. In early June, Defense Secretary Yogendra Narain said that both countries should prepare for "mutual destruction" if Pakistan

---

[128] BBC News (2001).
[129] Shukla (2002).
[130] *The Hindu* (2002).
[131] Dugger (2002b).
[132] Roy-Chaudhury (2004, 107).
[133] Khan (2004, 88).
[134] Dugger (2002a).
[135] Dugger (2002a).
[136] Roy-Chaudhury (2004, 108).

launched a nuclear attack.[137] Narain further suggested that India's "nuclear button" was ready: "Everything is finalised. It is in the hands of the civilian government and we don't expect any delay in issuing orders."[138] Defense Minister Fernandes conveyed a similar threat. When asked about the risk of Musharraf exercising the nuclear option, Fernandes said, "if he should finally take that kind of step, perhaps out of desperation, he should realize that India can survive a nuclear attack, but Pakistan cannot."[139] These statements were framed as deterrent nuclear threats, but they nonetheless could have been interpreted as nuclear blackmail since India was trying to change Pakistan's behavior during the 2001–2002 crisis.

The American and Pakistani Responses

India's threats were directed at two states: Pakistan and the United States. Its brinkmanship behavior was intended, in part, to raise Pakistan's expected costs of continued resistance, thereby increasing the likelihood of capitulation from Islamabad. At the same time, taking a page out of Pakistan's playbook from the Kargil War, India sought to place international pressure on Pakistan by manipulating the risk of nuclear war.[140] The United States would force Pakistan to accept India's demands, officials in New Delhi hoped, to stave off a potentially catastrophic conflict. However, in neither case did India's brinkmanship have its intended effect.

First, the possibility of nuclear war did not compel Pakistan to meet India's demands. There is little evidence that Pakistan viewed India's nuclear threats as sincere. As political scientist Vipin Narang writes, "Islamabad did not fear a nuclear response from Delhi over subconventional attacks."[141] We cannot say with certainty that Pakistani officials ruled out the possibility of an Indian nuclear attack entirely, but they were generally dismissive of India's nuclear signals. India itself questioned the credibility of its nuclear threats during the border confrontation. According to Sood and Sawhney, "Probably the single most important realization which emerged from the June [2002] standoff

---

[137] Roy-Chaudhury (2004, 112).
[138] *The Telegraph* (2002).
[139] Richardson (2002).
[140] Chari et al. (2007, 154).
[141] Narang (2014, 277).

with Pakistan is that there is a need to honestly re-examine India's nuclear weapons credibility."[142]

Signaling failures undermined the effectiveness of India's nuclear brinkmanship. New Delhi repeatedly sent muddled and contradictory nuclear signals. During critical moments of the crisis, India publicly asserted that the nuclear option was not being considered immediately after taking actions or making statements that were seemingly intended to manipulate the risk of nuclear war. It is easy to see how this kind of inconsistency could lead one to question the sincerity of India's nuclear threats. Consider the following examples. India tested Agni missiles in the early stages of the confrontation, as noted previously, but then publicly downplayed the significance of the test. Within hours of General Padmanabhan's January 11 nuclear threat, Defense Minister Fernandes chastised the army chief for making inflammatory comments and suggested that nuclear issues should not be dealt with "in a cavalier manner."[143] Yet Fernandes himself made veiled nuclear threats both before and after the general's statements. The Indian government again quelled nuclear fears after Narain's particularly direct (and therefore potentially effective) threat in June: "The Government makes it clear that India does not believe in the use of nuclear weapons," the statement issued by New Delhi said.[144] These contradictory messages made it difficult for Pakistan to receive the appropriate signal, assuming that India did, in fact, intend to raise the possibility of nuclear escalation with its missile tests, verbal threats, and missile deployments.[145] Rahul Roy-Chaudhury, who previously held a position in the Indian National Security Council Secretariat in the Prime Minister's Office, put it best:

Although India attempted to convey clear messages, its nuclear signals appeared confusing and, at times, were at cross-purposes with one another. It is also not clear whether these signals were even perceived as intended by Pakistan or by other parties. If they were, it is not clear whether they were fully understood, or even taken cognizance of, especially by Pakistan.[146]

Why would India send such contradictory nuclear signals throughout the crisis? New Delhi wanted to coerce Pakistan, of course, but it

[142] Sood and Sawhney (2003, 179).
[143] Roy-Chaudhury (2004, 107).
[144] Roy-Chaudhury (2004, 112).
[145] Chari et al. (2007, 174).
[146] Roy-Chaudhury (2004, 101).

also sought to "win" the crisis in the court of public opinion. Consistent brinkmanship behavior may have helped achieve the former objective, but it likely would have complicated the latter. To get (and keep) international public opinion on its side, India had to play the role of victim, while painting Pakistan as aggressive and irresponsible. The government thus decided, according to Ambassador C.V. Ranganathan, the chairman of India's National Security Advisory Board, that "there should be nothing provocative done by India since it was quite clear that international opinion was in favor of India."[147] Because openly brandishing its arsenal would probably be perceived as a provocative act, some Indian officials sought to minimize the role of nuclear weapons in the crisis. There was thus constant pressure to take the nuclear card off the table after it had been played. This made it hard for India to make clear and consistent nuclear threats. Concerns about international blowback ultimately curtailed India's brinkmanship behavior, just as nuclear skepticism theory would expect.

Second, in terms of the U.S. reaction to India's brinkmanship, Washington did lean on Pakistan to comply with India's demands. But Islamabad met few, if any, of these conditions for peace. At the same time, U.S. interventions were not one-sided. The risk of nuclear war caused the United States to pressure India, too. U.S. officials repeatedly called on India to demobilize and resume negotiations with Pakistan. The message that Washington conveyed to New Delhi, as summarized by one Pentagon official, was, "We know you are pissed. And you have a right to be pissed. But you won't make the situation any better by going to war."[148] As the crisis heated up in early June 2002, the United States placed additional pressure on New Delhi by banning travel to India and evacuating all nonessential embassy and consulate personnel.[149] In the view of many American officials, these measures "helped convince New Delhi to seek a face-saving exit from the crisis."[150] Somewhat paradoxically, then, India's brinkmanship behavior had the unintended effect of constraining its own actions.

---

[147] Stolar (2008, 13).
[148] Nayak and Krepon (2006, 38).
[149] The degree to which Washington intentionally used these policies to coerce India is still debated. Chari et al. (2007, 170–171).
[150] Nayak and Krepon (2006, 34).

Pakistan's Nuclear Brinkmanship and India's Response

India was not the only country to engage in nuclear brinkmanship during the border confrontation. Pakistan also invoked its nuclear arsenal on numerous occasions. Like India, it conducted missile tests, issued verbal nuclear threats, and deployed nuclear-capable missiles along the border.[151] Yet whereas India's nuclear signals were meant to coerce, Pakistan's were meant to deter. We would expect, then, that Pakistan's threats had a higher likelihood of success, based on nuclear skepticism theory. This appears to have been the case.

Analysts continue to debate the role of Pakistan's nuclear arsenal in the border crisis.[152] Some argue that nuclear weapons had little effect on India's decision to end Operation Parakram. Based on this line of thinking, other factors – especially U.S. pressure – were more important in restraining India.[153] But there are some indications that Indian officials also worried about nuclear escalation. Speaking during a closed-door meeting, Prime Minister Vajpayee reportedly expressed concern about Pakistan using nuclear weapons if India expanded the conflict by crossing the LoC.[154] In light of the conflicting evidence, it is difficult to know to what degree Pakistan's nuclear brinkmanship deterred India from attacking. It seems clear, however, that Pakistan's nuclear threats were relatively more credible than India's. As Sood and Sawhney conclude, India "was deterred by Pakistan's nukes more than Pakistan was by India's putative nuclear second-strike capability."[155] Although other factors help account for this disparity, the fact that Islamabad was trying to defend the status quo – not reverse it – played a role in how its threats were perceived vis-à-vis India's.

---

[151] For a detailed discussion of Pakistani nuclear threats during this crisis, see Sood and Sawhney (2003), Chari et al. (2007), Kapur (2007), and Narang (2014).

[152] For example, Ganguly and Hagerty (2005), Kapur (2007), and Narang (2014).

[153] Sood and Sawhney (2003, 97).

[154] Sood and Sawhney (2003, 106).

[155] Sood and Sawhney (2003, 83). See also Narang (2014, 278).

Korean Crisis, 2013

If anyone is capable of nuclear blackmail today, it should be North Korea. The world's newest nuclear power is widely viewed as belligerent and unpredictable. In the eyes of the international community, the leaders in Pyongyang are madmen capable of doing things that more "rational" leaders would not dare contemplate. Many therefore believe that a trigger-happy North Korea can bully and intimidate its adversaries by raising the prospect of nuclear war. As former U.S. presidential candidate Mitt Romney declared, North Korea can "thumb its nose at the world with impunity" because it has the bomb.[156]

However, Pyongyang has not derived much coercive leverage from its nuclear arsenal to date. North Korea's possession of the bomb may have deterred the United States and others from launching attacks against the so-called Hermit Kingdom. Yet, for things other than deterrence, its nuclear arsenal has had limited utility. North Korea's inability to blackmail its enemies is not for lack of trying. Since conducting its first nuclear test in 2006 – and especially since Kim Jong Un came to power in 2011 – Pyongyang has issued several coercive nuclear threats. Yet these threats have mostly fallen on deaf ears.

The most serious case of North Korean nuclear coercion to date occurred in 2013.[157] This crisis ensued after North Korea launched a satellite into space on December 12, 2012, in violation of an international ban on North Korean missile tests. In response, the UN Security Council passed a resolution that condemned the test and broadened economic sanctions against Pyongyang. North Korea then raised the specter of nuclear war.

North Korea's Nuclear Brinkmanship

Pyongyang conducted a third nuclear test on February 12, 2013, and threatened to hit South Korea and the United States with "lighter

---

[156] Romney (2011, 90).

[157] An earlier episode is also noteworthy. On April 23, 2012, North Korea accused the South Korean media of slandering Pyongyang and threatened to "reduce all the ratlike groups and the bases for provocations to ashes in three or four minutes ... by unprecedented peculiar means." See Choe (2012). This not-so-subtle reference to nuclear weapons did not have a discernible effect on South Korea's behavior.

and smaller nukes."[158] This prompted the Security Council to pass an additional resolution that reprimanded North Korea. Washington further conducted joint military exercises with Seoul as a show of resolve. North Korea responded by upping the ante: it unilaterally voided the 1953 armistice, which ended the Korean War, and threatened to exercise "the right to a pre-emptive nuclear attack to destroy the strongholds of the aggressors."[159] It also released a video showing President Barack Obama enveloped in a sea of nuclear flames.[160] In addition, military leaders threatened to launch kamikaze nuclear strikes against the United States: "Stalwart pilots, once given a sortie order, will load nuclear bombs, instead of fuel for return, and storm enemy strongholds to blow them up," said air force commander Ri Pyong-chol.[161]

One might question the sincerity of these threats, given that launching a nuclear attack against the United States or its allies would likely be suicidal. Kim, who presumably understood this, used nuclear brinkmanship to make his threats appear credible. He placed military units on high alert, cut off communication with South Korea, moved missiles to North Korea's east coast, and test-fired short-range missiles in the Sea of Japan.[162] North Korea also conducted live-fire drills near the disputed sea border with South Korea, further raising the possibility of inadvertent escalation.[163] Additionally, it restarted a plutonium production reactor at Yongbyon that had been shut down since 2007, allowing the country to potentially expand its nuclear arsenal.[164] At the height of the crisis, Pyongyang warned foreigners to evacuate because the Korean Peninsula was on the brink of nuclear war. Kim's behavior led Fidel Castro to assert that the 2013 confrontation carried the most significant risk of nuclear war since the Cuban missile crisis.[165]

---

[158] Choe (2013b).
[159] Bruton and Johnston (2013).
[160] Lee (2014b, 92).
[161] Choe (2013a).
[162] Carter and Voigt (2013) and Smith-Spark (2013).
[163] Choe (2013a).
[164] Carter and Voigt (2013).
[165] Osnos (2013).

North Korea clearly played a dangerous game. It did so in part to extract concessions from its enemies at the bargaining table. Pyongyang sought, in particular, to end the crippling UN-backed sanctions against it, and to curtail joint U.S.-South Korean military exercises.[166] Pyongyang also desired international recognition as a legitimate nuclear power.[167] North Korea did not obtain any of these objectives, despite instigating a potentially dangerous crisis.

The U.S. Response

Responding to Kim's provocations, U.S. president Barack Obama asserted that North Korea would not be able to "create a crisis and elicit concessions."[168] This proved to be correct. Stringent sanctions against North Korea remained in place following months of hostile rhetoric. The United States and South Korea showed little sign of ending their joint military exercises. If anything, the crisis may have strengthened the U.S. commitment to defend South Korea. And North Korea was no closer to being recognized as a nuclear power after the crisis.[169] Thus, Kim's nuclear threats failed. In the second half of 2013, after months of hostile rhetoric, North Korea pursued a more concil-iatory foreign policy towards its rivals, likely realizing that nuclear coercion had yielded few dividends.

The United States was not totally dismissive of North Korea's nuclear threats. U.S. Secretary of Defense Chuck Hagel indicated, "We have to take seriously every provocative, bellicose word and action [from North Korea]," adding that Kim's recent actions and rhetoric had "ratcheted up the danger."[170] Ultimately, however, Washington doubted North Korea's willingness to launch a nuclear attack, despite Kim's best efforts to make his threats seem credible. The United States

---

[166] Discerning North Korea's intentions is notoriously difficult, but these were Pyongyang's stated conditions for coming to the negotiating table. Mullen (2013).

[167] Birsel and Nebehay (2013).

[168] BBC News (2013).

[169] Thomas Countryman, U.S. Assistant Secretary of State for International Security and Non-Proliferation, dismissed this demand as "neither realistic nor acceptable." Birsel and Nebehay (2013).

[170] Londono (2013).

had calculated even before the crisis began, in the words of Director of National Intelligence James Clapper, that "North Korea would consider using nuclear weapons only under narrow circumstances" – namely, only if "it perceived its regime to be on the verge of military defeat and risked an irretrievable loss of control."[171] Because of its relatively low stakes, the 2013 crisis did not reach the point where U.S. officials believed that North Korea would launch a nuclear attack.

Nuclear Superiority: A Relevant Factor?

Did the nuclear balance play a role in the 2013 crisis? Due to the short time since this crisis, there is very little information in open sources that speaks to this question. The best we can do at this point is offer a brief conjecture. It appears that the U.S. nuclear arsenal was relevant in the 2013 crisis. Part of what made North Korea's nuclear threats seem so unbelievable is that, if they were carried out, the United States would have almost certainly retaliated with atomic strikes. The U.S. second-strike capability, then, probably frustrated North Korea's efforts to engage in nuclear blackmail.

It is doubtful, however, that the nuclear balance per se had a major effect on U.S. decision making. To argue otherwise, one would have to demonstrate that North Korea's threats would have worked if it had possessed more nuclear weapons than the United States. This is a difficult case to make because the problems that are so fundamental to nuclear blackmail – namely, the relatively low stakes in coercive crises and the high political costs of carrying out threats – still would have existed. Indeed, these issues stymied U.S. attempts to coerce North Korea before Pyongyang acquired nuclear weapons. As we will see below, in a similar crisis nearly half a century earlier, the United States was unable to coerce a nonnuclear North Korea.

Political Fallout

Pyongyang's actions caused significant political blowback. Kim's aggressive brinkmanship alarmed China, North Korea's most important ally.[172] Beijing criticized North Korea following its third nuclear test, and seemed to grow increasingly weary of its ally's antics.

---

[171] Clapper (2012, 6–7).
[172] Lee (2014b, 90).

As Xi Jinping, China's president, said during the crisis, "No one should be allowed to throw a region and even the whole world into chaos for selfish gains," an apparent reference to North Korea's nuclear behavior.[173] Some Chinese writers even called on Beijing to "abandon North Korea" on the grounds that it had become too much of a liability.[174] China seems unlikely to pull the plug on its alliance with North Korea, but Pyongyang's belligerence certainly caused Chinese elites to think hard about the utility of continuing to support Kim's regime.

The 2013 Korean crisis thus reaffirms one key aspect of nuclear skepticism theory: that practicing nuclear brinkmanship can be politically costly. In North Korea's case, its aggressive behavior strained a critical alliance. Even attempting atomic blackmail carries significant costs for the challenger, which is one reason that this tactic is used so infrequently.

Less Serious Nuclear Crises

The above cases, in our view, represent some of the clearest failures of nuclear blackmail. In these six cases, states failed to coerce their adversaries despite making serious nuclear threats. As we noted earlier in this chapter, however, nuclear powers failed at coercive diplomacy on several other occasions in which a plausible threat of nuclear strikes loomed in the background. These crises carried a lower risk of nuclear escalation, but they nevertheless illustrate the logic of nuclear skepticism theory.

Seizure of the USS Pueblo, 1968

On January 22, 1968, North Korea seized the USS *Pueblo*, a U.S. intelligence vessel operating in the Sea of Japan. President Lyndon Johnson demanded that Pyongyang return the ship and its crew, or face the possibility of a military attack. Twelve months later, Washington backed down. It admitted to spying on North Korea and apologized for the incident. Pyongyang then returned the crew members, but the ship remains in North Korea today.

---

[173] Hatton (2013).
[174] Yuwen (2013).

Although this standoff is not typically viewed as a nuclear crisis,[175] it included underappreciated atomic elements. The United States deployed a naval task force to the Sea of Japan during the standoff. At least one of the aircraft carriers operating in the region, the *Enterprise*, had nuclear weapons on board. Journalist Jack Cheevers argues that not only were nuclear weapons present, but that they were ready to be used at any point: "two jets bearing nuclear bombs sat ready for instant takeoff," he writes, "[with] pilots in their cockpits at all times."[176] The United States also deployed nuclear-capable aircraft, including B-52 bombers, to the region.[177] Although President Lyndon Johnson and other senior U.S. officials were not enthuiastic about launching nuclear attacks against North Korea, these military deployments could be seen as implicit nuclear threats. At the very least, it would be a mistake to assume that nuclear weapons played no role in this crisis: declassified documents reveal that Washington considered using nuclear weapons if North Korea escalated the crisis by invading South Korea.[178]

However, North Korea stood firm in the face of American military signals. We do not know the degree to which officials in Pyongyang worried about U.S. nuclear attacks, and we probably never will. Yet Pyongyang's behavior – particularly its resistance in the face of a looming nuclear shadow – strongly suggests that it did not view the nuclear option as credible.

Falklands War, 1982

In April 1982, Argentina invaded and occupied a chain of British island possessions: the Falkland Islands, South Georgia, and the South Sandwich Islands. Britain responded by deploying a naval task force to the South Atlantic, hoping that the prospect of military force would convince Argentina to withdraw from the islands. Nuclear weapons played a role in the crisis, albeit a relatively minor one. British frigates at the time routinely carried nuclear depth charges for use in antisubmarine warfare. Tactical nuclear weapons, therefore,

---

[175] One exception, however, is Blechman and Kaplan (1978).
[176] Cheevers (2013, 231).
[177] Mobley (2001, 112).
[178] Spivy (2014).

were aboard many of the vessels that Britain deployed to the South Atlantic. Britain later consolidated its nuclear forces on two carriers – HMS *Hermes* and HMS *Invincible* – which together carried 65% of the British stockpile of WE.177A nuclear depth charges. In late May, amid growing concerns that Argentina might sink carriers with nuclear weapons aboard, the government decided to return the depth bombs to Britain.[179]

Britain sent another noteworthy signal: it conducted military exercises off the coast of Scotland with Vulcan bombers, a key delivery vehicle for British nuclear weapons, and then deployed those aircraft to Ascension Island in the South Atlantic.[180] The bombers had been retooled to deliver conventional bombs, and the government did not seriously consider equipping them with nuclear weapons. However, as noted in recently declassified minutes from a cabinet meeting on April 16, "the Vulcans were associated in the public mind with their longstanding nuclear role."[181] Britain may have exploited the aircraft's perceived atomic connection to intimidate Argentina.[182]

Some scholars discount British nuclear brinkmanship during the crisis on the grounds that the government had no intention of using atomic weapons against Argentina. In the official history of the Falklands War, for example, Lawrence Freedman writes that nuclear employment "was never taken seriously as a realistic possibility."[183] According to this view, the nuclear signals sent by Britain were an unfortunate byproduct of standard operating procedure, and London had no interest in practicing nuclear coercion. However, the nuclear option may not have been so farfetched. According to Sir Michael Quinlan, a former top official in the Ministry of Defense, Margaret Thatcher "would have been prepared actually to consider

---

[179] Freedman (2005, 50). There are rumors, which have yet to be substantiated, that nuclear weapons were aboard the battleship HMS *Sheffield*, which sank following an attack by Argentine forces. Freedman (2005, 21).

[180] BBC News (1982b).

[181] U.K. Cabinet Office (1982, 3).

[182] We did not find any direct evidence of this, but the government clearly used the Vulcan deployment as a political signal. London did not intend to attack the Argentine mainland with Vulcans, but it also believed that "there might be some military advantage in the Argentines being afraid of that." U.K. Cabinet Office (1982, 3).

[183] Freedman (2005, 49).

nuclear weapons had the Falklands gone sour on her." If, for example, Argentina sank one of the carriers, Thatcher indicated to Quinlan that she "would have been willing to face up to the real eventuality of [nuclear] use." This is a stunning revelation: as Quinlan recalled, that fact that the prime minister said such a thing "raised my eyebrows and my hair slightly."[184]

In any case, the military junta in Argentina stood firm, and did not appear to take nuclear threats seriously. Castro Madero, head of the Argentine National Atomic Energy Commission said during the conflict, "I don't think a country with nuclear arms will use them against a country that doesn't have them."[185] He also characterized discussions of nuclear use as "psychological action" against his country.[186] Other officials agreed that British nuclear threats were not credible. Based on interviews with officers in the Argentine military, scholar T.V. Paul concludes that "the junta considered the chances of Britain using its nuclear forces in the event of its losing the conventional battle and discounted such a possibility. It was viewed as highly improbable, as Britain would incur the world's wrath by breaking the tradition of non-use."[187] General Sir Hugh Beach, who served in the British Army for forty years, echoed these sentiments: "No doubt the Argentine Government judged – correctly – that the British would not risk the opprobrium of breaching the taboo on nuclear use over such distant islands."[188] Britain ultimately had to launch an amphibious invasion, and eventually regained control over the disputed territories.

Taiwan Strait Crisis, 1995–1996

In May 1995, the United States allowed Taiwanese president Lee Teng-hui to visit Cornell University, his alma mater. This seemingly innocuous move triggered a Sino-American crisis over the international status of Taiwan. Beijing interpreted the approval of Lee's visa as evidence that the United States supported Taiwan's quest for independence. Over the next several months – until Taiwan's presidential election

---

[184] BBC Radio 4 (2013).
[185] BBC News (1982a).
[186] BBC News (1982a).
[187] Paul (2009, 152).
[188] Beach (2011, 11). General Beach retired from the army in 1981, and he did not actively participate in the Falklands campaign.

in March 1996 – China sought to curtail U.S. support for Taiwan and reverse Lee's push towards greater international recognition.[189] The resulting dispute was the most serious Sino-American confrontation since the 1958 Taiwan Strait crisis, which we examine in the next chapter.[190]

During the crisis, in October 1995, Chinese Lieutenant General Xiong Guangkai made an apparent nuclear threat. In a conversation with American diplomat Charles Freeman, Xiong expressed doubt that the United States would respond militarily to Chinese military maneuvers in the Taiwan Strait. Invoking nuclear weapons, the general said, "you do not have the strategic leverage that you had in the 1950s when you threatened nuclear strikes on us. You were able to do that because we could not hit back. But if you hit us now, we can hit back. So you will not make those threats. In the end you care more about Los Angeles than you do about Taipei."[191] Chinese officials also reportedly told Freeman that China would sacrifice "millions of men" and "entire cities" to prevent Taiwanese independence, apparently suggesting that Beijing was resolved to fight a nuclear war if necessary.[192] It is important to note that these statements appear to constitute *deterrent* nuclear threats, and Freeman himself later characterized them as such.[193] However, they were made at a time when Beijing was trying to influence, and arguably change, U.S. policy on Taiwan.[194] It would not be surprising, then, if Xiong's remarks were seen in Washington as nuclear blackmail. Either way, U.S. officials took notice.

According to media reports, the general's words received "uneasy attention" in the U.S. government.[195] Anthony Lake, President Clinton's national security advisor, directly responded to the threat

---

[189] Ross (2000) contends that Beijing's objectives were coercive in nature. One could also argue, however, that China mostly wanted to deter Taiwan and the United States from taking further actions towards Taiwanese independence. The line between deterrence and coercion is particularly blurry in this crisis, at least when it comes to China's goals. By contrast, it is quite clear that the United States was trying to deter China, not coerce it into revising the status quo.

[190] Bush and O'Hanlon (2007, 2).

[191] Freeman (1998).

[192] Tyler (1996).

[193] Freeman (1998).

[194] Ross (2000).

[195] Gellman (1998).

in a private conversation with Liu Huaqiu, a senior Chinese official. "I remember leaning forward," Lake later recalled, "and telling him [Liu] that not only were Americans insulted and the president insulted but I, at a personal level, had been insulted by threatening Los Angeles with nuclear weapons."[196]

China took other actions during the crisis that could be interpreted as nuclear signals. Perhaps most notably, during a military exercise dubbed "Strait 961," which lasted from March 8 to March 25, 1996, China test-fired nuclear-capable M-9 missiles. One of these missiles actually flew above the Taiwanese capital city before landing off the coast.[197] Chinese media reports called attention to the fact that the missiles belonged to the Second Artillery, China's nuclear rocket force.[198] Beijing carried out missile tests at other points in the crisis, too.[199] It also detonated a nuclear explosive device underground at its Lop Nur test site.[200]

Despite these apparent nuclear signals, China was mostly unable to extract significant concessions from Taiwan or the United States. Washington stated that its Taiwan policy "is not going to change," and refused Beijing's demand for an official communiqué that would address visits of Taiwanese leaders to the United States and reaffirm both states' support of a one-China policy.[201] It would also be hard to characterize China's coercive diplomacy as successful vis-à-vis Taiwan. Beijing wanted to oust President Lee from power and weaken his push towards independence – but Lee was reelected in March 1996, and continued to seek greater international status for Taiwan. Even if China's threats resulted in modest gains, as some have argued, there is no evidence that nuclear weapons played any role in the outcome of the crisis.[202] Thus, China's nuclear threats may have attracted international attention, but they did not cause a discernible change in U.S. or Taiwanese behavior. This is a notable conclusion given that this case represents one of the most widely discussed nuclear threats of the post–Cold War era.

[196] Gellman (1998).
[197] Gellman (1998).
[198] Gellman (1998).
[199] Thies and Bratton (2004, 564).
[200] Thies and Bratton (2004).
[201] Ross (2000, 97).
[202] Ross (2000).

Conclusion

This chapter has offered additional evidence in favor of nuclear skepticism theory. The case studies showed that nuclear threats may be dismissed by targets as not credible even when challengers engage in potentially dangerous brinkmanship. Indeed, in all of the crises analyzed above, states tried – and failed – to coerce their adversaries by raising the specter of nuclear attacks.

The case evidence illuminated two key aspects of our theory. First, it showed that credibility problems are pervasive in nuclear coercion. The political costs of carrying out nuclear threats and the relatively low stakes in coercive crises frequently seemed to undermine attempts at atomic blackmail. Second, the cases demonstrate that nuclear brinkmanship does not always help states overcome credibility problems. Targets routinely dismissed nuclear threats, even when challengers tried to make them believable. This happened, in part, because of signaling failures. Countries repeatedly failed to decipher what their opponents were trying to convey with nuclear-related preparations or deployments. As this evidence suggests, manipulating the risk of war is not as easy as nuclear coercion theory implies.

Of course, none of this implies that nuclear coercion *never* works. We noted in the introduction to Part III that states sometimes do make concessions after receiving nuclear threats. In the next chapter, we analyze ten apparently successful cases of nuclear blackmail.

6 | Think Again: Reassessing Nuclear Victories

The previous chapter analyzed clear failures of nuclear coercion. We showed that in six serious nuclear crises, and three less severe cases, countries failed to coerce their adversaries despite engaging in nuclear brinkmanship. In this chapter, we turn our attention to cases in which nuclear blackmail seemingly worked. These crises are apparent outliers for nuclear skepticism theory and fertile ground for evidence in support of the nuclear coercionist school. Indeed, the leaders involved in these episodes – as well as many scholars who have studied them – asserted that nuclear weapons were useful for military blackmail.

However, it is important to treat leaders' claims about nuclear coercion with some caution. Heads of state have political and psychological incentives to declare victory, so their claims of success cannot always be taken at face value. Consider the 1946 Iran crisis, during which President Truman allegedly issued the first coercive nuclear threat of the post–World War II era. "We're going to drop it on you," the president purportedly told Soviet Foreign Minister Andrei Gromyko, unless Soviet troops were removed from northern Iran within forty-eight hours.[1] In his memoirs, Truman implies that his "blunt message" forced the Soviets out of Iran.[2] If true, this would be clear evidence of nuclear blackmail at work. There is only one problem with Truman's threat: he never actually made it. We now know that he (and others) either invented a story about a nuclear ultimatum or misremembered how events actually transpired.[3] This episode provides a cautionary lesson to scholars: when evaluating whether nuclear coercion works, it is important to comprehensively examine the historical record, not just rely on assertions from crisis participants. This chapter

[1] *Time* (1980, 13).
[2] Truman (1956, 95).
[3] Thorpe (1978) and Bundy (1988, 232–233).

evaluates claims about nuclear coercion by analyzing a large body of evidence – including declassified documents whenever possible.

We critically assess ten crises that are widely regarded as successful instances of nuclear coercion, focusing our attention on the seven most serious cases. None of these crises provides unequivocal evidence that nuclear coercion works. In each instance, at least one of three factors mitigates the conclusion that a nuclear threat resulted in a coercive victory. First, factors other than nuclear weapons often played a significant role in states' decisions to back down. Second, on close inspection, some crisis outcomes were not truly "victories" for the coercer. Third, when nuclear weapons have helped countries in crises, they have aided in deterrence rather than coercion.

This does not imply that these cases are entirely unsupportive of the nuclear coercionist view. At one point or another, each of these crises has been cited by scholars as evidence for the notion that nuclear weapons provide states with coercive leverage. When looking at the basic facts of each crisis, it is not difficult to see why one might reach that conclusion. However, in each of these cases, the picture is murkier than it might appear at first glance.

Korean War, 1950–1953

Just five years after using atomic bombs against Japan in 1945, the United States found itself embroiled in another war in East Asia. North Korea invaded South Korea in June 1950, and the United States rushed to the South's defense. The war was the first since World War II to involve a nuclear-armed country, and when Chinese troops turned the tide of the war by routing U.S. forces in December 1950, the United States faced a serious crisis. The crisis provided several opportunities to use nuclear weapons as coercive tools.

U.S. Nuclear Threats: Eisenhower's Attempt to End the War

The most well-known instance of brinkmanship during the Korean War came in 1953. After more than two years of bloody stalemate, President Dwight D. Eisenhower sought a way of compelling China and North Korea to terminate hostilities. Atomic weapons provided one possible answer. Indeed, Eisenhower had suggested using atomic weapons against North Korean forces as early as 1950.[4] The

---

[4] Crane (2000, 72–73).

deployment of low-yield tactical nuclear weapons in the intervening years had made this option even more attractive. Upon taking office in January 1953, Eisenhower and Secretary of State Dulles began seriously exploring the nuclear option.

During a National Security Council (NSC) meeting on February 11, 1953, Eisenhower suggested using nuclear weapons to attack Kaesong, where enemy troops were believed to be massing in preparation for an offensive. According to notes from this meeting, Eisenhower "expressed the view that we should consider the use of tactical atomic weapons on the Kaesong area, which provided a good target for this type of weapon."[5] This echoed the view of several of his advisers, including Dulles, who began advocating for the use of nuclear weapons just weeks after Eisenhower's election in 1952.[6] Dulles argued at the February 11 NSC meeting that the United States should work to erase the "false distinction" between conventional and atomic weapons.[7] Indeed, Eisenhower appeared to believe that the U.S. public had already abandoned this distinction.[8] Paul Nitze, who was director of Policy Planning at the State Department, was another advocate of using nuclear weapons. Nitze argued that atomic weapons would be "militarily effective" and would involve at most only minor "political disadvantages."[9] Eisenhower continued to press for a nuclear option, stressing the idea again during NSC meetings in early May.[10]

Eventually, contingency plans were drawn up that involved the use of atomic weapons. On May 19, the Chairman of the Joint Chiefs of Staff recommended a course of action that involved the "extensive strategical and tactical use of atomic bombs."[11] Eisenhower and the NSC quickly approved the Joint Chiefs' plan "in the event that current truce negotiations break down and it is decided to extend the war in

---

[5] U.S. Department of State (1953e, 770).

[6] James (1993, 116).

[7] U.S. Department of State (1953e, 770). Dulles made a similar argument during a March 31 NSC meeting; see U.S. Department of State (1953d, 827).

[8] Eisenhower expressed this view to British prime minister Anthony Eden after the war had ended. See Shuckburgh (1986, 114).

[9] Quoted in Tannenwald (2007, 141). This reversed a position Nitze had voiced in 1950, when he argued that the political costs of using nuclear weapons in Korea would be prohibitive, and could lead to Soviet intervention (U.S. Department of State, 1950, 1041–42).

[10] U.S. Department of State (1953f, 977) and U.S. Department of State (1953g, 1014).

[11] U.S. Department of State (1953a, 1062).

an effort to gain a military decision."[12] The idea was that the United States would be prepared to implement the plan within nine to twelve months.[13] The following day, Dulles met with Indian prime minister Jawaharlal Nehru, informing him that "if the armistice negotiations collapsed, the United States would probably make a stronger rather than a lesser military exertion, and that this might well extend the area of conflict."[14] Dulles expected – and intended – that this message would be passed on to the Chinese government.[15] Eisenhower later claimed that the message was that "we intended to move decisively without inhibition in our use of weapons."[16] Four days later, in the Nevada desert, the United States conducted its first and only test of an artillery-fired atomic shell. "The implication was plain," according to one historian: the United States would use atomic weapons if the war did not end soon.[17] Shortly after Eisenhower approved the nuclear contingency plan, China agreed to U.S. conditions for an armistice agreement, and a truce was signed a month later.

Did Brinkmanship Work? A Net Assessment

Both Eisenhower and Dulles later claimed that the threat of nuclear attack coerced China into ending the war on U.S. terms. Eisenhower, for instance, asserted years later that the "danger of an atomic war" was what brought China to the bargaining table.[18] Some scholars agree with his assessment: Hastings, for instance, argues that once the Soviets and Chinese became convinced that the Eisenhower administration was willing to use nuclear weapons, they sped up armistice negotiations.[19] In this view, nuclear weapons coerced China into ending the Korean War.[20]

---

[12] U.S. Department of State (1953h, 1067).
[13] Foot (1985, 223).
[14] U.S. Department of State (1953b, 1068).
[15] Adams (1961, 48).
[16] Eisenhower (1963, 181).
[17] Hastings (1987, 319).
[18] Adams (1961, 49).
[19] Hastings (1987, 320). George and Smoke (1974, 239–40) and Merrill and Peleg (1984, 35) also seem to agree with this thesis. Keefer (1996, 287) and Ryan (1989, 152–65) note several other historians who share this view.
[20] Whether Eisenhower was actually willing to use nuclear weapons is unclear, and remains a subject of intense debate. See, for example, Keefer (1986), Gaddis (1987, 123–29), Trachtenberg (1988, 30–49), and Jackson (2005).

But there are several problems with this story. First, although the Eisenhower administration was engaged in extensive discussions about atomic weapons behind the scenes, it appears that little of this was conveyed to the Chinese. The clearest attempt to use nuclear threats to bring the Chinese to the bargaining table appears to be Dulles's conversation with Nehru on May 21, 1953, which a contemporary account called an "unmistakable warning" to China.[21] But the warning was hardly unmistakable. If Dulles mentioned atomic weapons to Nehru, he did not include it in his write-up of the conversation. When Nehru followed up with Dulles to ask what he meant, Dulles simply changed the subject, declining to either reinforce or clarify his earlier statements.[22] Indeed, up to this point the Eisenhower administration had declined to deploy bombers and atomic weapons to the Korean theater.[23]

Regardless of what Dulles actually said or implied during the May meeting, Nehru denied that he transmitted any message to Chinese officials,[24] and neither Chinese nor Soviet archives make any mention of it.[25] Although Mao was aware that the Eisenhower administration sought a tougher approach for ending the war, he privately expressed doubt that Eisenhower would use nuclear weapons to do it. Instead, Mao believed that "getting tough" meant that the United States would conduct amphibious assaults on the Korean coastline – not use nuclear weapons – and ordered military preparations in anticipation of such tactics.[26] If a nuclear signal was sent, then, it was muted. More likely, it was missed altogether.[27]

[21] Shepley (1956, 72).

[22] U.S. Department of State (1953c).

[23] Eisenhower's assistant claimed that the United States transferred missiles with atomic warheads to Okinawa in the spring of 1953, in hopes that China and the Soviet Union would detect the deployment (e.g., Adams, 1961, 48). Dingman (1988, 82–87), however, rejects this interpretation, arguing that there is no evidence of such deployments; Ryan (1989, 156) also calls reports of the Okinawa nuclear deployments in 1953 "obviously erroneous." To be sure, Eisenhower eventually approved the transfer of nuclear weapons to military custody in preparation for overseas deployment, but this did not happen until days before the armistice was signed. See Gaddis (1997, 108) and Rosenberg (1983, 27).

[24] Reid (1981, 45), Foot (1988, 104).

[25] Zhang (1992, 133), Stueck (1995, 329). Although Lewis and Xue (1988, 14) assert that Chinese officials knew of Dulles's threat, they cite only a single unpublished paper from 1985 to support this claim.

[26] Zhang (1992, 136–37), Jian (2001, 114), Stueck (2002, 172).

[27] Dingman (1988, 85) calls Eisenhower's approach "milder, nonnuclear persuasive diplomacy" rather than atomic diplomacy. Betts (1987, 42–47)

Second, the timing of Chinese concessions in the spring of 1953 casts doubt on the importance of U.S. nuclear threats. The most significant breakthrough in negotiations between the United States and China occurred shortly after the death of Josef Stalin on March 5. Throughout the war Stalin had pressed Mao to adopt a tough stance toward the United States, but immediately upon his death the Soviet Union pressed for a more conciliatory approach, beginning with Premier Georgi Malenkov's "peace offensive" speech at Stalin's funeral on March 9.[28] The main sticking point in armistice negotiations at that point had been the issue of prisoners of war. Tens of thousands of captured Chinese and North Korean POWs – many of whom had been forcibly conscripted – did not wish to return home,[29] and the United States and China sharply disagreed about whether they should be repatriated against their will. In late March, however, the Chinese government made two key concessions: first, it agreed to an exchange of sick and wounded prisoners, an idea that the United States had suggested without success only a month earlier; second, it would allow Communist POWs to be transferred to a neutral country if they chose. The offer set off weeks of negotiations in which the two sides haggled over the details of POW repatriation while fierce fighting continued on the battlefield. But the deadlock was broken. After several concessions by both sides, China finally agreed to a deal on June 8, paving the way for a final armistice.[30]

The timing of these events does not square with the view that U.S. nuclear threats broke the logjam. The main reason is that China's concession occurred nearly two months *before* Dulles's May 21 meeting with Nehru. Dulles's supposed ultimatum therefore could not have been responsible. What, then, explains the critical Chinese concession on March 30? Many historians have offered a straightforward answer: Josef Stalin's death created the conditions for a compromise. Stalin's death had two effects. First, it removed a key source of pressure on China to maintain a hardline stance in the armistice negotiations. Stalin had sought to prolong the war in part because it tied down American forces and drained U.S. resources away from Europe, while

likewise calls the administration's signals "faint" and "elliptical." Friedman (1975, 90) goes further, calling Dulles' supposed ultimatum a "fable."

[28] Brady (2009, 19–22).

[29] Goodman (1978, 356).

[30] Vatcher (1958) and Foot (1990).

also giving Soviet intelligence analysts an opportunity to observe how the U.S. military performed in combat.[31] Now, the most powerful advocate of continuing the war was gone. Second, it brought into power a new Soviet regime, which quickly signaled that Soviet support for the Chinese war effort was waning. Indeed, within two weeks of Stalin's death, the Soviet Council of Ministers proposed to Mao and Kim Il Sung the very concessions that China would make just days later.[32] Even if pressure from Stalin had not been responsible for China's willingness to continue the war, the prospect of declining Soviet support suddenly forced China to rethink its approach. Some historians see Stalin as an obstacle; others see him as China's protector. Either way, his death offers a more convincing explanation for the armistice than atomic blackmail.[33]

A second problem with the nuclear coercion hypothesis is that it overlooks the fact that nuclear threats failed multiple times prior to 1953. The Truman administration on several occasions employed far more colorful nuclear signals than Eisenhower ever did. Like Eisenhower, Truman had his advisers seriously explore the nuclear option, up to the point of devising a tentative list of targets.[34] While Eisenhower never used military deployments to communicate nuclear threats, however, Truman deployed nuclear-configured B-29 bombers as well as operational atomic weapons to the region in 1951.[35] These deployments came on the heels of a November 30, 1950 press conference in which Truman sparked a global uproar by suggesting that the use of nuclear weapons was under "active consideration," and that the decision to use them would be left to "the military commander in the field."[36] Perhaps most provocatively, in October 1951 the

---

[31] Gaddis (1997, 108) and Weathersby (1998, 102, 109–10).

[32] *Cold War International History Project Bulletin* (1995, 80–81).

[33] Weathersby (1998, 108) argues that Stalin's death caused "a radical change" in the Soviet stance toward the war. Many scholars have concurred with this assessment; see, for example, Hinton (1967, 178–84), Gaddis (1997, 108–09), Stueck (2002, 173–74), Rose (2011, 134–35), and Burr and Kimball (2015, 22–23).

[34] General Douglas MacArthur submitted the list of targets in December 1950. Foot (1985, 114–15) and Betts (1987, 36) argue that this constituted an actual request for nuclear bombs, but Gaddis (1987, 116) contends that MacArthur was only responding to requests from the Joint Chiefs of Staff to explore hypothetical scenarios, and never formally requested the weapons.

[35] See Cumings (2010, 156–57) and Tannenwald (2007, 117–26).

[36] Truman (1950).

United States conducted Operation Hudson Harbor, in which B-29 bombers were flown over North Korea on simulated atomic bombing runs, dropping dummy bombs or heavy conventional weapons.[37] Yet if these signals were designed to coerce North Korea, China, or the Soviet Union, they failed. The war dragged on for nearly two more years, and it was Eisenhower, not Truman, who succeeded in ending it.

Did nuclear threats play a role in ending the Korean War? Ultimately, the evidence for this claim is circumstantial at best, relying primarily on the close correlation of Dulles's "ultimatum" to Nehru and the POW agreement two weeks later. No direct evidence exists that the risk of nuclear escalation played a role in China's decision to accept the essence of U.S. demands regarding the POW issue. This is not to say that the case is closed: too much remains unknown, particularly regarding deliberations in Moscow and Beijing, to reach definitive conclusions about the role of nuclear coercion in 1953. But the case for nuclear coercion is, by any measure, a weak one. A scholar who has examined Chinese archival documents concluded:

There is no evidence to show that the Beijing leadership... paid any significant attention to whether or not the Americans would use nuclear weapons in Korea... When Mao and the other CCP leaders analyzed the means Washington might use to put pressure on the Communists, *they did not even bother to mention the atomic bomb.*[38]

Indochina War, 1954

In December 1946, war broke out in Southeast Asia between the French Union and the Viet Minh. The Viet Minh, led by Ho Chi Minh, sought to unite all of Vietnam under an independent Communist state – the Democratic Republic of Vietnam (DRVN). France resisted this path, however, and hoped to maintain control over Vietnam and its other colonial possessions in Indochina. After seven years of fighting, the French military position began to unravel. In March 1954, the Viet Minh launched an attack against the French garrison at Dien Bien Phu. Surrounded and outnumbered, French forces appeared to be on the cusp of a crushing defeat. As the French desperately tried to hold on at Dien Bien Phu, representatives for the relevant stakeholders

---

[37] Keefer (1996, 300).
[38] Jian (2001, 111). Emphasis added.

– the DRVN, France, the State of Vietnam, Cambodia, Laos, China, Britain, the Soviet Union, and the United States – gathered in Geneva to negotiate a political settlement to the war.

U.S. Nuclear Brinkmanship and the War's Resolution

The prospect of a French defeat in Indochina worried President Eisenhower and some of his advisors. They feared, in particular, that a Viet Minh victory would facilitate the spread of Communism throughout the region. As Admiral Arthur Radford, chairman of the Joint Chiefs of Staff, told Eisenhower on March 24, events in Indochina "can well lead to the loss of all of S.E. Asia to Communist domination."[39] The president certainly wanted to avoid such an outcome. "My god, we must not lose Asia," he told a group of U.S. Senators one month before the siege at Dien Bien Phu began.[40] As the situation worsened at Dien Bien Phu, the United States considered ramping up its military aid to France.

President Eisenhower and his national security team discussed launching massive air strikes against Viet Minh positions to save the French garrison at Dien Bien Phu. However, despite his concerns about Southeast Asia going Communist, the president was not enthusiastic about openly intervening in Indochina. He placed three main conditions on U.S. military intervention: (1) support from Britain and other allies; (2) the complete independence of Vietnam, Laos, and Cambodia; and (3) French assurances that they would keep their forces in Indochina.[41] It was also essential, Eisenhower believed, for Congress to authorize any use of U.S. military force. These conditions were virtually impossible to meet, making it unlikely that the United States would swoop in to save the day at Dien Bien Phu. Yet Eisenhower seemed tempted by the possibility of carrying out strikes *covertly* – if they would be decisive. He told two reporters in a private meeting on April 1, if the United States did bomb the Communists at Dien Bien Phu, "we'd have to deny it forever."[42]

[39] Quoted in U.S. Department of Defense (2004, 155).
[40] Quoted in Herring and Immerman (1984, 346).
[41] Bundy (1988, 265).
[42] Bundy (1988, 262).

At various points during the crisis, U.S. officials privately considered the nuclear option. According to then-Vice President Richard Nixon's memoirs, Washington hatched a plan, known as Operation Vulture, to use tactical nuclear weapons at Dien Bien Phu.[43] A secret "advance study group" in the Pentagon concluded that "three tactical A-weapons, properly employed, would be sufficient to smash the Vietminh effort" in Dien Bien Phu.[44] Some U.S. officials – particularly Radford and Nathan Twining, the chief of staff of the air force – strongly supported this conclusion, and openly advocated nuclear use. As Twining later said, "There was only one way to save [Dien Bien Phu] that late and Radford and I were the only ones that agreed ... what we thought would be – and I still think it would have been a good idea – was to take three small tactical A-bombs ... You could take all day to drop a bomb, make sure you put it in the right place. No opposition. And clean those Commies out of there ... and the French would come marching out of Dien Bien Phu in fine shape."[45]

On April 7, Radford's assistant, Captain George Anderson, made the case for using nuclear weapons to the counselor of the State Department, Douglas MacArthur II.[46] Eleven days later, Radford raised the nuclear option in a lunch meeting with Secretary of State Dulles and Secretary of Defense Charles Wilson.[47] There is no public record of this meeting, but their conversation may have spawned a historically disputed exchange between Dulles and French Foreign Minister Georges Bidault in Paris on April 23. By some accounts, Dulles offered Bidault two atomic bombs for use against the Viet Minh.[48] It seems unlikely that Dulles made a formal offer to hand over American nuclear weapons. However, he may have solicited Bidault's views on the nuclear option in Indochina. According to historian Fredrik Logevall, Dulles inquired in general terms about the French view on "potentially using two or three tactical nuclear weapons against these enemy positions."[49] If nothing else, this encounter

---

[43] Nixon (1978, 150).
[44] U.S. Department of State (1954a, 1271).
[45] Quoted in Bundy (1988, 267).
[46] U.S. Department of State (1954a, 1271).
[47] Bundy (1988, 268).
[48] Logevall (2012, 498).
[49] Jackson (2014).

suggests that Washington had not totally ruled out the possibility of using nuclear weapons in Indochina.

The nuclear option came up again during a NSC meeting on April 29. Some officials believed that using nuclear weapons would send a strong signal to China. According to National Security Advisor Robert Cutler's account of the meeting, the "view was expressed that U.S. use of 'new weapon' [a euphemism for a nuclear bomb] in Vietnam would tend to deter Chinese aggression in retaliation, and that failure to use the 'new weapon' in Vietnam would tend to increase chance of Chinese aggression in retaliation."[50] Eisenhower and Nixon seemed to like the idea of transferring a small number of weapons to France, as Dulles allegedly suggested to his French counterpart one week previously. The two agreed that "we might *consider* saying to the French that we had never yet given them any 'new weapons' and if they wanted some *now* for possible use, we might give them a few."[51] The possibility of using nuclear weapons stayed on the minds of U.S. officials for another week, if not longer. On May 6, Dulles suggested that the NSC needed to address a critical question: "Is the U.S. prepared to acquiesce in the clearly engineered Communist aggression in and taking over of Indo-China – with Red Chinese support – even though we evaluate this loss as very serious to the free world and even though we have the military means to redeem the situation? (The A-bomb)."[52]

At least two notable public nuclear threats accompanied private discussions of nuclear use. First, during an April 23 speech to the NATO Council, Dulles said that the United States and its allies must agree to use nuclear weapons "whenever or wherever it would be of advantage to do so, taking account of all relevant factors." This statement may have been intended to "keep Moscow and Beijing guessing" about how the West might respond in Indochina, but Dulles did not refer to Vietnam specifically.[53] A second threat explicitly made the connection between Indochina and America's nuclear arsenal. Radford asserted that "any United States intervention in Indochina should be on an all-out basis, including use of atomic weapons."[54] These statements

[50] U.S. Department of State (1954b, 1447).
[51] U.S. Department of State (1954b, 1447). See also Logevall (2012, 499). Emphasis in original.
[52] Dulles (2011).
[53] Logevall (2012, 499).
[54] Quoted in Trachtenberg (2013, 18).

may have had an element of bravado, but they also reflected a genuine interest in the nuclear option among some U.S. officials.

Overall, however, U.S. nuclear brinkmanship was mostly muted. Washington did little to publicly signal its resolve to use atomic bombs. There was no nuclear alert, and there is no evidence that the United States conspicuously deployed nuclear forces in a way that would have attracted attention in Beijing or Moscow. Thus, as Richard Betts points out, the American nuclear option "did not function as a coercive signal since it never surfaced in a way that might impress Moscow, Beijing, or the Vietminh."[55]

As nuclear skepticism theory predicts, Washington worried about the political blowback that would inevitably result from carrying out a coercive nuclear threat against Vietnam – or from even considering this possibility. MacArthur, the State Department counselor, worried that "The fact that we were considering such steps [using nuclear weapons] in Indochina would in turn cause a great hue and cry throughout the parliaments of the free world, and particularly among some of our NATO allies ... Furthermore, in addition to the Soviet propaganda, many elements in the free world would portray our desire to use such weapons in Indochina as proof of the fact that we were testing out weapons on native peoples and were in fact prepared to act irresponsibly and drop weapons of mass destruction on the Soviet Union whenever we believed it was necessary to do so."[56]

In the end, the United States did not intervene to save the French at Dien Bien Phu. The garrison finally fell on May 7. The next day, diplomats in Geneva began working towards a negotiated settlement. Yet the United States held out the possibility of military intervention in Indochina. Washington believed that it could strengthen France's hand in Geneva by leaving ambiguous the question of whether it would be willing to intervene.[57] The Communists might be more willing to make concessions, based on this line of thinking, if they believed that the alternative was active American participation in the Indochina conflict.

On July 21, the belligerents agreed to a ceasefire, bringing an end to the Indochina War. The ceasefire agreement temporarily divided Vietnam in half, granting control of the north to the Communist Viet

---

[55] Betts (1987, 53).

[56] U.S. Department of State (1954a, 1271–72).

[57] U.S. Department of Defense (2004, 171).

Minh and control of the south to the anticommunist State of Vietnam. France also agreed to withdraw its forces from Indochina and
grant independence to Cambodia, Laos, and the State of Vietnam. The
terms of the Geneva agreement turned out to be highly consequential,
as they set the stage for American involvement in Vietnam over the
next two decades.

Did Nuclear Coercion Work?

Some have argued that U.S. nuclear threats forced the Communists –
including China, the Soviet Union, and the Viet Minh – to make
concessions during the Geneva negotiations.[58] "Nuclear coercion
'worked' in 1954," argues Marc Trachtenberg, because the Communists were forced to accept an anticommunist state in South Vietnam.[59]
According to this line of thinking, the Viet Minh had considerable
leverage after their victory at Dien Bien Phu, and they should have
secured more territory as a result. They did not, according to this view,
because the Chinese and the Soviets, who were worried that America
would intervene and potentially use nuclear weapons, pressured the
Viet Minh to accept a suboptimal arrangement. In short, U.S. nuclear
blackmail forced the Communists to "draw in their horns and accept
a political settlement in Indochina that was less advantageous to them
than circumstances would otherwise have warranted."[60]

The lack of nuclear signaling in 1954 raises doubts about how serious the United States was about using nuclear weapons to coerce the
Communists over Indochina. However, it is important to consider the
possibility that Washington did not need any signals because the Chinese and the Soviets already knew that the possibility of a nuclear
strike loomed in the background. The implicit possibility of nuclear
attack, one could argue, was enough to coerce the Communists in
Geneva.[61] This view is not entirely without merit.

Some officials – especially Anthony Eden, who was British deputy
prime minister during the crisis – believed that nuclear threats helped
the West in Geneva. Eden claimed that "this was the first international

---

[58] See, for example, Bundy (1988, 271–73) and Trachtenberg (2013).
[59] Trachtenberg (2013, 22).
[60] Trachtenberg (2013, 22).
[61] Trachtenberg (2013, 20).

meeting at which I was sharply conscious of the deterrent power of the hydrogen bomb. I was grateful for it. I do not believe that we should have got through the Geneva Conference and avoided a major war without it."[62] It is difficult to judge how the Chinese and the Soviets perceived the possibility of a U.S. nuclear threat at Geneva, since the relevant archives are not yet available. China and the Soviet Union certainly wanted to keep the United States out of Indochina. It is also clear that officials in Beijing and Moscow worried that a failure to strike a deal at Geneva might lead to American intervention.[63] Leaders in these states therefore wanted to see the war end. But did they accept a suboptimal deal because of U.S. nuclear threats?

The best piece of evidence in the affirmative appears to be a statement made by Soviet Premier Nikita Khrushchev in August 1961, during the Berlin Wall crisis. "There was a time," he said, "when the American Secretary of State Dulles brandished thermonuclear bombs and followed a policy of 'from positions of strength' with regard to the socialist countries...That was barefaced atomic blackmail, but it had to be reckoned with at the time because we did not possess sufficient means of retaliation...But today the situation has changed radically."[64] This statement is suggestive, but it is less impressive when viewed in context of the speech in which it appeared. First, Khrushchev did not specify which historical episode he had in mind. During his entire speech, he did not mention Indochina once; instead, the quotation appears in the context of remarks about Germany. It seems unlikely that Khrushchev was offering a stunning admission of being blackmailed in 1954. Second, it is ambiguous whether Khrushchev was referring to threats against the Soviet Union, China, or North Korea, all of whom were "socialist countries" during Dulles's tenure and arguably the targets of Dulles' nuclear diplomacy.

Indeed, Khrushchev's hints notwithstanding, several factors confound the nuclear coercionist interpretation of this crisis. First, factors other than Chinese and Soviet pressure helped bring the Viet Minh to the negotiating table. Indeed, the DRVN had its own reasons to seek a political settlement.[65] In particular, Viet Minh commanders continued

---

[62] Quoted in Bundy (1988, 271).

[63] Herring (2002, 48).

[64] Khrushchev (1961, 145). This is a key piece of evidence cited by Trachtenberg (2013, 21).

[65] Logevall (2012, 561).

to worry, even after the victory at Dien Bien Phu, about low morale among their troops and an unfavorable balance of forces.[66]

Second, even if Beijing and Moscow persuaded the Viet Minh to accept the Geneva agreement, it is far from obvious that U.S. nuclear threats caused the Communists to take action. Mao Zedong did not appear to be concerned about the possibility of an American nuclear attack during the crisis, and neither did Soviet leaders.[67] They had several reasons to question the credibility of the American nuclear threat. Using nuclear weapons would have been costly for the United States: it would have, for example, turned international public opinion against Washington and severely strained alliance relationships, particularly its partnership with Britain. It is also not clear that nuclear weapons would have been militarily useful in Indochina, due to the lack of viable targets.[68] In addition, the experience of the Korean War underscored America's reluctance to use nuclear weapons during a conventional war. Why, then, in the absence of nuclear signals to persuade them otherwise, would the Communists be overly worried about a nuclear attack in Indochina one year later?

There is a third problem with the assertion that nuclear blackmail worked in 1954: it presumes that the crisis resulted in a victory for the United States. However, U.S. officials viewed the Geneva agreement as a failure – or, at best, a deal that was tolerable. Throughout the crisis, the United States maintained that it was unacceptable to negotiate *any* territory away to the Communists. Dulles believed that even a partial Viet Minh victory would be "disastrous," and that "partition of Vietnam ... was synonymous with defeat."[69] It would be better to have no agreement at all, Washington believed, than one that rewarded Communist aggression.[70] It is not surprising, then, that U.S. officials repeatedly tried to torpedo the Geneva negotiations.[71] When it became clear that the Geneva agreement would include a partition

---

[66] Logevall (2012, 561).
[67] On Mao's views, see Shu (1999, 199). Again, this conclusion is necessarily tentative given the lack of Chinese and Soviet documents in the public record.
[68] Chinese officials emphasized these points when explaining America's unwillingness to use nuclear weapons in the 1950s. See Powell (1965, 58).
[69] Logevall (2012, 461, 470).
[70] Logevall (2012, 567).
[71] Statler (2007, 97).

of Vietnam, the White House was clearly unhappy. Dulles told members of Congress that the deal would be "something we would have to gag about," and he said to French prime minister Pierre Mendès France, "What you sign in Geneva will be bad."[72] The United States apparently wanted nothing to do with the Geneva deal.

On top of this, U.S. threats may have been intended to force a Viet Minh retreat at Dien Bien Phu – not necessarily to obtain a better settlement at Geneva.[73] This is how Wei Guoqing, the Chinese military advisor to the Viet Minh, interpreted U.S. actions: "the true purpose of Washington's threat," Wei believed, "was to compel the Viet Minh to withdraw from Dien Bien Phu."[74] This shows, yet again, how military signals may be misinterpreted. If this was the central objective of the American threat, it clearly failed. Instead of retreating, Viet Minh forces dug in their heels and prepared for the final offensive at Dien Bien Phu.

In sum, despite making veiled nuclear threats, the United States failed to impose its will on the Communists during the Indochina crisis. If nuclear coercion worked in 1954, it did so only in the most minimal sense. When measured against the Eisenhower administration's objectives, the Geneva agreement represented a failure for U.S. coercive diplomacy. And U.S. threats did not save the French garrison at Dien Bien Phu. Even if one views the outcome of the Indochina crisis as desirable for the United States, the evidence suggesting that nuclear coercion contributed to the war's resolution is spotty and circumstantial.

First Taiwan Strait Crisis, 1954–1955

At the tail end of the Chinese civil war, the defeated Nationalist government, led by Chiang Kai-shek, fled to Taiwan. Chiang's forces also occupied offshore islands located within ten miles of the Chinese mainland – most notably, Quemoy (Jinmen) and Matsu (Mazu). These islands were widely viewed as a staging point for a possible future invasion of China, making the Nationalist presence there threatening to

---

[72] Logevall (2012, 592, 600).

[73] These two things were related, of course, given that a Viet Minh victory at Dien Bien Phu would have strengthened their position at the bargaining table.

[74] Zhai (2000, 48).

Mao's new government in Beijing. On September 3, 1954, the Chinese military began artillery strikes against Quemoy, killing two Americans. The United States perceived this move as a precursor to an invasion of the offshore islands and, potentially, Taiwan itself. Beijing's aims in fact appear to have been more modest: the shelling of Quemoy was meant, in part, to protest growing defense ties between the United States and Taiwan. Yet the events of September 3 triggered a tense nine-month crisis that brought the Eisenhower administration to the nuclear brink.[75]

Towards the Nuclear Brink: U.S. Nuclear Threats

The United States bolstered its military presence in the Western Pacific following the September 3 shelling of Quemoy. Within days, Washington had positioned three aircraft carriers, one cruiser, and three destroyer divisions in the vicinity of the offshore island.[76] In private, U.S. officials discussed the nuclear option. Some in the president's inner circle believed that the United States should defend Taiwan with nuclear weapons, if necessary. A formerly top secret memorandum prepared by Secretary of State Dulles on September 12, for example, concluded that "Quemoy cannot be held *indefinitely* without a general war with Red China in which the Communists are defeated" and defending the island "would probably lead to our initiating the use of atomic weapons."[77] For the next three months, the crisis simmered – but it did not come to a boil.

In early December, the United States entered into a mutual defense treaty with Taiwain, pledging to defend it from Chinese aggression. One month later, China escalated the crisis by attacking the Tachen Islands north of Quemoy and Matsu and seizing the tiny nearby island of Ichiang. Eisenhower now believed that "the time had come to draw the line."[78] His administration decided that it must fight to defend Taiwan and potentially use force to preserve the Nationalist position in Quemoy and Matsu.[79] Congress passed the Formosa Resolution on

---

[75] For additional details, see Chang (1988), Chang and Di (1993), and Zhang (1992, 189–224).
[76] Soman (2000, 124).
[77] U.S. Department of State (1954c, 611). Emphasis in original.
[78] Bundy (1988, 275).
[79] Bundy (1988, 275).

January 29, giving the president broad authorization to intervene military if China attacked Taiwan. China nonetheless continued building up military forces on the mainland, directly across from Quemoy and Matsu. Some U.S. officials took this as a sign that a Chinese invasion was imminent.[80]

Washington soon began ratcheting up the nuclear pressure. On January 22, 1955 – one week before the passage of the Formosa Resolution – the *Washington Star* called attention to the fact that "the Seventh Fleet was equipped with tactical nuclear bombs and any action to attack Taiwan would have to go through [them] first."[81] More explicit nuclear threats from within the administration soon followed. On February 13, Eisenhower approved Operation Teacup, a series of tactical nuclear weapon tests designed, in part, to intimidate Beijing.[82] Then, over a three-day period in March, three key U.S. officials publicly invoked nuclear weapons. During a press conference on March 15, Dulles indicated that tactical weapons would be used in a general war in Asia. The next day, when asked to respond to Dulles's statement, Eisenhower implied that nuclear weapons could be used "as you would use a bullet or anything else;" he later indicated that this statement was indeed meant to signal resolve to China.[83] Vice President Richard Nixon similarly warned China to refrain from further aggression the following day, stating that "tactical atomic weapons are now conventional and will be used against the targets of any aggressive force."[84] The next week, Robert Carney, the Chief of Naval Operations, publicly revealed that the United States was planning nuclear attacks against mainland China.[85] Shortly thereafter, on April 2, China detected four waves of U.S. aircraft over its territory, which it viewed as an attempt to "increase tension in the Far East."[86]

The documents suggest that Eisenhower was prepared to use tactical nuclear weapons against China – but he was not enthusiastic about the possibility. According to notes from a meeting in the president's office on March 11, Eisenhower believed that "if we had to intervene

[80] Chang (1988, 106).
[81] Quoted in Zhang (1992, 220).
[82] Betts (1987, 59).
[83] Betts (1987, 59).
[84] Chang (1988, 108).
[85] Schwartz and Derber (1990, 86–87).
[86] Lieberman (1955).

with conventional weapons, such intervention might not be decisive; that the time might come when the U.S. might have to intervene with atomic weapons, but that should come only at the end, and we would have to advise our allies first."[87] Indeed, U.S. nuclear weapons were deployed in the vicinity: in addition to the nuclear bombs aboard U.S. naval vessels near the Strait, the United States placed eight-inch howitzers that could fire nuclear munitions on Quemoy.[88] According to General Curtis LeMay, the head of the Strategic Air Command (SAC), a B-36 crew was in position at Guam. Air units had been given a list of targets, he wrote, and were "ready for immed[iate] execution."[89]

In early April, Eisenhower and his advisors hatched a plan that, if implemented, might have provoked war with China: Washington would ask Chiang to withdraw from the offshore islands, and U.S. forces would impose a naval blockade of the Taiwan Strait. The proposed blockade was a textbook attempt at risk manipulation: the U.S. naval presence in the Strait would increase the likelihood of a deliberate or accidental military clash, potentially causing the crisis to spiral out of control. The White House certainly recognized this: Radford told Eisenhower that it would only be a matter of time before Chinese aircraft fired upon U.S. ships. On April 20, Radford traveled to Taipei to present their plan to Chiang. The Taiwanese leader balked at the proposal and refused to pull his forces out of Quemoy and Matsu.[90]

However, while the U.S. delegation was in Taipei, Chinese premier Zhou Enlai made an unexpected announcement from Bandung, Indonesia, where officials were convening for the first Afro-Asian conference. Zhou indicated a willingness to negotiate and reduce tensions in the Taiwan Strait.[91] This brought an end to the crisis, although this would not be the last time that the United States would employ nuclear brinkmanship against China over the Taiwan question.

The Role of Nuclear Threats in China's Decision to Back Down

According to folk wisdom, the 1954–1955 Taiwan Strait crisis is an example of successful nuclear brinkmanship. American crisis

[87] U.S. Department of State (1955, 159).
[88] Schwartz and Derber (1990, 87).
[89] Quoted in Schwartz and Derber (1990, 87).
[90] Chang (1988, 115–16).
[91] Bundy (1988, 279).

participants – notably Dulles and Eisenhower – certainly believed this to be true.[92] So did many scholars writing during the Cold War.[93] The view that U.S. nuclear threats resulted in a crisis victory for the United States largely persists today, even among analysts who are generally skeptical about the coercive utility of nuclear weapons. Historian Bradford Lee, for instance, calls the 1954–1955 dispute "the only case [of those in the early Cold War period] in which nuclear compellence may have played a key role."[94]

Nuclear coercion theory points to the timing of events to support the view that nuclear blackmail worked. China caved, according to this logic, shortly after Washington made a series of nuclear threats in March 1955. There is also some evidence that China received American nuclear signals, and that officials in Beijing worried about the possibility of nuclear escalation. Zhou Enlai complained about the United States "brandishing atomic weapons" in January and three months later accused Eisenhower of "openly boasting of nuclear missiles as conventional weapons and preparing for nuclear war."[95] Moreover, on February 12, Guo Moruo, the chairman of the Sino-Soviet Friendship Organization, openly spoke to the Chinese people about nuclear war, underscoring the fact that U.S. officials were "mad dogs [that] may jump over a wall."[96] Mao's initiation of China's own nuclear weapons program during the crisis also suggests that he worried about nuclear escalation and wanted to protect his country from future atomic blackmail.[97]

On the basis of this evidence, it would be hard to argue that nuclear weapons were irrelevant during the first crisis in the Taiwan Strait. This does not mean, however, that nuclear coercion played a decisive role in China's decision to back down. A close look at the available evidence leads us to question the degree to which this crisis supports the nuclear coercionist school.

To begin, it is important to consider what exactly U.S. nuclear threats may have accomplished. China clearly believed that U.S. nuclear brinkmanship was meant to *coerce* Beijing. According to a

---

[92] See, for example, Shepley (1956, 72, 77).
[93] For instance, Betts (1987, 54–62).
[94] Lee (2014a, 386).
[95] Zhang (1992, 220).
[96] Quoted in Zhang (1992, 221).
[97] Lewis and Xue (1988, 34–39) and Zhang (1992, 222).

Chinese document delivered by Zhou Enlai to Soviet ambassador Eugene in May 1955, China understood U.S. demands to be threefold: abandon its policy of liberating Taiwan, acknowledge the legitimacy of the U.S. occupation of Taiwan, and admit that there are "two Chinas."[98] Yet despite U.S. nuclear brinkmanship, China refused to accede to any of these demands: China did not walk away from its policy of liberating Taiwan, nor did it accept the legitimacy of Chiang's government or the U.S. military presence on the island.[99]

One might argue, alternatively, that U.S. nuclear threats coerced Chinese officials by bringing them to the negotiating table. There are two problems with this line of thinking. First, the link between Zhou Enlai's conciliatory remarks in Bandung and U.S. nuclear brinkmanship is tenuous. Zhou appeared to believe that his Bandung statement simply reaffirmed China's existing policy and therefore was not a significant concession. Moreover, Zhou's speech was an "impromptu response" to discussions with some of his Asian colleagues and was not necessarily authorized by anyone in Beijing.[100] Second, and more importantly, China did not make any significant concessions during the subsequent talks, agreeing only to a temporary cease-fire on the offshore islands – a cease-fire that would be broken three years later. To the extent that nuclear coercion was tried, it appears to have been largely unsuccessful.

At best, the 1954–1955 Taiwan Strait crisis represents a victory for nuclear *deterrence*. U.S. nuclear threats may have deterred China from launching further attacks against Taiwan or the offshore islands. But here too, there are reasons to be circumspect. First, there are serious doubts about whether China ever intended to launch an invasion in the first place.[101] The Chinese documentary record suggests that Beijing viewed the shelling of Quemoy as a limited response to growing U.S. activity in the region.[102] China apparently felt the need to protest the U.S. defense treaty with Taiwan, to avoid the perception that Chiang's government was legitimate. But Beijing was not necessarily looking for war with the United States.[103] At the time, according to Chinese

---

[98] Chinese Foreign Ministry (1955).
[99] Chang and Di (1993, 1523).
[100] Chang and Di (1993, 1520).
[101] Lewis and Xue (1988, 27) and Soman (2000, 134–37).
[102] See Chang and Di (1993, 1507).
[103] Fravel (2007/08, 60).

crisis participants, China did not even have a military plan – let alone the intent – to seize Quemoy and Matsu.[104] Second, Zhou's April 1955 conciliatory statement was hardly the end of the Sino-American dispute over Taiwan. China was not deterred from initiating future provocations – just three years later, China once again shelled Quemoy, triggering another serious crisis.

Second Taiwan Strait Crisis, 1958

In early 1958, as Taiwan began to move large numbers of troops to disputed offshore islands in the Taiwan Strait, the Chinese military devised a plan for a new campaign against the island of Quemoy.[105] Mao approved these plans, hoping to "probe the attitude of the Americans in Washington, testing their determination."[106] On August 23, the Chinese army put these plans into action, firing more than 40,000 artillery shells onto Quemoy. The next day, a Chinese force attempted to capture Tungting, a small island nearby. Chinese patrol torpedo boats attacked two Nationalist ships on August 24 and successfully prevented resupply shipments from landing on Quemoy for two weeks, putting significant pressure on the Taiwanese garrison there. The United States again found itself playing a game of chicken in the Taiwan Strait.

U.S. Nuclear Brinkmanship and the Chinese Response

Washington's response to the shelling of Quemoy in 1958 was strikingly similar to its moves during the 1954–1955 crisis. Almost immediately, the U.S. bolstered its military presence in the area, hoping to deter a Chinese invasion of Quemoy – but without emboldening the Taiwanese government to take actions that might drag the United States into an unwanted war. Two aircraft carrier groups were sent to the region from the Middle East, along with shipments of military equipment and ammunition. Prior to the crisis, the United States had already been bolstering its military position in response to an ongoing

---

[104] Chang and Di (1993, 1507).
[105] Jian (2001, 172).
[106] Soman (2000, 175) and Jian (2001, 183–84).

Chinese buildup.[107] Once the Chinese shelling began, Eisenhower reinforced those units with additional aircraft carriers, destroyers, and submarines.[108] Most important, the United States began escorting resupply ships to the offshore islands.

As the Eisenhower administration considered its options, the possible use of nuclear weapons quickly came to the fore. The Joint Chiefs of Staff argued in August, shortly before China began shelling Quemoy, that "in the event of an assault or an interdiction, effective U.S. intervention would necessitate *nuclear bombing of mainland bases*" in China.[109] Other U.S. officials, particularly Dulles, seemed to once again embrace the nuclear option. While discussing nuclear weapons with General Twining, who was chairman of the Joint Chiefs of Staff during the crisis, Dulles complained that "there was no use of having a lot of stuff and never being able to use it."[110] On August 25, Washington told the commander of the U.S. Pacific Command that if China invaded the islands the U.S. military response would likely be conventional, but that U.S. forces should make preparations "to use atomic weapons to extend deeper into Chinese Communist territory if necessary."[111]

In public, Washington began signaling its resolve to defend Taiwan. On September 4, Dulles issued a statement in which he declared that Quemoy was essential to the security of Taiwan, and that "acquiescense" to Chinese aggression "would threaten peace everywhere."[112] The same day, Curtis LeMay, who was by this time vice chief of air staff, embarked on a high-profile trip to Taiwan.[113] The implicit U.S. deterrent threat was clear: "U.S. DECIDES TO USE FORCE IF REDS INVADE QUEMOY," read the *New York Times* headline the

---

[107] Soman (2000, 174).

[108] Halperin (1966, 134–36). See also O'Neill (1958) and Van Staaveren (1962).

[109] U.S. Department of State (1958a, 56). Emphasis added.

[110] Quoted in Bundy (1988, 279).

[111] Quoted in Betts (1987, 68). Remarkably, however, the Pacific Air Force command misinterpreted this guidance to mean that Eisenhower had now decided firmly against the use of nuclear weapons. See Betts (1987, 70–71). A reiteration of these instructions on September 6 took pains to clarify that nuclear weapons could only be used with explicit permission of the president – permission that Eisenhower had not yet granted. See Halperin (1966, xii, 113, 285–87).

[112] Dulles (1958b, 2).

[113] Soman (2000, 181).

following day.[114] In response to these actions, Khrushchev complained to Eisenhower in a September 7 letter that "military leaders in the United States are trying also, with the tacit agreement of the American Government, to resort to atomic blackmail against China."[115]

As the crisis persisted, the United States ratcheted up its nuclear brinkmanship. On September 17, the United States landed three nuclear-capable eight-inch artillery guns on Quemoy, reinforcing what national media called a "nuclear-equipped armada."[116] Ten days later, Air Force Secretary James Douglas alluded to U.S. nuclear capabilities in the Taiwan Strait, declaring in a speech approved by the State Department that "our most modern fighters are on the spot, ready to meet the threat of the Chinese Communists. And make no mistake, our fighter-bombers and light bombers are as capable of using high-explosive bombs as more powerful weapons."[117]

But by the time U.S. nuclear rhetoric escalated, the crisis had cooled considerably. Chinese artillery fire against Quemoy had tapered off, with less than 5,000 shells fired between August 31 and September 7, compared to 40,000 on the first day of the crisis alone.[118] It did not resume in earnest until the second American-escorted supply convoy landed on Quemoy on September 8.

On the diplomatic front, on September 6 Zhou Enlai extended an offer – immediately accepted by the United States – to "sit down at the negotiation table with the Americans to discuss how to relax and eliminate the tension in the Taiwan Strait."[119] Ambassadorial talks, which were the primary means of direct communication between Washington and Beijing, had been suspended for nine months. The resumption of these talks on September 15 in Warsaw was a notable achievement for Mao.

Moreover, at the same time, the United States was putting pressure on the government of Chiang Kai-shek to remove its military forces from the offshore islands. Dulles expressed concern about Taiwanese activities that the Chinese might find "provocative," and suggested that the United States might seek a resolution to the crisis that involved

[114] *New York Times* (1958).
[115] Khrushchev (1958, 12).
[116] Raymonds (1958, 17).
[117] Frankel (1958, 10).
[118] Halperin (1966, 160, 213).
[119] Quoted in Jian (2001, 188).

securing Taiwanese jurisdiction over the offshore islands while also demilitarizing them.[120] Dulles went further in a September 30 news conference, stating that "if there were a cease-fire in the area which seemed to be reasonably dependable, I think it would be foolish to keep these large forces on these islands. We thought that it was rather foolish to put them there" in the first place. He added, "there is nobody that is less anxious to have a war than President Eisenhower is."[121]

The Chinese responded positively to these overtures. On October 6, Mao ordered that Chinese forces should hold their fire – even if they were bombarded by U.S. forces.[122] The following day, the Chinese defense minister, Peng Dehuai, announced that this unilateral cease-fire would hold for one week. The cease-fire was extended for two weeks on October 13, although firing resumed on October 20 in response to an alleged U.S. naval intrusion into Chinese territorial waters.[123] On October 25, Peng announced that shelling of Quemoy would resume only on odd-numbered days, allowing Taiwanese forces to receive supplies on even-numbered days. All cease-fires were conditional on the U.S. not escorting Taiwanese supply ships to Quemoy, to which the United States agreed.[124] Two months later, China stopped shelling the island altogether, bringing the crisis to a close.

Did Nuclear Threats Succeed in 1958?

The 1958 crisis has been widely interpreted as a success for U.S. nuclear diplomacy. Mao admitted to being stunned by the ferocious reaction to his probe: "I did not expect that the entire world would be so deeply shocked."[125] U.S. officials were certainly pleased with the outcome, as Washington had stood firm in the face of a blatant challenge to its resolve.

---

[120] U.S. Department of State (1958c, 157).

[121] Dulles (1958a, 8).

[122] Jian (2001, 200).

[123] Halperin (1966, 471). Jian (2001, 201) indicates that the October 20 barrage lasted just one hour, while Halperin (1966, 471–72) reports that it continued until October 24.

[124] Halperin (1966, 484, 495–96).

[125] *Cold War International History Project Bulletin* (1995, 216). See also Whiting (1975, 265).

But does the crisis illustrate the coercive value of nuclear threats? Here, the evidence is much more ambiguous. First, just like in 1954–1955, the outcome of the crisis was not really a *coercive* victory for the United States. American nuclear threats issued during the 1958 crisis seemed to be largely deterrent in nature. At best, the United States achieved a return to the status quo ante, with the Chinese continuing to claim the offshore islands but refraining from direct military confrontation. For its part, the United States made some key concessions, agreeing to restart ambassadorial talks and putting pressure on the Taiwanese government to vacate Quemoy. Indeed, one of the central U.S. objectives during the crisis was to restrain Taiwanese behavior and avoid provoking an escalation of the crisis. To that end, the outcome was less than satisfactory for Chiang, who had hoped for more aggressive U.S. action against the Chinese. By the end of 1958, at Eisenhower's insistence, Taiwan actually reduced the size of its garrison in Quemoy by 15,000 troops.[126] The Chinese government, by contrast, made few concessions, aside from drawing down the limited probe it had initiated. All of these facts complicate the view that the United States coerced the Chinese during the crisis.

Second, there are plausible reasons to doubt whether nuclear threats made the difference in convincing Mao to deescalate the crisis. By the time the nuclear dimension of the 1958 crisis became clear, around mid-September, the Chinese had already begun to deescalate, and U.S. anxiety about a Chinese invasion had largely passed. While U.S. officials discussed the possible use of nuclear weapons from the beginning, these discussions were not conducted in public, and it is doubtful that the Chinese were aware of the extent to which U.S. military advisers viewed atomic weapons as a necessity.

U.S. military movements at the outset of the crisis certainly carried the whiff of a nuclear threat. But the United States already had considerable nuclear assets in the area well before the Chinese launched the August 23 attacks on Quemoy.[127] Five SAC B-47 bombers were placed on alert in Guam for possible nuclear strikes against the Chinese mainland – but this too was ordered before the Chinese shelling

---

[126] Halperin (1966, 543).

[127] Nuclear-capable Matador missiles were deployed in Taiwan (and had been test-fired several months earlier), and the United States had Mk-6, Mk-36, and Mk-39 nuclear bombs in Guam and Okinawa. U.S. Department of Defense (1978, B2–B5).

began.[128] Although the United States sent additional forces as soon as the crisis erupted, the Chinese were already well aware that the U.S. had nuclear assets in the area. Yet Mao elected to initiate the crisis anyway.

Indeed, Chinese behavior during the 1958 crisis suggests that nuclear threats were not driving Mao's calculations. China's most aggressive military actions during the crisis occurred on September 8, when it fired 53,310 artillery shells against Quemoy and incoming supply convoys, and on September 11, when it fired more than 60,000 shells.[129] In addition, the People's Liberation Army (PLA) fired more than 10,000 shells per day on five separate occasions between September 19 and October 1, and continued to engage Nationalist pilots in aerial combat until at least October 10.[130] This behavior occurred after Dulles's September 4 press conference, and after Khrushchev accused the United States of atomic blackmail. Thus, the Chinese continued to escalate even after Washington approached the proverbial brink.

Instead, Mao's behavior during the crisis seems to have been driven by tactical considerations unrelated to U.S. nuclear brinkmanship. In particular, once the Communist air force lost air superiority in the Strait and Mao no longer had the ability to stop the American-escorted convoys, continued shelling would only have highlighted China's inability to interdict Taiwan's supply routes. Once the blockade was broken, trying in vain to enforce it would only compound China's embarrassment.[131] In other words, China's conventional military weakness – particularly in the air – loomed far larger than its vulnerability to nuclear attack.

While the Chinese showed a considerable appetite for risky behavior during the crisis, Eisenhower did not. The United States went to great lengths to avoid actions that carried a risk of provocation or inadvertent escalation, opting instead for carefully controlled deterrence and support operations. From the outset, U.S. naval escorts of supply convoys were kept a minimum of three miles from Quemoy to avoid engagements with PLA artillery batteries.[132] While ultimately effective,

---

[128] Nalty (1968, 19).
[129] Halperin (1966, 213, 298–99).
[130] Halperin (1966, 298–303, 307). See also Van Staaveren (1962, 38).
[131] See Halperin (1966, 485–89).
[132] Eisenhower (1965, 297–99).

this restriction limited the utility of the convoys and infuriated Chiang Kai-shek. Even the normally hawkish Dulles was so concerned about provoking a conflict that on September 11 he suggested that Washington should cease operations within the territorial waters claimed by China, despite the fact that the United States did not officially recognize those boundaries.[133] Thus, at the same time as they were devising nuclear plans behind closed doors, American officials sought to restrain Taiwanese behavior and avoid provoking the Chinese.

Overall, the 1958 crisis provides little support for the coercionist view of nuclear weapons. While the United States prevailed in the crisis, its victory lay in preventing further Chinese aggression rather than extracting concessions. Further, the coercionist school would expect to see the United States gradually escalating the crisis, invoking its nuclear edge until China could no longer stomach the risk of nuclear attack. Yet this expectation is not borne out by the historical record. The Eisenhower administration, while making a firm commitment to Taiwan's defense, sought at every turn to minimize risk, opting instead to simply counter Mao's blockade strategy and wait him out. In the end, Mao concluded that he had achieved his dual purposes of mobilizing domestic support and probing American resolve, and the two countries returned to the status quo ante.

Cuban Missile Crisis, 1962

Beginning in September 1962, the Soviet Union introduced nuclear weapons – including medium-range R-12 missiles and intermediate-range R-14 missiles – into Cuba. In mid-October, an American U-2 spy plane captured photos of missile sites under construction on the island. After learning of the nuclear deployments on October 16, Kennedy appeared puzzled by Khrushchev's intentions. "It's a goddamn mystery to me," he declared to his advisors when asked what the Soviet leader was thinking.[134] However, Khrushchev's motives were far from mysterious: he hoped to defend Fidel Castro's regime, which was vulnerable to American aggression, augment the Soviet capacity to hit the U.S. mainland with nuclear missiles, and gain an advantage in Berlin after

---

[133] Soman (2000, 188).
[134] Allison and Zelikow (1999, 81).

failing to expel western forces from the city from 1958 to 1961.[135] Either way, the Soviet missile deployments were unacceptable to the United States. Kennedy had previously warned Khrushchev that "the gravest issues would arise" if Moscow introduced bases or ballistic missiles in Cuba.[136] America's realization that the Soviet leader had disregarded this threat triggered a tense thirteen-day crisis that brought the two superpowers to the brink of nuclear war.

U.S. Nuclear Brinkmanship and the Soviet Response

The United States considered two main options to deal with the missiles in Cuba: (1) launching air strikes against the missile sites, and (2) setting up a naval quarantine. Kennedy and several of his advisors initially favored a swift conventional attack. As the president said at the onset of the crisis, "We're certainly going to ... take out these ... missiles ... We ought to be making *those* preparations."[137] However, Kennedy's team ultimately agreed on the latter option, deciding against the immediate use of force in Cuba.

In an address to the nation on October 22, the president announced the creation of a quarantine around the island and demanded that the Soviet Union remove the missiles. The threat of military escalation – including, potentially, an invasion of Cuba – loomed in the background if Moscow did not dismantle and remove the missiles. As Kennedy wrote to Khrushchev in a private letter on the day of his public address, "I must tell you that the United States is determined that this threat to the security of this hemisphere be removed. At the same time, I wish to point out that the action we are taking [the quarantine] is the minimum necessary to remove the threat to the security of the nations of this hemisphere. The fact of this minimum response should not be taken as a basis, however, for any misjudgment on your part."[138]

As Washington pursued a peaceful resolution to the crisis, it also prepared for war. Early in the crisis, on October 20, the Joint Chiefs of Staff told U.S. military commanders worldwide that "the state of tension in Cuba could lead to military action."[139] The United States

---

[135] See Fursenko and Naftali (1997, 166–83) and Dobbs (2008, 33–34).
[136] Quoted in Allison and Zelikow (1999, 79).
[137] Quoted in Fursenko and Naftali (1997, 224–225). Emphasis in original.
[138] U.S. Department of State (1962, 166).
[139] Fursenko and Naftali (1997, 234).

prepared for an attack by deploying planes to Puerto Rico, increasing the number of SAC bombers on active duty, and bolstering its naval presence in the Carribean under the guise of a secret exercise called ORTSAC ("Castro" spelled backwards).[140] Then, on October 24, two days after Kennedy announced the quarantine, Washington took an unprecedented step. For the first and only time in its history, the United States military moved to DEFCON 2 – one step away from imminent nuclear war. It placed ICBMs on alert and mobilized SAC for war to signal its resolve.[141] As General David Burchinal later explained, "We had SAC bombers on nuclear alert with weapons in the bomb-bays on civilian airfields all over the U.S. . . . all these moves were signals the Soviets could see and we knew they could see them. We got everything we had . . . ready and aimed and we made damn sure they saw it."[142] As a result of the nuclear alert, military commanders were given launch authority over some nuclear forces. This raised the possibility, however unlikely it may have been, that nuclear weapons could be launched inadvertently.

On October 27, a day known in the White House as "Black Saturday," a U-2 based in Alaska inadvertently strayed into Soviet airspace, leading some in Moscow to fear that a preemptive nuclear attack was imminent. The U-2 returned to American airspace without a military confrontation, but the outcome of this episode could have been catastrophic. Khrushchev certainly took notice: he wrote to Kennedy that the U-2 "could be easily taken for a nuclear bomber, which might push us to a fateful step; and all the more so since the U.S. Government and Pentagon long ago declared that you are maintaining a continuous nuclear bomber patrol?"[143] Kennedy did not intend to provoke a nuclear war, but U.S. brinkmanship nonetheless threatened to take the superpowers down that path. On the very same day, Soviet anti-aircraft batteries shot down a different U-2 over Cuba, killing the pilot. For the coercionist school, these incidents illustrate how nuclear crises create an intrinsic risk of inadvertent escalation.[144]

As events seemed to spiral out of control, both Kennedy and Khrushchev desperately sought a way out of the crisis. On the night

[140] Fursenko and Naftali (1997, 237).
[141] Sagan (1985, 108–09).
[142] Quoted in Trachtenberg (1985, 157).
[143] Quoted in Allison and Zelikow (1999, 240).
[144] Schelling (1960, chapter 8).

of October 27, Robert Kennedy and Soviet ambassador Anatoly Dobrynin met to discuss a resolution to the crisis. By Kennedy's telling, he delivered a clear threat to Dobrynin: "if they did not remove those bases, we would remove them."[145] The two then struck a compromise that brought an end to the Cuban affair: the Soviets would remove the missiles from Cuba if, in exchange, the United States publicly pledged not to invade the island. In addition, Washington privately agreed to remove nuclear-armed Jupiter missiles from Turkey that had been deployed close to Soviet territory since 1961.

The Role of Nuclear Weapons: A Mixed Assessment

The Cuban missile crisis is widely viewed as a case of successful nuclear blackmail.[146] During the crisis, Secretary of State Dean Rusk famously said, "We're eyeball to eyeball, and the other fellow just blinked."[147] This statement came to exemplify the belief that the United States prevailed against the Soviet Union in a game of atomic chicken. It is easy to see why this view is so pervasive: Washington did, in fact, compel the Soviets to heed its demands after threatening to unleash a nuclear war. But to what degree did U.S. nuclear threats contribute to the outcome of the crisis?

There are some indications that Washington's threats fueled Khrushchev's fears of nuclear war, just as nuclear coercion theory would expect. When explaining the need to withdraw the missiles to the Presidium on October 28, Khrushchev said, "we found ourselves face to face with the danger of war and of nuclear catastrophe, with the possible result of destroying the human race. In order to save the world, we must retreat."[148] Two days later, Khrushchev justified his actions to a visiting Czechoslovak delegation: a U.S. attack on Cuba "would mean nuclear war. We could not be certain that they would not do so [use nuclear weapons]. The presence of our missiles provoked them too much ... That is why we issued the statement [on October 28] that we would dismantle the missiles if the USA declared it swore not to attack Cuba."[149]

---

[145] Kennedy (1969, 86).
[146] For example, Trachtenberg (1985) and Betts (1987, 109–23).
[147] Quoted in Dobbs (2008, 88).
[148] Fursenko and Naftali (1997, 284).
[149] National Security Archive (2002a).

However, a close look at the historical record suggests that the evidence in favor of the nuclear coercionist view is less definitive than it may initially seem. Three factors complicate the standard narrative of the crisis.

First, the timing of events leads one to question the degree to which U.S. nuclear brinkmanship affected Soviet capitulation over the Cuban missiles. Khrushchev decided midday on October 25, nine days into the crisis, that he needed to defuse the situation. He no longer believed that the Soviets could keep the missiles in Cuba without a war.[150] The Soviet leader told his colleagues during a formal meeting of the Presidium that the missiles must be dismantled. However, it is unlikely that U.S. nuclear brinkmanship caused Khrushchev's about-face. Moscow detected the U.S. move to DEFCON 2, but news of the U.S. nuclear alert "probably had not yet reached the Kremlin" by the time Khrushchev decided to remove the missiles.[151] Based on the available evidence, he decided to back down before receiving word of the nuclear alert – and before either the U-2 incidents or Robert Kennedy's ultimatum, which occurred two days later.

Second, the Soviet Union was conventionally outgunned in the Caribbean. Lieutenant General Nikolai Beloborodov, who commanded the Soviet nuclear arsenal in Cuba, indicated that Washington's ten-to-one advantage in conventional forces left an indelible impression: "The U.S. forces, using their proximity to Cuba, numerical superiority in air forces and naval power and the presence of a strong group of marines, clearly demonstrated their intention to unleash a war."[152] This statement implies that U.S. conventional signaling influenced Moscow's decision to back down. Indeed, several key U.S. officials believed that U.S. conventional superiority – not America's nuclear arsenal – played the decisive role in the outcome of the crisis. For example, then-Secretary of Defense Robert McNamara observed that the Soviets "were finally forced out, but it was not through the threat of use of nuclear weapons."[153] "It was our tremendous conventional power in the region," he went on to say, "which forced the Soviets to take those missiles out."[154] Henry Kissinger, who

---

[150] Fursenko and Naftali (1997, 259).
[151] Fursenko and Naftali (1997, 258, 260).
[152] Beloborodov (1990).
[153] Charlton (1987, 23).
[154] Charlton (1987, 23).

did not participate in the crisis but played a key role in future nuclear crises, apparently agreed: "Khrushchev withdrew from Cuba because we had *local* superiority," he said.[155] This evidence does not imply that the risk of nuclear war had no effect on Khrushchev – it probably did to some extent. Yet it is difficult to disentangle the effects of U.S. nuclear and conventional power on Khrushchev's ultimate retreat.

Third, the crisis was not necessarily a slam dunk victory for the United States. To be sure, the United States achieved its central objective: compelling the Soviets to remove the missiles from Cuba. It is misleading to imply, however, that Kennedy resolutely stood firm while Khrushchev "blinked." In fact, one could argue that Kennedy blinked too.[156] The president said in private a few weeks after the crisis subsided that the intermediate-range Soviet nuclear missiles in Cuba served as "a substantial deterrent to me."[157] Kennedy's concerns about nuclear escalation were evident during the crisis: he feverishly searched for a diplomatic solution, even after a U-2 was shot down over Cuba on "Black Saturday." In the end, the president offered a last-minute concession to Khrushchev, pledging to remove nuclear missiles from Turkey. Washington may have won the crisis, but not without making some concessions.

Questioning the Effects of Nuclear Superiority

Nuclear relativists sometimes claim that the United States won the crisis because it had a larger nuclear arsenal than the Soviet Union.[158] Indeed, according to contemporary estimates, Washington possessed more than five times as many nuclear-capable long-range missiles as Moscow in 1962, and more than three times as many

---

[155] Charlton (1987, 55). Emphasis in original. However, Kissinger also added, "On top of it, what made it easier was that we also had strategic superiority."

[156] Blanton (2012, 11).

[157] Dobbs (2008, 229). Kennedy made this statement without knowing the extent to which the Soviet Union had deployed tactical nuclear weapons in Cuba. Based on satellite imagery, CIA director John McCone told Kennedy that Moscow may have introduced tactical nuclear weapons, in addition to the medium-range missiles, but the president lacked definitive information about these deployments. He did not know, for example, that the Soviets had short-range nuclear missiles pointed at the American military base in Guantanamo Bay. See Taylor (2012).

[158] For example, Betts (1987, 120–23).

long-range bombers.[159] Yet even if the danger of nuclear war influenced Khrushchev's decision to capitulate, it is far from obvious that nuclear superiority mattered to the degree that nuclear relativists assert.

First, nuclear superiority did not provide solace to U.S. officials during the crisis. Dean Rusk, Robert McNamara, George Ball, Roswell Gilpatric, Theodore Sorensen, and McGeorge Bundy – all key participants in the crisis – later wrote: "American nuclear superiority was not in our view a critical factor, for the fundamental and controlling reason that nuclear war, already in 1962, would have been an unexampled catastrophe for both sides ... No one of us ever reviewed the nuclear balance for comfort in those hard weeks."[160] Rusk later added, "We did not count missiles on either side." McNamara echoed, "nuclear played a zero role in Cuba."[161] General Maxwell Taylor, chairman of the Joint Chiefs of Staff during the crisis, shared this view. He argued, "Our great superiority in nuclear weapons contributed little to the outcome of the Cuba crisis."[162]

Some scholars dismiss these statements because they were made in the midst of a fierce debate about U.S. nuclear policies during the Reagan administration.[163] Yet President Kennedy expressed similar sentiments during the crisis, and his views cannot be ascribed so easily to partisan politics.[164] When discussing how the Soviet missile deployment influenced the nuclear balance of power, Kennedy said, "What difference does it make? They've got enough to blow us up now anyway."[165] On another occasion, he expressed shock when the Pentagon told him that 600,000 people would die if one Soviet missile hit an American city: "That's the total number of casualties in the Civil War," he said, "And we haven't gotten over that in a hundred years."[166] Despite the fact that he held nuclear superiority, it is not clear that Kennedy was any less afraid than his Soviet counterpart.

[159] American Security Council (1967, 32).
[160] Rusk et al. (1982).
[161] Herken (1985, 167).
[162] Taylor (1982).
[163] See, for example, Gavin (2012a).
[164] Kennedy also questioned the coercive utility of nuclear weapons, regardless of the nuclear balance. He believed that nuclear forces were "only good for deterring." Dobbs (2008, 229).
[165] Quoted in Trachtenberg (1985, 148).
[166] Dobbs (2008, 229).

Second, it was Khrushchev who initiated the crisis. The Soviet leader still believed – despite his failures in the Berlin crises – that he could blackmail the United States with nuclear weapons. In May 1962, Khrushchev told the Presidium that introducing nuclear missiles in Cuba "will be an offensive policy."[167] He did not elaborate on what this meant, but Khrushchev may have hoped to use the Cuban missiles to coerce the United States over Berlin, Laos, and a nuclear test ban. Khrushchev later suggested that the missiles were there simply to protect Cuba from a U.S. invasion, but it is clear that he also had coercive intentions. According to the nuclear relativist logic, Khrushchev should have recognized the folly in this position. He ought to have anticipated that he would lose any future crisis over Cuba, and refrained from placing missiles on the island. That he opted for such a gamble in the first place suggests that nuclear superiority provides at best a partial explanation for the dynamics of this crisis. This raises the question, as Kennedy himself wondered: why did Khrushchev believe that he could get away with introducing the missiles?[168]

Newly available documents provide some clues. Khrushchev believed that "we will win this operation" because the missiles could be presented to the United States as a *fait accompli.*[169] He instructed the Presidium, "Carry this out secretly. Then declare it."[170] His plans were dashed when U.S. intelligence detected the missiles before all of the relevant military equipment had arrived on the island. This supports a key provision of our nuclear skepticism theory – namely, that *faits accomplis* backed by nuclear weapons are hardly a recipe for guaranteed success. Khrushchev tried – and failed – to use his nuclear arsenal as a shield to protect an aggressive gambit in Cuba.

Third, other aspects of Soviet behavior during the crisis are inconsistent with the nuclear relativist logic. A key component of the coercionist argument is that nuclear superiority emboldens states to push harder in crises. This line of thinking implies that states are more likely to manipulate risk when they have a superior nuclear arsenal.

---

[167] Presidium of the Central Committee of the Communist Party of the Soviet Union (2012, 303).

[168] See Fuhrmann and Sechser (2014a) for a general discussion of why countries deploy nuclear weapons abroad.

[169] Fursenko and Naftali (2006, 440).

[170] Presidium of the Central Committee of the Communist Party of the Soviet Union (2012, 303).

Many scholars assume that this was the case during the Cuban missile crisis: the U.S. went to DEFCON 2, and the Soviet Union did nothing to signal its resolve, "equivalent to a threatened dog's rolling over belly-up."[171] Yet this characterization of Soviet behavior during the crisis is misleading. In fact, we now know that the Soviet Union took dangerous gambles with its arsenal as well. Moscow introduced tactical nuclear weapons in Cuba, in addition to the medium-range missiles that precipitated the crisis. The smaller tactical weapons, which were meant primarily for use in the event of an American invasion, were deployed throughout the standoff. According to General Anatoly Gribkov, Defense Minister Rodion Malinovsky orally authorized Soviet field commanders, before they departed for Cuba, to use these weapons if the United States attacked.[172] Khrushchev initially supported the predelegation of launch authority: "If there is a [U.S.] landing," he instructed, "[use] the tactical atomic weapons, but [not] the strategic weapons until [there is] an order."[173] Moscow later explicitly prohibited local commanders from using *any* nuclear weapons without authorization from central command, and debates persist about when (and if) local commanders had the ability to fire tactical weaponry. Yet, as Savranskaya and Blanton conclude, "in all likelihood, tactical nuclear weapons would most definitely be used in a first salvo if U.S. forces had landed in Cuba."[174] Questions of political authorization aside, Moscow technically had no way to prohibit the tactical weapons from being launched, just as it could not stop local commanders from shooting down the U.S. spy plane.

A second case of risk manipulation involved Soviet submarines that were sent to Cuba armed with nuclear-tipped torpedoes. The submarine commanders were given instructions about when they were to use nuclear weapons. According to Ryurik Ketov, who served aboard one of the submarines, Vice-Admiral Anatoly Rassokho ordered the crew to use the torpedoes if they were attacked underwater, shot at while on the surface, or received orders from Moscow to fire. Rassokho then added, "I suggest to you, commanders, that you use your nuclear weapons first, and then you will figure out what to do after

---

[171] Betts (1987, 120).
[172] Savranskaya and Blanton (2013). A written order providing these instructions is publicly available, but it is not signed.
[173] Quoted in Fursenko and Naftali (2006, 471).
[174] Savranskaya and Blanton (2013).

that."[175] The officers aboard the submarines therefore had a good deal of leeway regarding launch authority of their torpedoes. A dangerous moment ensued when the U.S. navy attempted to force several of these submarines to the surface. In one instance, the Americans hit a Soviet submarine (known as B-59) with a small depth charge. The commander of B-59, Valentin Savitsky, reportedly believed that he was under attack, and he ordered the officer in charge of the nuclear torpedo to prepare it for battle readiness. Then Savitsky said, "Maybe the war has already started up there, while we are doing somersaults here. We're going to blast them now! We will die, but we will sink them all."[176] Another officer, Vasili Archipov, reportedly calmed Savitsky down, and the submarine ultimately came to the surface.[177] While cooler heads prevailed, this episode provides another fitting illustration of crisis risk manipulation. Although this submarine incident is rarely discussed in the scholarly literature, it was no less dangerous than the American U-2 episode. There was one key difference, though: there is no evidence that Kennedy knew about the nuclear-tipped torpedoes, further underscoring the challenges associated with nuclear signaling during crises.

Finally, subsequent events cause us to question the effects of nuclear superiority in 1962. The two superpowers experienced a second crisis over Cuba in September 1970, when U.S. intelligence detected the construction of a Soviet submarine base on the island. Washington believed that the presence of this base, which was located in the port of Cienfuegos, violated a key pledge made by the Soviets at the end of the Cuban missile crisis – namely, that they would not reintroduce offensive nuclear weapons in Cuba.[178] Washington quietly signaled that it would not tolerate a nuclear submarine base ninety miles from the U.S. mainland. National Security Advisor Henry Kissinger told Anatoly Dobrynin that the United States viewed the continued construction of the base with the "utmost gravity."[179] The implication of Kissinger's statement was clear: the Soviets would face the prospect of U.S. military action if they did not dismantle the Cienfuegos base. Faced with the possibility of another public confrontation, the Soviets ultimately

[175] National Security Archive (2002c).
[176] Quoted in National Security Archive (2002b).
[177] National Security Archive (2002b).
[178] Garthoff (1983, 46–48).
[179] Kissinger (1979, 647).

heeded the American demand and indicated that there would not be a naval base in Cuba.[180] Thus, the United States got its way – just as it had in 1962.

Yet the nuclear balance had changed dramatically between 1962 and 1970. During the Cuban missile crisis, the United States had a clear strategic nuclear advantage over the Soviet Union, but by 1970 the Soviets had achieved virtual nuclear parity with the United States.[181] As Christopher Gelpi argues, during the Cienfuegos crisis, "Nixon and Kissinger were faced with a Soviet Union that was roughly their nuclear equal."[182] This change in the nuclear balance, according to the nuclear coercionist school, should have emboldened the Soviets and lessened U.S. coercive bargaining leverage. However, this was not the case. Moscow actually behaved less belligerently during the Cienfuegos crisis than it did in 1962, when it was in a position of extreme nuclear inferiority. Moreover, the onset of nuclear parity did not seem to constrain the United States during the Cienfuegos crisis. As Kissinger later argued, "We used more or less the same tactics [as Kennedy used in 1962] and we achieved more or less the same result."[183] That the United States had an *easier* time coercing the Soviet Union once the nuclear balance became far less favorable confounds the conventional wisdom about nuclear coercion.

To conclude, of all the crises in the atomic age, the Cuban missile crisis may offer the best evidence for nuclear coercionist school, and it is perhaps the most significant outlier for nuclear skepticism theory. We would expect, then, that this crisis would provide troves of "slam dunk" evidence in favor of the coercionist view. However, it does not. Although there are some indications that U.S. nuclear brinkmanship intimidated Khrushchev into backing down, the evidence is in fact quite murky. Instead of offering clear support for the nuclear coercionist position, the evidence supports elements of both theories.

Sino-Soviet Border Conflict, 1969

In the mid-1960s, China and the Soviet Union very nearly reached an agreement defining the Sino-Soviet boundary along the Ussuri and

[180] Garthoff (1983, 49).
[181] Jervis (1989, 43). See also Lewis (1981).
[182] Gelpi (2003, 125).
[183] Quoted in Jervis (1989, 43).

Amur rivers, which would have settled a border dispute that had
been a point of contention in Sino-Soviet relations for more than a
century.[184] Negotiations collapsed in 1964, however, and in the subsequent five years the Soviet Union adopted a more assertive stance
toward China. First, the Soviets bolstered their military position in the
Far East. By 1969, almost thirty Soviet infantry divisions were stationed along the border with China, compared to half that number
five years earlier.[185] Moreover, in the late 1960s, the Soviets deployed
tactical nuclear missiles and nuclear-capable cruise missiles along the
Sino-Soviet border and began conducting large-scale military maneuvers near China.[186] Second, the Soviets initiated a more aggressive
border patrolling stance, forcibly expelling Chinese troops, fishermen,
and peasants they encountered on disputed territory.[187] As a consequence of this new posture, the number of violent incidents between
Soviet and Chinese border patrols began to increase. Chinese leaders
began to worry that their weakening bargaining position vis-à-vis the
Soviet Union would invite coercion or even invasion, and sought to
teach Moscow a "bitter lesson" to show that they could not easily be
pushed around.[188]

On March 2, 1969, a Chinese infantry unit ambushed Soviet border guards occupying Zhenbao Island in the Ussuri River. On March
15, the stunned Soviets struck back, this time using tanks, aircraft,
armored vehicles, and heavy-caliber artillery. The two sides had experienced thousands of border incidents in the preceding five years –
including several on Zhenbao Island – but these clashes were by far
the most violent. The second attack alone, which involved more than
2,000 troops on the Chinese side, inflicted roughly 60 Soviet and 800
Chinese casualties.[189]

The March clashes ignited a tense eight-month standoff between
China and the Soviet Union. Soviet leaders were so taken aback by the

---

[184] For background, see Robinson (1972), Fravel (2008, 119–23), and Gerson
(2010, 10–15).
[185] U.S. Central Intelligence Agency (1970c) and U.S. Central Intelligence Agency
(1970d, 3).
[186] U.S. Central Intelligence Agency (1970b, 24–25), U.S. Department of State
(1969), U.S. Central Intelligence Agency (1970d, 9), and Whiting (2001, 2).
See also Robinson (1981, 269–73).
[187] Wich (1980, 98) and Fravel (2008, 206–07).
[188] Yang (2000, 28).
[189] Robinson (1981, 277) and Robinson (2003, 201–02).

Chinese assault that they moderated the brusque unilateral approach they had followed since 1964 and requested to restart the border talks that Khrushchev had terminated five years earlier. Rather than continuing to rely on aggressive military tactics for securing their territorial goals, the Soviets aimed instead to bring the Chinese back to the negotiating table, where China could then be pressed to accept a border agreement that favored the Soviet Union.[190] Indeed, the Soviets were so keen to reopen negotiations that Soviet premier Alexei Kosygin attempted to make a direct telephone call to Mao on March 21, only to be humiliated when the operator on the Chinese side cursed him as a "revisionist element" and refused to connect the call.[191] In short, the Soviets' central goal during the crisis was to secure territory, and Soviet leaders saw negotiations as the best avenue for achieving that goal.

Soviet Nuclear Brinkmanship and the Chinese Response

The Soviets' primary fear following the March 2 clash was that it signaled a broader Chinese campaign against Soviet positions on the border. Their immediate objective therefore was to avoid further incidents like the attack on Zhenbao and deter the Chinese from launching a wider offensive. While the Soviet leadership tried to open negotiations with the Chinese, the Red Army made preparations for war.

In the immediate aftermath of the second attack, the Soviets placed their Strategic Rocket Forces on high alert, moved mobile missile launchers into firing positions, and ramped up air reconnaissance activity in Chinese airspace. As this alert was initiated, two Chinese-language radio broadcasts from Moscow warned of the Soviet Union's nuclear superiority over China, declaring ominously that "the whole world knows that the main striking force of the Soviet Armed Forces is its rocket units... They are capable of carrying nuclear warheads many times stronger than all the explosives used in past wars put together."[192]

When the Chinese ignored Soviet calls for negotiations, the Soviets responded by ratcheting up military preparations. The Soviets moved

---

[190] Robinson (1981) and Gerson (2010, 28).

[191] Quoted in Lüthi (2008, 341–42).

[192] Quoted in Gerson (2010, 29). The alert is discussed in U.S. Central Intelligence Agency (1970b, 50). See also Lüthi (2012, 383).

additional troop divisions to the Far East and began major military exercises in the Amur River area, taking the unusual step of inviting journalists and foreign visitors to observe these measures.[193] The Chinese, however, were unmoved, viewing Soviet actions as "an empty show of strength, a show that was designed for others to watch."[194] When China finally replied to Soviet proposals in late May, it agreed to talks only on the condition that the Soviets acknowledge the inequality of existing boundary agreements.

As the summer wore on, the Soviets began to lose patience. The Soviet military continued to reinforce ground units in the Far East, and began conducting war games simulating possible attacks against China.[195] In June, Soviet bomber units in Siberia and Mongolia engaged in practice strikes against targets made to resemble Chinese nuclear facilities.[196] The Soviet military also began initiating more border incidents, including a major clash on August 13, marking a departure from the policy of comparative restraint it had followed since the March attacks.[197] By early August, a classified U.S. National Intelligence Estimate concluded that "for the first time, it is reasonable to ask whether a major Sino-Soviet war could break out in the near future."[198]

At the same time, the Soviets also began to escalate the severity of their coercive threats. Whereas the Soviets previously had relied mainly on radio broadcasts and unattributed newspaper editorials to issue threats in the early days of the crisis, Soviet officials now began to adopt more explicit rhetoric in conversations with foreign diplomats. On August 18, a mid-level State Department official was stunned when a Soviet Embassy officer abruptly asked over lunch how the United States would react to a strike on Chinese nuclear installations.[199] U.S. intelligence officials learned that Soviet officials had simultaneously approached Communist allies in Europe with similar inquiries –

---

[193] Kaplan (1981, 140–41) and Gelman (1982, 35).

[194] Zhou (1997).

[195] Garthoff (1985, 238n).

[196] Whiting (1980b, 336) and Whiting (1980a, 99–100).

[197] U.S. Central Intelligence Agency (1970b, 65). See also Robinson (1981, 279–80) and Gerson (2010, 33).

[198] U.S. Central Intelligence Agency (1969, 1).

[199] U.S. Department of State (2001b). See also Kissinger (1979, 183).

information that was quickly shared with the press.[200] Around the same time, a Soviet military official in Tehran sought out his American counterpart to state that the Soviets "would not hesitate to use nuclear weapons against the Chinese if they attacked with major forces."[201] These overtures contrasted sharply with the Soviet Union's previous approach of distancing government officials from nuclear rhetoric.

Perhaps most significantly, in August the Soviet air force conducted an "unprecedented" stand-down of its forces in the Far East.[202] From a military perspective, the move was significant because it allowed all aircraft to be brought to a state of high combat readiness simultaneously – a sign of a possible attack.[203]

There remains debate about whether the Soviets genuinely considered launching a nuclear strike in 1969.[204] However, Chinese officials grew anxious enough to issue emergency mobilization orders to PLA border units, initiate civilian evacuations from border areas, and call on citizens to stockpile supplies and begin digging air raid shelters in preparation for war.[205] The Chinese also agreed to a hastily arranged September 11 meeting between Premier Kosygin and Zhou Enlai at the Beijing airport, at which the two sides exchanged reassurances and laid the groundwork for a resumption of talks.

Tensions began to ease following the September 11 meeting, but not before the Soviets transmitted one final nuclear threat. A Soviet journalist believed to be a mouthpiece for the Soviet government authored an article in the *London Evening News* on September 16, stating that a Soviet air strike against Chinese nuclear installations was under serious consideration in Moscow and remarking that the Soviet Union "prefers using rockets to manpower."[206] The message was clear: the Soviets wanted to convince China that an attack was imminent. The Chinese received the message, and redoubled their preparations for

---

[200] Kissinger (1979, 184).

[201] U.S. Department of State (2001a).

[202] U.S. Central Intelligence Agency (1970b, 65).

[203] Sources differ on whether the Soviet stand-down occurred in early August or from late August through early September. See U.S. Central Intelligence Agency (1970b) and Kissinger (1979, 183).

[204] Goldstein (2003, 62–65) cites several Soviet sources suggesting that plans were at least drawn up, while Gerson (2010, 43–44) contends that the Soviets never "seriously contemplated" a nuclear attack.

[205] Yang (2000, 36–37) and Fravel (2008, 215).

[206] *New York Times* (1969).

war – preparations which may have included placing nuclear forces on alert.[207] Chinese slogans published in advance of the country's twentieth anniversary celebrations warned of "atomic war."[208] Shortly afterward, Zhou agreed to Soviet proposals for full-scale negotiations, and the crisis drew to a close when talks began in Beijing on October 20.

The Wages of Nuclear Diplomacy

In many ways, the Sino-Soviet crisis unfolded as brinkmanship theorists would expect. According to brinkmanship theory, nuclear crises are competitions in risk taking in which both sides "rock the boat" until the risk of an accidental or inadvertent war becomes intolerable for one side.[209] This turns out to be a poor description of almost every nuclear crisis since 1945: in most crises, leaders work feverishly to mitigate – not magnify – the risk that they will lose control. But it describes Soviet behavior in 1969 quite well. When the Soviet Union's initial bluster failed to impress the Chinese, Soviet leaders gradually intensified the pressure, spreading semi-official rumors of nuclear strike plans and engaging in increasingly aggressive behavior along the border. Further, the Soviet Union enjoyed unequivocal nuclear superiority over China, whose nuclear arsenal in 1969 remained small and unsophisticated.[210] The 1969 crisis therefore ought to be a sparkling example of brinkmanship theory in action.

Indeed, the received wisdom on the crisis holds that it was an unqualified success for Soviet coercive nuclear threats. Kissinger, for example, writes that "it seemed to me that in the war of nerves China had backed down."[211] Scholars have reached similar conclusions: Gerson concludes that "the Soviets had now sufficiently convinced Beijing

---

[207] See especially Yang (2000, 39–41), Lewis and Xue (2006, 56–70), and Gerson (2010, 48–52). The precise nature of the nuclear alert, however, remains uncertain, since it is not clear whether China had any operational missile units during the crisis. See Lewis (2014, 23–28).

[208] Komine (2008, 107). Komine cites an internal State Department report from the Bureau of Intelligence and Research, "Communist China: War Fears and Domestic Politics," dated September 18, 1969. See also Yang (2000, 39).

[209] See Schelling (1960, 187–203) and Schelling (1966, 92–105).

[210] See, for example, Goldstein (2003, 67–71).

[211] Kissinger (1979, 186).

that its nuclear threats were credible" and that, as a result, "the Soviets had successfully coerced – or, more precisely, compelled – China to come to the negotiating table."[212]

But a closer look tells a different story. What did the Soviets actually gain from their brinkmanship behavior in 1969? In fact, they gained very little. At most, Soviet threats seem to have persuaded the Chinese government to participate in negotiations over the border dispute. But once negotiations commenced, China proceeded to stonewall the Soviets on virtually every major point of contention. China agreed to a few minor crisis-management safeguards, including limits on border patrolling and the establishment of a direct governmental hotline from Beijing to Moscow.[213] But the major concessions during the talks were made by the Soviets, not the Chinese: indeed, the Soviet Union accepted China's preferred line of demarcation, effectively relinquishing claims to roughly 600 river islands. By early February 1970, the Soviets had withdrawn from many of the islands they had previously controlled, including Zhenbao.[214] Wich puts it succinctly: "It was Moscow that repeatedly made the concessions, and the Chinese remained in possession of the disputed island that had sparked the fighting."[215] If the 1969 crisis is a success for nuclear coercion, it is a feeble one.

The crisis poses other awkward puzzles for brinkmanship theory as well. One is that China's decision to meet Kosygin on September 11 was driven mainly by fear of an attack against its nuclear facilities, not its population centers. Brinkmanship theory argues that nuclear weapons coerce because of their ability to inflict "catastrophe": millions of deaths and massive economic destruction. Yet this is not what Chinese leaders feared when they agreed to negotiate. Chinese deterrent threats throughout the crisis mainly tried to dissuade Moscow from attempting a *limited* strike, not a massive nuclear barrage.[216] If

---

[212] Gerson (2010, 46).

[213] Robinson (1981, 281) and Garthoff (1985, 240–41).

[214] Wich (1980, 212) and Fravel (2008, 216). See also Gelman (1982, 45).

[215] Wich (1980, 276). McGeorge Bundy (1988, 533) likewise writes: "Nuclear threats were uttered, but the most that can be claimed for them is that they persuaded Zhou Enlai to meet Kosygin for a talk at the Beijing airport. They did not make him say very much, and in the end it was the Soviets who took the lead in easing the crisis."

[216] During their September 11 meeting, for example, Zhou warned Kosygin: "You say that you will take preemptive measures to destroy our nuclear

nuclear weapons mattered in the 1969 crisis, it was not for the reasons envisioned by brinkmanship theorists.[217]

Eventually, Chinese leaders did begin to fear a wider nuclear attack. Their anxiety peaked on two occasions. First, they worried that the Soviets would exploit a Chinese national holiday to launch a surprise attack on October 1, and undertook extensive military preparations in anticipation of such an attack. Second, Mao reportedly began to "panic" about a Soviet attack in the days leading up to the October 20 negotiations, fearing that the plane carrying Soviet diplomats would instead be armed with nuclear air-to-surface missiles. Mao was so convinced that the Soviets were planning a sneak attack that he ordered an evacuation of top leaders from Beijing, reasoning that "one atomic bomb may eliminate all of us."[218]

For brinkmanship theory, there are two inconvenient facts here. First, the timing of events belies the view that China's decision to negotiate was driven by a credible nuclear threat against Beijing. The Soviet nuclear threat was most credible in the days just before negotiations began on October 20. But by this point, China had already agreed to Soviet demands: Zhou met with Kosygin on September 11 and by late September had agreed to the October 20 start date. In other words, Chinese concessions preceded the credibility of the threat, not vice versa. Second, it is noteworthy that even as Mao supposedly grew frantic about the prospect of a Soviet attack in mid-October, he made no effort to appease the Soviets with additional concessions. Indeed, Chinese negotiators promptly adopted a hardline stance toward the Soviets as soon as the talks began.

In short, the events of the 1969 crisis offer little support for the view that nuclear weapons are useful tools of coercion. The Soviets' belligerent behavior during the crisis succeeded in creating a credible

---

facilities. If you do so, we will declare that this is war, and that this is aggression. We will rise in resistance. We will fight to the end." See Yang (2000, 38). Similar deterrent threats are cataloged in Gerson (2010, 43,47).

[217] Indeed, a 1970 National Intelligence Estimate concluded that the Chinese agreed to negotiate mainly to avoid "risking their nuclear installations." See U.S. Central Intelligence Agency (1970a, 8).

[218] Yang (2000, 36). These events are also recounted by Lewis and Xue (2006, 59–70) and Gerson (2010, 48–52). Lewis and Xue (2006, 57) translate Mao's warning somewhat differently, as "even one atomic bomb will kill many of us."

threat of nuclear attack, but in the end they could not translate that credibility into bargaining leverage.

Yom Kippur War, 1973

On October 6, 1973, a coalition of Arab forces, led by Egypt and Syria, attacked Israel on two fronts: the Egyptian army moved into the Sinai Peninsula, while the Syrians crossed the ceasefire line in the Golan Heights. Arab forces made unexpected gains in the initial days of the conflict, resulting in significant losses for the Israeli Defense Forces.[219] The unfavorable military situation created a sense of panic in Jerusalem. By some accounts, after visiting the command centers on both fronts, Defense Minister Moshe Dayan said, "this is now a war for the land of Israel," implying that the survival of the Jewish state was at risk.[220] In a moment of desperation, Israel allegedly used its nuclear arsenal to blackmail the United States.

Declassified minutes from a meeting of the war cabinet on October 9 reveal that Israeli officials, including Prime Minister Golda Meir, believed that success in the war could hinge on securing immediate military aid from Washington.[221] However, the United States was initially reluctant to resupply Israeli forces, in part because Washington did not want to harm its relations with the Arab world. "The best result," Secretary of State Henry Kissinger calculated early in the war, "would be if Israel came out a little ahead but got bloodied in the process, and if the U.S. stayed clean."[222] Washington was therefore in no hurry to openly assist its struggling ally. Israel may have used nuclear brinkmanship to force the United States to act.

Israeli Nuclear Brinkmanship and the U.S. Response

In the early stages of the war, Israel increased the readiness level of its Jericho missile batteries, one of Israel's key nuclear delivery systems.[223] The United States detected the Jericho alert, and at least some officials

---

[219] Just three days into the war, Israel lost forty-nine planes and 500 tanks.
[220] *Haaretz* (2013).
[221] Israel State Archives (1973).
[222] Isaacson (2005, 514).
[223] Colby et al. (2013, 34).

in Washington viewed it as a clear attempt to secure U.S. military aid. William B. Quandt, who served on the NSC during the war, later wrote,

We did know around this time [October 9]...that Israel had placed its Jericho missiles on alert. I did not not know what kind of warheads they had, but it did not make much sense to me that they would be equipped with conventional ordnance...Without being told in so many words, we knew that a desperate Israel might activate its nuclear option. This situation, by itself, created a kind of blackmail potential. "Help us or else ..."[224]

Hermann Eilts, who was an adviser in the State Department during the war, shared this view: "the Israelis were opening some of the nuclear hatches, so to speak, of the missiles, and this was intended ...to influence us to get off of our tails and to get some equipment to Israel."[225]

Some sources suggest that Meir authorized equipping thirteen Jerichos and eight F-4 Phantom fighters with nuclear weapons.[226] However, no reliable evidence substantiates the notion that she authorized a nuclear alert, though it is plausible that Dayan authorized the change in status of the Jerichos without the prime minister's approval. Arnan "Sini" Azaryahu, who provides the only credible Israeli eyewitness testimony on the nuclear dimension of the 1973 Yom Kippur War, indicates that the prime minister closed the door on the nuclear option. According to Azaryahu, after a meeting of the war cabinet adjourned on October 7, on his way out the door, Dayan asked Meir to make technical preparations for a "nuclear option for demonstration."[227] This suggestion triggered sharp criticism from two ministers in the war cabinet, Yisrael Galili and Yigal Allon, who indicated that "we shouldn't panic." Meir agreed, and she told Dayan to "forget it." The prime minister said, according to Azaryahu's account, "we will fight with conventional weapons without involving any other means, directly or indirectly."[228] Israel therefore appears to have exercised some restraint, even in a moment of frenzy.

---

[224] Quandt (1991).
[225] Parker (2001, 121).
[226] For example, Sale (2002).
[227] It is not clear what Dayan meant by "demonstration," but one possibility was to conduct nuclear explosions over unpopulated areas in Egypt or Syria.
[228] Cohen (2008).

The Effects of Israel's Nuclear Signals

Many have argued that Israeli nuclear blackmail worked, even though Israel was probably further from the nuclear brink than is often assumed.[229] According to this view, the prospect of nuclear escalation forced the United States to do something it preferred not to – namely, equip the the Israeli military with planes and munitions. To be sure, the Israelis got what they wanted following their implicit nuclear threat: the United States began a large scale airlift to resupply Israel on October 13, a week after the outbreak of the war. But did Israeli nuclear signals cause this shift in U.S. policy?

The historical record does not allow us to answer this question with certainty. However, the evidence suggesting that the Jericho alert influenced U.S. policy is tenuous. Based on an exhaustive review of classified and unclassified U.S. sources, a study by the Center for Naval Analyses concluded that "neither any involved American official (including Quandt) nor any piece of official documentation lends credence to the proposition that specific Israeli nuclear weapons activity had a material impact on U.S. decision making regarding the resupply airlift or any other facet of the war."[230] Kissinger issued an unequivocal denial when asked about Israeli nuclear coercion three years after the war: "The airlift was decided on the evening of the 12th. The Israelis' nuclear capability didn't have a god damn thing to do with it."[231] Statements such as this should be viewed cautiously because U.S. officials might have incentives to deny that they were coerced, even if they were. Still, the lack of confirmation from any of the key players on the U.S. side casts doubt on the notion that Israeli nuclear coercion worked in 1973.

If senior U.S. officials worried about the possibility of Israeli nuclear escalation during the first week of the war, they certainly did not act like it. Washington dawdled when it came to implementing the airlift, allowing a bureaucratic spat to delay the arrival of supplies by several days.[232] One would assume that the Nixon administration would have

---

[229] For example, Hersh (1991, 225–40) and Narang (2014, 187–89).

[230] Colby et al. (2013). The mention of Quandt is important because, as Cohen (2012, 81) notes, Quandt saw reports of Israeli nuclear signaling as "critical to the American decision to initiate the airlift to Israel."

[231] U.S. Department of State (1976).

[232] Isaacson (2005, 515–22).

begun to resupply Israel immediately, beginning on October 9, if it genuinely believed that Israel was on the cusp of launching a nuclear attack against its neighbors. As Quandt argues, if nuclear blackmail occurred, "we were surprisingly slow to respond with a decision on a massive infusion of arms for Israel."[233]

Instead, at least three other factors can account for the onset of the airlift. First, the Soviet Union began openly resupplying the Arab armies on October 8, motivating Washington to reciprocate by sending equipment to Israel.[234] As Rodger Davies, Deputy Assistant Secretary of State, told the Yemeni ambassador on October 10, "there is growing evidence of a massive Soviet resupply of aircraft and ammunition to the Arab states and this will put great pressure on the U.S. to resupply Israel."[235] The Soviet airlift ultimately "engaged Nixon's fighting instincts," and pushed the United States into action.[236] Second, the U.S. was inspired to action by Egyptian president Anwar Sadat's rejection of a ceasefire resolution at the UN. As Kissinger explained, the resolution's failure made it necessary to bolster Israel's military situation so that "[the Arabs] would have to ask for a cease-fire rather than we." "This," he went on to say, "is the principal reason why we started the airlift on October 13."[237] Third, the Nixon administration faced significant domestic pressure.[238] All three of these considerations influenced U.S. policy at least as much as – and probably more than – Israel's nuclear signaling.

Arab Perceptions of Israeli Brinkmanship

Some have argued that the target of Israeli signaling was not the United States, but instead Egypt and Syria. According to this view, Israel's message was clear: limit the offensive or there will be dire consequences.[239] Did the Egyptians or the Syrians modify their behavior based on the apparent Jericho alert? Syrian forces halted their advance

---

[233] Quandt (1991).
[234] Israelyan (1995, 57).
[235] U.S. Department of State (1973a).
[236] Isaacson (2005, 519).
[237] U.S. Department of State (1973b, 694).
[238] Colby et al. (2013, 38).
[239] Hersh (1991, 227). However, since only the Soviet Union had the capability to detect changes to Israel's nuclear forces, the message would have to be passed along by the Soviets.

on October 7, leading some to speculate that "there may have been a veiled Israeli hint concerning nuclear weapons dropped in Damascus' ears" if the invasion did not stop.[240] Yet the evidence for this conjecture is thin. According to Murhaf Jouejati, officials in Damascus "knew that Israel had a massive nuclear capability, but did not take that option seriously."[241] Numerous factors unrelated to Israel's nuclear weapons can explain the abrupt halt to the Syrian offensive, including fuel and ammunition shortages, a desire to reorganize following two days of fighting, and concerns about exposing the army's flank.[242]

This does not imply that Israel's nuclear weapons were irrelevant in 1973. Its arsenal likely deterred Egypt and Syria from adopting more ambitious war aims. The Arab states had fairly modest objectives – to recapture territory lost in the 1967 Six Day War – presumably because they knew prior to launching an attack that Israeli might resort to atomic weapons if its survival were on the line.[243] Indeed, Anwar Sadat acknowledged to Ezer Weizman, the Israeli defense minister, that he never intended to push deeper into the Sinai Peninsula because "he knew what Israel had," an apparent reference to atomic weapons.[244] Nuclear weapons, then, may have deterred further escalation of the war. But it does not appear that Israel's nuclear brinkmanship played any role in coercing the United States, Egypt, or Syria in 1973.

The U.S. Nuclear Alert: Did It Work?

Israel was not the only country to use nuclear brinkmanship during the Yom Kippur War – the United States used its nuclear arsenal for political purposes as well. A superpower showdown occurred at the end of the war that seemed "as ominous as any since the Cuban missile crisis."[245] Israel violated UN-backed cease-fire agreements on October 22 and 23, and seemed to be on the cusp of destroying Egypt's Third Army. Sadat, who hoped to avoid a humiliating defeat for Egypt, pleaded with Moscow and Washington to send troops to enforce the

---

[240] Van Creveld (1993, 102).
[241] Parker (2001, 119).
[242] Dunstan (2007, 166–67).
[243] Colby et al. (2013, 11).
[244] Colby et al. (2013, 10–11).
[245] Isaacson (2005, 529).

cease-fire. Soviet officials, many of whom wanted the United States to compel Israel to stop fighting, favored the proposal. However, the United States viewed it as a nonstarter. U.S. officials, particularly Kissinger, were unwilling to permit the reintroduction of Soviet troops into Egypt for any reason. In response to Washington's rejection of the proposal, Soviet leader Leonid Brezhnev sent a letter to Washington threatening to "consider the question of taking appropriate steps unilaterally" if the United States deemed it "impossible to act jointly with us in this manner."[246] Washington then sent a nuclear signal to Moscow: Kissinger placed U.S. forces at DEFCON 3, the highest state of peacetime military readiness, shortly before midnight on October 24.[247]

The nuclear alert was intended to do two things: deter the Soviet Union and coerce Egypt. Washington sought to prevent Moscow from sending troops by raising the possibility of nuclear war. At the same time, the United States wanted to apply pressure on Egypt. Washington sent a letter to Sadat shortly after authorizing the move to DEFCON 3 that contained an ultimatum – stop asking Moscow to send troops or there would be grave consequences. The letter, which was sent in Nixon's name, invoked the possibility of nuclear war: "I ask you to consider the consequences for your country if the two great nuclear countries were thus to confront each other on your soil."[248]

For his part, Kissinger argued that U.S. nuclear brinkmanship worked, claiming that "the Soviets had backed off" due to American resolve.[249] After all, Moscow refrained from deploying troops to Egypt after the U.S. nuclear alert. Egypt also seemed to comply with the U.S. demand. Cairo sent a prompt reply to Nixon's letter, indicating that it would request a UN peacekeeping force that excluded the permanent five members of the Security Council, which included the Soviet Union and the United States. On the surface, then, this appears to be a case of successful nuclear diplomacy.

---

[246] Isaacson (2005, 530).

[247] Nixon, who was distracted by the Watergate scandal, was asleep during the meeting where his advisers decided to alert American nuclear forces. Kissinger and Alexander Haig, Nixon's chief of staff, made a conscious decision not to wake up the president, believing that he was not in the right state of mind to make an important national security decision. See Israelyan (1993).

[248] Kissinger (2003, 351).

[249] Isaacson (2005, 532).

A close look at the evidence, however, suggests otherwise. There is little evidence that the U.S. nuclear threat had anything to do with Egypt's behavior at the end of the war. Egyptian officials, including Sadat, viewed the nuclear alert as an empty and meaningless gesture.[250] The Soviets detected the nuclear alert, but were not sure how to interpret it. Very few members of the Politburo recognized – at least initially – that Brezhnev's threat to unilaterally send troops to Egypt had triggered the move to DEFCON 3. Brezhnev openly wondered, "What has this [the U.S. nuclear alert] to do with the letter I sent to Nixon?"[251] A letter from Nixon arrived shortly thereafter, stating that the United States "must view your suggestion of unilateral action as a matter of the gravest concern involving incalculable consequences," but it did not connect the Soviet proposal to the nuclear alert.[252] Brezhnev fumed: "After having unilaterally declared a nuclear alert, they dare to criticize us! Something is wrong with the American logic."[253] Moreover, most Soviet officials did not take the DEFCON 3 alert seriously, viewing it as "blackmail, a step taken for the benefit of the American audience."[254] In the end, Moscow decided to disregard the nuclear alert. "Nixon is too nervous – let's cool him down," Brezhnev concluded.[255] This evidence underscores two key components of our nuclear skepticism theory: nuclear signals may not be interpreted properly, even if they are received; and those signals may have little effect even when they are received as intended.

There is one final problem with Kissinger's interpretation of the October 24 superpower crisis: it is too simplistic to imply that the Americans "won" and the Soviets "lost." Moscow's goal all along was to persuade the United States to pressure Israel to enforce a ceasefire, which Washington ultimately did.[256] Suggesting that the United States prevailed in a game of nuclear chicken in which Moscow blinked overlooks a more complicated picture.

[250] Israelyan (1995, 198).
[251] Israelyan (1995, 179).
[252] Nixon (1973, 2).
[253] Israelyan (1995, 188).
[254] Israelyan (1995, 202).
[255] Israelyan (1995, 182–83).
[256] Israelyan (1995, 186,190).

Evidence from Less Serious Nuclear Crises

Before concluding this chapter, we briefly turn our attention to three lower-profile cases in which nuclear blackmail also appears to have worked.

Suez Crisis, 1956

In response to Egyptian president Gamal Abdel Nassar's nationalization of the Suez Canal, British, French, and Israeli forces invaded the canal region in October 1956. Shortly thereafter, Soviet premier Nikolai Bulganin demanded that British and French troops halt their intervention and publicly raised the prospect of Soviet retaliation if they did not comply. Moscow also appeared to make veiled threats to use nuclear weapons: writing to British prime minister Anthony Eden on November 5, Bulganin asked rhetorically: "In what situation would Britain find herself if she was attacked by stronger states, possessing all types of modern destructive weapons?"[257] France and Britain quickly backed down, accepting a cease-fire just days after the operation began.

The critical question is whether the Soviet Union's possession of nuclear weapons contributed to this outcome. Robert Pape has argued that Soviet nuclear threats indeed played the decisive role, citing a personal telegram from British prime minister Anthony Eden that appears to implicate fears of Soviet unpredictability in his decision to back down.[258] Soviet leaders such as Nikita Khrushchev likewise believed that Moscow's nuclear brinkmanship had succeeded – a view that was shared by some British officials as well.[259] Yet other sources cast doubt on the notion that the prospect of a nuclear attack influenced British and French capitulation. Archival documents reveal that Khrushchev's perceptions of British and French calculations during the crisis were often incorrect.[260] Eden later suggested that widespread public opposition to the operation played a more important role than Soviet

[257] Fukuyama (1980, 6).
[258] Pape (1997, 116).
[259] Murphy (1964, 391), Cooper (1978, 197), Finer (1964, 417–418), and Fursenko and Naftali (2006, 126–37).
[260] Fursenko and Naftali (2006, 134–37).

threats.[261] Moreover, minutes from meetings of the British Cabinet during the crisis strongly suggest that the decision to halt military operations was induced not by Soviet belligerence but by American threats to block an International Monetary Fund package that Britain had hoped would stem its loss of gold reserves.[262] Shortly before Britain withdrew its forces from Suez, Britain's Foreign Secretary, Selwyn Lloyd, argued in a Cabinet meeting that "the economic considerations were now even more important than the political."[263] In light of this evidence, it is easy to see why Betts concluded that "there are no persuasive grounds" to believe that Soviet threats played a crucial role in the British decision to withdraw from the canal zone.[264]

The degree to which the Soviets engaged in nuclear brinkmanship is also questionable. Moscow made thinly veiled nuclear threats, but it did not attempt to manipulate risk with its nuclear arsenal by engaging in dangerous actions that raised the possibility of inadvertent escalation.[265] In fact, the Soviets appeared to take great care to avoid risky behavior, issuing threats only after it was already clear that offensive operations had been halted and a cease-fire was in place.[266] This made it easier for officials in London, Paris, and Washington to question the threat's credibility. Indeed, Eden's public relations adviser later characterized the threat as "twaddle," and the CIA concluded at the time that the Soviet ultimatum was a bluff.[267]

With so many factors pushing in the same direction and little motivation for the participants to reveal their true motives, a clear judgment here is unrealistic. At the very least, however, there is little support for the conclusion that nuclear weapons played a decisive role in compelling an end to the Suez operation in 1956.

Bangladesh War, 1971

In March 1971, conflict erupted in South Asia after Bangladesh, formerly known as East Pakistan, declared independence from

---

[261] Smolansky (1965, 596).

[262] Kirshner (1995, 68–70), Gorst and Johnman (1997, 126–45), Klug and Smith (1999), and Kelly (2000, 172–73).

[263] Gorst and Johnman (1997, 142).

[264] Betts (1987, 64).

[265] However, the United States did alert its strategic nuclear forces during the crisis (Betts, 1987, 64).

[266] Fukuyama (1980, 8) and Carnesale et al. (1983, 151).

[267] Betts (1987, 64–65) and Cooper (1978, 200).

Pakistan. With help from India, the Bangladeshi *Mukti Bahini* were on the verge of liberating East Pakistan by early December, just over eight months after the war started. As fighting subsided in the east, the United States feared that India planned to mount an offensive against West Pakistan, possibly with backing from Moscow. U.S. officials therefore decided on December 10 to deploy to the region a task force (known as "Task Force 74") that included the aircraft carrier *Enterprise*, the U.S. Navy's most impressive ship at the time.[268] This deployment appeared to constitute an implicit nuclear threat: there were seventy-five nuclear-armed bombers aboard the *Enterprise*, and the task force included a nuclear attack submarine.[269] The task force entered the Bay of Bengal on December 15. The next day, Indian prime minister Indira Gandhi agreed to an unconditional cease-fire, bringing an end to the conflict.

Henry Kissinger, who served as U.S. national security advisor during the crisis, claims in his memoirs that the deployment of the nuclear-armed task force caused India to stop fighting.[270] He contends, in particular, that the Soviet Union forced Gandhi to the negotiating table because of U.S. coercive measures. Others agree that U.S. nuclear threats helped bring an end to the war, and many Indian officials and strategists believe that New Delhi was a victim of nuclear blackmail in 1971. The *Enterprise* deployment embittered India, and may have contributed to its decision to seek a nuclear arsenal.[271]

However, there are several reasons to question whether U.S. nuclear measures played a role in ending the war. First, India did not seem to understand what Nixon was trying to accomplish with the *Enterprise* deployment. The U.S. signal, like so many others in the nuclear age, was misinterpreted. As Hall writes, "The Indian government ... found it extremely difficult to interpret the purpose of the naval force, or credibly link its mission to Nixon's objective of deterring military action against West Pakistan. For some four days Indian defense officials pondered the likely purpose of the U.S. task force; apparently they never reached a definitive conclusion."[272] It is unclear whether the Soviets had any better luck deciphering Nixon's intentions. Second, the timing of events is inconsistent with the coercionist story:

---

[268] Hall (1978, 188).
[269] Hall (1978, 188).
[270] Kissinger (1979, 913).
[271] Perkovich (1999, 165–66, 171, 230–31).
[272] Hall (1978, 192).

having lasted more than eight months, the war was effectively over by the time the *Enterprise* arrived in the Bay of Bengal.[273] Third, India's acceptance of a ceasefire agreement is better explained by other factors. New Delhi had already achieved its basic war aims, and it was clear that the international community was not prepared to tolerate military action against West Pakistan.[274] Indeed, in light of these considerations, one of the most thorough treatments of this crisis concludes flatly that "Soviet and Indian support for a cease-fire was not the result of U.S. military pressure generated by Task Force 74."[275]

Kashmir Crisis, 1990

India and Pakistan experienced a serious crisis over Kashmir in early 1990.[276] During the crisis, Pakistan may have used nuclear threats to coerce the United States. In particular, some have alleged that Pakistan prepared its nuclear arsenal to compel Washington to intervene on its behalf, thereby preventing India from launching an attack.[277] Washington did, in fact, become involved in the dispute. After a Pakistani-supported insurgency erupted in Indian-controlled Kashmir, both countries amassed troops near the border and began issuing military threats.[278] Sensing that events could escalate quickly, the United States sent then-Deputy National Security Advisor Robert Gates to the region in May.[279] Shortly thereafter, India announced that it would withdraw some of its deployed forces, and the crisis subsided.

---

[273] Ganguly and Hagerty (2005, 34).

[274] Van Hollen (1980, 356).

[275] Hall (1978, 136).

[276] This case could be viewed as South Asia's first real nuclear crisis. Pakistan may have sent nuclear signals as early as 1984, and Pakistani officials may have issued nuclear threats during the 1987 Brasstacks crisis (though they were ignored by India) (Langewiesche, 2005; Chari, 2013). However, these cases typically are not regarded as overt nuclear crises (Chari et al., 2007, 66–67). The 1990 crisis over Kashmir had a more significant nuclear component, but it is widely seen as less serious than subsequent Indo-Pakistani nuclear crises, particularly those of 1999 and 2001–02. Ganguly and Hagerty (2005, 82) argue that the 1990 crisis "was not a nuclear crisis *per se*; rather it was a political crisis between two hostile neighbours who had already fought three wars and who were secretly developing nuclear weapons."

[277] See, for example, Hersh (1993) and Narang (2014, 265–67).

[278] Ganguly and Hagerty (2005, 87–90).

[279] Narang (2014, 66).

To what extent is this a case of successful nuclear coercion? It seems plausible that Pakistan's nuclear capability influenced U.S. decision making to some degree.[280] However, the magnitude of Pakistan's nuclear brinkmanship has often been exaggerated. Journalist Seymour Hersh, for example, argues that Pakistani general Aslam Beg authorized technicians at Kahuta to assemble nuclear weapons. At that point, he alleges, Pakistan moved equipment from a storage site for nuclear bombs to a nearby air base where Islamabad was believed to house nuclear-capable F-16s.[281] However, these claims have been challenged by others, including officials who were involved in the crisis. For example, Robert Oakley, the U.S. ambassador to Pakistan, said, "we never had any credible evidence that the F-16s were fitted out to deliver a nuclear device; that Pakistan had a nuclear device that could be delivered by an F-16 ... Nor did we know anything about any nuclear devices being moved from point 'x' to point 'y,' if there were any." Oakley added, "we were not worried about a conflict becoming nuclear. There's always that potential, but there was nothing at that time [when Gates was sent to South Asia] to indicate that this was the case."[282] This evidence, combined with similar statements from other officials,[283] casts doubt on the effects of Islamabad's coercive nuclear threats in 1990.

On top of this, several nonnuclear factors can account for the rolling back of tensions in 1990. First, India realized that it could not achieve a swift military victory against Pakistan, and de-escalated the crisis. Second, both sides feared that they would not receive support from major power patrons if the crisis escalated. Third, war would have harmed the Indian and Pakistani economies at a time when both states were trying to attract foreign investment.[284] Islamabad and New Delhi thus had their own reasons to exercise restraint, regardless of U.S. pressure brought on by Pakistan's nuclear threats. The nuclear element may have mattered as well, but it was probably less important than is sometimes asserted. As Chari, Cheema, and Cohen conclude, nuclear weapons do not "appear to have been a determining factor

---

[280] The strongest evidence for this view comes from Narang (2014, 65–69).

[281] Hersh (1993). See also Narang (2014, 67).

[282] Krepon and Faruqee (1994, 21, 39–40).

[283] See Krepon and Faruqee (1994) for a host of officials who dispute Hersh's account of the nuclear dimensions of the crisis.

[284] Chari et al. (2007, 116–17).

... This aspect of the crisis has attracted the most publicity in the West, although the 'nuclear' dimension was smaller than is made out in some accounts."[285]

At best, the 1990 crisis is a case of *indirect* nuclear coercion: a coercer (Pakistan) threatened to attack its adversary (India) to force a third party (the United States) to act. But there is scant evidence that Pakistan's nuclear threats had coercive effects on India itself. Pakistan may have conveyed a verbal nuclear threat to India. When meeting with officials in New Delhi during the crisis, Pakistan's minister of foreign affairs, Yaqub Khan, made several statements that could be construed as references to nuclear attack.[286] It is unclear whether Indian leaders perceived these statements as atomic threats, although some have argued that they did.[287] In any case, neither verbal threats nor the alleged Pakistani nuclear alert appears to have forced India to revise the status quo.[288]

If Pakistan readied its nuclear arsenal, officials in New Delhi did not seem to notice or care.[289] As Indian foreign minister S.K. Singh said, the government "failed to see Pakistan's 'burgeoning' nuclear capability as a major... threat to ourselves."[290] George Perkovich substantiates this view when discussing Gates' trip to South Asia: "the American team did not find the Indians worrying explicitly about a nuclear threat from Pakistan. The Indians did not know of the activity detected by American intelligence and Gates did not tell them about it ... India perceived the situation in terms of domestic politics, instability in Kashmir, and Pakistani subversion, not a nuclear threat."[291] Even those who argue that Pakistani nuclear threats coerced the United States acknowledge that they had little effect on India.[292]

---

[285] Chari et al. (2007, 117).
[286] An example of one such statement is Khan's remark that "the clouds are roaring with thunder." See Chari et al. (2007, 101).
[287] Ganguly and Hagerty (2005, 105).
[288] However, some have argued that Pakistan's nuclear threats deterred India from launching a war. See, for example, Ganguly and Hagerty (2005, 104–07).
[289] Chari et al. (2007, 104).
[290] Quoted in Kapur (2007, 111).
[291] Perkovich (1999, 310).
[292] Narang (2014, 266).

Conclusion

The chapter critically assessed ten apparently successful cases of nuclear coercion. These cases should have provided the clearest evidence in favor of the view that nuclear blackmail works. However, none of them unequivocally supports the nuclear coercionist school. In each case, there is some doubt – often considerable doubt – about whether nuclear weapons provided states with coercive leverage. Indeed, several of these crises provide strong support for nuclear skepticism theory, highlighting the challenges that countries face when attempting to employ nuclear signals for coercive purposes.

It is worth noting that the cases that provide the strongest support for the nuclear coercionist view – including the Cuban missile crisis – happened in the early days of the Cold War. The world has changed dramatically since that time. It is hard to argue that cases from the 1950s and 1960s tell us much about the role of nuclear weapons in world politics today. There is scant evidence that nuclear blackmail has worked since the collapse of the Soviet Union. The nuclear crises of the last quarter-century illustrate the coercive limits, rather than the virtues, of nuclear weapons.

PART IV

Conclusions

7 | *Nuclear Coercion in Myth and Reality*

What is the role of nuclear weapons in world politics? The political effects of nuclear weapons were central to the study of international relations during the Cold War. However, after the collapse of the Soviet Union, many people assumed that nuclear weapons were no longer relevant. Careful thinking about nuclear deterrence ground to a halt.

Events soon reminded us that nuclear weapons did not disappear with the end of the Cold War. India and Pakistan tested nuclear weapons in 1998. The United States invaded Iraq in 2003, in part due to concerns about Saddam Hussein's nuclear ambitions. North Korea withdrew from the Non-Proliferation Treaty and joined the nuclear club, carrying out its first successful nuclear explosion in 2006. Iran recently appeared to be on the cusp of building nuclear weapons. Clearly, nuclear weapons continue to influence the contemporary international landscape in many ways. Yet the field of international relations has been unable to answer critical questions about this new nuclear era.

One of those unanswered questions is how nuclear weapons shape the dynamics of coercion in international politics. An emerging wisdom – which we call the "nuclear coercionist" school – holds that nuclear weapons provide states with tremendous political leverage. According to this view, nuclear powers have special advantages in international diplomacy. Not only are they better able to deter attacks against themselves and their allies, but they can also win crises with greater ease and extract political concessions more effectively than nonnuclear countries. Nuclear weapons, according to coercionist logic, are useful for much more than self-defense – they also help states engage in military coercion.

This book has challenged this notion. It has offered an alternative theoretical approach, nuclear skepticism theory, that better explains the role of nuclear weapons in international affairs. This perspective argues that nuclear weapons do not help states throw their weight around in world politics. The reason is that it is exceedingly difficult to make coercive nuclear threats believable. Nuclear blackmail does not work because threats to launch nuclear attacks for offensive political purposes fundamentally lack credibility.

Three main factors work to undermine the credibility of coercive nuclear threats. First, nuclear weapons generally do not help states achieve coercive objectives by force. They are not useful for seizing territory, and they are often militarily redundant to a coercer's conventional capabilities. Second, the political, military, and economic costs of launching a nuclear attack are prohibitive, particularly if a challenger's political objectives are offensive in nature. And third, coercion by its very nature generally is a lower-stakes enterprise for coercers, in contrast to deterrence. These problems combine to render nuclear arsenals unhelpful in most coercive contexts.

The preceding chapters marshaled a vast array of evidence supporting the skeptical view. We first examined broad historical trends, analyzing whether nuclear-armed states tend to make more effective coercive threats (Chapter 3) or achieve better settlements in territorial disputes (Chapter 4). The evidence shows, quite simply, that they do not. Next, we took a close look at the most serious nuclear crises that have occurred over the last seventy years – cases in which countries tried to invoke their nuclear arsenals for coercive leverage. On several occasions, these states failed despite making serious nuclear threats (Chapter 5). Even when we examined episodes of successful coercion, however, the historical evidence did not clearly confirm – and in some cases clearly refuted – the importance of nuclear weapons in making those threats work (Chapter 6). Taken together, the weight of the evidence shows that nuclear weapons provide states with little coercive leverage. Nuclear arsenals may be good for self-defense, but they do not allow countries to dominate world politics.

Our conclusions arrive at a critical juncture. Now, as much as ever, it is important for policymakers and scholars to understand the role of nuclear weapons in international relations. Yet there is considerable confusion about what states can and cannot accomplish with nuclear arsenals. Informed observers hold many beliefs about the political effects of nuclear weapons that are wrong – and possibly dangerous.

Nuclear Coercion: A Reality Check

Since the beginning of the atomic age, nuclear weapons have captured the world's imagination. When English physicist James Chadwick discovered the neutron in the early 1930s, he launched more than a decade of frenetic progress in atomic research. In 1938, German physicists discovered how to split a uranium atom's nucleus by bombarding it with neutrons. The following year, Enrico Fermi proposed and tested a method for turning this "fission" process into a controlled chain reaction. With the outbreak of World War II, the quest to control the atom became more urgent, as scientists quickly grasped the possible military applications of atomic fission. These possibilities were realized in 1945, with the successful detonation of the first atomic weapon.

Seven decades have passed since the first man-made atomic explosion. During this time, a popular narrative has gradually emerged about the role that nuclear weapons play in world politics. This narrative equates the unprecedented destructive power of nuclear weapons with equally unprecedented political power. In nuclear folklore, a nuclear weapon is the ultimate coercive bargaining tool. This is why nations have made tremendous sacrifices to obtain it – and to keep it from their rivals. If international diplomacy is a high-stakes game of poker, then a nuclear weapon is a royal flush.

Like any good legend, the folklore surrounding nuclear weapons is based partly in reality. It starts with an irrefutable observation: nuclear weapons are the most destructive weapons known to man. But this simple fact has grown into an elaborate mythology, fueled by scholars, political leaders, and journalists. Ten beliefs in particular have shaped our thinking about nuclear weapons for much of the nuclear age. On close inspection, however, these beliefs do not stand up to scrutiny.

Myth #1: Nuclear Weapons Are a Diplomatic Magic Wand

The first and most important of these myths is that nuclear weapons are effective tools of coercive diplomacy. Leaders in possession of nuclear weapons, according to this line of thinking, can manipulate the behavior of other countries with relative ease. They can do so because nuclear weapons impose tremendous punishment: if a state resists a demand made by a nuclear power, it could suffer catastrophic consequences. Opponents of nuclear states therefore have no choice but to heed the wishes of their militarily superior counterparts. In particular, nuclear threats succeed where conventional threats may fail. As Robert Pape argues, "nuclear coercion works better than conventional coercion."[1]

This view, which is central to the nuclear coercionist perspective, is widely held within governmental circles. Since the onset of the atomic age, many world leaders – including Mao Zedong, John F. Kennedy, Saddam Hussein, and George W. Bush – have suggested that nuclear arsenals provide coercive benefits, either for themselves or for their nuclear-armed enemies. This belief is particularly pervasive today in the context of the ongoing crisis over Iran's nuclear program: many officials have argued that a nuclear Iran would be able to bully and intimidate other countries – including the United States.

Scholars also have trumpeted the political and diplomatic benefits of nuclear arsenals. In his classic book on nuclear blackmail, Richard Betts reached a guardedly optimistic conclusion about the efficacy of nuclear coercion: "Attempts to exploit nuclear leverage in the past," he argued, "seem useful at best and not costly at worst."[2] Since Betts' study was published, analysts have grown even more optimistic in their assessments. In the post–Cold War era, the notion that atomic arsenals confer coercive bargaining power has gained widespread acceptance. A growing number of studies seem to take for granted the idea that nuclear weapons are useful for things other than deterrence. One recent study, for example, argues that nuclear proliferation "directly affects the local balance of power, increasing newly nuclear states' bargaining leverage vis-à-vis their neighbors."[3] Another contends that nuclear weapons allow states to achieve "success in diplomatic wrangling."[4] Numerous other studies express similar views.[5]

Our study suggests a very different conclusion. The historical record overwhelmingly refutes the notion that nuclear weapons help states bully and intimidate their rivals. Our statistical tests revealed that

---

[1] Pape (1996, 9).

[2] Betts (1987, 218).

[3] Dittmeier (2013, 494). Indeed, Dittmeier claims that regional nuclear powers can extract even more coercive leverage from their arsenals than the superpowers could.

[4] Gartzke and Jo (2009, 217).

[5] See, for example, Bueno de Mesquita and Riker (1982), Horowitz and Reiter (2001), Gelpi and Griesdorf (2001), Beardsley and Asal (2009b), and Thayer and Skypek (2013).

nuclear powers are no better than other states at extracting coercive concessions from their rivals. Further, our analysis of nineteen historical cases demonstrated that nuclear coercion rarely works at all. New nuclear powers like India, Pakistan, and North Korea have experienced the same frustrations that the United States and the Soviet Union did during the Cold War. Just like the superpowers, these countries have had little success using the threat of nuclear war to extract concessions from their adversaries.

Scholars sometimes assume that military capabilities – and especially nuclear capabilities – work something like money: those with more of it can purchase whatever they want. Our research suggests otherwise. Nuclear weapons are not the currency of power in international relations. Instead, they more closely resemble "Monopoly" money: while they can be very useful under specific circumstances, they are of little value in most other contexts. As a deterrent to invasion or large-scale attack, nuclear weapons are undoubtedly valuable. For coercion, however, their utility is minimal.

Myth #2: Nuclear Weapons Give America Coercive Leverage

A related myth suggests that the United States has a special ability to extract political leverage from its nuclear arsenal. Many scholars and American officials believe that Washington can, in fact, advance its interests abroad more effectively because it has nuclear weapons. In a recent book, for instance, Paul Bracken calls the atomic bomb "a most useful weapon" for the United States, in part, because it helps America prevail in crises.[6] Proponents of this view often point to the Korean War (1953), the Indochina War (1954), the Taiwan Strait crises (1954–1955 and 1958), and the Cuban missile crisis (1962) as illustrative examples. In these cases, analysts argue, the United States compelled its opponents to make concessions by raising the possibility of nuclear escalation.[7]

By this reasoning, if the United States did not have nuclear weapons today, it would be unable to coerce its adversaries. Reducing or eliminating the U.S. nuclear arsenal would undermine Washington's political leverage and cause it to lose – or be unable to initiate – future crises. Many scholars and policymakers have opposed calls for U.S.

---

[6] Bracken (2012, 32–58).
[7] See, for example, Betts (1987), Trachtenberg (1991), and Pape (1996).

nuclear arsenal reductions on these grounds. Conventional weapons, one study argues, are no substitute for the "unique deterrent and coercive roles of nuclear weapons for advancing the interests of the United States."[8] Instead, this study concludes, a robust nuclear arsenal is necessary to "provide deterrent and coercive capabilities the United States has needed in the past, depends on now, and will in the future."

There is no question that the United States at times has tried to use its nuclear arsenal for coercive purposes. Indeed, Washington has used nuclear brinkmanship in an attempt to overturn the status quo more frequently than any other country. However, even a charitable reading of the evidence reveals that the U.S. record of nuclear diplomacy is not particularly enviable. While nuclear weapons seem to have played a role in several serious crises during the 1950s and 1960s, historical analysis casts doubt on the notion that nuclear threats were decisive in any of these cases. In most cases, factors other than the U.S. nuclear arsenal better account for the final outcome. Even in the Cuban missile crisis – the case that offers the clearest evidence in favor of the nuclear coercionist view – the evidence that U.S. nuclear brinkmanship caused the Soviet Union to back down is circumstantial.

Things only get worse for the nuclear coercionist perspective when we look beyond this episode. The Cold War offers several instructive examples of the coercive limits of U.S. nuclear weapons. For example, the U.S. nuclear arsenal did not help secure the return of the *Pueblo* from North Korea in 1968, even though the United States deployed nuclear forces to the region. U.S. coercive diplomacy failed during the *Mayaguez* dispute with Cambodia (1975) and the hostage crisis with Iran (1979). American threats of military force likewise did not compel Saddam Hussein to withdraw from Kuwait prior to the 1991 Persian Gulf War, a failure that is particularly notable in light of new evidence from captured Iraqi documents showing that he and his advisors thought that the United States might actually carry out nuclear strikes against Iraq.[9] Iraq stood firm in the face of U.S. coercive threats despite

---

[8] Thayer and Skypek (2013, 44).

[9] On November 2, 1990, two months before the start of Operation Desert Storm, Izzat Ibrahim al-Duri, one of Saddam's closest advisors, argued in a meeting, "We must also expect that the United States could hit us with a nuclear bomb. If the United States hits us and after six or seven months did not get the result [it wanted]. . . it is possible that it would use nuclear bombs to strike two or three cities." Quoted in Palkki (2014, 16).

believing that the nuclear option was plausible. Washington ultimately got its way, but it had to fight a costly war to push Iraqi forces out of Kuwait.

In the post–Cold War era, nuclear weapons have provided even fewer coercive benefits to the United States. Consider some recent U.S. failures of coercive diplomacy. Despite possessing a formidable nuclear arsenal, Washington failed to compel Serbian forces to evacuate Kosovo without a fight, terminate North Korea's nuclear program, make Afghanistan hand over al Qaeda leaders, or coerce Russian forces into leaving the Crimean peninsula. If nuclear weapons had blackmail benefits for the United States, these failures should have been victories.

Of course, the United States has also prevailed in several recent crises. For example, it coerced Haiti's military junta into stepping down and restoring Jean-Bertrand Aristide to power in 1994, compelled Iraq to readmit weapons inspectors in 1998, and coerced Syria into surrendering its chemical weapons in 2013–2014. Yet nuclear weapons had little to do with these successes. When the United States has prevailed in post–Cold War disputes, it has been because of its overwhelming conventional military power.

None of this implies that Washington could eliminate its nuclear arsenal without suffering any strategic setbacks. As we have made clear, dismantling the U.S. nuclear arsenal could have potentially serious consequences for America's ability to deter enemies. But the U.S. ability to bully adversaries would remain largely unaffected.

Myth #3: Dictators Are Better at Nuclear Coercion

In 1968, vice-presidential candidate and retired Air Force general Curtis LeMay lamented that the United States and its allies were too squeamish about using nuclear weapons. "We have a phobia about nuclear weapons," he complained. "The public opinion in this country and through the world throw up their hands in horror when you mention nuclear weapons just because of the propaganda that's been fed to them."[10] This attitude, LeMay argued, put the United States at a significant disadvantage in world politics, giving U.S.

---

[10] Carter (1995, 359).

adversaries "courage they didn't have before."[11] Four years earlier, presidential candidate Barry Goldwater expressed a similar view, calling opposition to nuclear weapons in the United States "silly and sissified."[12] In this view, public aversion to nuclear weapons harms the ability of the United States to use those weapons to the nation's advantage.

This anxiety has deep intellectual roots. Since Tocqueville fretted about the lack of "military spirit" in democracies, observers have worried that democratic countries are hamstrung in international conflicts.[13] International politics is a dangerous business, these scholars argue, but democracies are often hesitant to get their hands bloody. They are too reticent to kill, too sensitive to casualties – and too open about both. Wright's 1965 *Study of War* is emblematic of this school of thought: "in the game of power diplomacy, democracies pitted against autocracies are at a disadvantage. They cannot make effective threats unless they really mean war; they can seldom convince either themselves or the potential enemy that they really do mean war; and they are always vulnerable to the dissensions of internal oppositions."[14]

The implication of this logic is clear: autocratic countries are better at coercion in general, and nuclear coercion in particular. Liberal democracies cannot make nuclear threats effectively, in this view, because nobody will believe them. By contrast, nuclear threats from ruthless dictators like Stalin or Mao are more likely to be credible – after all, these leaders were willing to kill millions of their own citizens to achieve their political objectives; why would they shy away from doing the same to a foreign country?

Our research suggests that this view is half-right and half-wrong. Democracies do indeed have a difficult time using nuclear weapons for coercion. Britain, for example, gained no political advantages from its nuclear weapons while attempting to avoid military action against Argentina in 1982. More recently, India failed to coerce Pakistan into sponsoring cross-border violence in the 2001–2002 crisis. Even when democracies have successfully coerced their adversaries – as Israel

---

[11] Flint (1968).

[12] Mohr (1965, 120).

[13] de Tocqueville (2000 [1840], 648).

[14] Wright (1965, 842). A similar argument has been made more recently by Merom (2003), among others.

appeared to do in the 1973 Yom Kippur War – nuclear weapons played a negligible role.

The bright side for democracies, however, is that autocracies fare just as poorly. The Soviet Union accumulated a long list of failed attempts at nuclear coercion, including the Berlin crises in the 1950s and 1960s. Even its apparent victory against China in 1969 turned out to be hollow. And North Korea, a brutal dictatorship that has repeatedly proclaimed its enthusiasm for war with the United States, was unable to use nuclear threats to gain concessions in the 2013 crisis. The lesson is clear: democracies fail at nuclear coercion not because they are democracies, but because nuclear coercion rarely succeeds.

Myth #4: Nuclear Brinkmanship Solves the Problem of Credibility

Coercive nuclear threats face an inherent credibility problem. In most cases, targets simply doubt that a coercer will truly use its nuclear weapons to enforce its demands – especially if the target can retaliate with its own nuclear weapons. This is why nuclear blackmail rarely works. However, some scholars have argued that there is a solution to this credibility problem. They call it "nuclear brinkmanship" – the deliberate creation of risk in a crisis. Countries can coerce their adversaries, these scholars argue, by taking dangerous escalatory actions that raise the possibility of accidental or unauthorized nuclear use. A state might back down in a crisis because it worries about events spiraling out of control, even if it knows that its opponent would never make a conscious and deliberate decision to authorize a nuclear attack. Thus, by manipulating the risk of inadvertent war, countries can extract coercive value from their arsenals even when nuclear use is seemingly irrational.[15]

The coercionist school often points to the Cuban missile crisis as the archetypal example of nuclear brinkmanship. During the crisis, Nikita Khrushchev wrote a letter to John F. Kennedy in which he expressed fear that the two leaders were pulling on the ends of a rope in which Kennedy had tied a knot of war. "A moment may come," the Soviet leader suggested, "when that knot will be tied so tight that even he who

---

[15] Schelling (1960, 1966).

tied it will not have the strength to untie it, and then it will be necessary to cut that knot," leading to nuclear war.[16] Khrushchev recognized that neither he nor Kennedy desired war, but he nonetheless worried that their actions would inadvertently produce that outcome. This fear, according to brinkmanship theory, caused Khrushchev to back down, leading to a crisis victory for the United States.

The idea that states can effectively engage in nuclear coercion by ratcheting up the shared risk of a catastrophic confrontation is widely accepted, and is often taken for granted in theoretical work on nuclear deterrence.[17] Many policymakers agree that countries can make seemingly unbelievable threats credible by walking toward the end of the proverbial cliff. As John Foster Dulles, President Eisenhower's Secretary of State, famously put it in a 1956 issue of *Life* magazine, "The ability to get to the verge without getting into the war is the necessary art. If you cannot master it, you inevitably get into war. If you try to run away from it, if you are scared to go to the brink, you are lost." But just how effective are these threats that, in Schelling's words, "leave something to chance"?

History shows that these threats often fail to pay political dividends. Richard Nixon, Nikita Khrushchev, and Kim Jong Un all followed the brinkmanship script. These leaders did precisely what is needed to effectively engage in nuclear blackmail, according to the nuclear coercionist school: they used brinkmanship to manipulate the risk of inadvertent war and cultivated the image of an irrational madman. Yet even these men failed to effectively engage in nuclear blackmail. Taking risky actions that bid up the risk of nuclear war should lead to coercive victories, based on the conventional wisdom. Why, then, do these threats sometimes fail?

Nuclear coercion theory assumes that countries will notice when their opponents take dangerous escalatory measures during crises and that they will understand what these moves are meant to convey. The reality of world politics is quite different. Indeed, a close look at the historical record reveals that nuclear alerts and other forms of brinkmanship are frequently misinterpreted – assuming the recipient even notices that its adversary has attempted to manipulate the risk of nuclear war.

[16] Quoted in Kennedy (1969, 89).
[17] See, for example, Powell (1988, 1990).

Consider the 1958–1959 Berlin crisis. At the height of the confrontation, Khrushchev moved nuclear missiles into East Germany, giving the Soviet Union the ability to destroy cities in Western Europe. Forward-deploying nuclear forces during a crisis seems to be a fairly clear attempt to manipulate risk. However, it does not appear that President Eisenhower realized what his Soviet counterpart had done. Based on the available evidence, word about the missile deployment did not reach the president until after Khrushchev had already retracted his failed ultimatum.

Nixon's 1969 nuclear alert is also informative. During this episode, the Soviet Union noticed that the United States was conducting nuclear preparations, but it did not understand the message that Nixon was trying to communicate. We now know, based on declassified documents, that Nixon ordered the alert in hopes of coercing a favorable end to the Vietnam War. The Soviet Union, he hoped, would help get the North Vietnamese to the negotiating table if there was a risk of nuclear escalation. However, Moscow did not realize that U.S. nuclear brinkmanship was related to the Vietnam War. At the time of the alert, the Soviets were embroiled in the Ussuri River crisis with China. Moscow believed that, if anything, Washington was trying to prevent the Sino-Soviet conflict from escalating further. Soviet leaders obviously could not comply with Nixon's demands if they did not understand what the president was asking them to do. Thus, U.S. brinkmanship failed partially because of a major signaling failure.

Nuclear signals have also been garbled in South Asia. During the 1999 Kargil War, India appeared confused as to whether Pakistan had readied its nuclear arsenal and, if it had, whether it did so for offensive or defensive purposes. Similarly, in the 2001–2002 border confrontation, Indian nuclear signals – including missile deployments, verbal threats, and missile tests – apparently were not picked up in Islamabad.

The seemingly elegant solution to the problem of nuclear credibility therefore is not so elegant after all. The risk of accidents may be present in some nuclear crises, but it has rarely shaped their outcomes.

Myth #5: Every Crisis Carries an Inherent Risk of Nuclear War

There is a view among theoreticians of nuclear strategy that nuclear weapons cast a pervasive shadow over all of international politics. The whiff of nuclear attack is always in the air, the logic goes, whenever nuclear powers go about their business. Whether in quiet diplomatic exchanges or during headline-grabbing crises, nuclear weapons lurk in the background, shaping the course of events. This view rests on an important but unspoken assumption: that the mere existence of nuclear weapons makes nuclear war a real possibility in every confrontation involving a nuclear-armed country. Leaders do not always stand on the edge of the nuclear cliff, but they are conscious of where it is. Even a minor crisis could push them over the edge if they are not careful.

The implication is straightforward for any leader confronting a nuclear-armed adversary: the risk of nuclear attack can never be trivialized or ignored. In other words, nuclear powers need not brandish – or even mention – their arsenals in order to enjoy the bargaining power they convey. As one scholar writes: "nuclear weapons are an ever-present factor lurking in the background of political conflicts between nuclear-armed states. They can shape bargaining dynamics whether or not the states actually engage in direct armed-conflict, or explicitly threaten nuclear use."[18] Nuclear war, in this view, is always possible, no matter how small the crisis.

Our research suggests that the reality is quite different. Nuclear strategists may find it difficult to put nuclear weapons out of their minds, but national leaders do not. The vast majority of crises in international relations involve virtually no nuclear danger at all, even when nuclear states face off. One reason is that there are relatively few moments during a crisis in which an accident might plausibly lead to a nuclear exchange. It strains credulity to imply, as nuclear coercion theory sometimes does, that the 1994 Haiti crisis carried a risk of nuclear war. None of the crisis participants believed, to our knowledge, that there was any chance of an event that might result in the use of nuclear weapons. To insert nuclear weapons into a crisis, leaders must invoke their arsenals by alerting nuclear forces, conspicuously deploying relevant missiles or bombers, or making verbal threats. They cannot simply count on the nuclear shadow doing the job for them.

Myth #6: We Don't Know Enough About Nuclear Coercion

A skeptic might contend that history provides few examples of successful nuclear coercion simply because countries rarely attempt it.

[18] Kroenig (2013, 153).

It is not that nuclear weapons cannot coerce, in other words, it is that they are invoked only in the most extreme, severe circumstances. Even if coercion is common in international politics, coercion with nuclear weapons might not be. Indeed, Tannenwald has argued that there is an unspoken international "taboo" that forbids leaders not only from using nuclear weapons, but from even suggesting the possibility of using them.[19] If this is the case, leaders may shy away from even attempting to extract coercive leverage from their nuclear arsenals. In short, successful nuclear coercion is rare because leaders are too hesitant to try it. We therefore have too little evidence to draw any firm conclusions about its efficacy.

It is true that brinkmanship occurs in a relatively small percentage of all disputes involving nuclear actors. At the same time, leaders have attempted to use nuclear weapons for coercion more often than many people realize. Chapters 5 and 6 analyzed nineteen different episodes in which leaders made coercive nuclear threats of varying severity. In some cases, such as the 1956 Suez crisis, leaders' references to nuclear weapons were vague, with leaders alluding only to unspecified severe consequences that might follow if their demands were not met. In many other cases, however, nuclear threats were more explicit. In the 1961 Berlin crisis, Nikita Khrushchev specified the exact number of atomic bombs that he would use against Britain and France. North Korean military officers in 2013 flatly stated that their pilots would "load nuclear bombs" to use against the United States. And in several other cases, nuclear powers mobilized nuclear-capable forces, moved nuclear assets, and initiated nuclear alerts to make their threats more intimidating. While leaders have rarely succeeded in using their nuclear forces for coercion, it is not for a lack of trying.

Myth #7: The Cuban Missile Crisis Proves That Nuclear Coercion Works

The Cuban missile crisis was perhaps the single tensest moment of the Cold War, and it had a deep and enduring impact on the American psyche. But its impact was not limited to the general public: the crisis also quickly became the archetype for how scholars think about nuclear

---

[19] Tannenwald (1999, 2007).

coercion.[20] Early studies of coercive diplomacy adopted this crisis as the primary model for understanding how crises begin, escalate, and end.[21] Contemporary scholars of international relations continue to draw inspiration from this episode as the paradigmatic case of crisis bargaining.

The high profile of the Cuban missile crisis in international relations scholarship has led many to assume that the Cuban missile crisis is emblematic of a typical nuclear crisis. Historian Frank Gavin, for example, calls the period culminating in the Cuban missile crisis "the most important and most representative case" for understanding nuclear dynamics.[22] If the Cuban missile crisis is indeed the most representative case of nuclear diplomacy, then there is a clear implication: nuclear coercion works. Indeed, scholars often generalize from the Cuba episode that nuclear weapons are effective coercive tools, especially when combined with brinkmanship tactics. One prominent nuclear security scholar at Harvard voiced precisely this view, arguing that the case "proves" the efficacy of nuclear diplomacy: "After all, the Soviets put the missiles in, there was a risk of war, and then they took them out."[23]

But the fact is that the Cuban missile crisis is not representative of the broader pattern of nuclear diplomacy. The crisis was anomalous in at least two ways. First, nuclear-armed coercers – whether nuclear-superior or not – typically do not prevail the way the United States did in 1962. As we demonstrated in Chapter 3, when nuclear states issue explicit coercive threats, those threats typically end in failure. Moreover, even when those threats appear to succeed, often the reason has nothing to do with the risk of nuclear war, as the case studies in Chapter 6 showed. The Cuban missile crisis appears to show that nuclear coercion works, when in fact the opposite is true.

Second, the Cuban missile crisis gives the misleading impression that nuclear states frequently engage in risky brinkmanship tactics during confrontations. Both the United States and the Soviet Union took

---

[20] As an illustration of the impact of the crisis on academic research, a search of Google Scholar finds more than 1,000 books and articles with the phrase "Cuban missile crisis" in the title alone.

[21] For example, Schelling (1966), George and Smoke (1974) and Snyder and Diesing (1977).

[22] Gavin (2014).

[23] The unnamed Harvard scholar is quoted in Wilson (2012, 147).

actions that increased the risk of accidental war in 1962, including
alerting nuclear assets, moving opposing forces into close proximity,
and deploying nuclear-armed platforms to the conflict zone. But our
assessment of the historical record shows that this was an extreme
instance of brinkmanship, not a representative one. In most crises,
leaders are not preoccupied with the possibility of "blundering into
disaster,"[24] as U.S. and Soviet leaders were in 1962.

In short, scholars are likely to draw misleading inferences about
nuclear crisis bargaining if they use the Cuban missile crisis as their
primary inspiration. While the episode undoubtedly carries some useful lessons for contemporary scholars and policymakers, it is time to
stop thinking of it as the paradigmatic case of nuclear diplomacy.

Myth #8: Nuclear Weapons Provide a Shield for Aggression

Do nuclear arsenals enable states to act more aggressively? One view
suggests that nuclear-armed countries can use low-level violence with
relative impunity, knowing that their targets will hesitate to retaliate
due to the possibility of nuclear escalation. Nuclear weapons, then,
may serve as shields for aggression. This thinking reflects an old idea
known as the "stability-instability" paradox, and it is widely accepted
today.[25]

Proponents of this view draw heavily on evidence from South Asia.
Pakistan's risky ventures after testing nuclear weapons in 1998, they
contend, show that nuclear weapons have emboldening effects. For
example, during the Kargil operation, Pakistani troops swiftly grabbed
territory and presented New Delhi with a *fait accompli*: accept the
new status quo or fight to regain lost territory. Pakistani officials
believed – wrongly as it turned out – that the possibility of nuclear
escalation would deter India from attempting to reclaim the land militarily. Drawing in part on the Pakistani experience, many analysts
worry that Iran would be similarly emboldened if it acquired nuclear
weapons.[26] They argue that Tehran would be more likely to support
terrorism, launch minor military incursions, and initiate crises if it
possessed a nuclear deterrent.

---

[24] Robert McNamara, quoted in Blight et al. (1987, 177).
[25] The term was coined by Snyder (1965).
[26] For example, Kahl et al. (2012).

If true, the above logic implies that nuclear powers can use *faits accomplis* to change the status quo in their favor. They can simply take (or do) what they want without warning and threaten nuclear retaliation if anyone tries to restore the status quo ante. By acting in this way, countries can turn coercive threats, which are almost always incredible, into deterrent threats, which are more credible. Nuclear weapons, then, may provide states with indirect coercive benefits. Russia's seizure of Crimea in early 2014 illustrates how this might work. Vladimir Putin did not say to Ukraine, "hand over this territory or we will flatten Kiev with nuclear weapons." Instead, Russian troops swiftly grabbed territory without warning and used the implicit threat of military escalation to deter Ukraine from reclaiming it. There was no direct nuclear coercion in this case, but Russia's nuclear arsenal may have nevertheless helped Putin get what he wanted.[27]

We put the shield argument to the test, and found it to be wanting. There is scant evidence that countries behave more aggressively after they get nuclear weapons. Nuclear weapons do not make states more likely to (1) issue coercive threats, (2) make military challenges to the territorial status quo, (3) escalate ongoing conflicts over territory, or (4) resolve territorial disputes in their favor using military force.[28]

This does not imply that states are never emboldened by their nuclear arsenals. We do not doubt, for example, that nuclear weapons played a role in motivating Pakistan to initiate the Kargil War. And Russia may indeed have employed a nuclear shield in the case of Crimea. However, we should use caution when generalizing from one or two cases. Individual events are not necessarily indicative of a broader pattern. In this book we have analyzed a large number of countries over a long period of time, and we have looked for nuclear-backed aggression in a variety of different contexts. Our findings are clear: on the whole, nuclear weapons do not appear to encourage international aggression. If there is a stability-instability paradox, the instability leg of the conundrum is decidedly weak.[29]

Countries rarely have used nuclear shields to challenge the status quo. Moreover, attempts to do so have usually failed. It is important

---

[27] Applebaum (2015).

[28] We find, in particular, that military challenges by nuclear states fail to produce significant changes in the territorial status quo 70% of the time. See also Sechser (2009).

[29] These findings are also consistent with those of Bell and Miller (2015).

to remember that the 1999 Kargil venture did not produce a change in the territorial status quo. Even if nuclear weapons facilitated the Pakistani land grab, they did not help Islamabad "win" the broader dispute with India. The Cuban missile crisis offers another useful illustration. Khrushchev saw the operation to install ballistic missiles in Cuba as a *fait accompli*: he believed that he could install missiles on the island, declare their presence to the United States, and Washington would be forced to accept the new status quo. This view turned out to be misguided: the United States detected the missiles before they were fully operational and ultimately forced Khrushchev to remove them. Nuclear-backed *faits accomplis* sound plausible in theory, but are often frustrated in practice.

Myth #9: We Must Attack New Proliferators

Officials in Washington and elsewhere routinely express anxiety about the prospect of further nuclear proliferation. In the late 1940s, they worried about a Soviet atomic bomb. The prospect of a Chinese nuclear arsenal haunted U.S. policymakers during the 1960s. Concerns about India, Pakistan, and North Korea came next. Today, the possibility of Iran building nuclear weapons is widely viewed as a major threat to national and international security.

A specific concern that leaders have voiced, going back to the dawn of the nuclear age, is that new proliferators will be able to blackmail the rest of the world if they obtain atomic arsenals. For example, in the 1960s, many U.S. officials believed that China's international influence would expand if it obtained a nuclear arsenal. Declassified documents show that Washington worried about bowing to the demands of a nuclear-armed Beijing. As one document from that era stated, "The Chinese Communists seem determined to eject the United States from Asia. We can be sure that they will be seeking ways to exploit their nuclear weapons for this end ... Our structure of bases and alliances will be subjected to ever greater pressure."[30] This is similar to what many policymakers recently have said about Iran. One Arab official put it in particularly stark terms: "What happens after Iran gets a nuclear bomb? The next day they will tell the king of Bahrain to hand over power to the opposition. They will tell Qatar to send the

---

[30] U.S. Department of Defense (1978, 4).

American Air Force home. And they will tell King Abdullah [of Saudi Arabia], 'This is how much oil you may pump and this is what the price of oil will now be.'"[31]

To prevent new proliferators from bullying other states, many observers argue, military action is necessary – before it is too late. Indeed, in the atomic age, this has been a common refrain.[32] To forestall nuclear proliferation, the United States seriously considered attacking China in the 1960s and North Korea in the 1990s. In 2003, President Bush justified the invasion of Iraq, in part, as a means to prevent Saddam Hussein from obtaining nuclear weapons. The Soviet Union thought about preventive strikes against proliferators, too, particularly China and South Africa. And Israel has actually carried out attacks against nuclear facilities in Iraq (1981) and Syria (2007).

In recent years, many observers advocated for military strikes against Iran.[33] Proponents of the military option argued that an attack, while not necessarily desirable, was the best way to stop Iran from getting the bomb. A failure to act, they argued, would lead to disastrous consequences. Unless the United States (or Israel) bombs Iranian nuclear plants, Tehran would cross the nuclear threshold and, in the process, transform geopolitics in the Middle East. Iran is in a unique position to use nuclear weapons offensively, many suggest, because of its revolutionary fervor. Its leaders are fanatical, unpredictable, and potentially even irrational.

This book has cast considerable doubt on these claims. Nuclear weapons have little coercive value, even for revolutionary regimes or bloodthirsty dictators. Josef Stalin could not use nuclear blackmail against the United States. Neither could Nikita Khrushchev, Mao Zedong, or the Kims in North Korea. Could Iranian leaders bring the United States to its knees just because it possessed a few nuclear bombs? Seventy years worth of data suggests that the answer is no.

This does not mean, of course, that we should welcome an Iranian bomb, as some have argued.[34] There are many potential consequences associated with nuclear proliferation. Nuclear arsenals deter aggression, thereby providing greater security for their owners and

[31] Quoted in Pollack (2013, 78).
[32] For an overview of preventive strikes against nuclear programs, see Fuhrmann and Kreps (2010) and Kreps and Fuhrmann (2011).
[33] See, for example, Podhoretz (2007) and Bolton (2010, 2015).
[34] Waltz (2012).

potentially their allies.[35] In addition, one state's acquisition of nuclear weapons could encourage others to proliferate. As former U.S. Secretary of State George Shultz put it, "proliferation begets proliferation." Nuclear proliferation could also lead to potentially dangerous accidents.[36] Thus, there are reasons to worry about the consequences of an Iranian nuclear capability. Fears about nuclear blackmail, however, should not be among them.

Myth #10: Nuclear Superiority Matters

There were lively debates during the Cold War about the relevance of strategic nuclear superiority. Some argued that the nuclear balance – the destructive potential of one state's nuclear arsenal relative to its opponent – had little bearing on who prevailed in international disputes.[37] Many others contended, however, that states could only derive political leverage from their nuclear arsenals if they possessed strategic superiority.[38] According to this view, nuclear superiority is necessary for states to realize the coercive potential of their nuclear arsenals.

A debate about nuclear superiority has reemerged in recent years, with some scholars making strong claims about the political benefits of relatively large nuclear arsenals. Nuclear superiority, they contend, swings the balance of resolve in favor of the superior state, causing them to push harder in crises and ultimately prevail.[39] States with nuclear inferiority, by contrast, cannot achieve their coercive objectives, even if they have a survivable second strike capability. By this logic, the United States would have lost the Cuban missile crisis had it possessed fewer nuclear weapons than the Soviet Union in 1962.

This argument has implications for contemporary policy debates on nuclear arms control. In April 2010, Russia and the United States signed an agreement limiting the number of deployed strategic nuclear weapons by either country to 1,550. Further nuclear reductions may be on the horizon. But the logic of nuclear superiority suggests that additional cuts to the American nuclear arsenal are a bad idea. If the

---

[35] See, for example, Waltz (1981), Jervis (1989), Narang (2014), and Fuhrmann and Sechser (2014b).
[36] Sagan (1993); Schlosser (2013).
[37] For instance, see Blechman and Kaplan (1978) and Jervis (1979, 1989).
[38] See Betts (1987, 212–34) for a relevant discussion.
[39] McDonough (2006, 67).

United States goes to lower numbers, arms control critics contend, it will sacrifice coercive leverage.

The notion that more power equals greater influence is intuitive. But it is not supported by real-world events. The reality is that nuclear superiority is not nearly as beneficial as nuclear coercion theory asserts.

First, states rarely behave as if nuclear superiority provides them with advantages in coercive bargaining. Contrary to the preceding logic, nuclear superiority is not associated with greater risk taking in international disputes. Our analysis in this book demonstrates that states with nuclear advantages are not more likely to engage in military escalation after issuing coercive threats (Chapter 3) or during territorial disputes (Chapter 4). Moreover, the case studies we evaluated in Chapters 5 and 6 revealed that nuclear-inferior states are often the biggest risk-takers in serious nuclear crises. A strategically inferior Soviet Union relied more heavily on brinkmanship during the Berlin crises (1958–59 and 1961), as did Pakistan in the midst of the Kargil War and North Korea during the 2013 crisis with the United States. The Cuban missile crisis seemingly confirms the linkage between nuclear superiority and resolve, but, as we documented, the Soviets took significant and underappreciated risks in that case, too.

Second, there is no relationship between nuclear superiority and coercive victories.[40] On average, nuclear-superior states are neither more likely to issue successful coercive threats nor more likely to achieve favorable territorial dispute settlements. In some cases, countries with superior nuclear arsenals have indeed prevailed. However, a close examination of the evidence calls into question whether the nuclear balance actually caused these states to win. The United States achieved its aims in the Berlin crises of the 1950s and 1960s, for example, but this was mostly because it was trying to preserve the status quo, rather than change it – not because it possessed a larger nuclear arsenal than the Soviet Union.

In short, those who criticize nuclear arms control on the grounds that it will undermine U.S. coercive leverage do not have much evidence to substantiate their view. Our analysis suggests that the United States could engage in further nuclear arms reductions without harming its international influence.

---

[40] See Sechser and Fuhrmann (2013b,c).

The Relevance of Nuclear Weapons Today

One might be tempted to conclude from this book that nuclear weapons have become obsolete in contemporary international relations. Are nuclear weapons simply relics, serving only as grim reminders of a bygone age? This argument has been made before, and continues to be made today. Robert McNamara argued as early as 1983 that nuclear weapons "serve no military purpose whatsoever. They are totally useless – except only to deter one's opponent from using them."[41] McNamara's opinions foreshadow those of John Mueller, who has written about what he calls the "essential irrelevance" of nuclear weapons.[42] Other scholars recently have made arguments along similar lines.[43] While these authors share our pessimism about the efficacy of nuclear blackmail, they go much further, claiming that atomic weapons are not useful for deterrence either.

For these observers, the fact that nuclear powers have been attacked on several occasions is evidence that nuclear deterrence does not work. China, for example, launched a full-scale assault against U.S. forces during the Korean War. Syria and Egypt launched strikes against Israel in 1973. Iraq fired Scud missiles at Israel during the 1991 Persian Gulf War. And India and Pakistan fought the Kargil War in 1999. For deterrence critics, these examples prove that nuclear weapons do not promote international stability or protect their possessors, as is commonly assumed. As Ward Wilson put it, "The bullet proof vest, it turns out, is made of cheesecloth."[44]

We do not share this view. Many of the problems that make coercive nuclear threats incredible are less acute in deterrence contexts. Most notably, nuclear deterrent threats are often more credible because the stakes for nuclear defenders tend to be higher than they are for nuclear coercers. Indeed, a defender's very survival may be on the line. In part for this reason, the costs of carrying out a nuclear deterrent threat are likely to be lower, since it would be responding to aggression rather than striking first. It is therefore easier for states to make deterrent threats believable. It is not hard to imagine, for example, that the United States would use nuclear forces to defend Washington, D.C. It

---

[41] McNamara (1983, 79).
[42] Mueller (1988, 2009).
[43] For instance, see Tannenwald (2007) and Wilson (2013).
[44] Wilson (2013, 86).

is much more difficult to believe that it would carry out nuclear attacks for coercive reasons, like forcing China to abandon possessions in the South China Sea.

To be sure, nuclear powers are not invincible, and they have been attacked on occasion. However, this does not mean that atomic bombs are useless for deterrence. A preponderance of evidence suggests that they are useful for such a purpose.[45] Indeed, the effectiveness of nuclear deterrence was evident in some of the cases we evaluated in this book: Pakistan's deterrent nuclear threats, for example, probably played a role in limiting Indian aggression in 2001–2002. Nuclear states do not issue more effective coercive threats, but our evidence shows that they are less likely to be the targets of military blackmail. In other words, having a nuclear arsenal appears to protect countries from coercion, though it does not help them employ it.

Distinguishing between deterrence and coercion therefore provides us with a more nuanced view about the role of nuclear weapons in world politics. Nuclear arsenals may deter, but they do not coerce. It would be a mistake to assume that nuclear weapons are irrelevant just because they do not have coercive effects.

Thinking About the Future

Over the past decade, the future of nuclear weapons has been called into question. In 2007, a group of prominent former U.S. statesmen called for the United States to work toward the goal of "a world free of nuclear weapons."[46] Two years later, newly elected president Barack Obama declared "America's commitment to seek the peace and security of a world without nuclear weapons."[47] Even U.S. allies recently have called for the removal of U.S. nuclear weapons from Europe as a step toward eventual global nuclear disarmament.[48] And yet nuclear weapons remain a fixture of international politics. In the Ukraine crisis of 2014–2015, Russia explicitly invoked its nuclear arsenal as a warning to the United States. China has done the same in its dispute with Japan over the Senkaku Islands. And North Korea,

---

[45] Research that we have carried out elsewhere supports this view. See Fuhrmann and Sechser (2014b).

[46] Shultz et al. (2007).

[47] Obama (2009).

[48] Foradori (2013).

India, Pakistan, and Israel have shown no interest in echoing rhetoric about nuclear disarmament. It seems that nuclear weapons are here to stay.

Yet even if nuclear weapons remain a feature of international politics, it is worth considering whether their political effects could change. Could nuclear weapons become more useful tools of coercion in the future? What would be needed to bring about such a scenario?

The answer is a mixed one. On one hand, our analysis has revealed several limitations of nuclear brinkmanship that are unlikely to disappear. First, nuclear signaling is difficult: even when leaders have tried to send nuclear signals in the past, oftentimes those signals have been missed. Second, leaders during crises tend to fixate not on the risk of inadvertent nuclear attack, as brinkmanship theory expects, but instead on the likelihood of intentional nuclear use. Finally, leaders seek to assert maximal control over events during crises, even though brinkmanship theory sees the risk of accidents as the key source of states' leverage. It is difficult to see these features of crisis bargaining fading away in the future. The challenges of brinkmanship are time-tested.

Further, it is a simple fact of coercive diplomacy that the stakes for coercers tend to be lower than the stakes for defenders. One of the most consistent findings in the field of behavioral economics is that individuals are willing to pay higher costs to protect a possession than to acquire it. For this reason, defenders often enjoy a fundamental credibility advantage in international confrontations. Compellence, as Schelling pointed out, is harder than deterrence. Barring a fundamental shift in the way the human mind works, the inherent challenges of coercion are likely to remain with us in the future.

On the other hand, the credibility of coercive nuclear threats is not necessarily an immutable feature of international relations. Coercive nuclear threats have lacked credibility for the first seven decades of the nuclear age in part because of the backlash that would follow any use of nuclear weapons for coercive purposes. Yet if leaders someday decide that this backlash is no longer likely, then the barriers to using nuclear weapons for coercion would begin to weaken. If norms against using nuclear weapons dissolve, or if the use of nuclear weapons becomes broadly acceptable, then nuclear weapons could become more useful political instruments. The costliness of nuclear threats is an important reason nuclear weapons are poor tools of coercion. Those costs are dependent on the will of international and domestic actors to impose them. Over time, their will could weaken.

For now, however, the reality is that nuclear weapons and coercive diplomacy are a poor match. Leaders for decades have hoped that by acquiring nuclear weapons, their nations would gain the ability to assert their dominance in international political affairs. These leaders have been consistently disappointed. The evidence is overwhelming. Nuclear weapons continue to play a considerable role in international affairs, but they have sharp and significant limitations. Recognizing those limitations is the first step toward understanding how the nuclear revolution has reshaped our political world.

Appendix: Methods and Data

This appendix provides additional details about the statistical tests employed in Chapters 3 and 4. It consists of three main sections. First, it describes the variables used in the quantitative models of compellent threats (Chapter 3) and territorial dispute settlements (Chapter 4). Second, it discusses the methodology used to analyze compellent threats and presents detailed findings from a series of regressions. Third, it presents the methodology and findings from the territorial disputes analysis.

Variables

We used a number of variables to statistically analyze the role of nuclear weapons in coercive diplomacy. Unless otherwise noted, the variables pertaining to our analysis of compellent threats are from the Militarized Compellent Threats (MCT) data set, and the territorial dispute–related measures are from Huth and Allee's data set of territorial disputes.[1] We group the variables into five categories below.

Coercive outcome variables:

- COMPELLENCE SUCCESS. A dichotomous variable that is coded one if the target voluntarily complied with all demands of the challenger and the challenger did not have to use military force to achieve its desired outcome. The variable is coded zero otherwise.
- COMPELLENCE SUCCESS WITH FORCE. A dichotomous variable that codes compellent threats as successful even if the challenger used limited military force, as long as the target suffered fewer than 100 fatalities.

---

[1] Sechser (2011) and Huth and Allee (2002).

259

- PARTIAL COMPELLENCE SUCCESS. A variable that codes compellent threats as successful if the target complied with any – as opposed to all – of the challenger's demands.
- CHALLENGER TERRITORIAL CONCESSIONS. A dichotomous variable that is coded one if the challenger makes limited or major concessions in the current round of territorial negotiations and zero if it makes no concessions.
- TARGET TERRITORIAL CONCESSIONS. A dichotomous variable that is coded one if the target makes limited or major concessions in the current round of territorial negotiations and zero if it makes no concessions.

Military escalation variables:

- RESOLVE. A dichotomous variable that is coded one if the challenger employed demonstrations of force or engaged in military mobilizations during a compellent threat episode.
- MILITARY CHALLENGE. A dichotomous variable that is coded one if the challenger initiated a militarized dispute against the target in the context of a territorial dispute. The variable is coded zero otherwise.
- CHALLENGER MILITARY ESCALATION. A dichotomous variable that equals one if the challenger engaged in high escalation during an ongoing militarized dispute over territory, and zero otherwise.
- TARGET MILITARY ESCALATION. A dichotomous variable that equals one if the target engaged in high escalation during an ongoing militarized dispute over territory, and zero otherwise.

Nuclear status variables:

- NUCLEAR CHALLENGER. Dichotomous variable coded one if the challenger in a dyad possessed at least one nuclear weapon in a given year, and zero otherwise.[2]
- NUCLEAR TARGET. Dichotomous variable coded one if the target in a dyad possessed at least one nuclear weapon in a given year, and zero otherwise.
- NUCLEAR CHALLENGER × NUCLEAR TARGET. Interaction term between the two above nuclear variables. We use this variable, along with the two constituent components, to test the nuclear relativist hypothesis.

[2] Singh and Way (2004). We make one modification to the Singh and Way data on nuclear proliferation: we code Israel as a nuclear power beginning in 1967.

- CHALLENGER ARSENAL SIZE. Natural logarithm of the total number of nuclear weapons possessed by the challenger.[3]
- TARGET ARSENAL SIZE. Natural logarithm of the total number of nuclear weapons possessed by the target.[4]
- NUCLEAR SUPERIORITY. Coded one if the challenger had more nuclear weapons than the target, and zero otherwise.[5]
- NUCLEAR RATIO. Proportion of nuclear capabilities controlled by the challenger in each dyad.[6]
- DIFFERENCE IN ARSENAL SIZE. Natural logarithm of the difference between the arsenal sizes of the challenger and target.[7]
- CHALLENGER NUCLEAR SHOCK. Dichotomous variable coded one if the challenger acquired nuclear weapons after a territorial dispute began, and zero otherwise.
- TARGET NUCLEAR SHOCK. Dichotomous variable coded one if the target acquired nuclear weapons after a territorial dispute began, and zero otherwise.
- CHALLENGER NONSHOCK NUCLEAR WEAPONS. Dummy variable that equals one if the challenger acquired nuclear weapons before a territorial dispute began, and zero otherwise.
- TARGET NONSHOCK NUCLEAR WEAPONS. Dummy variable that equals one if the target acquired nuclear weapons before a territorial dispute began, and zero otherwise.
- CHALLENGER NUCLEAR SHOCK × TARGET NUCLEAR SHOCK. Interaction term.
- NUCLEAR CHALLENGER × STAKES. Interaction term used in our analysis of compellent threats to determine whether nuclear weapons benefit coercers in high-stakes crises only.

Additional variables for the analysis of compellent threats:

- STAKES. Dichotomous variable coded one if the challenger made a demand over territory or leadership – as opposed to more minor matters of policy and ideology – and zero otherwise.

---

[3] Fuhrmann and Sechser (2014b).
[4] Fuhrmann and Sechser (2014b).
[5] Fuhrmann and Sechser (2014b). When analyzing challengers' concessions in territorial dispute negotiations (Model 55), this variable measures whether the *target* had more nuclear weapons.
[6] Fuhrmann and Sechser (2014b).
[7] Fuhrmann and Sechser (2014b).

- CAPABILITY RATIO. Proportion of nonnuclear material capabilities controlled by the challenger in each dyad, based on the Composite Index of National Capabilities.[8]
- DISPUTE HISTORY. The total number of militarized interstate disputes that the challenger and target experienced over the previous fifteen years, based on the Correlates of War's Militarized Interstate Dispute (MID) data set.[9]
- POST-1945. Dichotomous variable equal to one if the year is after 1945 and zero otherwise.
- JOINT DEMOCRACY. Dichotmous variable coded one if the challenger and the target both scored six or higher on the Polity 21-point composite indicator of regime type, which ranges from −10 to +10.[10]
- CONTIGUITY. Dichotmous variable coded one if the challenger and target are geographically contiguous.[11]
- DISTANCE. The distance between the capital cities of the challenger and target, in kilometers.[12]

Additional variables for the analysis of territorial disputes:

- MILITARY RATIO. Ratio of the total capabilities possessed by the challenger, based on military expenditures, troops, and spending per troop. This measure ranges from zero to one, with larger values indicating a stronger challenger relative to the target.
- ALLIANCE. Dichotomous variable coded one if there was a defense pact or entente alliance between the challenger and the target, and zero otherwise.
- COMMON OPPONENT. Dichotomous variable that equals one if the challenger and target shared at least one common territorial dispute adversary, and zero if not.
- CHALLENGER ETHNIC VALUE. Dichotomous variable coded one if the challenger had co-ethnics located in the disputed territory, and zero otherwise.
- CHALLENGER STRATEGIC VALUE. Variable indicating whether territory was strategically valuable for the challenger. It is coded one

[8] Singer (1987).
[9] Maoz (2003).
[10] Marshall et al. (2009).
[11] We obtain this variable from Downes and Sechser (2012).
[12] These data were downloaded from Kristian Gleditsch's website: privatewww.essex.ac.uk/ ksg/data-5.html.

if the challenger used natural resources in the disputed territory for the production of weapons, or if the land was strategically located. The variable equals zero otherwise.

- TARGET ETHNIC VALUE. Dichotomous variable coded one if the target had co-ethnics located in the disputed territory, and zero if it did not. Note that territory can be ethnically valuable for challengers but not targets, and vice-versa.
- TARGET STRATEGIC VALUE. Dummy variable coded one if the disputed territory was strategically valuable for the target, based on the above criteria, and zero otherwise. Like ethnic value, the strategic utility of a territory can vary among the disputants.
- CHALLENGER OTHER DISPUTE. Variable coded one if the challenger was involved in another military conflict, and zero otherwise.
- TARGET OTHER DISPUTE. Variable coded one if the target was involved in another military conflict, and zero otherwise.
- DEMOCRATIC DISPUTE. Dummy variable coded one if both states in a dyad were democracies, based on the same criteria as in JOINT DEMOCRACY above.
- TIME SINCE LAST MILITARY CONFLICT. The number of years since the last military challenge in a territorial dispute. We include this variable, along with its square and its cube, to control for time dependence in our analysis of conflict initiation.[13]

Analysis of Compellent Threats

We analyze the relationship between nuclear weapons and coercive threats using the MCT data set.[14] The data set includes 210 compellent threats issued from 1918 to 2001. In Chapter 3, we use this data set to analyze how nuclear weapons influence coercive threat success and military escalation during threat episodes.

Compellent Threat Success

The main dependent variable, COMPELLENCE SUCCESS, indicates whether targets complied with challengers' demands. We employ probit regressions designed to estimate the probability that a compellent threat will succeed. This estimator is frequently employed to evaluate coercive threat outcomes that are coded dichotomously. We use robust standard errors clustered by dyad.

---

[13] Carter and Signorino (2010).
[14] Sechser (2011).

Table A.1 presents the results of the regressions that were discussed in Chapter 3. Models 1–7 evaluate the relationship between various measures of nuclear capability and the effectiveness of a challenger's compellent threats. As the table makes clear, nuclear weapons are not associated with higher success rates: in all seven regressions, the variables measuring a challenger's nuclear capability are either statistically insignificant (Models 1 and 3–6) or are negative and significant (Models 2 and 7), suggesting that nuclear weapons do not help – and may even hinder – coercive success.

The one possible exception to this statement can be found in Model 7: the variable NUCLEAR CHALLENGER × STAKES is positive and statistically significant. Because the key variable in these cases is an interaction term, we cannot look at statistical significance alone – we must evaluate marginal effects in order to assess the overall impact of nuclear possession on compellent threat outcomes.[15] We calculated the marginal effect of simultaneously changing NUCLEAR CHALLENGER and the associated interaction term from zero to one in high-stakes crises. The ninety percent confidence interval for this marginal effect includes zero $(-0.211, +0.135)$, indicating that the net impact of a challenger's possession of nuclear weapons is indistinguishable from zero, even in high-stakes crises.

We modified the original regressions in several ways:

(i) **Alternate dependent variables.** We used COMPELLENCE SUCCESS WITH FORCE (Table A.2) and PARTIAL COMPELLENCE SUCCESS (Table A.3) as alternate dependent variables.

(ii) **Prenuclear era.** We replicated the original regressions using a limited sample that includes only post-1945 observations (Table A.4).

(iii) **Resolve.** One might be concerned that nuclear weapons embolden challengers to escalate crises after making threats, in which case the effects of nuclear possession might manifest themselves through the RESOLVE variable. We showed in Chapter 3 (and below) that this is not true empirically. Nevertheless, we replicate our original models without RESOLVE to address concerns about post-treatment bias (Table A.5).

---

[15] Brambor et al. (2006).

Table A.1 *Probit estimates of compellent threat success.*

	1	2	3	4	5	6	7
NUCLEAR CHALLENGER	-0.311 (0.251)	-0.474† (0.253)					-0.812* (0.390)
NUCLEAR TARGET		-0.502 (0.836)					
NUCLEAR CHALLENGER × NUCLEAR TARGET		1.543 (1.141)					
CHALLENGER ARSENAL SIZE			0.00185 (0.0350)				
NUCLEAR SUPERIORITY				-0.274 (0.251)			
NUCLEAR RATIO					-0.537 (0.464)		
DIFFERENCE IN ARSENAL SIZE						0.00112 (0.0347)	
STAKES	0.0181 (0.200)	0.00177 (0.202)	0.0366 (0.202)	0.0186 (0.200)	0.0244 (0.200)	0.0365 (0.202)	-0.127 (0.225)
NUCLEAR CHALLENGER × STAKES							0.741† (0.429)
CAPABILITY RATIO	-0.298 (0.397)	-0.364 (0.399)	-0.476 (0.393)	-0.322 (0.396)	-0.304 (0.398)	-0.473 (0.393)	-0.265 (0.399)
DISPUTE HISTORY	-0.0311 (0.0240)	-0.0434† (0.0226)	-0.0380† (0.0223)	-0.0318 (0.0239)	-0.0325 (0.0236)	-0.0379† (0.0224)	-0.0268 (0.0249)
RESOLVE	1.107*** (0.249)	1.106*** (0.254)	1.073*** (0.254)	1.101*** (0.249)	1.096*** (0.250)	1.074*** (0.254)	1.107*** (0.251)
CONSTANT	-1.033** (0.400)	-0.920* (0.395)	-0.932* (0.399)	-1.018* (0.399)	-0.766† (0.441)	-0.935* (0.399)	-0.965* (0.407)
N	236	236	236	236	236	236	236

NOTE: Robust standard errors in parentheses, clustered by dyad. *** $p < 0.001$, ** $p < 0.01$, * $p < 0.05$, † $p < 0.10$.

Table A.2 *Probit estimates of compellent threat success.*

	8	9	10	11	12	13	14
NUCLEAR CHALLENGER	−0.321 (0.244)	−0.554* (0.247)					−0.569 (0.411)
NUCLEAR TARGET		1.520** (0.470)					
NUCLEAR CHALLENGER × NUCLEAR TARGET		−0.152 (0.755)					
CHALLENGER ARSENAL SIZE			0.00797 (0.0326)				
NUCLEAR SUPERIORITY				−0.278 (0.244)			
NUCLEAR RATIO					−0.849† (0.439)		
DIFFERENCE IN ARSENAL SIZE						0.00732 (0.0323)	
STAKES	0.140 (0.195)	0.134 (0.201)	0.160 (0.198)	0.141 (0.195)	0.140 (0.195)	0.160 (0.198)	0.0615 (0.221)
NUCLEAR CHALLENGER × STAKES							0.377 (0.470)
CAPABILITY RATIO	−0.646 (0.404)	−0.574 (0.405)	−0.858* (0.399)	−0.674† (0.402)	−0.576 (0.410)	−0.855* (0.398)	−0.631 (0.406)
DISPUTE HISTORY	−0.0407† (0.0246)	−0.0533* (0.0214)	−0.0488* (0.0230)	−0.0415† (0.0245)	−0.0396† (0.0239)	−0.0487* (0.0230)	−0.0387 (0.0253)
RESOLVE	1.147*** (0.233)	1.138*** (0.238)	1.106*** (0.238)	1.141*** (0.233)	1.151*** (0.233)	1.107*** (0.238)	1.146*** (0.233)
CONSTANT	−0.629 (0.406)	−0.625 (0.402)	−0.506 (0.406)	−0.612 (0.405)	−0.250 (0.424)	−0.508 (0.406)	−0.590 (0.414)
N	236	236	236	236	236	236	236

NOTE: Robust standard errors in parentheses, clustered by dyad. *** $p < 0.001$, ** $p < 0.01$, * $p < 0.05$, † $p < 0.10$.

Table A.3 *Probit estimates of compellent threat success.*

	15	16	17	18	19	20	21
NUCLEAR CHALLENGER	-0.321 (0.245)	-0.547* (0.238)					-0.372 (0.396)
NUCLEAR TARGET		1.324** (0.482)					
NUCLEAR CHALLENGER × NUCLEAR TARGET		0.206 (0.810)					
CHALLENGER ARSENAL SIZE			-0.00165 (0.0324)				
NUCLEAR SUPERIORITY				-0.279 (0.246)			
NUCLEAR RATIO					-0.922* (0.429)		
DIFFERENCE IN ARSENAL SIZE						-0.00407 (0.0320)	
NUCLEAR CHALLENGER × STAKES							0.0860 (0.438)
STAKES	-0.0955 (0.171)	-0.121 (0.175)	-0.0689 (0.174)	-0.0937 (0.171)	-0.102 (0.171)	-0.0694 (0.174)	-0.115 (0.195)
CAPABILITY RATIO	-0.546 (0.378)	-0.486 (0.378)	-0.730† (0.374)	-0.574 (0.377)	-0.455 (0.375)	-0.720† (0.373)	-0.543 (0.380)
DISPUTE HISTORY	-0.0349 (0.0216)	-0.0478* (0.0199)	-0.0415* (0.0206)	-0.0357† (0.0216)	-0.0334 (0.0204)	-0.0411* (0.0206)	-0.0345 (0.0223)
RESOLVE	1.006*** (0.218)	0.989*** (0.223)	0.979*** (0.221)	1.000*** (0.218)	1.011*** (0.218)	0.981*** (0.221)	1.005*** (0.218)
CONSTANT	-0.292 (0.340)	-0.258 (0.331)	-0.200 (0.339)	-0.276 (0.339)	0.118 (0.355)	-0.206 (0.339)	-0.281 (0.337)
N	236	236	236	236	236	236	236

NOTE: Robust standard errors in parentheses, clustered by dyad. *** $p < 0.001$, ** $p < 0.01$, * $p < 0.05$, † $p < 0.10$.

Table A.4 *Probit estimates of compellent threat success.*

	22	23	24	25	26	27	28
NUCLEAR CHALLENGER	-0.226 (0.298)	-0.381 (0.306)					-1.264** (0.428)
NUCLEAR TARGET		-0.155 (0.867)					
NUCLEAR CHALLENGER × NUCLEAR TARGET		1.157 (1.121)					
CHALLENGER ARSENAL SIZE			0.0330 (0.0406)				
NUCLEAR SUPERIORITY				-0.179 (0.296)			
NUCLEAR RATIO					-0.407 (0.539)		
DIFFERENCE IN ARSENAL SIZE						0.0322 (0.0404)	
STAKES	-0.0952 (0.264)	-0.106 (0.270)	-0.0707 (0.267)	-0.0927 (0.265)	-0.0900 (0.262)	-0.0720 (0.267)	-0.669† (0.380)
NUCLEAR CHALLENGER × STAKES							1.500** (0.518)
CAPABILITY RATIO	-0.217 (0.543)	-0.144 (0.579)	-0.613 (0.550)	-0.261 (0.537)	-0.197 (0.545)	-0.607 (0.548)	-0.138 (0.559)
DISPUTE HISTORY	-0.0158 (0.0241)	-0.0307 (0.0224)	-0.0259 (0.0228)	-0.0167 (0.0242)	-0.0171 (0.0241)	-0.0256 (0.0229)	0.000646 (0.0243)
RESOLVE	0.670* (0.333)	0.656† (0.342)	0.537 (0.356)	0.657* (0.333)	0.659* (0.334)	0.540 (0.355)	0.742* (0.368)
CONSTANT	-0.843† (0.487)	-0.811 (0.508)	-0.603 (0.509)	-0.818† (0.485)	-0.661 (0.513)	-0.607 (0.508)	-0.634 (0.506)
N	121	121	121	121	121	121	121

NOTE: Robust standard errors in parentheses, clustered by dyad. *** $p < 0.001$, ** $p < 0.01$, * $p < 0.05$, † $p < 0.10$.

Table A.5 *Probit estimates of compellent threat success.*

	29	30	31	32	33	34	35
NUCLEAR CHALLENGER	-0.181	-0.355					-0.685†
	(0.243)	(0.243)					(0.390)
NUCLEAR TARGET		-0.361					
		(0.819)					
NUCLEAR CHALLENGER × NUCLEAR TARGET		1.493					
		(1.124)					
CHALLENGER ARSENAL SIZE			0.0233				
			(0.0340)				
NUCLEAR SUPERIORITY				-0.153			
				(0.244)			
NUCLEAR RATIO					-0.343		
					(0.430)		
DIFFERENCE IN ARSENAL SIZE						0.0225	
						(0.0337)	
STAKES	0.157	0.139	0.170	0.158	0.159	0.169	0.00467
	(0.196)	(0.199)	(0.198)	(0.197)	(0.196)	(0.198)	(0.222)
NUCLEAR CHALLENGER × STAKES							0.767†
							(0.429)
CAPABILITY RATIO	-0.494	-0.535	-0.675†	-0.510	-0.490	-0.671†	-0.464
	(0.391)	(0.389)	(0.386)	(0.390)	(0.387)	(0.386)	(0.392)
DISPUTE HISTORY	-0.0278	-0.0395†	-0.0348	-0.0283	-0.0285	-0.0346	-0.0242
	(0.0225)	(0.0216)	(0.0212)	(0.0225)	(0.0223)	(0.0213)	(0.0233)
CONSTANT	-0.149	-0.577	-0.0708	-0.143	0.0148	-0.0728	-0.0734
	(0.348)	(0.343)	(0.348)	(0.347)	(0.395)	(0.348)	(0.356)
N	236	236	236	236	236	236	236

NOTE: Robust standard errors in parentheses, clustered by dyad. *** $p < 0.001$, ** $p < 0.01$, * $p < 0.05$, † $p < 0.10$.

None of these modifications alter the main substantive conclusion of the chapter: neither nuclear possession nor nuclear superiority is associated with more effective compellent threats. The interaction term NUCLEAR CHALLENGER × STAKES is statistically significant in Models 28 and 35, suggesting that nuclear-armed coercers might be more likely to succeed in high-stakes disputes. However, we again calculate the marginal effect of NUCLEAR CHALLENGER as STAKES shifts from zero to one, and the ninety percent confidence interval includes zero in both cases $(-0.112, +0.269; -0.117, +0.200)$

Our main findings are likewise consistent when we jointly model compellent threat initiation and outcome using a bivariate probit model that is commonly referred to as a Heckman probit model. Heckman models depend on appropriate exclusion restrictions.[16] In other words, for the model to be properly identified, there must be at least one variable in the selection equation (threat initiation) that is excluded from the outcome equation (threat success). The excluded variable must be strongly associated with the former outcome and unrelated to the latter. We satisfy this requirement by including POST-1945 in our threat initiation equation. This variable is coded one in all years after 1945 and zero otherwise.[17]

In addition to the various indicators of nuclear capability, we include two variables from the censored model in the selection equation: CAPABILITY RATIO and DISPUTE HISTORY. These variables are often included in models of threat initiation or crisis onset. Additionally, we include a variable that counts the number of years that have passed without compellent threats within each dyad (TIME SINCE LAST THREAT), its square, and its cube. These three variables control for possible temporal dependence in our data.

Table A.6 presents the findings from the censored probit analysis. These models emulate the models reported in Table A.1 using the Heckman method. The estimation sample for our threat initiation model includes all politically relevant dyads from 1918 to 2001.

The results in the threat success equation (see Table A.6) are similar to the findings from the standard probit analysis. In addition, the correlation between the disturbance terms in the two equations (ρ) is statistically insignificant in all seven models. This suggests that our

---

[16] Heckman (1979).

[17] For further details, see pp. 12–13 of the appendices for Sechser and Fuhrmann (2013a).

Table A.6 *Heckman probit estimates of compellent threat success.*

	36	37	38	39	40	41	42
DV: COMPELLENT THREAT SUCCESS							
NUCLEAR CHALLENGER	−0.283 (0.267)	−0.427 (0.293)					−0.752† (0.403)
NUCLEAR TARGET		−0.358 (0.900)					
NUCLEAR CHALLENGER × NUCLEAR TARGET		1.435 (1.226)					
CHALLENGER ARSENAL SIZE			0.0117 (0.0353)				
NUCLEAR SUPERIORITY				−0.242 (0.261)			
NUCLEAR RATIO					−0.522 (0.478)		
DIFFERENCE IN ARSENAL SIZE						0.0101 (0.0348)	
STAKES	0.0311 (0.204)	0.00367 (0.206)	0.0274 (0.202)	0.0288 (0.204)	0.0316 (0.204)	0.0274 (0.202)	−0.111 (0.231)
NUCLEAR CHALLENGER × STAKES							0.692 (0.428)
CAPABILITY RATIO	−0.341 (0.455)	−0.416 (0.436)	−0.562 (0.422)	−0.369 (0.447)	−0.335 (0.438)	−0.555 (0.422)	−0.306 (0.462)
DISPUTE HISTORY	−0.0411 (0.0320)	−0.0577† (0.0305)	−0.0557* (0.0278)	−0.0430 (0.0315)	−0.0442 (0.0313)	−0.0553* (0.0279)	−0.0373 (0.0332)
RESOLVE	1.046*** (0.255)	1.037*** (0.257)	0.989*** (0.259)	1.037*** (0.255)	1.031*** (0.258)	0.990*** (0.259)	1.037*** (0.256)
CONSTANT	−0.457 (1.278)	−0.169 (1.273)	0.118 (1.215)	−0.374 (1.252)	−0.0891 (1.178)	0.105 (1.211)	−0.382 (1.311)

Table A.6 (Continued)

DV: COMPELLENT THREAT INITIATION

	(1)	(2)	(3)	(4)	(5)	(6)	(7)
NUCLEAR CHALLENGER	−0.0708 (0.0851)	−0.146† (0.0838)					−0.0707 (0.0851)
NUCLEAR TARGET		−0.636** (0.231)					
NUCLEAR CHALLENGER × NUCLEAR TARGET		0.625† (0.338)					
CHALLENGER ARSENAL SIZE			−0.0163 (0.0118)				
NUCLEAR SUPERIORITY				−0.0304 (0.0863)			
NUCLEAR RATIO					0.192 (0.126)		
DIFFERENCE IN ARSENAL SIZE						−0.0125 (0.0119)	
CAPABILITY RATIO	0.454*** (0.0869)	0.350*** (0.0860)	0.473*** (0.0876)	0.437*** (0.0883)	0.354*** (0.0953)	0.462*** (0.0890)	0.453*** (0.0869)
DISPUTE HISTORY	0.0629*** (0.00730)	0.0635*** (0.00764)	0.0628*** (0.00741)	0.0627*** (0.00725)	0.0628*** (0.00722)	0.0626*** (0.00736)	0.0629*** (0.00730)
POST-1945	−0.470*** (0.0899)	−0.389*** (0.0846)	−0.460*** (0.0884)	−0.485*** (0.0910)	−0.523*** (0.0854)	−0.468*** (0.0898)	−0.470*** (0.0900)
TIME SINCE LAST THREAT	−0.0609*** (0.0125)	−0.0612*** (0.0129)	−0.0613*** (0.0126)	−0.0606*** (0.0125)	−0.0602*** (0.0124)	−0.0609*** (0.0126)	−0.0608*** (0.0125)
TIME SINCE LAST THREAT SQUARED	0.00187*** (0.000426)	0.00193*** (0.000452)	0.00189*** (0.000427)	0.00185*** (0.000424)	0.00183*** (0.000424)	0.00187*** (0.000425)	0.00186*** (0.000428)
TIME SINCE LAST THREAT CUBED	−0.0000153*** (0.00000383)	−0.000016*** (0.00000409)	−0.0000155*** (0.00000382)	−0.0000151*** (0.00000381)	−0.0000149*** (0.00000381)	−0.0000153*** (0.00000381)	−0.0000152*** (0.00000385)
CONSTANT	−2.608*** (0.141)	−2.547*** (0.135)	−2.619*** (0.142)	−2.597*** (0.141)	−2.641*** (0.118)	−2.613*** (0.142)	−2.608*** (0.141)
ρ	−0.148 (0.329)	−0.197 (0.341)	−0.277 (0.304)	−0.167 (0.321)	−0.181 (0.312)	−0.275 (0.303)	−0.148 (0.334)
N	129,352	129,352	129,352	129,352	129,352	129,352	129,352

NOTE: Robust standard errors in parentheses, clustered by dyad. *** $p < 0.001$, ** $p < 0.01$, * $p < 0.05$, † $p < 0.10$.

initial findings appear not to be biased due to the exclusion of some missing explanatory variable that predicts both threat initiation and success. Overall, these results indicate that states possessing nuclear weapons are not more likely than nonnuclear countries to make successful compellent threats, even when we account for the factors that motivate states to issue demands in the first place.

Military Escalation During Coercive Crises

As noted in Chapter 3, for our analysis of military escalation we strive to replicate an existing model that produces findings consistent with the nuclear coercionist position.[18] Doing so should make it more difficult to find evidence in favor of nuclear skepticism theory. The dependent variable for this analysis is RESOLVE. In addition to various measures of nuclear status, we include the following independent variables: STAKES, CAPABILITY RATIO, DISPUTE HISTORY, JOINT DEMOCRACY, CONTIGUITY, and DISTANCE.[19]

Table A.7 reports the findings from this analysis. The results are striking: regardless of how we measure nuclear status, nuclear powers are *not* more likely than nonnuclear states to escalate coercive crises militarily.

Analysis of Territorial Disputes

We use a data set of 348 territorial disputes from 1919 to 1995 to study how nuclear weapons affect bargaining over territory.[20] As in Chapter 3, our quantitative analysis in Chapter 4 addressed dispute outcomes and intracrisis behavior.

Territorial Dispute Outcomes

To the extent possible, we follow the methodology used by Huth and Allee in their analysis of territorial concessions.[21] The decisions made by challengers and targets during territorial dispute negotiations

---

[18] Kroenig et al. (2015).
[19] Note that the latter three variables were not included in our analysis of compellent threat success. Adding them to the above models, however, produces similar findings.
[20] Huth and Allee (2002).
[21] Huth and Allee (2002, 189–230).

Table A.7 *Probit estimates of military escalation.*

	43	44	45	46	47	48	49
NUCLEAR CHALLENGER	0.237	0.165					-0.0356
	(0.273)	(0.277)					(0.383)
NUCLEAR TARGET		-0.0957					
		(0.707)					
NUCLEAR CHALLENGER × NUCLEAR TARGET		–					
		–					
CHALLENGER ARSENAL SIZE			0.0567				
			(0.0446)				
NUCLEAR SUPERIORITY				0.211			
				(0.271)			
NUCLEAR RATIO					0.315		
					(0.506)		
DIFFERENCE IN ARSENAL SIZE						0.0550	
						(0.0447)	
NUCLEAR CHALLENGER × STAKES							0.559
							(0.462)
CAPABILITY RATIO	-1.007**	-1.001**	-1.008**	-0.996**	-0.982*	-1.004**	-0.970**
	(0.378)	(0.378)	(0.370)	(0.377)	(0.382)	(0.370)	(0.373)
JOINT DEMOCRACY	-0.330	-0.316	-0.312	-0.333	-0.340	-0.314	-0.302
	(0.213)	(0.212)	(0.211)	(0.212)	(0.209)	(0.211)	(0.209)
STAKES	0.464*	0.465*	0.438*	0.462*	0.455*	0.436*	0.359
	(0.195)	(0.197)	(0.198)	(0.195)	(0.194)	(0.198)	(0.227)
DISPUTE HISTORY	0.000421	-0.00118	0.000673	0.000694	0.00221	0.000858	0.00233
	(0.0175)	(0.0166)	(0.0171)	(0.0175)	(0.0169)	(0.0171)	(0.0176)
CONTIGUITY	0.346+	0.321	0.347+	0.342+	0.330+	0.346+	0.398*
	(0.193)	(0.201)	(0.192)	(0.193)	(0.190)	(0.192)	(0.200)
DISTANCE	0.000124**	0.000122**	0.000103*	0.000125**	0.000126**	0.000104*	0.000131**
	(0.0000477)	(0.0000474)	(0.0000516)	(0.0000477)	(0.0000476)	(0.0000517)	(0.0000473)
CONSTANT	0.628+	0.646+	0.669+	0.628+	0.480	0.668+	0.608
	(0.380)	(0.389)	(0.382)	(0.380)	(0.432)	(0.382)	(0.379)
N	236	229	236	236	236	236	236

NOTE: Robust standard errors in parentheses, clustered by dyad. *** $p <0.001$, ** $p <0.01$, * $p <0.05$, † $p <0.10$.
NUCLEAR CHALLENGER × NUCLEAR TARGET is dropped from Model 44 because it predicts failure (i.e., RESOLVE=0) perfectly.

are obviously related: whether a challenger makes concessions may depend on the target's willingness to give some ground, and vice versa. A proper statistical analysis of territorial dispute concessions should account for this strategic interaction while controlling for factors that could influence whether either party capitulates. To do so, we use a bivariate probit model that jointly analyzes the decisions made by challengers and targets. This method is widely used in political science – including in research on territorial disputes – when separate decisions by two actors are interrelated.[22] We cluster the standard errors by dispute since the data set includes multiple rounds of negotiations over the same contested territory.

The findings from the initial bivariate probit analysis of territorial dispute concessions are displayed in Table A.8. Our statistical models account for the nuclear status of the challenger and the target, as well as several key control variables.[23] Both equations in each model include MILITARY RATIO, ALLIANCE, COMMON OPPONENT, and DEMOCRATIC DISPUTE as controls. The other covariates change based on the dependent variable. For example, when analyzing the challenger's decision to make concessions, we are primarily interested in the variable NUCLEAR TARGET. In contrast, NUCLEAR CHALLENGER is the key variable when studying the target's concessions. In all of the models shown in Table A.8, ρ is statistically significant, indicating that the disturbance terms in the two equations are correlated. This reaffirms our decision to rely on bivariate probit models, as opposed to independent probits that separately accounted for the behavior of challengers and targets.

Neither challengers nor targets are more likely to concede when facing nuclear-armed adversaries, undermining the nuclear coercionist argument but supporting nuclear skepticism theory (Model 50). This result holds when we distinguish between nuclear shocks and nuclear weapons acquired before disputes began (Model 51). Moreover, nuclear weapons do not appear to provide states with bargaining advantages even when their opponents are nonnuclear (Models 52 and 53). There is therefore no support for the nuclear relativist hypothesis.

---

[22] See Huth and Allee (2002, 190).
[23] Introducing additional control variables from Huth and Allee's data set produces similar results.

Table A.8 *Bivariate probit estimates of concessions during territorial dispute negotiations.*

	50	51	52	53
DV: CHALLENGER DECISION TO OFFER CONCESSIONS				
NUCLEAR TARGET	−0.0898 (0.0851)		−0.125 (0.134)	
TARGET NUCLEAR SHOCK		0.0122 (0.0855)		0.0399 (0.142)
TARGET NONSHOCK NUCLEAR WEAPONS		−0.435** (0.142)		−0.581** (0.194)
NUCLEAR CHALLENGER			−0.236 (0.220)	
NUCLEAR CHALLENGER × NUCLEAR TARGET			0.112 (0.291)	
CHALLENGER NUCLEAR SHOCK				−0.141 (0.224)
CHALLENGER NUCLEAR SHOCK × TARGET NUCLEAR SHOCK				−0.143 (0.289)
CHALLENGER NONSHOCK NUCLEAR WEAPONS				−0.355 (0.340)
CHALLENGER NONSHOCK NUCLEAR WEAPONS × TARGET NONSHOCK NUCLEAR WEAPONS				– –
MILITARY RATIO	0.667*** (0.158)	0.668*** (0.158)	0.695*** (0.163)	0.703*** (0.162)
ALLIANCE	0.203† (0.112)	0.193† (0.112)	0.192† (0.114)	0.170 (0.114)
COMMON OPPONENT	0.0991 (0.0976)	0.110 (0.0945)	0.0936 (0.0963)	0.106 (0.0927)

CHALLENGER STRATEGIC VALUE	0.0404	0.0784	0.0326	0.0713
	(0.0777)	(0.0749)	(0.0766)	(0.0745)
CHALLENGER ETHNIC VALUE	−0.0487	−0.0374	−0.0535	−0.0457
	(0.0692)	(0.0691)	(0.0707)	(0.0691)
CHALLENGER OTHER DISPUTE	−0.111†	−0.123†	−0.100	−0.111†
	(0.0669)	(0.0673)	(0.0666)	(0.0667)
DEMOCRATIC DISPUTE	0.105	0.0975	0.105	0.0927
	(0.136)	(0.134)	(0.138)	(0.134)
CONSTANT	−0.603**	−0.617***	−0.586***	−0.600***
	(0.102)	(0.103)	(0.105)	(0.103)

DV: TARGET DECISION TO OFFER CONCESSIONS

NUCLEAR CHALLENGER	−0.0532		−0.297	
	(0.113)		(0.228)	
CHALLENGER NUCLEAR SHOCK		−0.0252		−0.348
		(0.143)		(0.262)
CHALLENGER NONSHOCK NUCLEAR WEAPONS		−0.0169		−0.231
		(0.165)		(0.348)
TARGET NUUCLEAR WEAPONS			−0.0996	
			(0.129)	
NUCLEAR CHALLENGER × NUCLEAR TARGET			0.352	
			(0.290)	
TARGET NUCLEAR SHOCK				−0.0394
				(0.154)
CHALLENGER NUCLEAR SHOCK × TARGET NUCLEAR SHOCK				0.340
				(0.326)
TARGET NONSHOCK NUCLEAR WEAPONS				−0.249
				(0.198)

Table A.8 (*Continued*)

DV: TARGET DECISION TO OFFER CONCESSIONS

CHALLENGER NONSHOCK NUCLEAR WEAPONS × TARGET NONSHOCK NUCLEAR WEAPONS				—
				—
MILITARY RATIO	0.609***	0.597***	0.615***	0.614***
	(0.154)	(0.153)	(0.165)	(0.164)
ALLIANCE	0.193†	0.198†	0.189†	0.180
	(0.110)	(0.110)	(0.112)	(0.113)
COMMON OPPONENT	0.0846	0.0887	0.0727	0.0825
	(0.0921)	(0.0924)	(0.0896)	(0.0905)
TARGET STRATEGIC VALUE	−0.0360	−0.0293	−0.0353	−0.0271
	(0.0815)	(0.0824)	(0.0805)	(0.0823)
TARGET ETHNIC VALUE	−0.0442	−0.0283	−0.0548	−0.0488
	(0.0754)	(0.0775)	(0.0752)	(0.0771)
TARGET OTHER DISPUTE	0.102	0.0991	0.113†	0.112†
	(0.0663)	(0.0674)	(0.0655)	(0.0661)
DEMOCRATIC DISPUTE	0.190	0.190	0.196	0.190
	(0.133)	(0.133)	(0.136)	(0.135)
CONSTANT	−0.686***	−0.693***	−0.655***	−0.659***
	(0.0997)	(0.0997)	(0.105)	(0.105)
ρ	0.857***	0.858***	0.857***	0.859***
	(0.0191)	(0.0188)	(0.0190)	(0.0187)
N	1,528	1,528	1,528	1,528

NOTE: Robust standard errors in parentheses, clustered by territorial dispute. *** $p < 0.001$, ** $p < 0.01$, * $p < 0.05$, † $p < 0.10$. CHALLENGER NONSHOCK NUCLEAR WEAPONS × TARGET NONSHOCK NUCLEAR WEAPONS is dropped from Model 53 because of collinearity.

If anything, nuclear weapons are negatively associated with extracting concessions: TARGET NONSHOCK NUCLEAR WEAPONS is negative and statistically significant in the challenger equation (Models 51 and 53). Challengers therefore appear less likely to concede when facing predispute nuclear powers.

We replicate our empirical tests using the same alternate measures of nuclear status that we employed in Chapter 3: CHALLENGER ARSENAL SIZE (or TARGET ARSENAL SIZE when appropriate), NUCLEAR SUPERIORITY, NUCLEAR RATIO, and DIFFERENCE IN ARSENAL SIZE. The findings, which are displayed in Table A.9, continue to support our theory. An opponent's nuclear status is generally unrelated to whether a state makes territorial concessions. TARGET ARSENAL SIZE is negative and statistically significant (Model 54, challenger equation), meaning that the likelihood of challengers making concessions declines as the target's nuclear arsenal size increases. However, the statistical significance of TARGET ARSENAL SIZE is relatively weak ($p < 0.10$).

Military Escalation During Territorial Disputes

Chapter 4 looks at military escalation in two ways. First, it examines the use of military force in disputes over territory. Second, it evaluates escalatory behavior within ongoing military confrontations.

For the analysis of dispute initiation, we use a data set that includes 6,542 "opportunities" for challengers to initiate military confrontations. The dependent variable is MILITARY CHALLENGE. This measure accounts for the actions of challengers only – as opposed to both challengers and targets. We therefore use simpler probit regressions to analyze how the challenger's nuclear status influences the probability of a military challenge, while controlling for other relevant factors. Our models include the same covariates as we used in the preceding analysis, along with three additional measures designed to control for temporal dependence: TIME SINCE LAST MILITARY CONFLICT, TIME SINCE LAST MILITARY CONFLICT SQUARED, and TIME SINCE LAST MILITARY CONFLICT CUBED. We use robust standard errors clustered by territorial dispute.

Table A.10 presents the results from the probit analysis. Consistent with nuclear skepticism theory, nuclear challengers are no more likely than their nonnuclear counterparts to initiate military challenges to the status quo (Model 58). As Model 59 shows, the results are similar

Table A.9 *Bivariate probit estimates of concessions during territorial dispute negotiations.*

	54	55	56	57
DV: CHALLENGER DECISION TO OFFER CONCESSIONS				
TARGET ARSENAL SIZE	-0.0214† (0.0115)			
NUCLEAR SUPERIORITY		-0.115 (0.0845)		
NUCLEAR RATIO			0.205 (0.224)	
DIFFERENCE IN ARSENAL SIZE				-0.0343 (0.0396)
MILITARY RATIO	0.653*** (0.153)	0.656*** (0.156)	0.639*** (0.158)	0.766*** (0.158)
ALLIANCE	0.207† (0.115)	0.206† (0.113)	0.208† (0.113)	0.196† (0.111)
COMMON OPPONENT	0.106 (0.0953)	0.0999 (0.0970)	0.102 (0.0973)	0.0890 (0.0998)
CHALLENGER STRATEGIC VALUE	0.0404 (0.0759)	0.0407 (0.0772)	0.0403 (0.0769)	0.0370 (0.0787)
CHALLENGER ETHNIC VALUE	-0.0396 (0.0692)	-0.0445 (0.0695)	-0.0460 (0.0696)	-0.0590 (0.0712)
CHALLENGER OTHER DISPUTE	-0.110† (0.0666)	-0.111† (0.0669)	-0.111† (0.0669)	-0.106 (0.0673)
DEMOCRATIC DISPUTE	0.108 (0.136)	0.109 (0.136)	0.108 (0.138)	0.0993 (0.133)
CONSTANT	-0.599*** (0.0970)	-0.598*** (0.100)	-0.700*** (0.124)	-0.642*** (0.0967)

DV: TARGET DECISION TO OFFER CONCESSIONS

CHALLENGER ARSENAL SIZE	-0.00415 (0.0198)			
NUCLEAR SUPERIORITY		-0.0906 (0.179)		
NUCLEAR RATIO			0.0686 (0.219)	
DIFFERENCE IN ARSENAL SIZE				-0.0326 (0.0420)
MILITARY RATIO	0.596*** (0.153)	0.615*** (0.154)	0.570*** (0.162)	0.651*** (0.155)
ALLIANCE	0.197† (0.110)	0.194† (0.110)	0.198† (0.110)	0.192† (0.110)
COMMON OPPONENT	0.0876 (0.0920)	0.0836 (0.0917)	0.0849 (0.0917)	0.0740 (0.0915)
TARGET STRATEGIC VALUE	-0.0390 (0.0817)	-0.0369 (0.0816)	-0.0353 (0.0807)	-0.0344 (0.0812)
TARGET ETHNIC VALUE	-0.0340 (0.0758)	-0.0390 (0.0751)	-0.0446 (0.0754)	-0.0544 (0.0745)
TARGET OTHER DISPUTE	0.0984 (0.0663)	0.101 (0.0663)	0.106 (0.0660)	0.110† (0.0668)
DEMOCRATIC DISPUTE	0.190 (0.133)	0.190 (0.133)	0.193 (0.136)	0.192 (0.132)
CONSTANT	-0.686*** (0.100)	-0.689*** (0.0999)	-0.705*** (0.123)	-0.693*** (0.0991)
ρ	0.857** (0.0192)	0.857** (0.0191)	0.857** (0.0190)	0.857** (0.187)
N	1,528	1,528	1,528	1,528

NOTE: Robust standard errors in parentheses, clustered by territorial dispute. *** $p < 0.001$, ** $p < 0.01$, * $p < 0.05$, † $p < 0.10$.

Table A.10 Probit estimates of military challenges over territory.

	58	59	60	61
NUCLEAR CHALLENGER	-0.0396 (0.181)		-0.182 (0.244)	
CHALLENGER NUCLEAR SHOCK		0.112 (0.154)		0.0150 (0.200)
CHALLENGER NONSHOCK NUCLEAR WEAPONS		-1.007** (0.386)		-1.019** (0.383)
NUCLEAR TARGET			-0.124 (0.106)	
NUCLEAR CHALLENGER × NUCLEAR TARGET			0.579† (0.320)	
TARGET NUCLEAR SHOCK				0.0171 (0.107)
CHALLENGER NUCLEAR SHOCK × TARGET NUCLEAR SHOCK				0.259 (0.285)
TARGET NONSHOCK NUCLEAR WEAPONS				-0.613* (0.240)
CHALLENGER NONSHOCK NUCLEAR WEAPONS × TARGET NONSHOCK NUCLEAR WEAPONS			—	—
MILITARY RATIO	0.397** (0.126)	0.414** (0.125)	0.382** (0.130)	0.384** (0.131)
ALLIANCE	0.0695 (0.0955)	0.0770 (0.0944)	0.0634 (0.0933)	0.0706 (0.0914)

COMMON OPPONENT	−0.249**	−0.264**	−0.264**	−0.271**
	(0.0791)	(0.0798)	(0.0789)	(0.0785)
STRATEGIC VALUE	0.193**	0.193**	0.215**	0.228**
	(0.0745)	(0.0733)	(0.0752)	(0.0737)
ETHNIC VALUE	0.236**	0.223**	0.222**	0.214**
	(0.0740)	(0.0732)	(0.0737)	(0.0723)
CHALLENGER OTHER DISPUTE	0.256**	0.253**	0.251**	0.242**
	(0.0626)	(0.0622)	(0.0619)	(0.0621)
DEMOCRATIC DISPUTE	−0.380*	−0.371*	−0.388*	−0.369†
	(0.186)	(0.185)	(0.188)	(0.189)
TIME SINCE LAST MILITARY CONFLICT	−0.144**	−0.145**	−0.145**	−0.145**
	(0.0150)	(0.0151)	(0.0151)	(0.0151)
TIME SINCE LAST MILITARY CONFLICT SQUARED	0.00509**	0.00509**	0.00518**	0.00509**
	(0.000756)	(0.000758)	(0.000764)	(0.000764)
TIME SINCE LAST MILITARY CONFLICT CUBED	−0.0000514**	−0.0000515**	−0.0000530**	−0.0000517**
	(0.0000101)	(0.0000101)	(0.0000103)	(0.0000102)
CONSTANT	−1.305**	−1.297**	−1.278**	−1.269**
	(0.108)	(0.108)	(0.110)	(0.111)
N	6,542	6,542	6,542	6,542

NOTE: Robust standard errors in parentheses, clustered by territorial dispute. *** $p < 0.001$, ** $p < 0.01$, * $p < 0.05$, † $p < 0.10$. CHALLENGER NONSHOCK NUCLEAR WEAPONS × TARGET NONSHOCK NUCLEAR WEAPONS is dropped from Model 61 because of collinearity.

when we distinguish between nuclear shocks and weapons acquired before disputes begin. CHALLENGER NUCLEAR SHOCK is statistically insignificant, while CHALLENGER NONSHOCK NUCLEAR WEAPONS is significant and negative. Thus, states are less likely to start military confrontations when they possess nuclear weapons prior to making a territorial claim.

Does the nuclear status of the target affect whether nuclear-armed challengers initiate military confrontations? We address this question by including NUCLEAR CHALLENGER × NUCLEAR TARGET along with the two constituent parts (Model 60). The interaction term is positive and significant at the ninety percent level, which seemingly suggests that nuclear challengers are more likely to initiate military challenges against other nuclear powers. However, the ninety-five percent confidence interval around the marginal effect of NUCLEAR CHALLENGER includes zero when the target is nuclear, and when it is nonnuclear.

Table A.11 substitutes the more nuanced measures of nuclear status for NUCLEAR CHALLENGER. The variables CHALLENGER ARSENAL SIZE (Model 62), NUCLEAR SUPERIORITY (Model 63), NUCLEAR RATIO (Model 64), and DIFFERENCE IN ARSENAL SIZE (Model 65) are all statistically insignificant. These results further underscore that a challenger's nuclear status has little effect on its propensity to use force during territorial disputes.

We turn now to our second analysis of escalation, which picks things up once a military confrontation has begun. The data set used for this analysis includes 374 military disputes over territory. There are two dependent variables of interest: CHALLENGER ESCALATION and TARGET ESCALATION. Because we are once again interested in the behavior of challengers and targets, we use bivariate probit to estimate how a country's nuclear status affects its willingness to escalate military conflicts. We include the same independent variables as we used in our analysis of concessions. The standard errors are clustered by territorial dispute.

Table A.12 displays the results.[24] We first consider how the challenger's nuclear status affects its propensity to escalate. In Model 66, NUCLEAR CHALLENGER is negative and statistically significant at the ninety percent level, suggesting that nuclear powers are less likely

---

[24] Model 67 does not converge when we include the nonshock nuclear variables.

Table A.11 *Probit estimates of military challenges over territory.*

	62	63	64	65
CHALLENGER ARSENAL SIZE	-0.0295 (0.0390)			
NUCLEAR SUPERIORITY		-0.147 (0.245)		
NUCLEAR RATIO			0.153 (0.164)	
DIFFERENCE IN ARSENAL SIZE				-0.0330 (0.0442)
MILITARY RATIO	0.415** (0.123)	0.414** (0.125)	0.353** (0.130)	0.418** (0.124)
ALLIANCE	0.0655 (0.0950)	0.0660 (0.0952)	0.0705 (0.0961)	0.0665 (0.0947)
COMMON OPPONENT	-0.254** (0.0791)	-0.252** (0.0793)	-0.250** (0.0798)	-0.256** (0.0790)
STRATEGIC VALUE	0.197** (0.0744)	0.196** (0.0742)	0.199** (0.0744)	0.199** (0.0740)
ETHNIC VALUE	0.229** (0.0737)	0.230** (0.0739)	0.242** (0.0736)	0.227** (0.0738)
CHALLENGER OTHER DISPUTE	0.257** (0.0621)	0.257** (0.0621)	0.254** (0.0619)	0.255** (0.0617)
DEMOCRATIC DISPUTE	-0.376* (0.186)	-0.381* (0.186)	-0.378* (0.185)	-0.377* (0.186)
TIME SINCE LAST MILITARY CONFLICT	-0.145** (0.0150)	-0.145** (0.0150)	-0.145** (0.0150)	-0.145** (0.0151)
TIME SINCE LAST MILITARY CONFLICT SQUARED	0.00509** (0.000758)	0.00510** (0.000759)	0.00512** (0.000754)	0.00511** (0.000760)
TIME SINCE LAST MILITARY CONFLICT CUBED	-0.0000513** (0.0000101)	-0.0000516** (0.0000101)	-0.0000518** (0.0000100)	-0.0000517*** (0.0000102)
CONSTANT	-1.304** (0.108)	-1.305** (0.108)	-1.364** (0.123)	-1.303** (0.108)
N	6,542	6,542	6,542	6,542

NOTE: Robust standard errors in parentheses, clustered by dyad. *** $p < 0.001$, ** $p < 0.01$, * $p < 0.05$, † $p < 0.10$.

Table A.12 *Bivariate probit estimates of military escalation.*

	66	67	68	69	70	71	72
DV: CHALLENGER ESCALATION							
NUCLEAR CHALLENGER	-0.410+		-0.334				
	(0.216)		(0.351)				
CHALLENGER NUCLEAR SHOCK		-0.334+					
		(0.177)					
NUCLEAR TARGET			-0.138				
			(0.312)				
NUCLEAR CHALLENGER × NUCLEAR TARGET			-4.768***				
			(0.507)				
CHALLENGER ARSENAL SIZE				-0.0555			
				(0.0605)			
NUCLEAR SUPERIORITY					-0.322		
					(0.349)		
NUCLEAR RATIO						-0.219	
						(0.395)	
DIFFERENCE IN ARSENAL SIZE							-0.0473
							(0.0591)
MILITARY RATIO	1.200***	1.189***	1.143***	1.194***	1.196***	1.202***	1.190***
	(0.274)	(0.273)	(0.291)	(0.276)	(0.278)	(0.278)	(0.277)
ALLIANCE	-0.236	-0.229	-0.259	-0.231	-0.230	-0.201	-0.229
	(0.248)	(0.248)	(0.252)	(0.249)	(0.249)	(0.244)	(0.249)
COMMON OPPONENT	-0.400*	-0.393*	-0.404*	-0.407*	-0.403*	-0.386*	-0.408*
	(0.191)	(0.191)	(0.190)	(0.191)	(0.191)	(0.190)	(0.192)
CHALLENGER STRATEGIC VALUE	0.669***	0.664***	0.677***	0.667***	0.663***	0.638***	0.666***
	(0.173)	(0.172)	(0.185)	(0.173)	(0.173)	(0.169)	(0.174)

	(1)	(2)	(3)	(4)	(5)	(6)	(7)
CHALLENGER ETHNIC VALUE	0.370*	0.377*	0.379*	0.369*	0.368*	0.381*	0.369*
	(0.153)	(0.154)	(0.157)	(0.154)	(0.155)	(0.156)	(0.155)
CHALLENGER OTHER DISPUTE	0.312*	0.309*	0.302*	0.317*	0.315*	0.325**	0.316*
	(0.127)	(0.126)	(0.132)	(0.125)	(0.125)	(0.125)	(0.125)
DEMOCRATIC DISPUTE	−5.891***	−5.897***	−5.824***	−5.883***	−5.871***	−5.863***	−5.876***
	(0.249)	(0.248)	(0.252)	(0.251)	(0.251)	(0.251)	(0.251)
CONSTANT	−1.800***	−1.802***	−1.756***	−1.801***	−1.801***	−1.720***	−1.801***
	(0.243)	(0.244)	(0.253)	(0.242)	(0.242)	(0.312)	(0.242)
DV: TARGET ESCALATION							
NUCLEAR TARGET	0.128		0.143				
	(0.187)		(0.264)				
TARGET NUCLEAR SHOCK		0.156					
		(0.184)					
NUCLEAR CHALLENGER			0.127				
			(0.327)				
NUCLEAR CHALLENGER × NUCLEAR TARGET			−5.146***				
			(0.440)				
CHALLENGER ARSENAL SIZE				0.0120			
				(0.0568)			
NUCLEAR SUPERIORITY					0.0906		
					(0.322)		
NUCLEAR RATIO						−0.0660	
						(0.453)	

Table A.12 (Continued)

DV: TARGET ESCALATION							
DIFFERENCE IN ARSENAL SIZE							0.0221
							(0.0553)
MILITARY RATIO	0.251	0.255	0.209	0.211	0.207	0.244	0.203
	(0.311)	(0.310)	(0.330)	(0.324)	(0.327)	(0.322)	(0.325)
ALLIANCE	−0.161	−0.157	−0.162	−0.176	−0.176	−0.177	−0.174
	(0.266)	(0.266)	(0.266)	(0.266)	(0.266)	(0.263)	(0.266)
COMMON OPPONENT	−0.113	−0.110	−0.0988	−0.124	−0.123	−0.124	−0.122
	(0.188)	(0.189)	(0.188)	(0.190)	(0.189)	(0.189)	(0.190)
TARGET STRATEGIC VALUE	0.451**	0.449**	0.429*	0.452**	0.451**	0.452**	0.449**
	(0.168)	(0.168)	(0.171)	(0.172)	(0.172)	(0.168)	(0.173)
TARGET ETHNIC VALUE	0.0691	0.0673	0.0927	0.0584	0.0600	0.0378	0.0603
	(0.139)	(0.138)	(0.149)	(0.140)	(0.141)	(0.134)	(0.140)
TARGET OTHER DISPUTE	0.171	0.174	0.170	0.176	0.174	0.191	0.175
	(0.134)	(0.134)	(0.138)	(0.134)	(0.135)	(0.132)	(0.134)
DEMOCRATIC DISPUTE	−0.632	−0.635	−0.547	−0.630	−0.626	−0.634	−0.625
	(0.613)	(0.611)	(0.654)	(0.621)	(0.623)	(0.628)	(0.622)
CONSTANT	−1.282***	−1.287***	−1.262***	−1.245***	−1.244***	−1.225***	−1.243***
	(0.230)	(0.228)	(0.231)	(0.216)	(0.216)	(0.279)	(0.216)
ρ	0.925***	0.925***	0.923***	0.925***	0.925***	0.926***	0.925***
	(0.296)	(0.295)	(0.296)	(0.293)	(0.293)	(0.293)	(0.293)
N	374	374	374	374	374	374	374

NOTE: Robust standard errors in parentheses, clustered by territorial dispute. *** $p < 0.001$, ** $p < 0.01$, * $p < 0.05$, † $p < 0.10$.

to escalate military confrontations once they have begun. This result holds when we focus on nuclear shocks (Model 67). The nuclear status of the target appears to influence whether nuclear challengers escalate disputes, based on the results from Model 68. Nuclear challengers are not more likely to escalate against nonnuclear targets, but they are considerably less likely to escalate when facing other nuclear powers. As we discussed in Chapter 4, escalation by nuclear challengers is exceedingly rare: conflict initiators with nuclear arsenals escalated disputes with nonnuclear targets on only four occasions from 1919 to 1995, and nuclear challengers never escalated against other nuclear states. However, because military disputes are rare to begin with (especially those involving nuclear powers), this evidence should be interpreted cautiously. We are particularly reluctant to draw strong conclusions based on these negative relationships given that all of the variables that account for the nuclear balance are statistically insignificant (Models 69–72).

Nuclear targets likewise are no more likely than their nonnuclear counterparts to escalate disputes. As in our analysis of challengers, the interaction term is negative and statistically significant (Model 68) but all of the other nuclear variables are insignificant, meaning that the target's possession of nuclear weapons has little bearing on its willingness to escalate military disputes.

References

Abe, Shinzo. 2012. "Asia's Democratic Security Diamond." *Project Syndicate* (27 December).

Adams, Sherman. 1961. *Firsthand Report: The Story of the Eisenhower Administration.* New York: Harper.

Allison, Graham T., and Philip Zelikow. 1999. *Essence of Decision: Explaining the Cuban Missile Crisis.* 2nd ed. New York: Longman.

Alterman, Jon B. 2003. "Coercive Diplomacy Against Iraq, 1990–98." In *The United States and Coercive Diplomacy,* edited by Robert J. Art and Patrick M. Cronin, pp. 275–303. Washington, D.C.: U.S. Institute of Peace.

American Security Council. 1967. *The Changing Strategic Military Balance: USA v. USSR.* Washington, D.C.: House Armed Services Committee.

Applebaum, Anne. 2015. "An Old Threat Made New: Why Nuclear Weapons Suddenly Matter More than Ever." *Slate.com* (2 April).

Art, Robert J. 1980. "To What Ends Military Power?" *International Security* 4(4): 3–35.

1996. "American Foreign Policy and the Fungibility of Force." *Security Studies* 5(4): 7–42.

2003. "Coercive Diplomacy: What Do We Know?" In *The United States and Coercive Diplomacy,* edited by Robert J. Art and Patrick M. Cronin, pp. 359–420. Washington, D.C.: U.S. Institute of Peace.

Art, Robert J., and Patrick M. Cronin, eds. 2003. *The United States and Coercive Diplomacy.* Washington, D.C.: U.S. Institute of Peace.

Asal, Victor, and Kyle Beardsley. 2007. "Proliferation and International Crisis Behavior." *Journal of Peace Research* 44(2): 139–55.

Baldwin, David A. 2002. "Power and International Relations." In *Handbook of International Relations,* edited by Walter Carlsnaes, Thomas Risse, and Beth A. Simmons, pp. 177–91. Thousand Oaks, Calif.: Sage.

BBC News. 1982a. "Argentine Comment on Nuclear Arms and on NATO Position." *BBC Summary of World Broadcasts* (28 May).

1982b. "Other Reports and Comment on Falklands Dispute." *BBC Summary of World Broadcasts* (20 April).

1998. "Pakistan Declares Nuclear 'Superiority.'" (29 June).

2001. "U.S. Adds Pressure on Pakistan." (26 December).

2013. "Obama: North Korea's Crisis-for-Concession Days Over." (7 May).

BBC Radio 4. 2013. "Margaret Thatcher: Potency and Paradox." (8 April).

Beach, Hugh. 2011. "What Price Nuclear Blackmail?" *Evidence Submitted to the Trident Commission.* British American Security Information Council. Available at www.basicint.org/node/1848.

Beardsley, Kyle, and Victor Asal. 2009a. "Nuclear Weapons as Shields." *Conflict Management and Peace Science* 26(3): 235–55.

2009b. "Winning with the Bomb." *Journal of Conflict Resolution* 53(2): 278–301.

Bell, Mark S. 2015. "Beyond Emboldenment: How Acquiring Nuclear Weapons Can Change Foreign Policy." *International Security* 40(1): 87–119.

Bell, Mark S., and Nicholas L. Miller. 2015. "Questioning the Effect of Nuclear Weapons on Conflict." *Journal of Conflict Resolution* 59(1): 74–92.

Beloborodov, Nikolai. 1990. *The War Was Averted (Soviet Nuclear Weapons in Cuba, 1962).* Washington, D.C.: Translated by Anna Melyakova and Svetlana Savranskaya for the National Security Archive.

Berejikian, Jeffrey D., and Bryan R. Early. 2013. "Loss Aversion and Foreign Policy Resolve." *Political Psychology* 34(5): 649–71.

Betts, Richard K. 1987. *Nuclear Blackmail and Nuclear Balance.* Washington, D.C.: Brookings Institution.

Birsel, Robert, and Stephanie Nebehay. 2013. "U.S. Rejects North Korean Demand for Nuclear Status." *Reuters* (23 April).

Black, Samuel. 2010. *The Changing Political Utility of Nuclear Weapons: Nuclear Threats from 1970 to 2010.* Washington, D.C.: Stimson Center.

Blair, Bruce. 1993. *The Logic of Accidental Nuclear War.* Washington, D.C.: Brookings Institution.

Blanton, Thomas. 2012. "The Cuban Missile Crisis Just Isn't What It Used to Be." *Cold War International History Project Bulletin,* edited by James G. Hershberg and Christian F. Ostermann, vol. 17/18, pp. 11–18. Washington, D.C.: Wilson Center.

Blechman, Barry M., and Stephen S. Kaplan. 1978. *Force without War: U.S. Armed Forces as a Political Instrument.* Washington, D.C.: Brookings Institution.

Blight, James G., Joseph S. Nye, and David A. Welch. 1987. "The Cuban Missile Crisis Revisited." *Foreign Affairs* 66(1): 170–88.

Bolton, John R. 2010. "Get Ready for a Nuclear Iran." *Wall Street Journal* (2 May).

　2015. "To Stop Iran's Bomb, Bomb Iran." *New York Times* (26 March).

Bracken, Paul. 2012. *The Second Nuclear Age: Strategy, Danger, and the New Power Politics*. New York: Times Books.

Brady, Steven J. 2009. *Eisenhower and Adenauer: Alliance Maintenance Under Pressure, 1953–1960*. Lanham, Md.: Rowman & Littlefield.

Brambor, Thomas, William Roberts Clark, and Matt Golder. 2006. "Understanding Interaction Models: Improving Empirical Analyses." *Political Analysis* 14(1): 63–82.

Brecher, Michael, and Jonathan Wilkenfeld. 1997. *A Study of Crisis*. Ann Arbor, Mich.: University of Michigan Press.

Brehm, J.W. 1956. "Post-Decision Changes in Desirability of Alternatives." *Journal of Abnormal Social Psychology* 52(3): 384–89.

Brighton, Terry. 2009. *Patton, Montgomery, Rommel: Masters of War*. New York: Three Rivers Press.

Brodie, Bernard. 1959. *Strategy in the Missile Age*. Princeton, N.J.: Princeton University Press.

Bruton, F. Brinley, and Ian Johnston. 2013. "UN Passes Sanctions Despite North Korea Threat of 'Pre-emptive Nuclear Attack.'" *NBC News* (7 March).

Bueno de Mesquita, Bruce, and William H. Riker. 1982. "An Assessment of the Merits of Selective Nuclear Proliferation." *Journal of Conflict Resolution* 26(2): 283–306.

Bundy, McGeorge. 1984. "The Unimpressive Record of Atomic Diplomacy." In *The Choice: Nuclear Weapons Versus Security*, edited by Gwyn Prins, pp. 42–54. London: Chatto and Windus.

　1988. *Danger and Survival: Choices about the Bomb in the First Fifty Years*. New York: Random House.

Burns, Robert. 1996. "U.S. Said to Have No Non-Nuclear Way to Destroy Suspect Libyan Plant." *Associated Press* (23 April).

Burr, William. 2012. *The 3AM Phone Call: False Warnings of Soviet Missile Attacks during 1979–80 Led to Alert Actions for U.S. Strategic Forces* (Electronic Briefing Book No. 371). Washington, D.C.: National Security Archive. Available at nsarchive.gwu.edu/nukevault/ebb371.

Burr, William, and Jeffrey Kimball. 2003. "Nixon's Secret Nuclear Alert: Vietnam War Diplomacy and the Joint Chiefs of Staff Readiness Test, October 1969." *Cold War History* 3(2): 113–56.

Burr, William, and Jeffrey P. Kimball. 2015. *Nixon's Nuclear Specter: The Secret Alert of 1969, Madman Diplomacy, and the Vietnam War*. Lawrence: University Press of Kansas.

Burr, William, and Jeffrey T. Richelson. 2000/2001. "Whether to 'Strangle the Baby in the Cradle': The United States and the Chinese Nuclear Program, 1960–64." *International Security* 25(3): 54–99.

Bush, Richard C., and Michael E. O'Hanlon. 2007. *A War Like No Other: The Truth About China's Challenge to America*. Hoboken, N.J.: Wiley.

Byman, Daniel. 2000/2001. "After the Storm: U.S. Policy Toward Iraq Since 1991." *Political Science Quarterly* 115(4): 493–516.

Byman, Daniel, and Matthew C. Waxman. 2002. *The Dynamics of Coercion: American Foreign Policy and the Limits of Military Might*. New York: Cambridge University Press.

Cable, James. 1994. *Gunboat Diplomacy, 1919–1991: Political Applications of Limited Naval Force*. 3rd ed. New York: St. Martin's.

Caldwell, Dan, and Robert E. Williams. 2012. *Seeking Security in an Insecure World*. Lanham, Md.: Rowman and Littlefield.

Carnesale, Albert, Paul Doty, Stanley Hoffman, Samuel P. Huntington, Joseph S. Nye, Scott D. Sagan, and Derek Bok. 1983. *Living with Nuclear Weapons*. Cambridge, Mass.: Harvard University Press.

Carter, Chelsea J., and Kevin Voigt. 2013. "North Korea's War of Words Escalates – Timeline of a Crisis." *CNN* (11 April).

Carter, Dan T. 1995. *The Politics of Rage: George Wallace, the Origins of the New Conservatism, and the Transformation of American Politics*. New York: Simon and Schuster.

Carter, David, and Curtis S. Signorino. 2010. "Back to the Future: Modeling Time Dependence in Binary Data." *Political Analysis* 18(3): 271–92.

Chang, Gordon H. 1988. "To the Nuclear Brink: Eisenhower, Dulles, and the Quemoy-Matsu Crisis." *International Security* 12(4): 96–123.

Chang, Gordon H., and He Di. 1993. "The Absence of War in the U.S.-China Confrontation over Quemoy and Matsu in 1954–1955: Contingency, Luck, Deterrence." *American Historical Review* 98(5): 1500–24.

Chari, P.R. 2013. "Nuclear Signaling in South Asia: Revisiting A. Q. Khan's 1987 Threat." *Carnegie Endowment for International Peace Proliferation Analysis* (14 November).

Chari, P.R., Pervaiz Iqbal Cheema, and Stephen P. Cohen. 2007. *Four Crises and a Peace Process: American Engagement in South Asia*. Washington, D.C.: Brookings Institution.

Charlton, Michael. 1987. *From Deterrence to Defense: The Inside Story of Strategic Policy*. Cambridge, Mass.: Harvard University Press.

Cheevers, Jack. 2013. *Act of War: Lyndon Johnson, North Korea, and the Capture of the Spy Ship Pueblo*. New York: Penguin.

Chengappa, Raj. 2000. *Weapons of Peace*. New Delhi: Harper Collins.

Chinese Foreign Ministry. 1955. "Summary of the Views of Afro-Asian Countries on the Taiwan Issue at the Afro-Asian Conference, May 27, 1955." Washington, D.C.: Wilson Center Digital Archive.

Choe, Sang-Hun. 2012. "North Korea Threatens South With Military Action." *New York Times* (23 April).

——— 2013a. "North Korea Issues Threat at Ceremony for Military." *New York Times* (25 April).

——— 2013b. "North Korea Threatens to Attack U.S. With 'Lighter and Smaller Nukes.'" *New York Times* (5 March).

Clapper, James. 2012. "Unclassified Statement for the Record on the Worldwide Threat Assessment of the U.S. Intelligence Community for the Senate Select Committee on Intelligence." 31 January.

Clausewitz, Carl von. 1976. *On War*. Ed. and trans. by Michael Howard and Peter Paret. Princeton, N.J.: Princeton University Press.

CNN. 1999. "Pakistan's Prime Minister Rallies Troops at Kashmir Front." (24 June).

Cohen, Avner. 2008. "Interview with Arnan Azaryahu ("Sini")." *The Avner Cohen Collection*. Available at digitalarchive.wilson center.org/document/117848.

——— 2012. *The Worst Kept Secret: Israel's Bargain with the Bomb*. New York: Columbia University Press.

Colby, Elbridge, Avner Cohen, William McCants, Bradley Morris, and William Rosenau. 2013. *The Israeli "Nuclear Alert" of 1973: Deterrence and Signaling in Crisis*. Washington, D.C.: Center for Naval Analyses.

Cold War International History Project Bulletin. 1995. "19 March 1953, Resolution, USSR Council of Ministers with Draft Letters from Soviet Government to Mao Zedong and Kim Il Sung and Directive to Soviet Delegation at United Nations." Vols. 6/7: 80–83.

Constable, Pamela. 1999. "Kashmir Duel Stirs Fears of an Expanded Conflict." *Washington Post Foreign Service* (28 May): A1.

Cooper, Chester L. 1978. *The Lion's Last Roar: Suez, 1956*. New York: Harper and Row.

Crane, Conrad C. 2000. "To Avert Impending Disaster: American Military Plans to Use Atomic Weapons During the Korean War." *Journal of Strategic Studies* 23(2): 72–88.

Cumings, Bruce. 2010. *The Korean War: A History*. New York: Random House.

de Tocqueville, Alexis. 2000 [1840]. *Democracy in America*. Edited by J.P. Mayer, translated by George Lawrence. New York: Harper Collins.

Dingman, Roger. 1988. "Atomic Diplomacy During the Korean War." *International Security* 13(3): 50–91.

Dittmeier, Christopher R. 2013. "Proliferation, Preemption, and Intervention in the Nuclearization of Second-Tier States." *Journal of Theoretical Politics* 25(4): 492–525.

Dobbs, Michael. 2008. *One Minute to Midnight: Kennedy, Khrushchev, and Castro on the Brink of Nuclear War.* New York: Knopf.

Dobrynin, Anatoly. 1969. "Memorandum of Conversation of the Ambassador of the USSR A.F. Dobrynin with Kissinger, July 12, 1969." History and Public Policy Program Digital Archive, SCCD, F. 5, Op. 61, D. 558, LI. 92–105. Translated by Mark H. Doctoroff. Washington, D.C.: Wilson Center Digital Archive.

Downes, Alexander B., and Todd S. Sechser. 2012. "The Illusion of Democratic Credibility." *International Organization* 66(3): 457–89.

Dugger, Celia W. 1999. "Atmosphere Is Tense as India and Pakistan Agree to Talks." *New York Times* (1 June).

——— 2002a. "India Tests Missile, Stirring a Region Already on Edge." *New York Times* (26 January).

——— 2002b. "Indian General Talks Bluntly of War and a Nuclear Threat." *New York Times* (12 January).

——— 2002c. "The Kashmir Brink." *New York Times* (20 June).

Dulles, John Foster. 1957. "Challenge and Response in United States Policy." *Foreign Affairs* 36(1): 25–43.

——— 1958a. "State Department Transcript of Remarks Made by Dulles at News Conference." *New York Times* (1 October): 8.

——— 1958b. "Text of Dulles Statement on the Far East." *New York Times* (5 September).

——— 2011. "Report by Secretary of State Dulles on Geneva and Indochina, NSC 195th Meeting, May 6, 1954." In *The Pentagon Papers: The Defense Department History of United States Decisionmaking on Vietnam,* Vol. 1, p. 500. Washington, D.C.: National Archives.

Dunstan, Simon. 2007. *The Yom Kippur War: The Arab-Israeli War of 1973.* New York: Osprey.

Eisenhower, Dwight D. 1963. *The White House Years: Mandate for Change, 1953–1956.* Garden City, NY: Doubleday.

——— 1965. *Waging Peace, 1956–1961.* Garden City, N.Y.: Doubleday.

Evans, Michael, and Philip Webster. 2002. "British Generals Prepare for Nuclear War Aftermath." *(London) Times* (24 May).

Fearon, James D. 1994. "Signaling Versus the Balance of Power and Interests: An Empirical Test of a Crisis Bargaining Model." *Journal of Conflict Resolution* 38(2): 236–69.

2002. "Selection Effects and Deterrence." *International Interactions* 28(1): 5–29.

Feaver, Peter D. 1995. "Optimists, Pessimists, and Theories of Nuclear Proliferation Management." *Security Studies* 4(4): 754–72.

Feldman, Shai. 1983. *Israeli Nuclear Deterrence: A Strategy for the 1980s.* New York: Columbia University Press.

Festinger, Leon. 1957. *A Theory of Cognitive Dissonance.* Stanford: Stanford University Press.

Finer, Herman. 1964. *Dulles over Suez: The Theory and Practice of His Diplomacy.* Chicago: Quadrangle.

Flint, Jerry M. 1968. "LeMay Explains His Nuclear Position." *New York Times* (28 October): 40.

Foot, Rosemary. 1985. *The Wrong War: American Policy and the Dimensions of the Korean Conflict, 1950–1953.* Ithaca, N.Y.: Cornell University Press.

1988. "Nuclear Coercion and the Ending of the Korean Conflict." *International Security* 13(3): 92–112.

1990. *A Substitute for Victory: The Politics of Peacemaking at the Korean Armistice Talks.* Ithaca, N.Y.: Cornell University Press.

Foradori, Paolo, ed. 2013. *Tactical Nuclear Weapons and Euro-Atlantic Security: The Future of NATO.* New York: Routledge.

Frankel, Max. 1958. "U.S. Called Ready to Use Atom Arms: Air Force Secretary Says Force Is Prepared to Deal With the Taiwan Area Crisis." *New York Times* (28 September): 10.

Fravel, M. Taylor. 2005. "Regime Insecurity and International Cooperation: Explaining China's Compromises in Territorial Disputes." *International Security* 30(2): 46–83.

2007/08. "Power Shifts and Escalation: Explaining China's Use of Force in Territorial Disputes." *International Security* 32(3): 44–83.

2008. *Strong Borders, Secure Nation: Cooperation and Conflict in China's Territorial Disputes.* Princeton, N.J.: Princeton University Press.

Freedman, Lawrence. 2005. *The Official History of the Falklands Campaign, Vol. 2: War and Diplomacy.* London: Routledge.

Freeman, Chas. 1998. "Did China Threaten to Bomb Los Angeles?" *Carnegie Endowment for International Peace Proliferation Brief* (22 March).

Friedman, Edward. 1975. "Nuclear Blackmail and the End of the Korean War." *Modern China* 1(1): 75–91.

Fuhrmann, Matthew. 2012. *Atomic Assistance: How "Atoms for Peace" Programs Cause Nuclear Insecurity.* Ithaca, N.Y.: Cornell University Press.

2016. "After Armageddon: Pondering the Potential Political Consequences of Using Nuclear Weapons." Typescript, Texas A&M University.

Fuhrmann, Matthew, and Sarah Kreps. 2010. "Targeting Nuclear Programs in War and Peace: A Quantitative Empirical Analysis, 1941–2000." *Journal of Conflict Resolution* 54(6): 831–59.

Fuhrmann, Matthew, Matthew Kroenig, and Todd S. Sechser. 2014. "The Case for Using Statistics to Study Nuclear Security." *H-Diplo/International Security Studies Forum* (2): 37–54.

Fuhrmann, Matthew, and Todd S. Sechser. 2014a. "Nuclear Strategy, Nonproliferation, and the Causes of Foreign Nuclear Deployments." *Journal of Conflict Resolution* 58(3): 455–80.

2014b. "Signaling Alliance Commitments: Hand-Tying and Sunk Costs in Extended Nuclear Deterrence." *American Journal of Political Science* 58(4): 919–35.

Fuhrmann, Matthew, and Jaroslav Tir. 2009. "Territorial Dimensions of Enduring Internal Rivalries." *Conflict Management and Peace Science* 26(4): 307–29.

Fukuyama, Francis. 1980. *Soviet Threats to Intervene in the Middle East 1956–1973*. Santa Monica, Calif.: Rand Corporation.

Fursenko, Aleksandr, and Timothy Naftali. 1997. *One Hell of a Gamble: Khrushchev, Castro, and Kennedy, 1958–1962*. New York: W.W. Norton.

2006. *Khrushchev's Cold War: The Inside Story of an American Adversary*. New York: W.W. Norton.

Gaddis, John Lewis. 1987. *The Long Peace: Inquiries into the History of the Cold War*. New York: Oxford University Press.

1997. *We Now Know: Rethinking Cold War History*. New York: Oxford University Press.

Ganguly, Sumit, and Devin T. Hagerty. 2005. *Fearful Symmetry: India-Pakistan Crises in the Shadow of Nuclear Weapons*. Seattle: University of Washington Press.

Ganguly, Sumit, and R. Harrison Wagner. 2004. "India and Pakistan: Bargaining in the Shadow of Nuclear War." *Journal of Strategic Studies* 27(3): 479–507.

Garnaut, John. 2013. "China Colonel Raises Nuclear Spectre." *The Age (Melbourne, Australia)* (23 January).

Garthoff, Raymond L. 1983. "Handling the Cienfuegos Crisis." *International Security* 8(1): 46–66.

1985. *Détente and Confrontation: American-Soviet Relations from Nixon to Reagan*. Washington, D.C.: Brookings Institution.

Gartzke, Erik, and Dong-Joon Jo. 2009. "Bargaining, Nuclear Proliferation, and Interstate Disputes." *Journal of Conflict Resolution* 53(2): 209–33.

Gartzke, Erik, Jeffrey M. Kaplow, and Rupal N. Mehta. 2014. "The Determinants of Nuclear Force Structure." *Journal of Conflict Resolution* 58(3): 481–508.

Gartzke, Erik, and Matthew Kroenig. 2009. "A Strategic Approach to Nuclear Proliferation." *Journal of Conflict Resolution* 53(2): 151–160.

Gavin, Francis J. 2012a. "Lessons from the Cuban Missile Crisis." *The National Interest Online* (26 October).

2012b. *Nuclear Statecraft: History and Strategy in America's Atomic Age.* Ithaca, N.Y.: Cornell University Press.

2014. "What We Talk About When We Talk About Nuclear Weapons: A Review Essay." *H-Diplo/International Security Studies Forum* (2): 11–36.

Gellman, Barton. 1998. "U.S. and China Nearly Came to Blows in '96: Tension Over Taiwan Prompted Repair of Ties." *Washington Post* (21 June): A1.

Gelman, Harry. 1982. *The Soviet Far East Buildup and Soviet Risk-Taking Against China.* Santa Monica, Calif.: Rand Corporation.

Gelpi, Christopher. 2003. *The Power of Legitimacy: Assessing the Role of Norms in Crisis Bargaining.* Princeton, N.J.: Princeton University Press.

Gelpi, Christopher, and Michael Griesdorf. 2001. "Winners or Losers? Democracies in International Crisis, 1918–94." *American Political Science Review* 95(3): 633–47.

Genba, Koichiro. 2012. "Japan-China Relations at a Crossroads." *New York Times* (20 November).

George, Alexander L., and William E. Simons. 1994. *The Limits of Coercive Diplomacy.* 2nd ed. Boulder, Colo.: Westview.

George, Alexander L., and Richard Smoke. 1974. *Deterrence in American Foreign Policy: Theory and Practice.* New York: Columbia University Press.

Gerson, Michael S. 2010. *The Sino-Soviet Border Conflict: Deterrence, Escalation, and the Threat of Nuclear War in 1969.* Arlington, Va.: Center for Naval Analyses.

Gibler, Douglas M. 2007. "Bordering on Peace: Democracy, Territorial Issues, and Conflict." *International Studies Quarterly* 51(3): 509–32.

Goldenberg, Suzanne. 2006. "Bush Threatened to Bomb Pakistan, Says Musharraf." *The Guardian* (22 September).

Goldstein, Lyle J. 2003. "Do Nascent WMD Arsenals Deter? The Sino-Soviet Crisis of 1969." *Political Science Quarterly* 118(1): 53–79.

Goodman, Alan E. 1978. *Negotiating While Fighting: The Diary of Admiral C. Turner Joy at the Korean Armistice Conference.* Stanford, Calif.: Hoover Institution Press.

Gorst, Anthony, and Lewis Johnman. 1997. *The Suez Crisis.* New York: Routledge.

Haaretz. 2013. "Dayan Told then IDF Chief: 'Whoever Gets Killed – Gets Killed.'" (11 September).

Haldeman, Harry R. 1978. *The Ends of Power.* New York: Times Books.

Hall, David K. 1978. "The Laotian War of 1962 and the Indo-Pakistani War of 1971." In *Force without War,* edited by Barry M. Blechman and Stephen S. Kaplan, pp. 135–221. Washington, D.C.: Brookings Institution.

Halperin, Morton H. 1966. *The 1958 Taiwan Straits Crisis: A Documented History.* Santa Monica, Calif.: Rand Corporation.

1987. *Nuclear Fallacy: Dispelling the Myth of Nuclear Strategy.* Cambridge, Mass.: Ballinger.

Harrison, Hope Millard. 2003. *Driving the Soviets up the Wall: Soviet-East German Relations, 1953–1961.* Princeton, N.J.: Princeton University Press.

Hastings, Max. 1987. *The Korean War.* New York: Simon and Schuster.

Hatton, Celia. 2013. "Is China Ready to Abandon North Korea?" *BBC News* (12 April).

Heckman, James J. 1979. "Sample Selection Bias as a Specification Error." *Econometrica* 47(1): 153–62.

Herken, Gregg. 1985. *Counsels of War.* New York: Knopf.

Herring, George C. 2002. *America's Longest War: The United States and Vietnam, 1950–1975.* 4th ed. Boston, Mass.: McGraw-Hill.

Herring, George C., and Richard H. Immerman. 1984. "Eisenhower, Dulles, and Dienbienphu: The Day We Didn't Go to War Revisited." *Journal of American History* 71(2): 343–63.

Hersh, Seymour M. 1991. *The Samson Option: Israel's Nuclear Arsenal and American Foreign Policy.* New York: Random House.

1993. "On the Nuclear Edge." *The New Yorker* (29 March).

Hinton, Harold C. 1967. "The Chinese Attitude." In *Sino-Soviet Relations and Arms Control,* edited by Morton C. Halperin, pp. 171–92. Cambridge, Mass.: MIT Press.

Horowitz, Michael C. 2009. "The Spread of Nuclear Weapons and International Conflict: Does Experience Matter?" *Journal of Conflict Resolution* 53(2): 234–57.

Horowitz, Michael C., and Dan Reiter. 2001. "When Does Aerial Bombing Work? Quantitative Empirical Tests, 1917–1999." *Journal of Conflict Resolution* 45(2): 147–73.

Horowitz, Michael C., Allan Stam, and Cali M. Ellis. 2015. *Why Leaders Fight.* New York: Cambridge University Press.

Hoyt, Timothy D. 2009. "Kargil: The Nuclear Dimension." In *Asymmetric Warfare in South Asia: The Causes and Consequences of the Kargil Conflict*, edited by Peter R. Lavoy, pp. 144–70. Cambridge: Cambridge University Press.

Huth, Paul K. 1996. *Standing Your Ground: Territorial Disputes and International Conflict*. Ann Arbor, Mich.: University of Michigan Press.

Huth, Paul K., and Todd L. Allee. 2002. *The Democratic Peace and Territorial Conflict in the Twentieth Century*. New York: Cambridge University Press.

Huth, Paul K., and Bruce Russett. 1984. "What Makes Deterrence Work? Cases from 1900 to 1980." *World Politics* 36(4): 496–526.

Isaacson, Walter. 2005. *Kissinger: A Biography*. 2nd ed. New York: Simon and Schuster.

Israel State Archives. 1973. "Minutes of a Consultation Held in the Prime Minister's Bureau, Tuesday, 9 October 1973, 07:30." *The Yom Kippur War, 1973: Special Publication*. Available at www.archives.gov.il/ArchiveGov_Eng/general/YomKippurWar/YK4/.

Israelyan, Victor. 1993. "Nuclear Showdown as Nixon Slept." *Christian Science Monitor* (3 November).

1995. *Inside the Kremlin During the Yom Kippur War*. State College, Penn.: The Pennsylvania State University Press.

Jackson, Julian. 2014. "Dien Bien Phu: Did the U.S. Offer France an A-Bomb?" *BBC News Magazine* (5 May).

Jackson, Michael Gordon. 2005. "Beyond Brinkmanship: Eisenhower, Nuclear War Fighting, and Korea, 1953–1968." *Presidential Studies Quarterly* 35(1): 52–75.

James, D. Clayton. 1993. *Refighting the Last War: Command and Crisis in Korea, 1950–1953*. New York: Free Press.

Jastrow, Robert. 1983. "Why Strategic Superiority Matters." *Commentary* 75(3): 27–32.

Jervis, Robert. 1976. *Perception and Misperception in International Politics*. Princeton: Princeton University Press.

1979. "Why Nuclear Superiority Doesn't Matter." *Political Science Quarterly* 94(4): 617–33.

1982. "Deterrence and Perception." *International Security* 7(3): 3–30.

1984. *The Illogic of American Nuclear Strategy*. Ithaca, N.Y.: Cornell University Press.

1989. *The Meaning of the Nuclear Revolution: Statecraft and the Prospect of Armageddon*. Ithaca, N.Y.: Cornell University Press.

Jian, Chen. 2001. *Mao's China and the Cold War*. Chapel Hill, N.C.: University of North Carolina Press.

Joeck, Neil. 2009. "The Indo-Pakistani Nuclear Confrontation: Lessons from the Past, Contingencies for the Future." In *Pakistan's Nuclear Future: Reining in the Risk,* edited by Henry Sokolski, pp. 19–61. Carlisle, Penn.: Strategic Studies Institute.

Kahl, Colin H., Melissa G. Dalton, and Matthew Irvine. 2012. *Risk and Rivalry: Iran, Israel and the Bomb.* Washington, D.C.: Center for a New American Security.

Kahn, Herman. 1960. *On Thermonuclear War.* Princeton, N.J.: Princeton University Press.

Kahneman, Daniel, Jack L. Knetsch, and Richard H. Thaler. 1990. "Experimental Tests of the Endowment Effect and the Coase Theorem." *Journal of Political Economy* 98(6): 1325–48.

Kahneman, Daniel, and Amos Tversky. 1979. "Prospect Theory: An Analysis of Decision under Risk." *Econometrica* 47(2): 263–92.

Kaplan, Stephen S. 1981. *Diplomacy of Power: Soviet Armed Forces as a Political Instrument.* Washington, D.C.: Brookings Institution.

Kapur, S. Paul. 2007. *Dangerous Deterrent: Nuclear Weapons Proliferation and Conflict in South Asia.* Palo Alto, Calif.: Stanford University Press.

2008. "Ten Years of Instability in a Nuclear South Asia." *International Security* 33(2): 71–94.

Kargil Review Committee. 2000. *From Surprise to Reckoning: The Kargil Review Committee Report.* New Delhi: Sage.

Karl, David J. 1996. "Proliferation Pessimism and Emerging Nuclear Powers." *International Security* 21(3): 87–119.

2001. "Lessons for Proliferation Scholarship in South Asia: The Buddha Smiles Again." *Asian Survey* 41(6): 1002–22.

2014. "Pakistan's Evolving Nuclear Weapon Posture: Implications for Deterrence Stability." *Nonproliferation Review* 21(3–4): 317–36.

Keefer, Edward C. 1986. "President Dwight D. Eisenhower and the End of the Korean War." *Diplomatic History* 10(3): 267–89.

1996. "Truman and Eisenhower: Strategic Options for Atomic War and Diplomacy in Korea." In *The Korean War: Handbook of the Literature and Research,* edited by Lester H. Brune, pp. 285–305. Westport, Conn.: Greenwood.

Kelly, Saul. 2000. "Transatlantic Diplomat: Sir Roger Makins, Ambassador to Washington and Joint Permanent Secretary to the Treasury." In *Whitehall and the Suez Crisis,* edited by Saul Kelly and Anthony Gorst, pp. 157–77. London: Frank Cass.

Kempe, Frederick. 2011. *Berlin 1961: Kennedy, Khrushchev, and the Most Dangerous Place on Earth.* New York: G.P. Putnam's Sons.

Kennedy, Robert F. 1969. *Thirteen Days: A Memoir of the Cuban Missile Crisis.* New York: Norton.

Khan, Feroz Hassan. 2004. "Nuclear Signaling, Missiles, and Escalation Control in South Asia." In *Escalation Control and the Nuclear Option in South Asia,* edited by Michael Krepon, Rodney W. Jones, and Ziad Haider, pp. 76–100. Washington, D.C.: Stimson Center.

Khrushchev, Nikita S. 1958. "Message from Khrushchev to Eisenhower on Crisis in the Taiwan Strait Area." *New York Times* (9 September): 12.

    1961. "Address by N.S, Khrushchev at a Soviet-Rumanian Friendship Meeting at the Grand Kremlin Palace, August 11, 1961." In *The Soviet Stand on Germany: 9 Key Documents Including Diplomatic Papers and Major Speeches by N.S. Khrushchev,* pp. 133–150. Oxford: Crosscurrents Press.

Kirshner, Jonathan. 1995. *Currency and Coercion: The Political Economy of International Monetary Power.* Princeton, N.J.: Princeton University Press.

Kissinger, Henry A. 1956. "Force and Diplomacy in the Nuclear Age." *Foreign Affairs* 34(3): 349–66.

    1979. *White House Years.* Boston, Mass.: Little, Brown, and Co.

    2003. *Crisis: The Anatomy of Two Major Foreign Policy Crises.* New York: Simon and Schuster.

Klug, Adam, and Gregor W. Smith. 1999. "Suez and Sterling, 1956." *Explorations in Economic History* 36(3): 181–203.

Komine, Yukinori. 2008. *Secrecy in U.S. Foreign Policy: Nixon, Kissinger and the Rapprochement with China.* Hampshire, UK: Ashgate.

Kraig, Michael R. 1999. "Nuclear Deterrence in the Developing World: A Game-Theoretic Treatment." *Journal of Peace Research* 36(2): 141–67.

Krepon, Michael, and Mishi Faruqee. 1994. *Conflict Prevention and Confidence-Building Measures in South Asia: The 1990 Crisis.* Washington, D.C.: Stimson Center Occasional Paper No. 17.

Kreps, Sarah E., and Matthew Fuhrmann. 2011. "Attacking the Atom: Does Bombing Nuclear Facilities Affect Proliferation?" *Journal of Strategic Studies* 34(2): 161–87.

Kroenig, Matthew. 2013. "Nuclear Superiority and the Balance of Resolve: Explaining Nuclear Crisis Outcomes." *International Organization* 67(1): 141–71.

Kroenig, Matthew, Miriam Krieger, and Hans Noel. 2015. "Dare to Fail: Nuclear Superiority, Threat Initiation, and Compellent Success." Typescript, Georgetown University.

Laird, Melvin. 1969. "Memorandum for Dr. Kissinger, 21 February 1969." In *Nixon's Nuclear Ploy: The Vietnam Negotiations and the Joint Chiefs of Staff Readiness Test, October 1969* (Electronic Briefing Book No. 81), edited by William Burr and Jeffrey Kimball. Washington, D.C.: National Security Archive. Available at nsarchive.gwu.edu/NSAEBB/NSAEBB81.

Langewiesche, William. 2005. "The Wrath of Khan." *The Atlantic* (November).

Lavoy, Peter R., ed. 2009a. *Asymmetric Warfare in South Asia: The Causes and Consequences of the Kargil Conflict.* Cambridge: Cambridge University Press.

Lavoy, Peter R. 2009b. "Introduction: The Importance of the Kargil Conflict." In *Asymmetric Warfare in South Asia: The Causes and Consequences of the Kargil Conflict,* edited by Peter R. Lavoy, pp. 1–38. Cambridge: Cambridge University Press.

Lee, Bradford A. 2014a. "American Grand Strategy and the Unfolding of the Cold War, 1945–1961." In *Successful Strategies: Triumphing in War and Peace from Antiquity to the Present,* edited by Williamson Murray and Richard Hart Sinnreich, pp. 353–402. Cambridge: Cambridge University Press.

Lee, Hong Yung. 2014b. "North Korea in 2013: Economy, Executions, and Nuclear Brinkmanship." *Asian Survey* 54(1): 89–100.

Lewis, Jeffrey G. 2014. *Paper Tigers: China's Nuclear Posture.* London: International Institute for Strategic Studies.

Lewis, John Wilson, and Litai Xue. 1988. *China Builds the Bomb.* Palo Alto, Calif.: Stanford University Press.

——— 2006. *Imagined Enemies: China Prepares for Uncertain War.* Stanford, Calif.: Stanford University Press.

Lewis, Kevin N. 1981. *The U.S.–Soviet Strategic Balance in the 1980s: Can We Meet the Challenge?* Santa Monica, Calif.: Rand Corporation.

Lieberman, Henry R. 1955. "Provocation by U.S. Planes Is Charged by Red Chinese." *New York Times* (3 April): A1.

Logevall, Fredrik. 2012. *Embers of War: The Fall of an Empire and the Making of America's Vietnam.* New York: Random House.

Londono, Ernesto. 2013. "U.S. Taking Serious Note of N. Korea's 'Provocative' Threats, Hagel Says." *Washington Post* (28 March).

Lüthi, Lorenz M. 2008. *The Sino-Soviet Split: Cold War in the Communist World.* Princeton, N.J.: Princeton University Press.

——— 2012. "Restoring Chaos to History: Sino-Soviet-American Relations, 1969." *China Quarterly* 210(June): 378–97.

Lyall, Jason, and Isaiah Wilson. 2009. "Rage against the Machines: Explaining Outcomes in Counterinsurgency Wars." *International Organization* 63(1): 67–106.

Malik, V.P. 2006. *Kargil War: From Surprise to Victory.* New Delhi: Harper Collins.

Mao, Zedong. 1995. "Speech, Mao Zedong at the Fifteenth Meeting of the Supreme State Council, 5 September 1958." *Cold War International History Project Bulletin 6/7*: 215–17.

Maoz, Zeev. 2003. "Dyadic MID Dataset, Version 2.0." Available at hdl.handle.net/1982.1/11489.

Marshall, Monty G., Ted Robert Gurr, and Keith Jaggers. 2009. "Polity IV Project: Political Regime Characteristics and Transitions, 1800–2009."

McDonough, David S. 2006. *Nuclear Superiority: The "New Triad" and the Evolution of Nuclear Strategy* (Adelphi Paper #383). London: International Institute for Strategic Studies.

McNamara, Robert S. 1983. "The Military Role of Nuclear Weapons: Perceptions and Misperceptions." *Foreign Affairs* 62(1): 59–80.

Mearsheimer, John J. 1984. "Nuclear Weapons and Deterrence in Europe." *International Security* 9(3): 19–46.

1993. "The Case for a Ukrainian Nuclear Deterrent." *Foreign Affairs* 72(3): 50–66.

2001. *The Tragedy of Great Power Politics.* New York: W. W. Norton.

Merchant, Livingston. 1959. "Secretary Dulles Wants to Support the U.S. Position in a Test of Nerves by Sending Atomic Weapons to West Germany, 27 February 1959." In *Berlin Crisis, 1958–1962,* p. BC00837. Washington, D.C.: Digital National Security Archive.

Merom, Gil. 2003. *How Democracies Lose Small Wars.* Cambridge: Cambridge University Press.

Merrill, John, and Ilan Peleg. 1984. "Nuclear Compellence: The Political Use of the Bomb." *Crossroads* 11: 19–39.

Mobley, Richard. 2001. "Pueblo: A Retrospective." *Naval War College Review* 54(2): 98–117.

Mohr, Charles. 1965. "Requiem for a Lightweight." *Esquire* (August): 67–71, 121–22.

Monk, Ray. 2012. *Robert Oppenheimer: A Life Inside the Center.* New York: Doubleday.

Montgomery, Alexander H., and Scott D. Sagan. 2009. "The Perils of Predicting Proliferation." *Journal of Conflict Resolution* 53(2): 302–28.

Morgan, Patrick M. 2003. *Deterrence Now.* New York: Cambridge University Press.

Morrow, James D. 1989. "Capabilities, Uncertainty, and Resolve: A Limited Information Model of Crisis Bargaining." *American Journal of Political Science* 33(4): 941–72.

Mueller, John. 1988. "The Essential Irrelevance of Nuclear Weapons: Stability in the Postwar World." *International Security* 13(2): 55–79.

———. 2009. *Atomic Obsession: Nuclear Alarmism from Hiroshima to al-Qaeda.* New York: Oxford University Press.

Mullen, Jethro. 2013. "North Korea Outlines Exacting Terms for Talks with U.S., South Korea." *CNN* (18 April).

Murphy, Robert D. 1964. *Diplomat among Warriors.* Garden City, N.Y.: Doubleday.

Nalty, Bernard C. 1968. *The Air Force Role in Five Crises, 1958–1965: Lebanon, Taiwan, Congo, Cuba, Dominican Republic.* Washington, D.C.: United States Air Force Historical Division Liaison Office.

Narang, Vipin. 2009. "Posturing for Peace: Pakistan's Nuclear Postures and South Asian Stability." *International Security* 34(3): 38–78.

———. 2013. "What Does It Take to Deter? Regional Power Nuclear Postures and International Conflict." *Journal of Conflict Resolution* 57(3): 478–508.

———. 2014. *Nuclear Strategy in the Modern Era: Regional Power Nuclear Postures and International Conflict.* Princeton, N.J.: Princeton University Press.

National Security Archive. 2002a. "Minutes of Conversation between the Delegation of the Czechoslovak Communist Party and the Communist Party of the Soviet Union, Moscow, October 30, 1962." In *The Cuban Missile Crisis after 40 Years: Conference Briefing Book,* edited by Thomas S. Blanton, Peter Kornbluh, Svetlana Savranskaya, and Malcolm Byrne.

———. 2002b. "Recollections of Vadim Orlov (USSR Submarine B-59), We Will Sink Them All, But We Will Not Disgrace Our Navy." In *The Cuban Missile Crisis after 40 Years: Conference Briefing Book,* edited by Thomas S. Blanton, Peter Kornbluh, Svetlana Savranskaya, and Malcolm Byrne.

———. 2002c. "Transcript of Excerpts from the Russian Documentary Program 'How it Happened,' 30 January 2001, ORT (Russian Television Channel 1) with Four Submarine Commanders who Participated in Operation Anadyr." In *The Cuban Missile Crisis after 40 Years: Conference Briefing Book,* edited by Thomas S. Blanton, Peter Kornbluh, Svetlana Savranskaya, and Malcolm Byrne.

Nayak, Polly, and Michael Krepon. 2006. *U.S. Crisis Management in South Asia's Twin Peaks Crisis.* Washington, D.C.: Henry L. Stimson Center.

New York Times. 1958. "U.S. Decides to Use Force if Reds Invade Quemoy." (5 September): 1.

1969. "Controversial Soviet Newsman Hints Russians Might Launch Attack on China." (18 September): 5.

2012. "Tough Choices in Dealing With Iran." (11 September).

Nitze, Paul H. 1956. "Atoms, Strategy, and Policy." *Foreign Affairs* 34(2): 187–98.

1976/77. "Deterring Our Deterrent." *Foreign Policy* (25): 190–210.

Nixon, Richard M. 1973. "Nixon Letter to Brezhnev, 25 October 1973, delivered to Soviet Embassy, 5:40 a.m."

1978. *RN: The Memoirs of Richard Nixon.* New York: Crossett and Dunlap.

1980. *The Real War.* New York: Warner Books.

Obama, Barack. 2009. Remarks by President Barack Obama in Prague as Delivered. Hradcany Square, Prague, Czech Republic (5 April). Available at www.whitehouse.gov/the_press_office/Remarks-By-President-Barack-Obama-In-Prague-As-Delivered/.

O'Neill, Arthur C. 1958. *Fifth Air Force in the Taiwan Straits Crisis of 1958.* Yokota Air Base, Japan: Pacific Air Force, Fifth Air Force, Office of Information Services, Director of Historical Services.

Organski, A. F. K. 1958. *World Politics.* New York: Knopf.

Osnos, Evan. 2013. "North Korea's Nuclear Game Theory." *The New Yorker* (5 April).

Palkki, David. 2014. "Calculated Ambiguity, Nuclear Weapons, and Saddam Hussein's Strategic Restraint." Typescript, Texas A&M University.

Pape, Robert A. 1996. *Bombing to Win: Air Power and Coercion in War.* Ithaca, N.Y.: Cornell University Press.

1997. "Why Economic Sanctions Do Not Work." *International Security* 22(2): 90–136.

2003. "The Strategic Logic of Suicide Terrorism." *American Political Science Review* 97(3): 343–61.

Parker, Richard. 2001. *The October War: A Retrospective.* Gainesville, Fla.: University of Florida Press.

Paul, T.V. 1998. "Power, Influence, and Nuclear Weapons: A Reassessment." In *The Absolute Weapon Revisited: Nuclear Arms and the Emerging International Order,* edited by T.V. Paul, Richard J. Harknett, and James J. Wirtz, pp. 19–46. Ann Arbor, Mich.: University of Michigan Press.

2009. *The Tradition of Non-Use of Nuclear Weapons.* Palo Alto, Calif.: Stanford University Press.

Perkovich, George. 1999. *India's Nuclear Bomb: The Impact on Global Proliferation.* Berkeley, Calif.: University of California Press.

Podhoretz, Norman. 2007. "The Case for Bombing Iran." *Commentary* (June): 17–23.

Pollack, Kenneth M. 2013. *Unthinkable: Iran, the Bomb, and American Strategy.* New York: Simon and Schuster.

Powell, Ralph L. 1965. "Great Powers and Atomic Bombs Are Paper Tigers." *China Quarterly* 23 (July): 55–63.

Powell, Robert. 1988. "Nuclear Brinkmanship with Two-Sided Incomplete Information." *American Political Science Review* 82(1): 155–78.

1990. *Nuclear Deterrence Theory: The Search for Credibility.* New York: Cambridge University Press.

2014. "Nuclear Deterrence Theory, Nuclear Proliferation, and National Missile Defense." *International Security* 27(4): 86–118.

Presidium of the Central Committee of the Communist Party of the Soviet Union. 2012. "Protocol No. 32, Session of 21 May 1962." In *Cold War International History Project Bulletin,* edited by James G. Hershberg and Christian F. Ostermann, vol. 17/18, p. 303. Washington, D.C.: Wilson Center.

Press, Daryl G., Scott D. Sagan, and Benjamin A. Valentino. 2013. "Atomic Aversion: Experimental Evidence on Taboos, Traditions, and the Non-Use of Nuclear Weapons." *American Political Science Review* 107(1): 188–206.

Quandt, William B. 1991. "How Far Will Israel Go?" *Washington Post Book World* (24 November): X7.

Raymonds, Jack. 1958. "U.S. Air-Sea Force Massed in Pacific: Nuclear-Equipped Armada, Poised for Attack, Called Most Powerful Ever." *New York Times* (17 September): 17.

Reid, Escott. 1981. *Envoy to Nehru.* New York: Oxford University Press.

Rice, Condoleezza. 2002. "Interview with Condoleezza Rice." *CNN* (8 September).

Richardson, Michael. 2002. "Q&A / George Fernandes: India and Pakistan Are Not Imprudent on Nuclear Option." *New York Times* (3 June).

Riedel, Bruce. 2009. "American Diplomacy and the 1999 Kargil Summit at Blair House." In *Asymmetric Warfare in South Asia: The Causes and Consequences of the Kargil Conflict,* edited by Peter R. Lavoy, pp. 130–43. Cambridge: Cambridge University Press.

Robinson, Thomas W. 1972. "The Sino-Soviet Border Dispute: Background, Development, and the March 1969 Clashes." *American Political Science Review* 66(4): 1175–1202.

1981. "The Sino-Soviet Border Conflict." In *Diplomacy of Power: Soviet Armed Forces as a Political Instrument,* edited by Stephen S. Kaplan, pp. 265–313. Washington, D.C.: Brookings Institution.

2003. "The Sino-Soviet Border Conflicts of 1969: New Evidence Three Decades Later." In *Chinese Warfighting: The PLA Experience Since 1949,* edited by Mark A. Ryan and David M. Finkelstein, pp. 198–214. Armonk, N.Y.: M.E. Sharpe.

Romney, Mitt. 2011. *No Apology: Believe in America.* New York: St. Martin's Griffin.

Rose, Gideon. 2011. *How Wars End: Why We Always Fight the Last Battle.* New York: Simon and Schuster.

Rosen, Stephen Peter. 2005. *War and Human Nature.* Princeton, N.J.: Princeton University Press.

Rosenberg, David Alan. 1983. "The Origins of Overkill: Nuclear Weapons and American Strategy, 1945–1960." *International Security* 7(4): 3–71.

Ross, Robert S. 2000. "The 1995–1996 Taiwan Strait Confrontation: Coercion, Credibility, and Use of Force." *International Security* 25(2): 87–123.

Roy-Chaudhury, Rahul. 2004. "Nuclear Doctrine, Declaratory Policy, and Escalation Control." In *Escalation Control and the Nuclear Option in South Asia,* edited by Michael Krepon, Rodney W. Jones, and Ziad Haider, pp. 101–118. Washington, D.C.: Stimson Center.

Rusk, Dean, Robert McNamara, George W. Ball, Roswell Gilpatric, Theodore Sorensen, and McGeorge Bundy. 1982. "The Lessons of the Cuban Missile Crisis." *Time* (27 September).

Russett, Bruce M. 2011. *Hegemony and Democracy.* New York: Routledge.

Ryan, Mark A. 1989. *Chinese Attitudes Toward Nuclear Weapons: China and the United States During the Korean War.* Armonk, N.Y.: M.E. Sharpe.

Sagan, Scott D. 1985. "Nuclear Alerts and Crisis Management." *International Security* 9(4): 99–139.

1993. *The Limits of Safety: Organizations, Accidents, and Nuclear Weapons.* Princeton, N.J.: Princeton University Press.

1996. "Why Do States Build Nuclear Weapons? Three Models in Search of a Bomb." *International Security* 21(3): 54–86.

2000. "The Commitment Trap: Why the United States Should Not Use Nuclear Threats to Deter Biological and Chemical Weapons Attacks." *International Security* 24(4): 85–115.

2001. "The Perils of Proliferation in South Asia." *Asian Survey* 41(6): 1064–86.

2004. "Realist Perspectives on Ethical Norms and Weapons of Mass Destruction." In *Ethics and Weapons of Mass Destruction: Religious and Secular Perspectives,* edited by Sohail H. Hashmi, pp. 73–95. New York: Cambridge University Press.

Sagan, Scott D., and Jeremi Suri. 2003. "The Madman Nuclear Alert: Secrecy, Signaling, and Safety in October 1969." *International Security* 27(4): 150–83.

Sagan, Scott D., and Kenneth N. Waltz. 2002. *The Spread of Nuclear Weapons: A Debate Renewed*. New York: W.W. Norton.

Sale, Richard. 2002. "Yom Kippur: Israel's 1973 Nuclear Alert." *UPI* (16 September).

Sanger, David. 2011. "In U.S.-Libya Nuclear Deal, a Qaddafi Threat Faded Away." *New York Times* (1 March).

Sanger, David E. 2006. "Suppose We Just Let Iran Have the Bomb." *New York Times* (19 March).

Saunders, Elizabeth N. 2014. "Transparency without Tears: A Pragmatic Approach to Transparent Security Studies Research." *Security Studies* 23(4): 689–98.

Savranskaya, Svetlana, and Thomas Blanton. 2013. *Last Nuclear Weapons Left Cuba in December 1962* (Electronic Briefing Book No. 449). Washington, D.C.: National Security Archive. Available at nsarchive.gwu.edu/NSAEBB/NSAEBB449.

Schelling, Thomas C. 1960. *The Strategy of Conflict*. Cambridge, Mass.: Harvard University Press.

1966. *Arms and Influence*. New Haven, Conn.: Yale University Press.

Schlosser, Eric. 2013. *Command and Control: Nuclear Weapons, the Damascus Accident, and the Illusion of Safety*. New York: Penguin.

Schwartz, Stephen C. 1998. *Atomic Audit: The Costs and Consequences of U.S. Nuclear Weapons Since 1940*. Washington, D.C.: Brookings Institution Press.

Schwartz, William, and Charles Derber. 1990. *The Nuclear Seduction: Why the Arms Race Doesn't Matter – and What Does*. Berkeley, Calif.: University of California Press.

Sechser, Todd S. 2009. "Should the United States or the International Community Aggressively Pursue Nuclear Nonproliferation Policies?" In *Controversies in Globalization: Contending Approaches to International Relations*, edited by Peter M. Haas, John A. Hird, and Beth McBratney, pp. 164–174. Washington, D.C.: CQ Press.

2010. "Goliath's Curse: Coercive Threats and Asymmetric Power." *International Organization* 64(4): 627–60.

2011. "Militarized Compellent Threats, 1918–2001." *Conflict Management and Peace Science* 28(4): 377–401.

2016a. "A Bargaining Theory of Coercion." Typescript, University of Virginia.

2016b. "Reputations and Signaling in Coercive Bargaining." *Journal of Conflict Resolution* (forthcoming).

2016c. "Sharing the Bomb: How Foreign Nuclear Deployments Shape Nonproliferation and Deterrence." *Nonproliferation Review* (forthcoming).

Sechser, Todd S., and Matthew Fuhrmann. 2013a. "Crisis Bargaining and Nuclear Blackmail." *International Organization* 67(4): 173–95.

2013b. "Debating the Benefits of Nuclear Superiority for Crisis Bargaining, Part II." *The Duck of Minerva* (25 March). Available at www.whiteoliphaunt.com/duckofminerva/2813/83/debating -the-benefits-of-nuclear-superiority-for-crisis-bargaining-part-ii.html.

2013c. "Debating the Benefits of Nuclear Superiority, Part III." *The Duck of Minerva* (28 March). Available at www.whiteoliphaunt .com/duckofminerva/2813/83/debating-the-benefits-of-nuclear-superi ority-part-iii.html.

2014. "Nuclear Weapons Are (Still) Poor Instruments of Blackmail." *H- Diplo/International Security Studies Forum* (2): 55–62.

Sechser, Todd S., and Abigail Post. 2015. "Hand-Tying versus Muscle-Flexing in Crisis Bargaining." Presented at the Annual Meeting of the American Political Science Association, San Francisco, September 1–4.

Seng, Jordan. 1997. "Less Is More: Command and Control Advantages of Minor Nuclear States." *Security Studies* 6(4): 50–92.

Shepley, James. 1956. "How Dulles Averted War." *Life* (16 January): 70–80.

Shin, Jiwoong, and Dan Ariely. 2004. "Keeping Doors Open: The Effect of Unavailability on Incentives to Keep Options Viable." *Management Science* 50(5): 575–86.

Shlaim, Avi. 1983. *The United States and the Berlin Blockade, 1948– 1949: A Study in Crisis Decision-Making*. Berkeley, Calif.: University of California Press.

Shu, Guang Zhang. 1999. "Between Paper and Real Tigers: Mao's View of Nuclear Weapons." In *Cold War Statesmen Confront the Bomb: Nuclear Diplomacy since 1945,* edited by John Gaddis, Philip Gordon, Ernest May, and Jonathan Rosenberg, pp. 194–215. Oxford: Oxford University Press.

Shuckburgh, Evelyn. 1986. *Descent to Suez: Diaries, 1951–56*. London: Weidenfeld & Nicolson.

Shukla, J.P. 2002. "No Weapons Will Be Spared for Self-Defence: PM." *The Hindu* (3 January).

Shultz, George P., William J. Perry, Henry A. Kissinger, and Sam Nunn. 2007. "A World Free of Nuclear Weapons." *Wall Street Journal* (4 January).

Simon, Michael. 2004. "Asymmetric Proliferation and Nuclear War: The Limited Usefulness of an Experimental Test." *International Interactions* 30(1): 69–85.

Singer, J. David. 1987. "Reconstructing the Correlates of War Dataset on Material Capabilities of States, 1816–1985." *International Interactions* 14(2): 115–32.

Singh, Sonali, and Christopher R. Way. 2004. "The Correlates of Nuclear Proliferation: A Quantitative Test." *Journal of Conflict Resolution* 48(6): 859–85.

Smith-Spark, Laura. 2013. "Report: North Korea Launches Fourth Short-Range Missile." *CNN* (19 May).

Smolansky, O.M. 1965. "Moscow and the Suez Crisis, 1956: A Reappraisal." *Political Science Quarterly* 80(4): 581–605.

Smyser, W.R. 2009. *Kennedy and the Berlin Wall.* Lanham, Md: Rowman and Littlefield.

Snyder, Glenn H. 1965. "The Balance of Power and the Balance of Terror." In *The Balance of Power,* edited by Paul Seabury, pp. 184–201. San Francisco, Calif.: Chandler.

Snyder, Glenn H., and Paul Diesing. 1977. *Conflict among Nations: Bargaining, Decision Making, and System Structure in International Crises.* Princeton, N.J.: Princeton University Press.

Soman, Appu Kuttan. 2000. *Double-Edged Sword: Nuclear Diplomacy in Unequal Conflicts: The United States and China, 1950–1958.* Westport, Conn.: Praeger.

Sood, V.K., and Pravin Sawhney. 2003. *Operation Parakram: The War Unfinished.* Thousand Oaks, Calif.: Sage.

Spivy, B.E. 2014. "Possible Responses to North Korean Attack on the Republic of Korea, May 14, 1968." In *USS Pueblo: LBJ Considered Nuclear Weapons, Naval Blockade, Ground Attacks in Response to 1968 North Korean Seizure of Navy Vessel, Documents Show* (Electronic Briefing Book No. 453) edited by John Prados and Jack Cheevers. Washington, D.C.: National Security Archive.

Statler, Kathryn C. 2007. *Replacing France: The Origins of American Intervention in Vietnam.* Lexington, Ky.: University Press of Kentucky.

Stolar, Alex. 2008. *To the Brink: Indian Decision-Making and the 2001–2002 Standoff.* Washington, D.C.: Henry L. Stimson Center.

Stueck, William. 1995. *The Korean War: An International History.* Princeton, N.J.: Princeton University Press.

——— 2002. *Rethinking the Korean War: A New Diplomatic and Strategic History.* Princeton, N.J.: Princeton University Press.

Sullivan, Patricia L. 2007. "War Aims and War Outcomes: Why Powerful States Lose Limited Wars." *Journal of Conflict Resolution* 51(3): 496–524.

Suri, Jeremi. 2008. "The Nukes of October: Richard Nixon's Secret Plan to Bring Peace to Vietnam." *Wired Magazine* (25 February).

Swami, Praveen. 2002. "Beating the Retreat." *Frontline Magazine* 19(22): 26 October.

Tannenwald, Nina. 1999. "The Nuclear Taboo: The United States and the Normative Basis of Nuclear Non-Use." *International Organization* 53(3): 433–68.

2007. *The Nuclear Taboo: The United States and the Nonuse of Nuclear Weapons Since 1945.* New York: Cambridge University Press.

Tatlow, Didi Kristen. 2012. "Rising Tension – and Stakes – in Japan-China Island Dispute." *International Herald Tribune* (14 September).

Taubman, William. 2003. *Khrushchev: The Man and His Era.* New York: Norton.

Taylor, Maxwell D. 2012. "Memo from Chairman JCS Maxwell Taylor from the President, Evaluation of the Effect on U.S. Operational Plans of Soviet Army Equipment Introduced into Cuba, 2 November 1962." In *Pentagon Estimated 18,500 U.S. Casualties in Cuba Invasion 1962, But If Nukes Launched, Heavy Losses Expected,* (Electronic Briefing Book No. 397) edited by William Burr. Washington, D.C.: National Security Archive. Available at nsarchive.gwu.edu/NSAEBB/NSAEBB397.

1982. "Reflections on a Grim October." *Washington Post* (5 October).

Thayer, Bradley A., and Thomas M. Skypek. 2013. "Reaffirming the Utility of Nuclear Weapons." *Parameters* 42(4): 41–45.

The Hindu. 2002. "Military Option if Diplomacy Fails." (4 January).

The Telegraph. 2002. "Nuclear Weapons Ruled Out." (2 June).

Thies, Wallace J., and Patrick C. Bratton. 2004. "When Governments Collide in the Taiwan Strait." *Journal of Strategic Studies* 27(4): 556–84.

Thompson, Llewellyn. 1958. "Pravda Article on Berlin Should Be Taken Seriously, Secret Cable, 1106, November 18, 1958." In *Berlin Crisis, 1958–1962,* p. BC00317. Washington, D.C.: Digital National Security Archive.

Thorpe, James A. 1978. "Truman's Ultimatum to Stalin on the 1946 Azerbaijan Crisis: The Making of a Myth." *Journal of Politics* 40(1): 188–95.

Time. 1980. "Good Old Days." (28 January): 13.

Tir, Jaroslav. 2005. "Keeping the Peace after Secession: Territorial Conflicts Between Rump and Secessionist States." *Journal of Conflict Resolution* 49(5): 713–41.

Trachtenberg, Marc. 1985. "The Influence of Nuclear Weapons in the Cuban Missile Crisis." *International Security* 10(1): 137–63.

1988. "A 'Wasting Asset': American Strategy and the Shifting Nuclear Balance, 1949–1954." *International Security* 13(3): 5–49.

1991. *History and Strategy.* Princeton, N.J.: Princeton University Press.

2013. "Audience Costs in 1954?" *H-Diplo/International Security Studies Forum* (1): 4–25.

Truman, Harry S. 1950. "The President's News Conference." *American Presidency Project* (30 November). Available at www.presidency.ucsb.edu/ws/index.php?pid=13673.

1956. *Memoirs, Volume 2: 1946–52: Years of Trial and Hope.* New York: Doubleday.

Tyler, Patrick E. 1996. "China Threatens Taiwan, It Makes Sure U.S. Listens." *New York Times* (24 January): A3.

Uhl, Matthias, and Vladimir I. Ivkin. 2001. "Operation Atom: The Soviet Union's Stationing of Nuclear Missiles in the German Democratic Republic, 1959." *Cold War International History Project Bulletin* 12/13(104): 299–307.

U.K. Cabinet Office. 1982. "Minutes of a Meeting Held at 10 Downing Street on Wednesday 16 April 1982 at 12 noon." *British National Archives* CAB 148/211.

U.S. Central Intelligence Agency. 1960. *Khrushchev on Nuclear Strategy.* Washington, D.C.: Office of Current Intelligence.

1969. *The USSR and China: National Intelligence Estimate 11/13–69.* Washington, D.C.: Directorate of Intelligence.

1970a. *Communist China's International Posture: National Intelligence Estimate 13-7-70.* Washington, D.C.: Directorate of Intelligence.

1970b. *The Evolution of Soviet Policy in the Sino-Soviet Border Dispute.* Washington, D.C.: Directorate of Intelligence.

1970c. *Military Forces Along the Sino-Soviet Border.* Washington, D.C.: Directorate of Intelligence.

1970d. *Recent Soviet Military Activity Along the Sino-Soviet Border.* Washington, D.C.: Directorate of Intelligence.

U.S. Department of Defense. 1964. "China as a Nuclear Power (Some Thoughts Prior to the Chinese Test)." Office of International Security Affairs, 7 October. In *The United States, China, and the Bomb*, edited by William Burr. Washington, D.C.: National Security Archive.

1978. *History of the Custody and Deployment of Nuclear Weapons, July 1945 through September 1977.* Washington, D.C.: Office of the Assistant to the Secretary of Defense for Atomic Energy.

2004. *The Joint Chiefs of Staff and the First Indochina War, 1947–1954.* Washington, D.C.: Office of the Chairman of the Joint Chiefs of Staff, Joint History Office.

U.S. Department of State. 1950. "Memorandum by the Director of the Policy Planning Staff (Nitze), November 4, 1950." *Foreign Relations of the United States, 1950: Korea,* pp. 1041–42.

1953a. "Memorandum by the Joint Chiefs of Staff to the Secretary of Defense (Wilson), May 19, 1953." *Foreign Relations of the United States, 1952–1954: Korea,* pp. 1059–63.

1953b. "Memorandum of Conversation, by the Secretary of State, May 21, 1953." *Foreign Relations of the United States, 1952–1954: Korea,* pp. 1068–69.

1953c. "Memorandum of Conversation, by the Secretary of State, May 22, 1953." *Foreign Relations of the United States, 1952–1954: Korea,* p. 1071.

1953d. "Memorandum of Discussion at a Special Meeting of the National Security Council on Tuesday, March 31, 1953." *Foreign Relations of the United States, 1952–1954: Korea,* pp. 825–27.

1953e. "Memorandum of Discussion at the 131st Meeting of the National Security Council, Wednesday, February 11, 1953." *Foreign Relations of the United States, 1952–1954: Korea,* pp. 769–72.

1953f. "Memorandum of Discussion at the 143d Meeting of the National Security Council, Wednesday, May 6, 1953." *Foreign Relations of the United States, 1952–1954: Korea,* pp. 975–79.

1953g. "Memorandum of Discussion at the 144th Meeting of the National Security Council, Wednesday, May 13, 1953." *Foreign Relations of the United States, 1952–1954: Korea,* pp. 1012–17.

1953h. "Memorandum of Discussion at the 145th Meeting of the National Security Council, Wednesday, May 20, 1953." *Foreign Relations of the United States, 1952–1954: Korea,* pp. 1064–68.

1954a. "Memorandum by the Counselor (MacArthur) to the Secretary of State, April 7, 1954." *Foreign Relations of the United States, 1952–1954: Indochina, Part 1,* pp. 1270–72.

1954b. "Memorandum by the Special Assistant to the President for National Security Affairs (Cutler) to the Under Secretary of State (Smith)." *Foreign Relations of the United States, 1952–1954: Indochina, Part 2,* pp. 1445–48.

1954c. "Memorandum Prepared by the Secretary of State: Washington, 12 September." *Foreign Relations of the United States, 1952–1954: China and Japan, Part 1,* pp. 611–13.

1955. "Memorandum for the Record, by the President's Special Assistant (Cutler): Washington, 11 March." *Foreign Relations of the United States, 1955–1957: China,* pp. 355–60.

1958a. "Memorandum from Acting Secretary of State Herter to Secretary of State Dulles." *Foreign Relations of the United States, 1958–1960: China*, pp. 56–57.

1958b. "Memorandum of Conversation: Bonn, 8 February." *Foreign Relations of the United States, 1958–1960: Berlin Crisis*, pp. 345–48.

1958c. "Memorandum of Conversation, September 8, 1958, 10:21–11:53a.m." *Foreign Relations of the United States, 1958–1960: China*, pp. 155–59.

1958d. "Telegram from the Embassy in the Soviet Union to the Department of State." (3 December).

1962. "Letter from President Kennedy to Chairman Khrushchev, October 22, 1962." *Foreign Relations of the United States, 1961–1963: Kennedy-Khrushchev Exchanges*, pp. 165–66.

1969. *Communist China: Peking Inflates Soviet War Threat*. Washington, D.C.: Bureau of Intelligence and Research.

1973a. "Memorandum of Conversation: The Middle East Conflict and U.S. Oil Interests." (10 October).

1973b. "Minutes of the Secretary of State's Staff Meeting, October 23, 1973, 4:35p.m." *Foreign Relations of the United States, 1969–1976: Arab-Israeli Crisis and War*, pp. 689–700.

1976. "TELCON: The Secretary/Jerry Schecter, April 3, 1976, 10:50a.m."

2001a. "U.S. Embassy Tehran Airgram A-383 to State Department: Soviet Chicom Hostilities, 4 September 1969." In *The Sino-Soviet Border Conflict, 1969: U.S. Reactions and Diplomatic Maneuvers*, edited by William Burr. Washington, D.C.: National Security Archive. Available at nsarchive.gwu.edu/NSAEBB/NSAEBB49.

2001b. "U.S. Reaction to Soviet Destruction of CPR Nuclear Capability; Significance of Latest Sino-Soviet Border Clash; Internal Opposition." In *The Sino-Soviet Border Conflict, 1969: U.S. Reactions and Diplomatic Maneuvers*, edited by William Burr. Washington, D.C.: National Security Archive. Available at nsarchive.gwu.edu/NSAEBB/NSAEBB49.

Van Creveld, Martin. 1993. *Nuclear Proliferation and the Future of Conflict*. New York: Free Press.

Van Hollen, Christopher. 1980. "The Tilt Policy Revisited: Nixon-Kissinger Geopolitics and South Asia." *Asian Survey* 20(4): 339–361.

Van Staaveren, Jacob. 1962. *Air Operations in the Taiwan Crisis of 1958*. Washington, D.C.: Air Force Historical Division Liaison Office.

Varadarajan, Siddharth. 2004. "Indo-Pak Fusion on Nuclear Doctrines." *Times of India* (19 June).

Vasquez, John A. 1993. *The War Puzzle*. New York: Cambridge University Press.

Vatcher, William Henry. 1958. Panmunjom: The Story of the Korean Military Armistice Negotiations. New York: Praeger.

Voeten, Erik. 2004. "Resisting the Lonely Superpower: Responses of States in the United Nations to U.S. Dominance." *Journal of Politics* 66(3): 729–54.

Walt, Stephen M. 2000. "Containing Rogues and Renegades: Coalition Strategies and Counter-Proliferation." In *The Coming Crisis: Nuclear Proliferation, U.S. Interests, and World Order,* edited by Victor A. Utgoff, pp. 191–226. Cambridge, Mass.: MIT Press.

Waltz, Kenneth N. 1981. *The Spread of Nuclear Weapons: More May Be Better* (Adelphi Paper No. 171). London: International Institute for Strategic Studies.

———. 2003a. "More May Be Better." In *The Spread of Nuclear Weapons: A Debate Renewed,* edited by Scott D. Sagan and Kenneth N. Waltz, pp. 3–45. New York: W. W. Norton.

———. 2003b. "Waltz Responds to Sagan." In *The Spread of Nuclear Weapons: A Debate Renewed,* edited by Scott D. Sagan and Kenneth N. Waltz, pp. 125–155. New York: W. W. Norton.

———. 2012. "Why Iran Should Get the Bomb: Nuclear Balancing Would Mean Stability." *Foreign Affairs* 91(4): 2–5.

Weathersby, Kathryn. 1998. "Stalin, Mao, and the End of the Korean War." In *Brothers in Arms: The Rise and Fall of the Sino-Soviet Alliance, 1945–1963,* edited by Odd Arne Westad, pp. 90–116. Palo Alto, Calif: Stanford University Press.

Wheeler, Earle. 1969. "Cable from JCS Chairman Wheeler to General Holloway, CINCSAC et al., 10 October 1969." In *Nixon's Nuclear Ploy: The Vietnam Negotiations and the Joint Chiefs of Staff Readiness Test, October 1969* (Electronic Briefing Book No. 81), edited by William Burr and Jeffrey Kimball. Washington, D.C.: National Security Archive. Available at nsarchive.gwu.edu/NSAEBB/NSAEBB81.

Whiting, Allen S. 1975. "Quemoy 1958: Mao's Miscalculations." *China Quarterly* 62(June): 263–70.

———. 1980a. "China and the Superpowers: Toward the Year 2000." *Daedalus* 109(4): 97–113.

———. 1980b. "Sino-American Detente." *China Quarterly* 82(June): 334–41.

———. 2001. "Letter from Allen S. Whiting to Henry Kissinger, 16 August 1969, Enclosing Report, 'Sino-Soviet Hostilities and Implications for U.S. Policy.'" In *The Sino-Soviet Border Conflict, 1969: U.S. Reactions and Diplomatic Maneuvers,* edited by William Burr. Washington, D.C.: National Security Archive. Available at nsarchive.gwu.edu/NSAEBB/NSAEBB49.

Wich, Richard. 1980. *Sino-Soviet Crisis Politics: A Study of Political Change and Communication.* Cambridge, Mass.: Harvard University Press.

Wiegand, Krista E. 2012. *Enduring Territorial Disputes: Strategies of Bargaining, Coercive Diplomacy, and Settlement.* Athens, Ga.: University of Georgia Press.

Wilson, Ward. 2012. "Myth, Hiroshima and Fear: How We Overestimated the Usefulness of the Bomb." *Cadmus* 1(5): 145–49.

2013. *Five Myths about Nuclear Weapons.* New York: Houghton Mifflin Harcourt.

Wright, Quincy. 1965. *A Study of War.* 2nd ed. Chicago: University of Chicago Press.

Xinhua. 2012. "Senior Military Official Urges No Slackness in Military Preparation." (14 September).

Yang Kuisong. 2000. "The Sino-Soviet Border Clash of 1969: From Zhenbao Island to Sino-American Rapprochement." *Cold War History* 1(1): 21–52.

Yuwen, Deng. 2013. "China Should Abandon North Korea." *Financial Times* (27 February).

Zhai, Qiang. 2000. *China and the Vietnam Wars, 1950–1975.* Chapel Hill, N.C.: University of North Carolina Press.

Zhang, Shu Guang. 1992. *Deterrence and Strategic Culture: Chinese-American Confrontations, 1949–1958.* Ithaca, N.Y.: Cornell University Press.

Zhou, Enlai. 1997. "Report, Zhou Enlai to Mao Zedong and Lin Biao, 3 April 1969." In *Zhou Enlai's Military Papers.* Washington, D.C.: Wilson Center, History and Public Policy Program Digital Archive.

Index